# FEMINIST EPISTEMOLOGIES

**Thinking Gender**
Edited by Linda Nicholson

Also published in the series

# FEMINIST EPISTEMOLOGIES

Edited and with
an Introduction by
**LINDA ALCOFF** and
**ELIZABETH POTTER**

**ROUTLEDGE**

**NEW YORK AND LONDON**

Published in 1993 by

Routledge
An imprint of Routledge, Chapman and Hall, Inc.
29 West 35 Street
New York, NY 10001

Published in Great Britain by

Routledge
11 New Fetter Lane
London EC4P 4EE

**Library of Congress Cataloging-in-Publication Data**

Feminist epistemologies / edited by Linda Alcoff and Elizabeth Potter.
    p.   cm. — (Thinking gender)
  Includes index.
  ISBN 0-415-90450-1. — ISBN 0-415-90451-X (pb)
  1. Feminist theory.  2. Knowledge, Theory of.  I. Alcoff, Linda
II. Potter, Elizabeth.  III. Series.
HQ1190.F45  1992
305.42′01—dc20                       92-11309
                                     CIP

ISBN 0-415-90450-1 (HB)
ISBN 0-415-90451-X (PB)

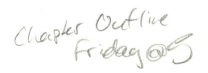
Chapter Outline
Friday @ 5

# Contents

# Acknowledgments

The editing of an anthology is, even more than other intellectual projects, a collaborative effort. We would like to thank the many people who responded to our call for papers by offering us their own thoughtful and interesting work. Had we not been constrained by space, time and the need for a coherent thematic, many more papers could have been included. We would also like to thank our contributors for their generosity and patience in helping this project to succeed. The philosophy departments at Hamilton College and Syracuse University gave us support and financial help for which we are grateful. Marianne Janack-Adams prepared our index and Maureen MacGrogan and Linda Nicholson provided crucial advice and encouragement. Linda wishes to thank Sam and Joe for stuffing and licking all those envelopes and Libby thanks Janet Halley whose belief helped constitute this book.

# 1

# Introduction: When Feminisms Intersect Epistemology

*Linda Alcoff and Elizabeth Potter*

Yesterday, "feminist epistemology" was an oxymoron; today, it has name recognition, but its referent is not yet clear. Our title, *Feminist Epistemologies,* is meant to indicate that the term does not have a single referent and, for reasons that we will explore later, it may never. Feminist theorists have used the term variously to refer to women's "ways of knowing," "women's experience," or simply "women's knowledge," all of which are alien to professional philosophers and to epistemology "proper"—that is, alien to a theory of *knowledge in general.* But this latter conception of proper epistemology leaves un-challenged the premise that a general account of knowledge, one that uncovers justificatory standards a priori, is *possible.* This is precisely the premise that feminist epistemologists have called into question. Feminist analyses in philosophy, as in other disciplines, have insisted on the significance and particularity of the context of theory. This has led many feminist epistemologists to skepticism about the possibility of a general or universal account of the nature and limits of knowl-edge, an account that ignores the social context and status of knowers. Is it likely that epistemological accounts of dominant knowledges, that is, knowledge produced and authorized by people in dominant polit-ical, social, and economic positions, can apply to subaltern knowl-edges as well?

"Feminist epistemology," as we use the term, marks the uneasy alliance of feminism and philosophy, an alliance made uneasy by this contradictory pull between the concrete and the universal. The au-thors included in this text are concerned with many of the problems that have vexed traditional epistemology, among them the nature of knowledge itself, epistemic agency, justification, objectivity, and whether and how epistemology should be naturalized. But their essays

1

are also informed by feminism and so treat these issues in new ways and introduce new problems including the politics of knowledge and the impact of the social status as well as the sexed body of the knower upon the production of knowledge.

Still, those working in feminist epistemology are engaged in a dialogue with one or more traditions in the history of epistemology. And the feminist orientation toward these mainstream views is varied; it involves appropriation and respect as well as criticism and rejection, and when the mainstream epistemology is already naturalistic, recognizing, for example, the contextual nature of justificatory standards, the feminist orientation reveals the progressive political possibilities of that epistemology. We view this dialogue as healthy and disagree with those who argue that any use of or engagement with the traditional problematics of epistemology leads to our co-optation. On the other hand, the essays in this volume demonstrate that a conservative approach that preserves traditional assumptions and strategies is not a virtue in feminist work. The history of feminist epistemology itself is the history of the clash between the feminist commitment to the struggles of women to have their understandings of the world legitimated and the commitment of traditional philosophy to various accounts of knowledge—positivist, postpositivist, and others—that have consistently undermined women's claims to know.

Feminism made its first incursions into philosophy in a movement from the margins to the center. Applied fields, most notably applied ethics, were the first areas in which feminist work was published. Not coincidentally, these areas were and are viewed by most professional philosophers as "on the periphery" of central philosophical work, where the virtue of centrality is accorded to work with a greater degree of abstraction from concrete material reality and with pretensions to universality. Feminist philosophers began work in the applied areas because feminism is, first and last, a political movement concerned with practical issues, and feminist philosophers understood their intellectual work to be a contribution to the public debate on crucial practical issues. At first, the more abstract areas of philosophy seemed distant from these concrete concerns. But from the applied areas we moved into more central ones as we began to see the problems produced by androcentrism in aesthetics, ethics, philosophy of science, and, finally and fairly recently, in the "core" areas of epistemology and metaphysics.[1]

Feminist work in epistemology, as in all other areas, began as a critique of the tradition (including a critique of the dominant narratives about just what that tradition *is*). Although this critique continues, constructive and reconstructive work in the theory of knowledge is emerging today. The essays in this volume reveal the contours of a new research program in epistemology, a research program moving beyond critique to reframe the problematic of knowledge. Our title, *Feminist Epistemologies*, should alert readers that this new research program is internally heterogeneous and irreducible to any uniform set of theses. The feminisms that make up this new problematic are diverse, often having in common only their commitment to unearth the politics of epistemology. But this recognition of the political commitments and effects implicit in every philosophical position has sparked a determination to reconstruct epistemology on newer, more self-conscious ground. This reconstruction also promises to reconfigure the borders between epistemology, political philosophy, ethics, and other areas of philosophy as we come to see the interrelationships and inseparability of heretofore disparate issues. Moreover, the distinctions between margin and center or periphery and core within the domain of philosophy itself give way. Once we recognize that values, politics, and knowledge are *intrinsically* connected, the hierarchies and divisions within philosophy will be replaced by more holistic and coherentist models. This volume demonstrates that the work of feminist philosophers is in the process of producing a new configuration of the scope, contours, and problematics of philosophy *in its entirety*.

Readers may be tempted to assume that because this anthology bears the word "feminist" in its title, the issues treated in it are limited or reduced to gender issues. Not so. Growing awareness of the many ways in which political relationships (that is, disparate power relations) are implicated in theories of knowledge has led to the conclusion that gender hierarchies are not the only ones that influence the production of knowledge. Cognitive authority is usually associated with a cluster of markings that involve not only gender but also race, class, sexuality, culture, and age. Moreover, developments in feminist theory have demonstrated that gender as a category of analysis cannot be abstracted from a particular context while other factors are held stable; gender can never be observed as a "pure" or solitary influence. Gender identity cannot be adequately understood—or even *perceived*—except as a component of complex interrelationships with other systems of identification and hierarchy. Thus, because gender as an abstract universal is not a useful analytical category and because research has revealed a plethora of oppressions at work in productions of knowledge, feminist epistemology is emerging as a research program with multiple dimensions. And feminist epistemology should not be taken as involving a commitment to gender as the primary axis of oppression, in any sense of "primary," or positing that gender is a

*[margin annotation: not just about gender issues]*

theoretical variable separable from other axes of oppression and sus-
ceptible to a unique analysis.

Why, then, retain the adjective "feminist"? We decided to retain
*Feminist Epistemologies* as the title of this collection because it serves
to identify work about which there is considerable curiosity; thus, its
title distinguishes this book as an appropriate resource for anyone
who seeks acquaintance with that body of work. As well, the term
"feminist" correctly identifies the history of this work. The articles
collected here under the rubric "feminist epistemologies" represent
the latest development of a good fifteen years of work that did in fact
begin (among those who identified with mainstream academic feminism) as work on gender issues in the theory of knowledge. The term
allows us to identify the historical trajectory of current work and to
see where we are coming from.

We find a strong consensus among feminists today that both the
term and the project of feminism itself must be more inclusive than
a focus on gender alone permits. If feminism is to liberate women, it
must address virtually all forms of domination because women fill the
ranks of every category of oppressed people. Indeed, the ontological
status of woman and even of women has shifted for academic feminists
in light of influential arguments showing that women, per se, do not
exist. There exist upper-caste Indian little girls; older, heterosexual
Latinas; and white, working-class lesbians. Each lives at a different
node in the web of oppressions. Thus, to refer to a liberatory project
as "feminist" cannot mean that it is only for or about "women," but
that it is informed by or consistent with feminism. It seeks, in current
feminist parlance, to unmake the web of oppressions and reweave the
web of life.

If the concept "woman" has lost its analytical credibility, the concept of a universal human nature is even less credible. Yet it is the
latter concept that allows mainstream epistemologists to ignore the
specificity of the knowing subject. Lorraine Code in "Taking Subjectivity into Account," argues that this inattention to the subjective elements involved in knowing and the illusion that knowing is universal
and perspectiveless are easy to maintain when the paradigm of knowledge is taken to be the observation of everyday simple objects, such
as sticks, apples, and patches of colors. In this type of knowing—
"perception at a distance"—the particular person who fills the role of
the knowing subject will make no difference. Any person would be
likely to see the object in the same way, and epistemologists have
concluded therefore that there is no point in "taking subjectivity into
account." The key epistemic attributes of knowers are then argued to
be "universal."

Code suggests that there is no justifiable reason to take "perception at a distance" as the paradigm case of knowing and the model for analyzing epistemic practices. Knowing others, which is arguably a more crucial practice in human knowledge acquisition given that most of our knowledge is interactive and dependent on others, would yield a very different "geography of the epistemic terrain" if taken as the paradigm case. However, Code does not want simply to replace one hegemonic paradigm of knowing with another but to show why the strategies for identifying necessary and sufficient conditions for "*S* knows that *p*" in the mainstream literature can never be successful until they pay as much attention to *S* as they pay to *p*.

Code also argues that mainstream epistemology creates the illusion of a universal subject through the excision of "unacceptable" points of view. She shows how Richard Foley's attempt to ground his account of knowledge on a first-person subjective foundationalism can only erect its "we subject" through the exclusion of "crazy," "bizarre," and "abnormal" others. It is toward the goal of overturning such "perspectival hierarchies" that some feminist epistemologists have developed what they call *standpoint epistemologies*, which seek to epistemically valorize some of the most discredited perspectives of knowledge. Sandra Harding is one of the best-known proponents of such a view.

In "Rethinking Standpoint Epistemology," Harding defends the feminist version of standpoint epistemology from some of the major criticisms it has received since it was first developed a decade ago. In particular, she establishes that standpoint epistemology is not in contradiction with the goal of achieving objective knowledge. If we dispense with the notion that the process of knowing is universal and we accept the idea that all knowing will substantively involve the standpoint or social and historical context of particular knowers, it may seem that we must give up on objectivity and embrace relativism. Harding argues here not only that this is not the case but also that standpoint epistemology will increase and strengthen our ability to achieve objectivity.

Harding's argument consists of two parts. First, she argues that even if researchers were to follow the most rigorous rules of traditional methods of research, they would not be able to achieve strong objectivity. This is because these methods leave unexamined the context of discovery, which is considered nonrational and therefore exempt from analysis, and because these methods neglect to identify the social desires, interests, and values that have shaped the sciences. Science presents itself as subjectless: the disembodied report of value-free, context-independent facts. But Harding argues that science does have a subject, which in our community is a group of dominant males, and that this subject has a standpoint, that is, a perspective involving assumptions and values based on the kinds of activities this group engages in. Traditional science leaves this standpoint unexamined and thus impoverishes the objectivity that science could achieve.

Harding further argues that the standpoint of this dominant group is epistemically limited with respect to the standpoint of various marginalized groups. When the dominant group is homogeneous, its shared assumptions stand little chance of identification, and when this group benefits from maintaining these assumptions, there is even less chance that the assumptions will be critically interrogated. As a remedy, Harding advocates a methodology that involves "starting thought from the lives of marginalized peoples." She argues that this will reveal more of the unexamined assumptions influencing science and will generate more critical questions, thus producing less partial and distorted accounts. And she urges that research done in this way can be—and needs to be—undertaken by everyone, not just by the marginalized themselves.

Bat-Ami Bar On is skeptical that the attribution of epistemic privilege to socially marginalized subjects can be sustained. Bar On's paper, "Marginality and Epistemic Privilege," provides a useful analysis of the contrast between feminist claims about epistemic privilege and Marx's claim that the standpoint of the proletariat is epistemically superior to that of the bourgeoisie. Feminist standpoint theory has differed from Marx in two crucial ways. First, Marx's argument for epistemic privilege was based on the idea that workers are both marginal and central in bourgeois society: marginal in relation to political and cultural power but central to the process of production. Their marginality means that they have less vested interest in maintaining bourgeois ideology, whereas their centrality gives them a privileged view of the real nature of capitalist production; it is these two elements in combination that confer on the working class an epistemic superiority. Feminist arguments, on the other hand, have argued from and established only the marginality of women. A second difference lies in the level of complexity by which oppression is understood. Where Marx basically theorized a single axis of oppression that revolved around class, feminists have theorized multiple axes. The result of this more complicated social grid is that the notion of a single center becomes displaced, which then problematizes the use of a margin/center ontology and raises new questions about the relationships between the multiple oppressed groupings.

Bar On also argues provocatively that feminist claims for women's epistemic privilege are based on a neo-Romantic conception of the subject that is emotional and nondualistic between mind and body or reason and passion. Further, she points out that feminist claims have emerged as a counterpoint to the Enlightenment strategies for claiming authority. As such, the feminist arguments have been framed within the Enlightenment's terms of discourse and replicate its repressive mechanisms for claiming the authority and privilege to silence others. Bar On argues that feminists must repudiate such strategies of domination. Besides, such arguments only succeed in actuality within the oppressed group itself, because claiming authority when one lacks the social power on which to base it "cannot yield the same results as the self-authorizing claims of the dominant group and are, therefore, merely normative, compelling only for those who are . . . usually members of the socially marginalized group who find them empowering."

On different grounds Helen Longino also takes issue with standpoint accounts. In "Subjects, Power and Knowledge: Description and Prescription in Feminist Philosophies of Science," Longino argues that most feminist philosophies of science, including standpoint epistemologies, those derived from feminist object relations theory, and traditional feminist empiricism, have very strong descriptive elements but are insufficiently normative. This is particularly worrisome because, although recognizing that mainstream accounts of natural processes have been developed from particular locations and reflect particular affective orientations, these feminist epistemologies argue only that certain locations and orientations are superior to others without providing norms by which we can decide among their conflicting claims about natural processes. This is because they do not provide norms for deciding which standpoint or orientation is epistemically superior. Longino offers normative criteria for indirectly evaluating competing theories, viz. whether they are produced by scientific communities socially structured to facilitate transformative criticism. Longino's position recognizes that cognitive needs can vary among communities and that this variation creates cognitive diversity, but she rejects relativism for socially constituted objectivity; however, socially constituted objectivity presents the paradox that knowledge requires consensus but consensus is reached only by quieting oppositional positions.

Longino solves the paradox by rejecting consensus in favor of multiple, sometimes incompatible theories that satisfy local standards. This solution is a strong one when supported, inter alia, by a model-theoretic theory of theories according to which two different models are incompatible only if both are taken to describe a single underlying reality rather than to pick out objects and events under different descriptions and to pick out different sets of relations among objects and events.

It is important to note that Longino's paradox arises from her commitment to the social nature of knowledge production. For many feminists, the entire endeavor to analyze epistemic agency in terms of a single knower, whatever her or his social position, is wrongheaded. In "Epistemological Communities," Lynn Hankinson Nelson argues that communities are the primary epistemic agents, not the isolated individual subject posited by traditional epistemology and not the socially situated though still isolated individual subject of a possible feminist epistemology. Communities, not individuals, are "the primary generators, repositories, holders, and acquirers" of knowledge. Nelson also rejects recent postmodern claims that there is no subject or agent of knowledge. These postmodern arguments set two dilemmas for feminist epistemology; the first is that either agents or knowledge are abstract Cartesian selves or they are "subjects in process" constituted by "the discourses and practices of their culture" and so cannot be the agents of knowledge. This dichotomy is related to a second one about evidence; either there is a foundation of knowledge or there are no standards for judging knowledge claims. Nelson argues that neither dichotomy is exhaustive, and the burden of her essay is to present an alternative view of the agents of knowledge as communities and of the evidence underpinning knowledge as communal, historical, and contingent.

The discovery of a bit of scientific knowledge, for example, is only possible within a system of theories and practices including metaphysical commitments, methods, and standards of evidence that emerged concomitantly with the process of coming to know that bit of knowledge—when that system is adopted by a community. That is, Nelson argues that this adoption is itself only possible "within a context of social arrangements and practices, puzzles, pressures, conflicts, and undertakings."

We find, then, that what counts as evidence depends in turn on the same communal system; on the metaphysical commitments and methods incorporated in current scientific practices; on theories and practices in other, related fields; and ultimately on "common-sense" knowledge and experience of macroscopic objects and events—all adopted by a community with certain social arrangements, practices, and so on. We should note that Nelson also holds experience to be fundamentally social, not something fundamentally ascribed to individuals. Thus, the sensory experiences that provide partial evidence for scientific claims depend on public theories and practices that allow individuals "to organize our sensory experiences into coherent and recoverable accounts."

Nelson uses the dispute between man-the-hunter theories of human development and feminist critiques of those theories as well as woman-the-gatherer theories to illustrate her contentions that the proper agents of knowledge are communities and that evidence is communal. Nelson's discussion of the dispute also reveals that although she rejects objectivism, she does not embrace the view that "anything goes." The epistemological community of feminist scholars critiquing man-the-hunter theory and producing the woman-the-gatherer alternative shares enough standards with proponents of man-the-hunter to allow sensible debate over what we know about human development.

Elizabeth Potter, in "Gender and Epistemic Negotiation," uses Wittgenstein's argument against the possibility of a private language to argue against epistemological individualism; thus, she joins Nelson and Longino in pressing philosophers to recognize that the primary agent of knowledge must be the community, not the individual. Gender politics intersects with the production of knowledge by the community at the point where epistemic decisions have to be made, that is, when the community must decide between competing beliefs. Potter argues that Mary Hesse's Network Model of scientific theories can be used to suggest how assumptions about gender enter into these decisions when the choice is underdetermined by experiential data. In Potter's view, these decisions can be seen as negotiations in which gender may be a variable. Actual observation by sociologists of scientists at work reveals that scientists make many epistemic decisions through micronegotiations, exchanges that may take only a few moments, but Potter suggests that we can also see the politics of gender at work in macronegotiations over knowledge to be found, for example, in the pages of academic journals or among groups of people, such as occurred in seventeenth-century England over the nature of air.

Elizabeth Grosz points out in "Bodies and Knowledges: Feminism and the Crisis of Reason" that the knower has been conceptualized not only as an individual but also as disembodied. "Reason" can present itself as universal, perspectiveless, and free of desire because it understands itself as purely mental. Although Grosz rejects such a notion, she does not want to replace the idea of the "purely mental" with a conception of the body as a precultural "purely physical," and one of the most interesting parts of her paper is its description of a new conceptualization of the body as sociocultural, inscribed, and marked by power in a way that transcends the binary logic of inside/ outside.

Grosz articulates a feminist project that does not seek to resolve the crisis of (masculine) reason through repairing its fissures or reintroducing those elements of corporeality that it cannot acknowledge, but to exacerbate its contradictions in order to displace its hegemony. She suggests that "if the body is an unacknowledged or an inadequately acknowledged condition of knowledges, and if the body is always sexually specific, concretely 'sexed,' this implies that the hegemony over knowledges that masculinity has thus far accomplished can be subverted, upset, or transformed through women's assertion of 'a right to know' independent of and autonomous from the methods and presumptions regulating the prevailing (patriarchal) forms of knowledge." Part of the reason why the masculinity of knowledge remains hidden is because it lacks a contrast that would force its sexuality into relief. Grosz believes that the project of developing the female body as the *subject* of knowledge will reveal the phallocentric and partial nature of dominant knowledges as well as help to create new possible ways of knowing and producing knowledge.

W. V. O. Quine's "Epistemology Naturalized" marked, though it did not originate, the growing conviction among pragmatists and other mainstream philosophers that philosophy should strengthen its connection to other human endeavors, particularly science. For Quine, epistemology should be reduced to a branch of neurophysiology, the science best equipped to reveal the origin and production of knowledge in the human brain. Others favor a reduction to various branches of evolutionary biology. Still others, such as Richard Rorty, argue that philosophy should be replaced not by one of the sciences but by history and literature. The authors in this collection who agree that epistemology should be naturalized disagree with malestream naturalization programs in two important ways. Nelson, Addleson, and Potter reject the assumption of epistemological individualism that the individual is the primary epistemic agent of knowledge. It follows that the use of sciences such as neurophysiology to study individual human brains or evolutionary biology to study the evolution of human individuals puts the epistemological cart before the horse. Addelson looks to interactionist sociology as a science of human groups to provide methods and theoretical tools for exploring the current production of knowledge, whereas sociology of an ethnomethodological bent and social history offer Potter the means to explore scientific knowledge production, especially that of the past. Although Nelson argues for naturalization in terms of an empirical science, she points out that given the present constitution of the empirical sciences, none of them is adequate for feminist epistemology.

These authors also differ from mainstream naturalization programs by rejecting the *reduction* of epistemology to science or to any other discipline. Instead, epistemology should be *grounded* in the science(s) offering the best way to understand how knowledge is produced, but the normative functions of epistemology, the evaluation and critique of knowledge production, and the recommendation of new social forms that can lead to new ways to make knowledge are still necessary and cannot be given up in favor of more description.

In "Knower/Doers and Their Moral Problems," Kathryn Pyne Addelson argues for a new moral epistemology that will replace many of the analytical units of traditional moral epistemology. In traditional moral philosophy, policy issues are reduced to controversies over "positions" about which an individual rationally makes up his or her mind. Addelson argues that it is more useful to borrow concepts from the symbolic interactionist tradition in sociology that allow us to see those who work on public problems as social worlds of "knower/doers" (her term) acting in public arenas. Moral epistemology then reveals who in fact defines public problems, especially moral problems; how people act collectively on those problems, particularly how they organize knowledge about the problems; and how they struggle (sometimes as women against women) to solve them. It is very important for feminists to use an empirical science that answers these questions, for then feminist academics can test their moral theories against actual practice to see who is empowered and who is disempowered when the theories are put into practice. Addelson envisions a new moral epistemology and moral theory requiring that feminists be engaged outside the academy in the "harsh world of public policy," testing our work against the needs of activist social worlds.

Addelson's concern with philosophy's effect is echoed in Alcoff and Dalmiya's concern that traditional epistemology has reduced much of women's knowledge to the status of "old wives' tales." For example, though midwives had a range of instrumental sophistication and success, their legitimacy as authoritative knowers has been gradually undermined and replaced with labels such as "ignorant" and "superstitious." In "Are 'Old Wives' Tales' Justified?," the question Alcoff and Dalmiya pose is whether there have been adequate *epistemic* reasons for this delegitimation. The key factor is traditional epistemology's focus on propositional knowledge, or "knowing that," as the paradigm of knowing. "Knowing how," or skilled activity, is consistently subordinated to "knowing that," creating a hierarchy of knowledges that replicates the mind/body and mental/manual hierarchies.

Thus, the fact that epistemology valorizes and emphasizes propositional knowledge contributes to the continued silencing and disauthorization of women as epistemically inferior throughout the world. Using an example from *The Mahābhārata*, they show that such a knowing that/knowing how hierarchy has not existed in every culture's understanding of knowledge and is as unnecessary as it is pernicious. Alcoff and Dalmiya then show why women's traditional knowledge, which includes both practical knowledge and what they call experiential knowledge, should in fact be taken as cognitive activities and what difference an acknowledgment of this fact will make for epistemology as a whole.

In "Feminism and Objective Interests: The Role of Transformation Experiences in Rational Deliberation," Susan Babbitt explores the relationship between rational choice and objective interests to show the inadequacy of liberal views of rational choice—those preserving the individual's perspective and holding that an act is rational if it is accessible to someone through a process of rational deliberation. John Rawls, for example, argues that a choice is rational if it is one a person would make if she or he possessed adequate instrumental reasoning abilities, full and complete information, and the capacity to vividly imagine the consequences of her or his actions. Babbitt shows that liberal views of rational choice are unable to distinguish personal transformations that change the interests and desires of an individual—even an individual who meets the three criteria specified by Rawls—in ways that we would say are good, bringing the person a "thicker" sense of autonomy and allowing her or him to flourish, from those transformations that do not. Liberals worry only about cases like brainwashing that transform an individual's subjective interests and desires for the worse and fail to see that they have ruled out a priori the personal and political transformations necessary to allow ideologically oppressed people to acquire new interests and desires and a new understanding of their social positions. Moreover, limiting the knowledge expressed in sentences and acquired as information excludes the nonpropositional understandings that many feminists, including Alice Walker, Gayatri Chakravorty Spivak, and Sarah Hoagland, indicate are necessary for ideologically oppressed *and oppressing* people to change. According to Babbitt, liberal views of rational choice have it backwards. Propositional information is unlikely to bring about personal and political transformation; instead, acting politically may allow the transformation necessary to make propositional information about one's rights and objective interests useful.

These essays, then, ask questions and pose problems that are new to many philosophers; they also reframe old questions and shift the emphases and purposes of epistemology. Who is the subject of knowledge? How does the social position of the subject affect the production of knowledge? What is the impact upon knowledge and reason of the subject's sexed body? Is all knowledge expressible in propositional form? How can objectivity be maximized if we recognize that perspective cannot be eliminated? Are the perspectives of the oppressed epistemically privileged? How do social categories such as gender affect scientists' theoretical decisions? What is the role of the social sciences in the naturalization of epistemology? What is the connection between knowledge and politics?

Readers of this volume are likely to have varied responses to these questions; some questions will seem old hat to feminists but bizarre to traditional philosophers. And the answers offered by authors in this volume will also elicit varied responses. Some answers will appear familiar to philosophers but alien to readers of feminist theory; other answers will seem obvious to feminists but disconcerting to traditional epistemologists. The variation is inevitable given the contradictory relationship of feminism to philosophy.

For mainstream philosophers, feminist work in philosophy is scandalous primarily because it is unashamedly a political intervention. The philosophical myth, like the myth of natural science, is that politics may motivate a philosopher to undertake philosophical work and that work may be put to better or worse political and social uses, but that a philosopher's work is good to the extent that its substantive, technical content is free of political influence. Holding to this myth, traditional philosophers conclude that one need not even read feminist philosophy to know, a priori, that it is bad philosophy.

The work presented here supports the hypothesis that politics intersect traditional epistemology. Yet it would be a serious misreading to interpret these essays as arguing for or resulting in a reduction of epistemology to politics. Instead, they raise a question about the adequacy of any account of knowledge that ignores the politics involved in knowledge. These essays show, even when they do not say, that to be *adequate*, an epistemology must attend to the complex ways in which social values influence knowledge, including the discernible social and political implications of its own analysis. This new criterion of adequacy, of course, makes it much harder to do good epistemology.

And it is just as difficult for feminist epistemologies as it is for old-fashioned epistemologies. For feminists, the purpose of epistemology is not only to satisfy intellectual curiosity, but also to contribute to an emancipatory goal: the expansion of democracy in the production of knowledge. This goal requires that our epistemologies make it possible to see how knowledge is authorized and who is empowered by it. It follows that feminist epistemologies should be self-reflexive, able to reveal their own social grounds, a revelation made all the more urgent because academic feminists are in a contradictory social position, seeking fundamental changes in the very institutions that empower us to speak and work. The worry for academic feminists is that we will commit the metonymic fallacy once again by assuming that what is liberatory for us is liberatory for all women. Ultimately, as Addleson points out in this volume, feminist epistemologies must be tested by their effects on the practical political struggles occurring in a wider frame of reference than the academy.

**Note**

1.  See the bibliography of feminist philosophy compiled by Susan Bernick in the "Newsletter on Feminism and Philosophy," Issue no. 90:1, Fall 1990, 116–121.

# 2

# Taking Subjectivity into Account

*Lorraine Code*

## 1. The Problem

Suppose epistemologists should succeed in determining a set of necessary and sufficient conditions for justifying claims that "*S* knows that *p*" across a range of "typical" instances. Furthermore, suppose that these conditions could silence the skeptic who denies that human beings can have certain knowledge of the world. Would the epistemological project then be completed? I maintain that it would not.

There is no doubt that a discovery of necessary and sufficient conditions that offered a response to the skeptic would count as a major epistemological breakthrough. But once one seriously entertains the hypothesis that knowledge is a *construct* produced by cognitive agents within social practices and acknowledges the variability of agents and practices across social groups, the possible scope even of "definitive" justificatory strategies for *S*-knows-that-*p* claims reveals itself to be very narrow indeed. My argument here is directed, in part, against the breadth of scope that many epistemologists accord to such claims. I am suggesting that necessary and sufficient conditions in the "received" sense—by which I mean conditions that hold for any knower, regardless of her or his identity, interests, and circumstances (i.e., her or his subjectivity)—could conceivably be discovered only for a narrow range of artificially isolated and purified empirical knowledge claims, which might be paradigmatic by fiat but are unlikely to be so 'in fact.'

In this essay I focus on *S*-knows-that-*p* claims and refer to *S*-knows-that-*p* epistemologies because of the emblematic nature of such claims in the Anglo-American epistemology. My suggestion is not that discerning necessary and sufficient conditions for the justification of such

15

claims is the sole, or even the central, epistemological preoccupation. Rather, I use this label, S-knows-that-p, for three principal reasons as a trope that permits easy reference to the epistemologies of the mainstream. First, I want to mark the positivist-empiricist orientation of these epistemologies, which is both generated and enforced by appeals to such paradigms. Second, I want to show that these paradigms prompt and sustain a belief that universally necessary and sufficient conditions can indeed be found. Finally—and perhaps most importantly—I want to distance my discussion from analyses that privilege scientific knowledge, as do S-knows-that-p epistemologies implicitly and often explicitly, and hence to locate it within an "epistemology of everyday lives."

Coincidentally—but only, I think, coincidentally—the dominant epistemologies of modernity with their Enlightenment legacy and later infusion with positivist-empiricist principles, have defined themselves around ideals of pure objectivity and value-neutrality. These ideals are best suited to govern evaluations of the knowledge of knowers who can be considered capable of achieving a "view from nowhere"[1] that allows them, through the autonomous exercise of their reason, to transcend particularity and contingency. The ideals presuppose a universal, homogeneous, and essential "human nature" that allows knowers to be substitutable for one another. Indeed, for S-knows-that-p epistemologies, knowers worthy of that title can act as "surrogate knowers," who are able to put themselves in anyone else's place and know his or her circumstances and interests in just the same way as she or he would know them.[2] Hence those circumstances and interests are deemed epistemologically irrelevant. Moreover, by virtue of their detachment, these ideals erase the possibility of analyzing the interplay between emotion and reason and obscure connections between knowledge and power. They lend support to the conviction that cognitive products are as neutral—as politically innocent—as the processes that allegedly produce them. Such epistemologies implicitly assert that if one cannot see "from nowhere" (or equivalently, from an ideal observation position that could be anywhere and everywhere)—if one cannot take up an epistemological position that mirrors the "original position" of "the moral point of view"—then one cannot know anything at all. If one cannot transcend subjectivity and the particularities of its "location," then there is no knowledge worth analyzing.

The strong prescriptions and proscriptions that I have highlighted reveal that S-knows-that-p epistemologies work with a closely specified kind of knowing. That knowledge is by no means representative of "human knowledge" or "knowledge in general" (if such terms retain a legitimate reference in these postmodern times), either diachronically (across recorded history) or synchronically (across the late twentieth-century epistemic terrain). Nor have *theories* of knowledge throughout the history of philosophy developed uniformly around these same exclusions and inclusions. Neither Plato, Spinoza, nor Hume, for example, would have denied that there are interconnections between reason and "the passions"; neither Stoics, Marxists, phenomenologists, pragmatists, nor followers of the later Wittgenstein would represent knowledge seeking as a disinterested pursuit, disconnected from everyday concerns. And these are but a few exceptions to the "rule" that has come to govern the epistemology of the Anglo-American mainstream.

The *positivism* of positivist-empiricist epistemologies has been instrumental in ensuring the paradigmatic status of S-knows-that-*p* claims and all that is believed to follow from them.[3] For positivist epistemologists, sensory observation in ideal observation conditions is the privileged source of knowledge, offering the best promise of certainty. Knowers are detached, neutral spectators, and the objects of knowledge are separate from them; they are inert items in the observational knowledge-gathering process. Findings are presented in *propositions* (e.g., S-knows-that-*p*), which are verifiable by appeals to the observational data. Each individual knowledge-seeker is singly and separately accountable to the evidence; however, the belief is that *his* cognitive efforts are replicable by any other individual knower in the same circumstances. The aim of knowledge seeking is to achieve the capacity to predict, manipulate, and control the behavior of the objects known.

The fact/value distinction that informs present-day epistemology owes its strictest formulation to the positivist legacy. For positivists, value statements are not verifiable and hence are meaningless; they must not be permitted to distort the facts. And it is in the writings of the logical positivists and their heirs that one finds the most definitive modern articulations of the supremacy of scientific knowledge (for which read "the knowledge attainable in physics"). Hence, for example, Karl Popper writes: "Epistemology I take to be the theory of *scientific knowledge*."[4]

From a positivistically derived conception of scientific knowledge comes the ideal objectivity that is alleged to be achievable by any knower who deserves the label. Physical science is represented as the site of ideal, controlled, and objective knowing at its best; its practitioners are held to be knowers *par excellence*. The positivistic separation of the contexts of discovery and justification produces the conclusion that even though information gathering (discovery) may sometimes be contaminated by the circumstantial peculiarities of everyday life, justificatory procedures can effectively purify the final cognitive product—knowledge—from any such taint. Under the aegis of positivism, attempts to give epistemological weight to the provenance of knowledge claims—to grant justificatory or explanatory significance to social- or personal-historical situations, for example—risk committing the "genetic fallacy." More specifically, claims that epistemological insight can be gained from understanding the psychology of knowers or analyzing their socio-cultural locations invite dismissal either as "psychologism" or as projects belonging to the sociology of knowledge. For epistemological purists, many of these pursuits can provide anecdotal information, but none contributes to the real business of epistemology.

In this sketch I have represented the positivist credo at its starkest because it is these stringent aspects of its program that have trickled down not just to produce the tacit ideals of the epistemological orthodoxy but to inform even well-educated laypersons' conceptions of what it means to be objective and of the authoritative status of modern science.[5] Given the spectacular successes of science and technology, it is no wonder that the scientific method should appear to offer the best available route to reliable, objective knowledge not just of matters scientific but of everything one could want to know, from what makes a car run to what makes a person happy. It is no wonder that reports to the effect that "Science has proved . . ." carry an immediate presumption of truth. Furthermore, the positivist program offered a methodology that would extend not just across the natural sciences, but to the human/social sciences as well. All scientific inquiry—including inquiry in the human sciences—was to be conducted on the model of natural scientific inquiry, especially as practiced in physics.[6] Knowledge of people could be scientific to the extent that it could be based on empirical observations of predictable, manipulable patterns of behavior.

I have focused on features of mainstream epistemology that tend to sustain the belief that a discovery of necessary and sufficient conditions for justifying S-knows-that-p claims could count as the last milestone on the epistemological journey. Such claims are distilled, simplified observational knowledge claims that are objectively derived, propositionally formulable, and empirically testable. The detail of the role they play varies according to whether the position they figure in is foundational or coherentist, externalist or internalist. My intent is not to suggest that S-knows-that-p formulations capture the essence of these disparate epistemic orientations or to reduce them to one common principle. Rather, I am contending that certain reasonably constant features of their diverse functions across a range of inquiries—features that derive at least indirectly from the residual prestige of positivism and its veneration of an idealized scientific methodology—produce epistemologies for which the places $S$ and $p$ can be indiscriminately filled across an inexhaustible range of subject matters. The legislated (not "found") context-independence of the model generates the conclusion that knowledge worthy of the name must transcend the particularities of experience to achieve objective purity and value neutrality. This is a model within which the issue of taking subjectivity into account simply does not arise.

Yet despite the disclaimers, hidden subjectivities produce these epistemologies and sustain their hegemony in a curiously circular process. It is true that, in selecting examples, the context in which $S$ knows or $p$ occurs is rarely considered relevant, for the assumption is that only in abstraction from contextual confusion can clear, unequivocal knowledge claims be submitted for analysis. Yet those examples tend to be selected—whether by chance or by design—from the experiences of a privileged group of people and to be presented as paradigmatic for all knowledge. Hence a certain range of contexts is, in effect, presupposed. Historically, the philosopher arrogated that privilege to himself, maintaining an investigation of his mental processes could reveal the workings of human thought. In Baconian and later positivist-empiricist thought, as I have suggested, paradigmatic privilege belongs more specifically to standardized, faceless observers or to scientists. (The latter, at least, have usually been white and male.) Their ordinary observational experiences provide the "simples" of which knowledge is comprised: observational simples caused, almost invariably, by medium-sized physical objects such as apples, envelopes, coins, sticks, and colored patches. The tacit assumptions are that such objects are part of the basic experiences of every putative knower and that more complex knowledge—or scientific knowledge—consists in elaborated or scientifically controlled versions of such experiences. Rarely in the literature, either historical or modern, is there more than a passing reference to knowing other people, except occasionally to a recognition (i.e., observational information) that this is a man—whereas that is a door or a robot. Neither with respect to material objects nor to other people is there any sense of how these "knowns" figure in a person's life.

Not only do these epistemic restrictions suppress the context in which objects are known, they also account for the fact that, apart from simple objects—and even there it is questionable—one cannot, on this model, know anything well enough to do very much with it. One can only *perceive* it, usually at a distance. In consequence, most of the more complex, contentious, and locationally variable aspects of cognitive practice are excluded from epistemological analysis. Hence the knowledge that epistemologists analyze is not of concrete or unique aspects of the physical/social world. It is of *instances* rather than particulars; the norms of formal sameness obscure practical and experiential differences to produce a picture of a homogeneous epistemic community, comprised of discrete individuals with uniform access to the stuff of which knowledge is made.

The project of remapping the epistemic terrain that I envisage is subversive, even anarchistic, in challenging and seeking to displace some of the most sacred principles of standard Anglo-American epistemologies. It abandons the search for and denies the possibility of the disinterested and dislocated view from nowhere. More subversively, it asserts the political investedness of most knowledge-producing activity and insists upon the accountability—the epistemic responsibilities—of knowing subjects to the community, not just to the evidence.[7]

Because my engagement in the project is specifically prompted by a conviction that *gender* must be put in place as a primary analytic category, I start by assuming that it is impossible to sustain the presumption of gender-neutrality that is central to standard epistemologies: the presumption that gender has nothing to do with knowledge, that the mind has no sex, that reason is alike in all men, and man "embraces" woman.[8] But gender is not an enclosed category, for it is always interwoven with such other sociopolitical-historical locations as class, race, and ethnicity, to mention only a few. It is experienced differently, and it plays differently into structures of power and dominance at its diverse intersections with other specificities. From these multiply describable locations, the world looks quite different from the way it might look from nowhere. Homogenizing those differences under a range of standard or typical instances always invites the question, "standard or typical for whom?"[9] Answers to that question must necessarily take subjectivity into account.

My thesis, then, is that a "variable construction" hypothesis[10] requres epistemologists to pay as much attention to the nature and situation—the location—of $S$ as they commonly pay to the content of $p$; I maintain that a constructivist reorientation requires epistemologists to take subjective factors—factors that pertain to the circumstances of the subject, $S$—centrally into account in evaluative and justificatory procedures. Yet the socially located, critically dialogical nature of the reoriented epistemological project preserves a realist orientation, ensuring that it will not slide into subjectivism. This caveat is vitally important. Although I shall conclude this essay with a plea for a hybrid breed of relativism, my contention will be that realism and relativism are by no means incompatible. Although I argue the need to excise the positivist side of the positivist-empiricist couple, I retain a modified commitment to the empiricist side for several reasons.

I have suggested that the stark conception of objectivity that characterizes much contemporary epistemology derives from the infusion of empiricism with positivistic values. Jettison those values, and an empiricist core remains that urges both the survival significance and emancipatory significance of achieving reliable knowledge of the physical and social world.[11] People need to be able to explain the world and to explain their circumstances as part of it; hence they need to be able to assume its 'reality' in some minimal sense. The fact of the world's intractability to intervention and wishful thinking is the strongest evidence of its independence from human knowers. Earthquakes, trees, disease, attitudes, and social arrangements are *there*, requiring different kinds of reaction and (sometimes) intervention. People cannot hope to transform their circumstances and hence to realize emancipatory goals if their explanations cannot at once account for the intractable dimensions of the world and engage appropriately with its patently malleable features. Therefore it is necessary to achieve some match between knowledge and "reality," even when the reality at issue consists primarily in social productions such as racism or tolerance, oppression or equality of opportunity. A reconstructed epistemological project has to retain an empirical-realist core that can negotiate the fixities and less stable constructs of the physical-social world, while refusing to endorse the objectivism of the positivist legacy or the subjectivism of radical relativism.

## 2. Autonomous Solidarity

Feminist critiques of epistemology and philosophy of science/social science have demonstrated that the ideals of the autonomous reasoner—the dislocated, disinterested observer—and the epistemologies they inform are the artifacts of a small, privileged group of educated, usually prosperous, white men.[12] Their circumstances enable them to believe that they are materially and even affectively autonomous and to imagine that they are nowhere or everywhere, even as they occupy an unmarked position of privilege. Moreover, the ideals of rationality and objectivity that have guided and inspired theorists of knowledge throughout the history of western philosophy have been constructed through processes of excluding the attributes and experiences commonly associated with femaleness and underclass social status: emotion, connection, practicality, sensitivity, and idiosyncrasy.[13] These systematic excisions of "otherness" attest to a presumed—and willed—belief in the stability of a social order that the presumers have good reasons to believe that they can ensure, because they occupy the positions that determine the norms of conduct and enquiry. Yet all that these convictions demonstrate is that ideal objectivity is a generalization from the *subjectivity* of quite a small social group, albeit a group that has the power, security, and prestige to believe that it can generalise its experiences and normative ideals across the social order, thus producing a group of like-minded practitioners ("we") and dismissing "others" as deviant, aberrant ("they").

Richard Foley's book *The Theory of Epistemic Rationality* illustrates my point. Foley bases his theory on a criterion of first-person persuasiveness, which he calls a "subjective foundationalism." He presents exemplary knowledge claims in the standard $S$-knows-that-$p$ rubric. Whether or not a propositional knowledge claim turns out to be warranted for any putative knower/believer will depend upon its being "uncontroversial," "argument-proof" *for that individual,* "in the sense that all possible arguments against it are implausible."[14] Foley is not concerned that his "subjective" appeal could force him into subjectivism or solipsism. His unconcern, I suggest, is precisely a product of the confidence with which he expands his references to $S$ into "we." Foley's appeals to $S$'s normality—to his being "one of us," "just like the rest of us"—to his not having "crazy, bizarre [or] outlandish beliefs,"[15] "weird goals," or "weird perceptions,"[16] underpin his assumption that in speaking for $S$ he is speaking for everyone—or at least for "all of *us.*" Hence he refers to what "any normal individual on reflection would be likely to think,"[17] without pausing to consider the presumptuousness of the terminology. There are no problems, no politics of "we-saying" visible here; this is an epistemology oblivious to its experiential and political specificity. Yet its appeals to a taken-for-granted normality, achieved through commonality, align it with all of the positions of power and privilege that unthinkingly consign to epistemic limbo people who profess "crazy, bizarre, or outlandish" beliefs and negate their claims to the authority that knowledge confers. In its assumed political innocence, it prepares the ground for the practices that make 'knowledge' an honorific and ultimately exclusionary label, restricting it to the products of a narrow subset of the cognitive activities of a closely specified group. The histories of women and other "others" attempting to count as members of that group are justifiably bitter. In short, the assumptions that accord $S$-knows-that-$p$ propositions a paradigmatic place generate epistemologies that derive from a privileged subjective specificity to inform sociopolitical structures of dominance and submission. Such epistemologies—and

Foley's is just one example—mask the specificity of their origins beneath the putative neutrality of the rubric.

Therefore, although subjectivity does not figure in any explicit sense in the formulaic, purely place-holder status of *S* in Foley's theory, there is no doubt that the assumptions that allow him to presume *S*'s normality—and apolitical status—in effect work to install a very specific conception of subjectivity in the *S*-place: a conception that demands analysis if the full significance of the inclusions and exclusions it produces are to be understood. These "subjects" are interchangeable only across a narrow range of implicit group membership. And the group in question is the dominant social group in western capitalist societies: propertied, educated, white men. Its presumed political innocence needs to be challenged. Critics must ask for whom this epistemology exists; whose interests it serves; and whose it neglects or suppresses in the process.[18]

I am not suggesting that *S*-knows-that-*p* epistemologies are the only ones that rely on silent assumptions of solidarity. Issues about the implicit politics of "we-saying" infect even the work of such an antifoundationalist, anti-objectivist, anti-individualist as Richard Rorty, whom many feminists are tempted to see as an ally in their successor-epistemology projects. Again, the manner in which these issues arise is instructive.

In that part of his work with which feminist and other revisionary epistemologists rightly find an affinity,[19] Rorty develops a sustained argument to the effect that the "foundational" (for which read "empiricist-positivist and rationalist") projects of western philosophy have been unable to fulfill their promise. That is to say, they have not been successful in establishing their claims that knowledge must—and can—be grounded in absolute truth and that necessary and sufficient conditions can be ascertained. Rorty turns his back on the (in his view) ill-conceived project of seeking absolute epistemic foundations to advocate a process of "continuing conversation rather than discovering truth."[20] The conversation will be informed and inspired by the work of such "edifying philosophers" as Dewey, Wittgenstein, Heidegger, and (latterly) Gadamer. It will move away from the search for foundations to look within communally created and communably available history, tradition, and culture for the only possible bases for truth claims. Relocating questions about knowledge and truth to positions within the conversations of humankind does seem to break the thrall of objectivist detachment and to create a forum for dialogic, cooperative debate of the epistemological issues of everyday, practical life. Yet the question is how open that forum would—or could—be; who would have a voice in Rorty's conversations? They are not likely, I suspect, to be those who fall under Foley's exclusions.

In his paper "Solidarity or Objectivity?", Rorty reaffirms his repudiation of objectivist epistemologies to argue that "for the pragmatist [i.e., for him, as pragmatist] . . . knowledge is, like 'truth,' simply a compliment paid to the beliefs which *we* think so well justified that, for the moment, further justification is not needed."[21] He eschews epistemological analysis of truth, rationality, and knowledge to concentrate on questions about "what self-image our society should have of itself."[22] Contending that philosophy is a frankly ethnocentric project and affirming that "'there is only the dialogue,' only *us*," he advocates throwing out "the last residue of transcultural rationality."[23] It is evidently his belief that communal solidarity, guided by principles of liberal tolerance—and of Nietzschean irony—will both provide solace in this foundationless world *and* check the tendencies of ethnocentricity to oppress, marginalize, or colonize.

Yet as Nancy Fraser aptly observes: "Rorty homogenizes social space, assuming tendentiously that there are no deep social cleavages capable of generating conflicting solidarities and opposing "we's".[24] Hence he can presume that there will be no disagreement about the best self-image of "our" society; he can fail to note—or at least to take seriously—the androcentricity, class-centricity, and all of the other centricities that his solidarity claims produce. The very goal of achieving "as much intersubjective agreement as possible," of extending "the reference of 'us' as far as we can,"[25] with the belief that tolerance will do the job when conflicts arise, is unlikely to convince members of groups who have never felt solidarity with the representers of the self-image of the society. The very promise of inclusion in the extension of that "we" is as likely to occasion anxiety as it is to offer hope. Naming ourselves as "we" empowers us, but it always risks disempowering others. The we-saying, then, of assumed or negotiated solidarity must always be submitted to critical analysis.

Now it is neither surprising nor outrageous that epistemologies should derive out of specific human interests. Indeed, it is much less plausible to contend that they do not; human cognitive agents, after all, have made them. Why would they not bear the marks of their makers? Nor does the implication of human interests in theories of knowledge, prima facie, invite censure. It does alert epistemologists to the need for case-by-case analysis and critique of the sources out of which claims to objectivity and neutrality are made.[26] More pointedly, it forces the conclusion that if the ideal of objectivity cannot pretend to have been established in accordance with its own demands, then it has no right to the theoretical hegemony to which it lays claim.

Central to the program of taking subjectivity into account that feminist epistemological inquiry demands, then, is a critical analysis of that very politics of "we-saying" that objectivist epistemologies conceal from view. Whenever an *S*-knows-that-*p* claim is declared paradigmatic, the first task is to analyze the constitution of the group(s) by whom and for whom it is accorded that status.

## 3. Subjects and Objects

I have noted that the positivist-empiricist influence on the principal epistemologies of the mainstream manifests itself in assumptions that verifiable knowledge—knowledge worthy of the name—can be analyzed into observational simples; that the methodology of the natural sciences, and especially physics, is a model for productive enquiry; and that the goal of developing a "unified science" translates into a "unity of knowledge" project in which all knowledge—including everyday and social-scientific knowledge about people—would be modeled on the knowledge ideally obtainable in physics. Reliance upon *S*-knows-that-*p* paradigms sustain these convictions. In the preceding section I have shown that these paradigms, in practice, are problematic with respect to the subjects (knowers) who occupy the *S* position, whose subjectivity and accountability are effaced in the formal structure. In this section I shall show that they are ultimately oppressive for subjects who come to occupy the *p* position—who become objects of knowledge—because their subjectivity and specificity are reduced to interchangeable, observable variables. When more elaborated knowledge claims are at issue—theories and interpretations of human behaviors and institutions are the salient examples here—these paradigms generate a presumption in favor of apolitical epistemic postures that is at best deceptive and at worst dangerous, both politically and epistemologically.

This last claim requires some explanation. The purpose of singling out *paradigmatic* knowledge claims is to establish exemplary instances that will map, feature by feature, onto knowledge that differs from the paradigm in content across a wide range of possibilities. Strictly speaking, paradigms are meant to capture just the formal, structural character of legitimate (appropriately verifiable) knowledge. But their paradigmatic status generates presumptions in favor of much wider resemblances across the epistemic terrain than the strictest reading of the model would permit. Hence it looks as if it is not just the paradigm's purely formal features that are generalizable to knowledge that differs not just in complexity but in kind from the simplified, paradigmatic example. Of particular interest in the present context is the fact that paradigms are commonly selected from mundane experiences of virtually indubitable facticity ("Susan knows that the door is open"); they are distilled from simple objects in the world that seem to be just neutrally *there*. There appear to be no political stakes in knowing such a fact. Moreover, it looks (at least from the vantage point of the epistemologist) as though the poorest, most "weird," and most marginalized of knowers would have access to and know about these things in exactly the same way. Hence the substitutionalist assumption that the paradigm relies on points to the conclusion that *all* knowing—knowing theories, institutions, practices, life forms, *and* forms of life—is just as objective, transparent, and apolitical an exercise.

My contention that subjectivity has to be taken into account takes issue with the belief that epistemologists need only to understand the conditions for propositional, observationally derived knowledge, and all the rest will follow. It challenges the concommitant belief that epistemologists need only to understand how such knowledge claims are made and justified by individual, autonomous, self-reliant reasoners to understand all the rest. Such beliefs derive from conceptions of detached and faceless cognitive agency that mask the variability of the experiences and practices from which knowledge is constructed.

Even if necessary and sufficient conditions cannot yet be established, say in the form of unassailable foundations or seamless coherence, there are urgent questions for epistemologists to address. They bear not primarily upon criteria of evidence, justification, and warrantability but upon the "nature" of inquirers: upon their interests in the inquiry, their emotional involvement and background assumptions, and their character; upon their material, historical, and cultural circumstances. Answers to such questions will rarely offer definitive assessments of knowledge claims and hence are not ordinarily open to the charge that they commit the genetic fallacy; but they can be instructive in debates about the worth of such claims. I am thinking of questions about how credibility is established, about connections between knowledge and power, about political agendas and epistemic responsibilities, and about the place of knowledge in ethical and aesthetic judgments. These questions are less concerned with individual, monologic cognitive projects than with the workings of epistemic communities as they are manifested in structures of authority and expertise and in the processes through which knowledge comes to inform public opinion. Such issues will occupy a central place in reconstructed epistemological projects that eschew formalism in order to engage with cognitive practices and to promote emancipatory goals.

The epistemic and moral/political ideals that govern inquiry in technologically advanced, capitalist, free-enterprise western societies are an amalgam of liberal-utilitarian moral values and the empiricist-positivist intellectual values that I have been discussing in this essay. These ideals and values shape both the intellectual enterprises that the society legitimates and the language of liberal individualism that maps out the rhetorical spaces where those enterprises are carried out. The ideal of tolerance and openness is believed to be the right attitude from which, initially, to approach truth claims. It combines with the assumptions that objectivity and value-neutrality govern the rational conduct of scientific and social-scientific research to produce the philosophical commonplaces of late twentieth-century anglo-American societies, not just in "the academy" but in the public perception—the "common sense," in Gramsci's terms—that prevails about the academy and the scientific community.[27] (Recall that for Rorty, tolerance is to ensure that postepistemological societies will sustain productive conversations.) I have noted that a conversational item introduced with the phrase "Science has proved . . ." carries a presumption in favor of its reliability *because of* its objectivity and value-neutrality—a presumption that these facts can stand up to scrutiny *because* they are products of an objective, disinterested process of inquiry. (It is ironic that this patently "genetic" appeal—that is, to the genesis of cognitive products in a certain kind of process—is normally cited to discredit other genetic accounts!) Open and fair-minded consumers of science will recognize its claims to disinterested, tolerant consideration.

I want to suggest that these ideals are inadequate to guide epistemological debates about contentious issues and hence that it is deceptive and dangerous to ignore questions about subjectivity in the name of objectivity and value-neutrality. (Again, this is why simple observational paradigms are so misleading.) To do so, I turn to an example that is now notorious, at least in Canada.

Psychologist Philippe Rushton claims to have demonstrated that "Orientals as a group are more intelligent, more family-oriented, more law-abiding and less sexually promiscuous than whites, and that whites are superior to blacks in all the same respects."[28] Presented as "facts" that "science [i.e., an allegedly scientific psychology] has proved . . ." by using an objective statistical methodology, Rushton's findings carry a presumption in favor of their reliability *because* they are products of objective research.[29] The "Science has proved . . ." rhetoric creates a public presumption in favor of taking them at face value, believing them true until they are proven false. It erects a screen, a blind, behind which the researcher, like any other occupant of the *S* place, can abdicate accountability to anything but "the facts" and can present himself as a neutral, infinitely replicable vehicle through which data passes en route to becoming knowledge. He can claim to have fulfilled his epistemic obligations if, "withdraw[ing] to his professional self,"[30] he can argue that he has been "objective," detached and disinterested in his research. The rhetoric of objectivity and value-neutrality places the burden of proof on the challenger rather than the fact-finder and judges her guilty of intolerance, dogmatism, or ideological excess if she cannot make her challenge good. That same rhetoric generates a conception of knowledge for its own sake that at once effaces accountability requirements and threatens the dissolution of viable intellectual and moral community.

I have noted that the "Science has proved . . ." rhetoric derives from the sociopolitical influence of the philosophies of science that incorporate and are underwritten by $S$-knows-that-$p$ epistemologies. Presented as the findings of a purely neutral observer who "discovered" facts about racial inferiority and superiority in controlled observation conditions so that he could not rationally withhold assent, Rushton's results ask the community to be equally objective and neutral in assessing them. These requirements are at once reasonable and troubling. They are reasonable because the empiricist-realist component that I maintain is vital to any emancipatory epistemology makes it a mark of competent, reasonable inquiry to approach even the most unsavory truth claims seriously, albeit critically. But the requirements are troubling in their implicit appeal to a doxastic subjective accountability. The implicit claim is that empirical inquiry is not only a neutral and impersonal process but also an inexorable one; it is compelling, even coercive, in what it turns up to the extent that a rational inquirer *cannot* withhold assent. He has no choice but to believe that $p$, however unpalatable the findings may be. The individualism and presumed disinterestedness of the paradigm reinforces this claim.

It is difficult, however, to believe in the coincidence of Rushton's discoveries; they could only be compelling in that strong sense if they could be shown to be purely coincidental—brute fact—something he came upon as he might bump into a wall. Talk about his impartial reading of the data assumes such hard facticity: the facticty of a blizzard or a hot sunny day. "Data" is the problematic term here, suggesting that facts presented themselves neutrally to Rushton's observing eye as though they were literally given, not sought or made. Yet it is not easy to conceive of Rushton's "data" in perfect independence from ongoing debates about race, sex, and class.

These difficulties are compounded when Rushton's research is juxtaposed against analogous projects in other places and times. In her book, *Sexual Science*,[31] Cynthia Russett documents the intellectual climate of the nineteenth century, when claims for racial and sexual equality were threatening upheavals in the social order. She notes that there was a concerted effort just at that time among scientists to produce studies that would demonstrate the "natural" sources of racial and sexual *in*equality. Given its aptness to the climate of the times, it is hard to believe that this research was "dislocated," prompted by a disinterested spirit of objective, neutral fact-finding. It is equally implausible, at a time when racial and sexual unrest is again threatening the complacency of the liberal dream—and meeting with strong conservative efforts to contain it—that it could be purely by coincidence that Rushton reaches the conclusion he does. Consider Rushton's contention that the brain has increased in size and the genitals have shrunk correspondingly over the course of human evolution; blacks have larger genitals, ergo. . . . Leaving elementary logical fallacies aside, it is impossible not to hear echoes of nineteenth-century medical science's "proofs" that excessive mental activity in women interferes with the proper functioning of the uterus; hence, permitting women to engage in higher intellectual activity impedes performance of their proper reproductive roles.

The connections Rushton draws between genital and brain size, and conformity to idealized patterns of good liberal democratic citizenship, trade upon analogous normative assumptions. The rhetoric of stable, conformist family structure as the site of controlled, utilitarian sexual expression is commonly enlisted to sort the "normal" from the "deviant" and to promote conservative conceptions of the self-image a society should have of itself.[32] The idea that the dissolution of "the family" (the nuclear, two-parent, patriarchal family) threatens the destruction of civilized society has been deployed to perpetuate white male privilege and compulsory heterosexuality, especially for women. It has been invoked to preserve homogeneous WASP values from disruption by "unruly" (not law-abiding, sexually promiscuous) elements. Rushton's contention that "naturally occurring" correlations can explain the demographic distribution of tendencies to unruliness leaves scant room for doubt about what he believes a society concerned about its self-image should do: suppress unruliness. As Julian Henriques puts a similar point, by a neat reversal, the "black person becomes the cause of racism whereas the white person's prejudice is seen as a natural effect of the information-processing mechanisms."[33] The "facts" that Rushton produces are simply presented to the scholarly and lay communities so that they allegedly "speak for themselves" on two levels: both roughly as data and in more formal garb as research findings. What urgently demands analysis is the process by which these "facts" are inserted into a public arena that is prepared to receive them, with the result that inquiry stops right where it should begin.[34]

My point is that it is not enough just to be more rigorously empirical in adjudicating such controversial knowledge claims with the expectation that biases that may have infected the "context of discovery" will be eradicated in the purifying processs of justification. Rather, the scope of epistemological investigation has to expand to merge with moral-political inquiry, acknowledging that "facts" are always infused with values and that both facts and values are open to ongoing critical debate. It would be necessary to demonstrate the innocence of descriptions (their derivation from pure data) and to show the perfect congruence of descriptions with "the described" in order to argue that descriptive theories have no normative force. Their assumed innocence licenses an evasion of the accountability that socially concerned communities have to demand of their producers of knowledge. Only the most starkly positivistic epistemology merged with the instrumental rationality it presupposes could presume that inquirers are accountable only to the evidence. Evidence is *selected*, not found, and selection procedures are open to scrutiny. Nor can critical analysis stop there, for the funding and institutions that enable inquirers to pursue certain projects and not others explicitly legitimize the work.[35] So the lines of accountability are long and interwoven; only a genealogy of their multiple strands can begin to unravel the issues.

What, then, should occur within epistemic communities to ensure that scientists and other knowers cannot conceal bias and prejudice or claim *a right not to know* about their background assumptions and the significance of their locations?

The crux of my argument is that the phenomenon of the disinterested inquirer is the exception rather than the rule; there are no dislocated truths, and some facts about the locations and interests at the source of inquiry are always pertinent to questions about freedom and accountability. Hence I am arguing, with Naomi Scheman, that

> Feminist epistemologists and philosophers of science [who] *along with others who have been the objects of knowledge-as-control* [have to] understand and . . . pose alternatives to the epistemology of modernity. As it has been central to this epistemology to guard its products from contamination by connection to the particularities of its producers, it must be central to the work of its critics and to those who would create genuine alternatives to remember those connections . . .[36]

There can be no doubt that research is—often imperceptibly—shaped by presuppositions and interests external to the inquiry itself, which cannot be filtered out by standard, objective, disinterested epistemological techniques.[37]

In seeking to explain what makes Rushton possible,[38] the point cannot be to exonerate him as a mere product of his circumstances and times. Rushton accepts grants and academic honors in his own name, speaks "for himself" in interviews with the press, and claims credit where credit is to be had. He upholds the validity of his findings. Moreover, he participates fully in the rhetoric of the autonomous, objective inquirer. Yet although Rushton is plainly accountable for the sources and motivations of his projects, he is not singly responsible. Such research is legitimized by the community and speaks in a discursive space that is available and prepared for it. So scrutinizing Rushton's "scientific" knowledge claims demands an examination of the moral and intellectual health of a community that is infected by racial and sexual injustices at every level. Rushton may have had reasons to believe that his results would be welcome.

Equally central, then, to a feminist epistemological program of taking subjectivity into account are case-by-case analyses of the political and other structural circumstances that generate projects and lines of inquiry. Feminist critique—with critiques that center on other marginalizing structures—needs to act as an "experimental control" in epistemic practice so that every inquiry, assumption, and discovery is analyzed for its place in and implications for the prevailing sex/gender system, in its intersections with the systems that sustain racism, homophobia, and ethnocentrism.[39] The burden of proof falls upon inquirers who claim neutrality. In all "objective" inquiry, the positions and power relations of *gendered* and otherwise located subjectivity have to be submitted to piece-by-piece scrutiny that will vary according to the field of research. The task is intricate, because the subjectivity of the inquirer is always also implicated and has to be taken into account. Hence, the inquiry is at once critical and self-critical. But this is no monologic, self-sufficient enterprise. Conclusions are reached and immoderate subjective omissions and commissions become visible in dialogic processes among inquirers and—in social science—between inquirers and the subjects of their research.

It emerges from this analysis that although the ideal objectivity of the universal knower is neither possible nor desirable, a realistic commitment to achieving empirical adequacy that engages in situated analyses of the subjectivities of both the knower and (where appropriate) the known is both desirable and possible. This exercise in supposing that the places in the $S$-knows-that-$p$ formula could be filled by asserting "Rushton knows that blacks are inferior" shows that simple, propositional knowledge claims that represent inquirers as purely neutral observers of unignorable data cannot be permitted to count as paradigms of knowledge. Objectivity *requires* taking subjectivity into account.

## 4. Knowing Subjects

Women—and other "others"—are *produced* as "objects of knowledge-as-control" by S-knows-that-*p* epistemologies and the philosophies of science/social science that they inform. When subjects become objects of knowledge, reliance upon simple observational paradigms has the consequence of assimilating those subjects to physical objects, reducing their subjectivity and specificity to interchangeable, observable features.

S-knows-that-*p* epistemologies take for granted that observational knowledge of everyday objects forms the basis from which all knowledge is constructed. Prima facie, this is a persuasive belief. Observations of childhood development (at least in materially advantaged, "normal" western families) suggest that simple observational truths are the first bits of knowledge an infant acquires in learning to recognize and manipulate everyday objects. Infants seem to be objective in this early knowing: they *come across* objects and learn to deal with them, apparently without preconceptions and without altering the properties of the objects. Objects ordinarily remain independent of a child's knowing; these same objects—cups, spoons, chairs, trees, and flowers—seem to be the simplest and surest things that every adult knows. They are *there* to be known and are reasonably constant through change. In the search for examples of what standard knowers know "for sure," such knowledge claims are obvious candidates. So it is not surprising that they have counted as paradigmatic.

I want to suggest, however, that when one considers how basic and crucial *knowing other people* is in the production of human subjectivity, paradigms and objectivity take on a different aspect.[40] If epistemologists require paradigms or other less formal exemplary knowledge claims, knowing other people in personal relationships is at least as worthy a contender as knowledge of everyday objects. Developmentally, learning what she or he can expect of other people is one of the first and most essential kinds of knowledge a child acquires. She or he learns to respond *cognitively* to the people who are a vital part of and provide access to her or his environment *long before* she or he can recognize the simplest physical objects. Other people are the point of origin of a child's entry into the material/physical environment both in providing or inhibiting access to that environment—

in *making* it—and in fostering entry into the language with which children learn to name. Their initial induction into language generates a framework of presuppositions that prompts children, from the earliest stages, to construct their environments variously, according to the quality of their affective, intersubjective locations. Evidence about the effects of sensory and emotional deprivation on the development of cognitive agency shows that a child's capacity to make sense of the world (and the manner of engaging in that process) is intricately linked with her or his caregivers' construction of the environment.

Traditionally, theories of knowledge tend to be derived from the experiences of uniformly educated, articulate, epistemically "positioned" adults who introspect retrospectively to review what they must once have known most simply and clearly. Locke's *tabula rasa* is one model; Descartes's radical doubt is another. Yet this introspective process consistently bypasses the epistemic significance of early experiences with other people, with whom the relations of these philosophers must surely have been different from their relations to objects in their environment. As Seyla Benhabib wryly notes, it is a strange world from which this picture of knowledge is derived: a world in which "individuals are grown up before they have been born; in which boys are men before they have been children; a world where neither mother, nor sister, nor wife exist."[41] Whatever the historical variations in childraising practices, evidence implicit in (similarly evolving) theories of knowledge points to a noteworthy constancy. In separated adulthood, the knowledge that enables a knower to give or withhold trust as a child—and hence to survive—is passed over as unworthy of philosophical notice. It is tempting to conclude that theorists of knowledge must either be childless or so disengaged from the rearing of children as to have minimal developmental awareness. Participators in childraising could not easily ignore the primacy of knowing and being known by other people in cognitive development, nor could they denigrate the role such knowledge plays throughout an epistemic history. In view of the fact that disengagement throughout a changing history and across a range of class and racial boundaries has been possible primarily for *men* in western societies, this aspect of the androcentricity of objectivist epistemologies is not surprising.

Knowing other people in relationships requires constant learning: how to be with them, respond to them, and act toward them. In this respect it contrasts markedly with the immediacy of common, sense-perceptual paradigms. In fact, if exemplary "bits" of knowledge were drawn from situations where people have to *learn* to know, rather than from taken-for-granted adult expectations, the complexity of knowing even the simplest things would not so readily be masked, and the fact that knowledge is *qualitatively* variable would be more readily apparent. Consider the strangeness of traveling in a country and culture where one has to suspend judgment about how to identify and deal with things like simple artifacts, flora and fauna, customs and cultural phenomena. These experiences remind epistemologists of how tentative the process of making everyday observations and judgments really is.

Knowledge of other people develops, operates, and is open to interpretation at various levels; it admits of degree in ways that knowing that a book is red does not. Such knowledge is not primarily propositional; I can know that Alice is clever and not *know* her very well at all in a "thicker" sense. Knowing "facts" (the standard $S$-knows-that-$p$ substitutions) is part of such knowing, but the knowledge involved is more than and different from its propositional parts. Nor is this knowledge reducible to the simple observational knowledge of the traditional paradigms. The fact that it is acquired differently, interactively, and relationally differentiates it both as process and as product from standard propositional knowledge. Yet its status as knowledge disturbs the smooth surface of the paradigm's structure. The contrast between its multidimensional, multiperspectival character and the stark simplicity of standard paradigms requires philosophers to reexamine the practice of granting exemplary status to those paradigms. "Knowing how" and "knowing that" are implicated, but they do not begin to tell the whole story.

The contention that people are *knowable* may sit uneasily with psychoanalytic decenterings of conscious subjectivity and postmodern critiques of the unified subject of Enlightenment humanism. But I think this is a tension that has to be acknowledged and maintained. In practice, people often know one another well enough to make good decisions about who can be counted on and who cannot, who makes a good ally and who does not. Yet precisely because of the fluctuations and contradictions of subjectivity, this process is ongoing, communicative, and interpretive. It is never fixed or complete; any fixity claimed for "the self" will be a fixity in flux. Nonetheless, I argue that something must be fixed to "contain" the flux even enough to permit references to and ongoing relationships with "this person." Knowing people always occurs within the terms of this tension.

Problems about determining criteria for justifying claims to know another person—the utter availability of necessary and sufficient conditions, the complete inadequacy of $S$-knows-that-$p$ paradigms—must account for philosophical reluctance to count this as knowledge that bears epistemological investigation. Yet my suggestion that such knowledge is a model for a wide range of knowledge and is not merely inchoate and unmanageable recommends itself the more strongly in view of the extent to which cognitive practice is grounded upon such knowledge. I am thinking not just of everyday interactions with other people, but of the specialized knowledge—such as Rushton's—that claims institutional authority. Educational theory and practice, psychology, sociology, anthropology, law, some aspects of medicine and philosophy, politics, history, and economics all depend for their credibility upon knowing people. Hence it is all the more curious that observation-based knowledge of material objects and the methodology of the physical sciences hold such relatively unchallenged sway as the paradigm—and paragon—of intellectual achievement. The results of according continued veneration to observational paradigms are evident in the reductive approaches of behaviorist psychology. They are apparent in parochial impositions of meaning upon the practices of other cultures which is still characteristic of some areas of anthropology, and in the simple translation of present-day descriptions into past cultural contexts that characterizes some historical and archaeological practice. But feminist, hermeneutic, and postmodern critiques are slowly succeeding in requiring objectivist social scientists to reexamine their presuppositions and practices. In fact, it is methodological disputes within the social sciences—and the consequent unsettling of positivistic hegemony—that, according to Susan Hekman, have set the stage for the development of a productive, postmodern approach to epistemology for contemporary feminists.[42]

I am not proposing that knowing other people should become *the* new epistemological paradigm but rather that it has a strong claim to exemplary status in the epistemologies that feminist and other case-by-case analyses will produce. I am proposing further that if epistemologists require a model drawn from "scientific" inquiry, then a reconstructed, interpretive social science, liberated from positivistic constraints, will be a better resource than natural science—or physics—for knowledge as such.

Social science of whatever stripe is constrained by the factual-informational details that constrain all attempts to know people; physical, historical, biographical, environmental, social-structural, and other *facts* constitute its "objects" of study. These facts are available for objective analysis, yet they also lend themselves to varying degrees of interpretation and ideological construction. Social science often focuses upon meanings, upon purposeful and learned behavior, preferences, and intentions, with the aim of explaining what Sandra Harding calls "the origins, forms and prevalence of apparently irrational but culturewide patterns of human belief and action."[43] Such phenomena cannot be measured and quantified to provide results comparable to the results of a controlled physics experiment. Yet this constraint neither precludes social-scientific objectivity nor reclaims the methodology of physics as paradigmatic. Harding is right to maintain that "the totally reasonable exclusion of intentional and learned behavior from the subject matter of physics is a good reason to regard enquiry in physics as atypical of scientific knowledge-seeking."[44] I am arguing that it is equally atypical of everyday knowledge-seeking. Interpretations of intentional and learned behavior are indeed subjectively variable; taking subjectivity into account does not *entail* abandoning objectivity. Rabinow and Sullivan put the point well: "Discourse being about something, one must understand the world in order to interpret it . . . Human action and interpretation are subject to many *but not infinitely many* constructions."[45] When theorists acknowledge the oddity and peculiar insularity of physics-derived paradigms with their suppression of subjectivity, it is clear that their application to areas of inquiry in which subjectivities are the "objects" of study has to be contested.

The problem about claiming an exemplary role for personal-knowledge paradigms is to show how the kinds of knowledge integral to human relationships could work in situations where the object of knowledge is inanimate. The case has to be made by analogy and not by requiring knowers to convert from being objective observers to being friends with tables and chairs, chemicals, particles, cells, planets, rocks, trees, and insects. There are obvious points of disanalogy, not the least of which derives from the fact that chairs and plants and rocks cannot reciprocate in the ways that people can. There will be none of the mutual recognition and affirmation between observer and observed that there is between people. But Heisenberg's "uncertainty principle" suggests that not even physical objects are inert in and untouched by observational processes. If there is any validity to this suggestion, then it is not so easy to draw rigid lines separating responsive from unresponsive objects. Taking knowledge of other people as a model does not, *per impossibile*, require scientists to begin talking to their rocks and cells or to admit that the process is not working when the rocks fail to respond. It calls, rather, for a recognition that rocks, cells, and scientists are located in multiple relations to one another, all of which are open to analysis and critique. Singling out and privileging the asymmetrical observer–observed relation is but one possibility.

A more stubborn point of disanalogy may appear to attach to the belief that it is *possible* to know physical objects, whereas it is never possible really to know other people. But this apparent disanalogy appears to prevent the analogy from going through because of another feature of the core presupposition of empiricist-objectivist theories.

According to the standard paradigms, empirical observation can produce knowledge that is universally and uncontrovertibly established for all time. Whether or not such perfect knowledge has ever been achieved is an open question; a belief in its possibility guides and regulates mainstream epistemologies and theories of science. The presumption that knowing other people is difficult to the point of near impossibility is declared by contrast with those paradigms, whose realization may only be possible in contrived, attenuated instances. By *that* standard, knowing other people, however well, does look like as pale an approximation as it was for Descartes, by contrast with the "clear and distinct ideas" he was otherwise able to achieve. The question, again, is why *that* standard, which governs so minuscule a part of the epistemic lives even of members of the privileged professional class and gender, should regulate legitimate uses of the label "knowledge."

If the empiricist-positivist standard were displaced by more complex analyses in which knowledge claims are provisional and approximate, knowing other people might not seem to be so different. Current upheavals in epistemology point to the productivity of hermeneutic, interpretive, literary methods of analysis and explanation in the social sciences. The skills these approaches require are not so different from the interpretive skills that human relationships require. The extent of their usefulness for the natural sciences is not yet clear. But one point of the challenge is to argue that natural-scientific enquiry has to be located differently, where it can be recognized as a sociopolitical-historical activity in which knowing who the scientist is can reveal important epistemological dimensions of her or his inquiry.

A recognition of the space that needs to be kept open for reinterpretation of the contextualizing that adequate knowledge requires becomes clearer in the light of the "personal" analogy. Though the analogy is not perfect, it is certainly no more preposterous to argue that people should try to know physical objects in the nuanced way that they know their friends than it is to argue that they should try to know people in the unsubtle way that they often claim to know physical objects.

Drawing upon such an interpretive approach across the epistemic terrain would guard against reductivism and rigidity. Knowing other people occurs in a persistent interplay between opacity and transparency, between attitudes and postures that elude a knower's grasp and patterns that are clear and relatively constant. Hence knowers are kept on their cognitive toes. In its need to accommodate change and growth, this knowledge contrasts further with traditional paradigms that deal, on the whole, with objects that can be treated as permanent. In knowing other people, a knower's subjectivity is implicated from its earliest developmental stages; in such knowing, her or his subjectivity is produced and reproduced. Analogous reconstructions often occur in the subjectivity of the person(s) she or he knows. Hence such knowledge works from a conception of subject–object relations different from that implicit in simple empirical paradigms. Claims to know a person are open to negotiation between knower and "known," where the "subject" and "object" positions are always, in principle, interchangeable. In the process, it is important to watch for discrepancies between a person's sense of her or his own subjectivity and a would-be knower's conception of how things are for her or him; neither the self-conception nor the knower-conception can claim absolute authority, because the limits of self-consciousness constrain the process as closely as the interiority of mental processes and experiential constructs and their unavailability to observation.

That an agent's subjectivity is so clearly implicated may create the impression that this knowledge is, indeed, purely subjective. But such a conclusion would be unwarranted. There *are* facts that have to be respected: facts that constitute "the person one is" at any historical moment.[48] Only certain stories can accurately be told; others simply cannot. "External" facts are obvious constraints: facts about age, sex, place and date of birth, height, weight, and hair color—the information that appears on a passport. They would count as objective even on a fairly traditional understanding of the term. Other information is reasonably objective as well: facts about marriage or divorce, childbirth, siblings, skills, education, employment, abode, and travel. But the intriguing point about knowing people—and another reason why it is epistemologically instructive—is that even knowing all the *facts* about someone does not count as knowing her as the person she is. No more can knowing all the facts about oneself, past and present, guarantee self-knowledge. Yet none of these problems raise doubts that there is such a creature as the person I am or the person anyone else is now. Nor do they indicate the impossibility of knowing other people. If the limitations of these accumulated factual claims were taken seriously with respect to empirical knowledge more generally, the limitations of an epistemology built from S-knows-that-p claims would be more clearly apparent.

That perfect, objective knowledge of other people is not possible gives no support to a contention *either* that "other minds" are radically unknowable *or* that people's claims to know one another never merit the label "knowledge." Residual assumptions to the effect that people are opaque to one another may explain why this knowledge has had minimal epistemological attention. Knowledge, as the tradition defines it, is *of* objects; only by assimilating people to objects can one hope to know them. This long-standing assumption is challenged by my claims that knowing other people is an exemplary kind of knowing and that subjectivity has always to be taken into account in making and assessing knowledge claims of any complexity.

## 5. Relativism After All?

The project I am proposing, then, requires a new *geography* of the epistemic terrain: one that is no longer primarily a physical geography, but a population geography that develops qualitative analyses of subjective positions and identities and the sociopolitical structures that produce them. Because differing social positions generate variable constructions of reality and afford different perspectives on the world, the revisionary stages of this project will consist of case-by-case analyses of the knowledge produced in specific social positions. These analyses derive from a recognition that knowers are always *somewhere*—and at once limited and enabled by the specificities of their locations.[47] It is an interpretive project, alert to the possibility of finding generalities and commonalities within particulars and hence of the explanatory potential that opens up when such commonalities can be delineated. But it is wary of the reductivism that results when commonalities are presupposed or forced. It has no ultimate foundation, but neither does it float free, because it is grounded in experiences and practices, in the efficacy of dialogic negotiation and of action.

All of this having been said, my argument in this essay points to the conclusion that necessary and sufficient conditions for establishing empirical knowledge claims cannot be found, at least where experientially significant knowledge is at issue. Hence it poses the question whether feminist epistemologists must, after all, "come out" as relativists. In view of what I have been arguing, the answer to that question will have to be a qualified "yes." Yet the relativism that my argument generates is sufficiently nuanced and sophisticated to escape the scorn—and the anxiety—that "relativism, after all" usually occasions. To begin with, it refuses to occupy the negative side of the traditional absolutism/relativism dichotomy. It is at once realist, rational, and significantly objective; hence it is not forced to define itself within or against the oppositions between realism and relativism, rationality and relativism, or objectivism and relativism.[48] Moreover, it takes as its starting point a recognition that the "positive" sides of these dichotomies have been caricatured to affirm a certainty that was never rightfully theirs.

The opponents of relativism have been so hostile, so thoroughly scornful in their dismissals, that it is no wonder that feminists, well aware of the folk-historical identification of women with the forces of unreason, should resist the very thought that the logic of feminist emancipatory analyses points in that direction.[49] Feminists know, if they know anything at all, that they have to develop the best possible explanations—the "truest" explanations—of how things are if they are to intervene effectively in social structures and institutions. The intransigence of material circumstances constantly reminds them that their world-making possibilities are neither unconstrained nor infinite; they have to be able to produce accurate, transformative analyses of things as they *are*. In fact, many feminists are vehement in their resistance to relativism precisely because they suspect—not without reason—that only the supremely powerful and privileged, the self-proclaimed sons of God, could believe that they can make the world up as they will and practice that supreme tolerance in whose terms all possible constructions of reality are equally worthy. Their fears are persuasive. Yet even at the risk of speaking within the oppositional mode, it is worth thinking seriously about the alternative. For there is no doubt that only the supremely powerful and privileged could believe, in the face of all the evidence to the contrary, that there is only one true view, and it is theirs; that they alone have the resources to establish universal, incontrovertible, and absolute Truth. Donna Haraway aptly notes that: "Relativism is a way of being nowhere and claiming to be everywhere";[50] but absolutism is a way of being everywhere while pretending to be nowhere—and neither one, in its starkest articulation, will do. For this reason alone, it is clear that the absolutism/relativism dichotomy needs to be displaced because it does not, as a true dichotomy must, use up all of the alternatives.[51]

The position I am advocating is one for which knowledge is always *relative to* (i.e., a perspective *on*, a standpoint *in*) specifiable circumstances. Hence it is constrained by a realist, empiricist commitment according to which getting those circumstances right is vital to effective action. It may appear to be a question-begging position, for it does assume that the circumstances can be known, and it relies heavily upon pragmatic criteria to make good that assumption. It can usually avoid regress, for although the circumstances in question may have to be specified *relative to* other circumstances, prejudgments, and theories, it is never (as with Neurath's raft) necessary to take away all of the pieces—all of the props—at once. Inquiry grows out of and turns back to practice, to action; inquirers are always in media res, and the res are both identifiable and constitutive of perspectives and possibilities for action. Practice will show, not once and for all but case by case, whether conclusions are reasonable and workable. Hence the position at once allows for the development of practical projects and for their corrigibility.

This "mitigated relativism" has a skeptical component: a consequence many feminists will resist even more vigorously than they will resist my claim for relativism. Western philosophy is still in thrall to an Enlightenment legacy that equates skepticism with nihilism: the belief that if no absolute foundations—no necessary and sufficient conditions—can be established, then there can be no knowledge.[52] Nothing is any more reasonable or rational than anything else; there is nothing to believe in. This is the skepticism that necessary and sufficient conditions are meant to forestall.

But there are other skepticisms which are resourceful, not defeatist. The ancient skepticisms of Pyrrho and Sextus Empiricus were declarations not of nihilism but of the impossibility of certainty, of the need to withhold definitive judgment. They advocated continual searching in order to prevent error by suspending judgment. They valued a readiness to reconsider and warned against hasty conclusions. These were skepticisms about the possibility of definitive knowledge but not about the existence of a (knowable?) reality. For Pyrrhonists, skepticism was a moral stance that was meant to ensure the inner quietude (*ataraxia*) that was essential to happiness.[53]

My suggestion that feminist epistemologists can find a resource in such skepticisms cannot be pushed to the point of urging that they take on the whole package. There is no question that the quietude of *ataraxia* could be the achievement that feminists are after. Nor could they take on a skepticism that would immobilize them by negating all possibilities for action: a quietism born of a theorized incapacity to choose or take a stand. So the skepticism that flavors the position I am advocating is better characterized as a common-sense, practical skepticism of everyday life than as a technical, philosophers' skepticism. It resembles the "healthy skepticism" that parents teach their children about media advertising and the skepticism that marks cautiously informed attitudes to politicians' promises.

Above all, feminists cannot opt for a skepticism that would make it impossible to know that certain practices and institutions are *wrong* and likely to remain so. The political ineffectiveness of universal tolerance no longer needs demonstrating: sexism is only the most obvious example of an undoubted intolerable. (Seyla Benhabib notes that Rorty's "admirable demand to 'let a hundred flowers bloom' is motivated by a desire to depoliticize philosophy."[54]) So even the skepticism that I am advocating is problematic in the sense that it has to be carefully measured and articulated if it is not to amount merely to "an apology for the existing order."[55] Its heuristic, productive dimensions are best captured by Denise Riley's observation that "an active skepticism about the integrity of the sacred category 'women' would be no merely philosophical doubt to be stifled in the name of effective political action in the world. On the contrary, it would be a condition *for* the latter."[56] It is in "making strange," loosening the hold of taken-for-granted values, ideals, categories, and theories, that skepticism demonstrates its promise.

Michel Foucault is one of the most articulate late twentieth-century successors of the ancient skeptics. A skeptic in his refusal of dogmatic unities, essences, and labels, Foucault examines changing practices of knowledge rather than taking the standard epistemological route of assuming a unified rationality or science. He eschews totalizing, universalist assumptions in his search for what John Rajchman calls the "invention of specific forms of experience which are taken up and transformed again and again."[57] His is a skepticism about the certainty and stability of systems of representation. Like the ancient skeptics, Foucault can be cast as a realist. He never doubts that there *are* things, institutions, and practices whose genealogies and archaeologies can be written. His position recommends itself for the freedom that its skeptical component offers. Hence he claims

> All my analyses are against the idea of universal necessities in human existence. They show the arbitrariness of institutions and show which space of freedom we can still enjoy and how many changes can still be made.[58]

Yet this is by no means an absolute freedom, for Foucault also observes

> My point is not that everything is bad, but that everything is dangerous, which is not exactly the same as bad. If everything is dangerous, then we always have something to do. So my position leads not to apathy but to a hyper- and pessimistic activism. . . . [T]he ethico-political choice we have to make . . . is to determine which is the main danger.[59]

One of the most urgent tasks that Foucault has left undone is that of showing how we can *know* what is dangerous.

There are many tensions within the strands that my skeptical-relativist recommendations try to weave together. For these I do not apologize. At this critical juncture in the articulation of emancipatory epistemological projects it is impossible to have all of the answers, to resolve all of the tensions and paradoxes. I have exposed some ways in which S-knows-that-*p* epistemologies are dangerous and have proposed one route toward facing and disarming those dangers: taking subjectivity into account. The solutions that route affords and the further dangers it reveals will indicate the directions that the next stages of this enquiry must take.[60]

## Notes

1. I allude here to the title of Thomas Nagel's book, *A View From Nowhere* (Oxford: Oxford University Press, 1986).

2. I owe the phrase *surrogate knower* to Naomi Scheman, which she coined in her paper "Descartes and Gender," presented to the conference "Reason, Gender, and the Moderns," University of Toronto, February 1990. I draw on this idea to make a set of points rather different from these in my "Who Cares? The Poverty of Objectivism for Moral Epistemology," in Alan Megill, ed., *Rethinking Objectivity Annals of Scholarship* 9 (1992).

3. For an account of the central tenets of logical positivism, a representative selection of articles, and an extensive bibliography, see A. J. Ayer, ed., *Logical Positivism* (New York: The Free Press, 1959).

4. Karl Popper, *Objective Knowledge* (Oxford: Clarendon Press, 1972), 108; emphasis in original.

5. Mary Hesse advisedly notes that philosophers of science would now more readily assert than they would have done in the heyday of positivism that facts in both the natural and social sciences are "value-laden." [See Mary Hesse, *Revolutions and Reconstructions in the Philosophy of Science* (Bloomington: Indiana University Press, 1980), 172–73.] I am claiming, however, that everyday conceptions of scientific authority are still significantly informed by a residual positivistic faith.

6. For classic statements of this aspect of the positivistic program see, for example, Rudolf Carnap, "Psychology in Physical Language"; and Otto Neurath, "Sociology and Physicalism," in Ayer, ed., *Logical Positivism.*

7. I discuss such responsibilities in my *Epistemic Responsibility* (Hanover, N.H.: University Press of New England, 1987).

8. See, for example, Joan Wallach Scott, "Is Gender a Useful Category of Historical Analysis?" in her book *Gender and the Politics of History* (New York: Columbia University Press, 1989).

9. Paul Moser, for example, in reviewing my *Epistemic Responsibility*, takes me to task for not announcing "the necessary and sufficient conditions for one's being epistemically responsible." He argues that even if, as I claim throughout the book, epistemic responsibility does not lend itself to analysis in those terms, "we could still provide necessary and sufficient conditions for the wide range of typical instances, and then handle the wayward cases independently" [Paul Moser, review of *Epistemic Responsibility*, in *Philosophical Books* 29 (1988): 154–56]. Yet it is precisely their "typicality" that I contest. Moser's review is a salient example of the tendency of dominant epistemologies to claim as their own even those positions that reject their central premises.

10. See p. 1 of this essay for a formulation of this thesis.

11. These aims are continuous with some of the aims of recent projects to naturalize epistemology by drawing on the resources of cognitive psychology. See especially W. V. Quine, "Epistemology Naturalized," in *Ontological Relativity and Other Essays* (New York: Columbia University Press, 1969), Hilary Kornblith, ed. *Naturalizing Epistemology*, (Cambridge, Mass.: MIT Press, 1985); and his paper "The Naturalistic Project in Epistemology: A Progress Report," presented to the American Philosophical Association, Los Angeles, April 1990; and Alvin I. Goldman, *Epistemology and Cognition* (Cambridge, Mass.: Harvard University Press, 1986). Feminist epistemologists who are developing this line of inquiry are Jane Duran, *Toward a Feminist Epistemology* (Savage, MD: Rowman & Littlefield, 1991); and Lynn Hankinson Nelson, *Who Knows: From Quine to a Feminist Empiricism* (Philadelphia: Temple University Press, 1990). Feminists who find a resource in this work have to contend with the fact that the cognitive psychology that informs it presupposes a constancy in "human nature," exemplified in "representative selves" who have commonly been white, male, and middle class. They have also to remember the extent to which appeals to "nature" have oppressed women and other marginal groups.

12. For an extensive bibliography of such critiques up to 1989, see Alison Wylie, Kathleen Okruhlik, Sandra Morton, and Leslie Thielen-Wilson, "Philosophical Feminism: A Bibliographic Guide to Critiques of Science," *Resources for Feminist Research/Documentation sur la Recherche Feministe* 19, 2 (June 1990): 2–36.

13. For an analysis of the androcentricity—the 'masculinity' of these ideals—and their 'feminine' exclusions in theories of knowledge see Genevieve Lloyd, *The Man of Reason* (Minneapolis: University of Minnesota Press, 1984); and Susan Bordo, *The Flight to Objectivity* (Albany: State University of New York Press, 1987). For discussions of the scientific context, see Evelyn Fox Keller, *Reflections on Gender and Science* (New Haven: Yale University Press, 1985); Sandra Harding, *The Science Question in Feminism* (Ithaca: Cornell University Press, 1986); and Nancy Tuana, ed., *Feminism and Science* (Bloomington: Indiana University Press, 1989).

14. Richard Foley, *The Theory of Epistemic Rationality* (Cambridge, Mass.: Harvard University Press, 1987), 48.

15. Ibid., 114.

16. Ibid., 140.

17. Ibid., 54.

18. I have singled out Foley's book because it is such a good example of the issues I am addressing. But he is by no means atypical. Space does not permit a catalogue of similar positions, but Lynn Hankinson Nelson notes that "Quine apparently assumes that at a given time "we" will agree about the question worth asking and the standards by which potential answers are to be judged, so he does not consider social arrangements as epistemological factors" (*Who Knows*, 170). Quine assumes, further, that "in the relevant community . . . we will all . . . see the same thing" (p. 184).

19. Here I am thinking of Richard Rorty, *Philosophy and the Mirror of Nature*, (Princeton: Princeton University Press, 1979); and *Consequences of Pragmatism* (Minneapolis: University of Minnesota Press, 1982).

20. *Philosophy and the Mirror of Nature*, 373.

21. Richard Rorty, "Solidarity or Objectivity?" in John Rajchman and Cornel West, eds., *Post-Analytic Philosophy* (New York: Columbia University Press, 1985), 7; emphasis added.

22. Ibid., 11.

23. Ibid., 15.

24. Nancy Fraser, "Solidarity or Singularity? Richard Rorty between Romanticism and Technocracy," in Nancy Fraser, *Unruly Practices: Power, Discourse and Gender in Contemporary Social Theory* (Minneapolis: University of Minnesota Press, 1989), 104.

25. Rorty, "Solidarity or Objectivity?," 5.

26. I borrow the idea, if not the detail, of the potential of case-by-case analysis from Roger A. Shiner, "From Epistemology to Romance Via Wisdom," in Ilham Dilman, ed., *Philosophy and Life: Essays on John Wisdom* (The Hague: Martinus Nijhoff, 1984), 291–314.

27. See Antonio Gramsci, *Selections from the Prison Notebooks*, trans. and ed. Quintin Hoare and Geoffrey Nowell Smith (New York: International Publishers, 1971).

28. Rudy Platiel and Stephen Strauss, *The Globe and Mail*, 4 February 1989. I cite the newspaper report because the media produce the public impact that concerns me here. I discuss neither the quality of Rushton's research practice nor the questions his theories and pedagogical practice pose about academic freedom. My concern is with how structures of knowledge, power, and prejudice grant him an epistemic place.

29. Commenting on the psychology of occupational assessment, Wendy Hollway observes: "That psychology is a science and that psychological assessment is therefore objective is a belief which continues to be fostered in

organizations." She further notes: "The legacy of psychology as science is the belief that the individual can be understood through measurement" [Wendy Hollway, "Fitting work: psychological assessment in organizations," in Julian Henriques, Wendy Hollway, Cathy Urwin, Couze Venn, and Valerie Walkerdine, *Changing the Subject: Psychology, social regulation and subjectivity* (London: Methuen, 1984), 35, 55].

30. The phrase is Richard Schmitt's, from "Murderous Objectivity: Reflections on Marxism and the Holocaust," in Roger S. Gottlieb, ed., *Thinking the Unthinkable: Meanings of the Holocaust* (New York: Paulist Press, 1990), 71. I am grateful to Richard Schmitt for helping me to think about the issues I discuss in this section.

31. Cynthia Eagle Russett, *Sexual Science: The Victorian Construction of Womanhood* (Cambridge, Mass.: Harvard University Press, 1989). In this connection, see also Lynda Birke, *Women, Feminism, and Biology* (Brighton: Harvester Press, 1986); and Janet Sayers, *Biological Politics* (London: Tavistock Publications, 1982).

32. The best-known contemporary discussion of utilitarian, controlled sexuality is Michel Foucault, *The History of Sexuality Volume I: An Introduction*, trans. Robert Hurley (New York: Vintage Books, 1980). In Foucault's analysis, sexuality is utilitarian both in reproducing the population and in cementing the family bond.

33. Julian Henriques, "Social psychology and the politics of racism," in Henriques et al., *Changing the Subject*, 74.

34. Clifford Geertz comments: "It is not . . . the validity of the sciences, real or would-be, that is at issue. What concerns me, and should concern us all, are the axes that, with an increasing determination bordering on the evangelical, are being busily ground with their assistance" ["Anti Anti-Relativism," in Michael Krausz, ed., *Relativism: Interpretation and Confrontation* (Notre Dame: University of Notre Dame Press, 1989), 20].

35. Philippe Rushton has received funding from the Social Sciences and Humanities Research Council of Canada and the Guggenheim Foundation in the USA, agencies whose status in the North American intellectual community confers authority and credibility. He has also received funding from the Pioneer Fund, an organization with explicit white supremacist commitments.

36. Naomi Scheman, "Commentary," in the Symposium on Sandra Harding's 'The Method Question' *APA Feminism and Philosophy Newsletter* 88.3 (1989): 42.

37. Helen Longino observes: ". . . How one determines evidential relevance, why one takes some state of affairs as evidence for one hypothesis rather than for another, depends on one's other beliefs, which we can call background beliefs or assumptions" (p. 43). And "When, for instance, background assumptions are shared by all members of a community, they acquire an invisibility that renders them unavailable for criticism" (p. 80). In *Science*

*as Social Knowledge: Values and Objectivity in Scientific Inquiry* (Princeton: Princeton University Press, 1990).

38.   Here I am borrowing a turn of phrase from Michel Foucault, when he writes in quite a different context: "And it was this network that made possible the individuals we term Hobbes, Berkeley, Hume, or Condillac" [Michel Foucault, *The Order of Things: An Archaeology of the Human Sciences* (New York: Random House, 1971), 63].

39.   I owe this point to the Biology and Gender Study Group, in "The Importance of Feminist Critique for Contemporary Cell Biology," in Nancy Tuana, ed., *Feminism and Science* (Bloomington: Indiana University Press, 1989), 173.

40.   The argument about the primacy of knowing other people is central to the position I develop in my *What Can She Know? Feminist Theory and the Construction of Knowledge* (Ithaca: Cornell University Press, 1991). Portions of this section of this essay are drawn, with modifications, from the book.

41.   Seyla Benhabib, "The Generalized and the Concrete Other," in Seyla Benhabib and Drucilla Cornell, eds., *Feminism As Critique* (Minneapolis: University of Minnesota Press, 1987), 85.

42.   See Susan Hekman, *Gender and Knowledge: Elements of a Postmodern Feminism* (Boston: Northeastern University Press, 1990), especially p. 3. For an introduction to these disputes, see Paul Rabinow & William M. Sullivan, eds., *Interpretive Social Science: A Second Look* (Berkeley: University of California Press, 1987).

43.   Sandra Harding, *The Science Question in Feminism* (Ithaca: Cornell University Press, 1986), 47. Harding contends that "a critical and self-reflective social science should be the model for all science, and . . . if there are any special requirements for adequate explanations in physics, they are just that— special" (Ibid., 44).

44.   Ibid., 46.

45.   Introduction, "The Interpretive Turn," in Rabinow and Sullivan, *Interpretive Social Science*, 13; emphasis added.

46.   The phrase is Elizabeth V. Spelman's, in "On Treating Persons as Persons," *Ethics* 88 (1978): 151.

47.   Here I borrow a phrase from Susan Bordo, "Feminism, Postmodernism, and Gender-Scepticism," in Linda Nicholson, ed., *Feminism/Postmodernism* (New York: Routledge, 1990), 145.

48.   I allude here to three now-classic treatments of the relativism question: Anne Seller, "Realism versus Relativism: Toward a Politically Adequate Epistemology," in Morwenna Griffiths and Margaret Whitford, eds., *Feminist Perspectives in Philosophy* (Bloomington: Indiana University Press, 1988); Martin Hollis and Steven Lukes, eds., *Rationality and Relativism* (Cambridge, Mass.: MIT Press, 1982), and Richard Bernstein, *Beyond Objectivism and Relativism* (Philadelphia: University of Pennsylvania Press, 1983).

49.   Sandra Harding resists endorsing relativism even in her discussions of standpoint and postmodern epistemologies. In a recent piece she introduces the neologism "interpretationism" as a solution, noting that "relativism is a consequence, but not always the intent, of interpretationism." (See her "Feminism, Science, and the Anti-Enlightenment Critiques," in Linda Nicholson, ed., *Feminism/Postmodernism*, 102, n. 5.) By contrast, I am uring the value of endorsing a reconstructed relativism, shorn of its enfeebling implications.

50.   Donna Haraway, "Situated Knowledges: The Science Question in Feminism and the Privilege of Partial Perspective," *Feminist Studies* 14, 3 (Fall 1988).

51.   See Nancy Jay, "Gender and Dichotomy," *Feminist Studies* 7 (1981) for a discussion of the exclusiveness of dichotomies.

52.   Peter Unger, in *Ignorance: A Case for Skepticism* (Oxford: Clarendon Press, 1975), argues that because no knowledge claim can meet the exacting standards of formulation in absolute terms, there is only conjecture, opinion, and fantasy. People are doomed to ignorance and should simply avow their skepticism.

53.   In thinking about Pyrrhonian skepticism I am indebted to David R. Hiley, "The Deep Challenge of Pyrrhonian Skepticism," *Journal of the History of Philosophy* 25, 2 (April 1987): 185–213.

54.   Seyla Benhabib, "Epistemologies of Postmodernism: A Rejoinder to Jean-Francois Lyotard," in Linda Nicholson, ed., *Feminism/Postmodernism*, 124.

55.   The phrase is Hiley's, p. 213.

55.   Denise Riley, *"Am I That Name?" Feminism and the Category of Women in History* (Minneapolis: University of Minnesota Press, 1988), 113.

57.   John Rajchman, *Michel Foucault: The Freedom of Philosophy* (New York: Columbia University Press, 1985), 3.

58.   Rux Martin, "Truth, Power, Self: An Interview with Michel Foucault, October 25, 1982," in Luther H. Martin, Huck Gutman and Patrick H. Hutton, eds., *Technologies of the Self: A Seminar with Michel Foucault* (Amherst: University of Massachusetts Press, 1988), 11.

59.   Michel Foucault, "On the Genealogy of Ethics: An Overview of Work in Progress." Afterword, in Hubert L. Dreyfus and Paul Rabinow, *Michel Foucault: Beyond Structuralism and Hermeneutics*, 2nd ed. (Chicago: University of Chicago Press, 1983), 231.

60.   Earlier versions of this paper were presented at the American Philosophical Association conference at Los Angeles and to the Departments of Philosophy at McMaster University and McGill University. I am grateful to participants in those discussions—especially to Susan Dwyer, Hilary Kornblith, and Doug Odegard—for their comments and to Linda Alcoff and Libby Potter for their valuable editorial suggestions.

3

# Rethinking Standpoint Epistemology: What Is "Strong Objectivity"?

*Sandra Harding*

---

> *"Feminist objectivity means quite simply situated knowledges."*
> —Donna Haraway[1]

## 1. Both Ways

For almost two decades, feminists have engaged in a complex and charged conversation about objectivity. Its topics have included which kinds of knowledge projects have it, which don't, and why they don't; whether the many different feminisms need it, and if so why they do; and if it is possible to get it, how to do so.[2] This conversation has been informed by complex and charged prefeminist writings that tend to get stuck in debates between empiricists and intentionalists, objectivists and interpretationists, and realists and social constructionists (including poststructuralists).[3]

Most of these feminist discussions have *not* arisen from attempts to find new ways either to criticize or carry on the agendas of the disciplines. Frequently they do not take as their problematics the ones familiar within the disciplines. Instead, these conversations have emerged mainly from two different and related concerns. First, what are the causes of the immense proliferation of theoretically and empirically sound results of research in biology and the social sciences that have discovered what is not supposed to exist: rampant sexist and androcentric bias—"politics"!—in the dominant scientific (and popular) descriptions and explanations of nature and social life? To put the point another way, how should one explain the surprising fact that politically guided research projects have been able to produce less partial and distorted results of research than those supposedly guided by the goal of value-neutrality? Second, how can feminists create re-

49

search that is *for* women in the sense that it provides less partial and distorted answers to questions that arise from women's lives and are not only about those lives but also about the rest of nature and social relations? The two concerns are related because recommendations for future scientific practices should be informed by the best accounts of past scientific successes. That is, how one answers the second question depends on what one thinks is the best answer to the first one.

Many feminists, like thinkers in the other new social liberation movements, now hold that it is not only desirable but also possible to have that apparent contradiction in terms—socially situated knowledge. In conventional accounts, socially situated beliefs only get to count as opinions. In order to achieve the status of knowledge, beliefs are supposed to break free of—to transcend—their original ties to local, historical interests, values, and agendas. However, as Donna Haraway has put the point, it turns out to be possible "to have *simultaneously* an account of radical historical contingency for all knowledge claims and knowing subjects, a critical practice for recognizing our own 'semiotic technologies' for making meanings, and a no-nonsense commitment to faithful accounts of a 'real' world. . . ."[4]

The standpoint epistemologists—and especially the feminists who have most fully articulated this kind of theory of knowledge—have claimed to provide a fundamental map or "logic" for how to do this: "start thought from marginalized lives" and "take everyday life as problematic."[5] However, these maps are easy to misread if one doesn't understand the principles used to construct them. Critics of standpoint writings have tended to refuse the invitation to "have it both ways" by accepting the idea of real knowledge that is socially situated. Instead they have assimilated standpoint claims either to objectivism or some kind of conventional foundationalism or to ethnocentrism, relativism, or phenomenological approaches in philosophy and the social sciences.

Here I shall try to make clear how it really is a misreading to assimilate standpoint epistemologies to those older ones and that such misreadings distort or make invisible the distinctive resources that they offer. I shall do so by contrasting the grounds for knowledge and the kinds of subjects/agents of knowledge recommended by standpoint theories with those favored by the older epistemologies. Then I shall show why it is reasonable to think that the socially situated grounds and subjects of standpoint epistemologies require and generate stronger standards for objectivity than do those that turn away from providing systematic methods for locating knowledge in history. The problem with the conventional conception of objectivity is not that it is too rigorous or too "objectifying," as some have argued, but that it is *not rigorous or objectifying enough;* it is too weak to accomplish even the goals for which it has been designed, let alone the more difficult projects called for by feminisms and other new social movements.[6]

## 2. Feminist Standpoint versus Spontaneous Feminist Empiricist Epistemologies

Not all feminists who try to explain the past and learn lessons for the future of feminist research in biology and the social sciences are standpoint theorists. The distinctiveness of feminist standpoint approaches can be emphasized by contrasting them with what I shall call "spontaneous feminist empiricist epistemology."[7]

By now, two forms of feminist empiricism have been articulated: the original "spontaneous" feminist empiricism and a recent philosophical version. Originally, feminist empiricism arose as the "spontaneous consciousness" of feminist researchers in biology and the social sciences who were trying to explain what was and what wasn't different about their research process in comparison with the standard procedures in their field.[8] They thought that they were just doing more carefully and rigorously what any good scientist should do; the problem they saw was one of "bad science." Hence they did not give a special name to their philosophy of science; I gave it the name "feminist empiricism" in *The Science Question in Feminism* to contrast feminist standpoint theory with the insistence of empiricism's proponents that sexism and androcentrism could be eliminated from the results of research if scientists would just follow more rigorously and carefully the existing methods and norms of research—which, for practicing scientists, are fundamentally empiricist ones.

Recently, philosophers Helen Longino and Lynn Hankinson Nelson have developed sophisticated and valuable feminist empiricist philosophies of science (Longino calls hers "contextual empiricism") that differ in significant respects from what most prefeminist empiricists and probably most spontaneous feminist empiricists would think of as empiricism.[9] This is no accident, because Longino and Nelson both intend to revise empiricism, as feminists in other fields have fruitfully revised other theoretical approaches—indeed, as feminist standpoint theorists revise the theory from which they begin. Longino and Nelson incorporate into their epistemologies elements that also appear in the standpoint accounts (many would say that they have been most forcefully articulated in such accounts)—such as the inescapable but also sometimes positive influence of social values and interests in the content of science—that would be anathema to even the spontaneous feminist empiricists of the late 1970s and early 1980s as well as to their many successors today. These philosophical feminist empiricisms are constructed in opposition partly to feminist standpoint theories, partly to radical feminist arguments that exalt the feminine and essentialize "woman's experience" (which they have sometimes attributed to standpoint theorists), and partly to the prefeminist empiricists.

It would be an interesting and valuable project to contrast in greater detail these important philosophical feminist empiricisms with both spontaneous feminist empiricism and with feminist standpoint theory. But I have a different goal in this essay: to show how strongly feminist reflections on scientific knowledge challenge the dominant prefeminist epistemology and philosophy of science that are held by all of those people inside and outside science who are still wondering just what are the insights about science and knowledge that feminists have to offer. In my view, this challenge is made most strongly by feminist standpoint epistemology.

One can understand spontaneous feminist empiricism and feminist standpoint theory to be making competing arguments on two topics—scientific method and history—in order to explain in their different ways the causes of sexist and androcentric results of scientific research.[10] As already indicated, spontaneous feminist empiricists think that insufficient care and rigor in following existing methods and norms is the cause of sexist and androcentric results of research, and it is in these terms that they try to produce plausible accounts of the successes of empirically and theoretically more adequate results of research. Standpoint theorists think that this is only part of the problem. They point out that retroactively, and with the help of the insights of the women's movement, one can see these sexist or androcentric practices in the disciplines. However, the methods and norms in the disciplines are too weak to permit researchers *systematically* to identify and eliminate from the results of research those social values, interests, and agendas that are shared by the entire scientific community or virtually all of it. Objectivity has not been "operationalized" in such a way that scientific method can detect sexist and androcentric assumptions that are "the dominant beliefs of an age"—that is, that are collectively (versus only individually) held. As far as scientific method goes (and feminist empiricist defenses of it), it is entirely serendipitous when cultural beliefs that are assumed by most members of a scientific community are challenged by a piece of scientific research. Standpoint theory tries to address this problem by producing stronger standards for "good method," ones that can guide more competent efforts to maximize objectivity.[11]

With respect to history, spontaneous feminist empiricists argue that movements of social liberation such as the women's movement function much like the little boy who is the hero of the folk tale about the Emperor and his clothes. Such movements "make it possible for people to see the world in an enlarged perspective because they remove the covers and blinders that obscure knowledge and observation."[12] Feminist standpoint theorists agree with this assessment, but argue that researchers can do more than just wait around until social movements happen and then wait around some more until their effects happen to reach inside the processes of producing maximally objective, causal accounts of nature and social relations. Knowledge projects can find active ways incorporated into their principles of "good method" to use history as a resource by socially situating knowledge projects in the scientifically and epistemologically most favorable historical locations. History can become the systematic provider of scientific and epistemological resources rather than an obstacle to or the "accidental" benefactor of projects to generate knowledge.[13]

It is spontaneous feminist empiricism's great strength that it explains the production of sexist and nonsexist results of research with only a minimal challenge to the fundamental logic of research as this is understood in scientific fields and to the logic of explanation as this is understood in the dominant philosophies of science. Spontaneous feminist empiricists try to fit feminist projects into prevailing standards of "good science" and "good philosophy." This conservativism makes it possible for many people to grasp the importance of feminist research in biology and the social sciences without feeling disloyal to the methods and norms of their research traditions. Spontaneous feminist empiricism appears to call for even greater rigor in using these methods and following these norms. However, this conservatism is also this philosophy's weakness; this theory of knowledge refuses fully to address the limitations of the dominant conceptions of method and explanation and the ways the conceptions constrain and distort results of research and thought about this research even when these dominant conceptions are most rigorously respected. Nevertheless, its radical nature should not be underestimated. It argues persuasively that the sciences have been blind to their own sexist and androcentric research practices and results. And it thereby clears space for the next question: are the existing logics of research and explanation really so innocent in the commission of this "crime" as empiricism insists, or are they part of its cause?[14]

The intellectual history of feminist standpoint theory is conventionally traced to Hegel's reflections on what can be known about the master/slave relationship from the standpoint of the slave's life versus that of the master's life and to the way Marx, Engels, and Lukacs subsequently developed this insight into the "standpoint of the proletariat" from which have been produced marxist theories of how class society operates.[15] In the 1970s, several feminist thinkers independently began reflecting on how the marxist analysis could be transformed to explain how the structural relationship between women and men had consequences for the production of knowledge.[16] However, it should be noted that even though standpoint arguments are most fully articulated as such in feminist writings, they appear in the scientific projects of all of the new social movements.[17] A *social* history of standpoint theory would focus on what happens when marginalized peoples begin to gain public voice. In societies where scientific rationality and objectivity are claimed to be highly valued by dominant groups, marginalized peoples and those who listen attentively to them will point out that from the perspective of marginal lives, the dominant accounts are less than maximally objective. Knowledge claims are always socially situated, and the failure by dominant groups critically and systematically to interrogate their advantaged social situation and the effect of such advantages on their beliefs leaves their social situation a scientifically and epistmologically disadvantaged one for generating knowledge. Moreover, these accounts end up legitimating exploitative "practical politics" even when those who produce them have good intentions.

The starting point of standpoint theory—and its claim that is most often misread—is that in societies stratefied by race, ethnicity, class, gender, sexuality, or some other such politics shaping the very structure of a society, the *activities* of those at the top both organize and set limits on what persons who perform such activities can understand about themselves and the world around them. "There are some perspectives on society from which, however well-intentioned one may be, the real relations of humans with each other and with the natural world are not visible."[18] In contrast, the activities of those at the bottom of such social hierarchies can provide starting points for thought—for *everyone's* research and scholarship—from which humans' relations with each other and the natural world can become visible. This is because the experience and lives of marginalized peoples, as they understand them, provide particularly significant *problems to be explained* or research agendas. These experiences and lives have been devalued or ignored as a source of objectivity-maximizing questions—the answers to which are not necessarily to be found in those experiences or lives but elsewhere in the beliefs and activities of people at the center who make policies and engage in social practices that shape marginal lives.[19] So one's social situation enables and sets limits on what one can know; some social situations—critically unexamined dominant ones—are more limiting than others in this respect, and what makes these situations more limiting is their inability to generate the most critical questions about received belief.[20]

It is this sense in which Dorothy Smith argues that women's experience is the "grounds" of feminist knowledge and that such knowledge should change the discipline of sociology.[21] Women's lives (our many different lives and different experiences!) can provide the starting point for asking new, critical questions about not only those women's lives but also about men's lives and, most importantly, the causal relations between them.[22] For example, she points out that if we start thinking from women's lives, we (anyone) can see that women are assigned the work that men do not want to do for themselves, especially the care of everyone's bodies—the bodies of men, babies, children, old people, the sick, and their own bodies. And they are assigned responsibility for the local places where those bodies exist as they clean and care for their own and others' houses and work places.[23] This kind of "women's work" frees men in the ruling groups to immerse themselves in the world of abstract concepts. The more successful women are at this concrete work, the more invisible it becomes to men as distinctively social labor. Caring for bodies and the places bodies exist disappears into "nature," as, for example, in sociobiological claims about the naturalness of "altruistic" behavior for females and its unnaturalness for males or in the systematic reticence of many prefeminist marxists actually to analyze who does what in everyday sexual, emotional, and domestic work, and to integrate such analyses into their accounts of "working class labor." Smith argues that we should not be surprised that men have trouble seeing women's activities as part of distinctively human culture and history once we notice how invisible the social character of this work is from the perspective of their activities. She points out that if we start from women's lives, we can generate questions about why it is that it is primarily women who are assigned such activities and what the consequences are for the economy, the state, the family, the educational system, and other social institutions of assigning body and emotional work to one group and "head" work to another.[24] These questions lead to less partial and distorted understandings of women's worlds, men's worlds, and the causal relations between them than do the questions originating only in that part of human activity that men in the dominant groups reserve for themselves—the abstract mental work of managing and administrating.

Standpoint epistemology sets the relationship between knowledge and politics at the center of its account in the sense that it tries to provide causal accounts—to explain—the effects that different kinds of politics have on the production of knowledge. Of course, empiricism also is concerned with the effects politics has on the production of knowledge, but prefeminist empiricism conceptualizes politics as entirely bad. Empiricism tries to purify science of all such bad politics by adherence to what it takes to be rigorous methods for the testing of hypotheses. From the perspective of standpoint epistemology, this is *far too weak a strategy* to maximize the objectivity of the results of research that empiricists desire. Thought that begins from the lives of the oppressed has no chance to get its critical questions voiced or heard within such an empiricist conception of the way to produce knowledge. Prefeminist empiricists can only perceive such questions as the intrusion of politics into science, which therefore deteriorates the objectivity of the results of research. Spontaneous feminist empiricism, for all its considerable virtues, nevertheless contains distorting traces of these assumptions, and they block the ability of this theory of science to develop maximally strong criteria for systematic ways to maximize objectivity.

Thus the standpoint claims that all knowledge attempts are socially situated and that some of these objective social locations are better than others as starting points for knowledge projects challenge some of the most fundamental assumptions of the scientific world view and the Western thought that takes science as its model of how to produce knowledge. It sets out a rigorous "logic of discovery" intended to maximize the objectivity of the results of research and thereby to produce knowledge that can be *for* marginalized people (and those who would know what the marginalized can know) rather than *for* the use only of dominant groups in their projects of administering and managing the lives of marginalized people.

## 3. What Are the Grounds for Knowledge Claims?

Standpoint theories argue for "starting off thought" from the lives of marginalized peoples; beginning in those determinate, objective locations in any social order will generate illuminating critical questions that do not arise in thought that begins from dominant group lives. Starting off research from women's lives will generate less partial and distorted accounts not only of women's lives but also of men's lives and of the whole social order. Women's lives and experiences provide the "grounds" for this knowledge, though these clearly do not provide foundations for knowledge in the conventional philosophical sense. These grounds are the site, the activities, from which scientific questions arise. The epistemologically advantaged starting points for research do not guarantee that the researcher can maximize objectivity in her account; these grounds provide only a necessary—not a sufficient—starting point for maximizing objectivity. It is useful to contrast standpoint grounds for knowledge with four other kinds: the "God-trick," ethnocentrism, relativism, and the unique abilities of the oppressed to produce knowledge.

*Standpoint Theories versus the "God-Trick"*

First, for standpoint theories, the grounds for knowledge are fully saturated with history and social life rather than abstracted from it. Standpoint knowledge projects do not claim to originate in purportedly universal human problematics; they do not claim to perform the "God-trick."[25] However, the fact that feminist knowledge claims are socially situated does not in practice distinguish them from any other knowledge claims that have ever been made inside or outside the history of Western thought and the disciplines today; all bear the fingerprints of the communities that produce them. All thought by humans starts off from socially determinate lives. As Dorothy Smith puts the point, "women's perspective, as I have analyzed it here, discredits sociology's claim to constitute an objective knowledge independent of the sociologists's situation. Its conceptual procedures, methods, and relevances are seen to organize its subject matter from a determinate position in society."[26]

It is a delusion—and a historically identifiable one—to think that human thought could completely erase the fingerprints that reveal its production process. Conventional conceptions of scientific method enable scientists to be relatively good at eliminating those social interests and values from the results of research that differ *within* the scientific community, because whenever experiments are repeated by different observers, differences in the social values of individual observers (or groups of them from different research teams) that have shaped the results of their research will stand out from the sameness of the phenomena that other researchers (or teams of them) report.[27] But scientific method provides no rules, procedures, or techniques for even identifying, let alone eliminating, social concerns and interests that are shared by all (or virtually all) of the observers, nor does it encourage seeking out observers whose social beliefs vary in order to increase the effectiveness of scientific method. Thus culturewide assumptions *that have not been criticized within the scientific research process* are transported into the results of research, making visible the historicity of specific scientific claims to people at other times, other places, or in other groups in the very same social order. We could say that standpoint theories not only acknowledge the social situatedness that is the inescapable lot of all knowledge-seeking projects but also, more importantly, transform it into a systematically available scientific resource.

### Standpoint Theories versus Ethnocentrism

Universalists have traditionally been able to imagine only ethnocentrism and relativism as possible alternatives to "the view from nowhere" that they assert grounds universal claims, so they think standpoint epistemologies must be supporting (or doomed to) one or the other of these positions. Is there any reasonable sense in which the ground for knowledge claimed by feminist standpoint theory is ethnocentric?

Ethnocentrism is the belief in the inherent superiority of one's own ethnic group or culture.[28] Do feminist standpoint theorists argue that the lives of *their own group or culture* is *superior* as a grounds for knowledge?[29] At first glance, one might think that this is the case if one notices that it is primarily women who have argued for starting thought from women's lives. However, there are several reasons why it would be a mistake to conclude from this fact that feminist standpoint theory is ethnocentric.

First, standpoint theorists themselves all explicitly argue that marginal lives that are not their own provide better grounds for certain kinds of knowledge. Thus the claim by women that women's lives provide a better starting point for thought about gender systems is not the same as the claim that *their own* lives are the best such starting points. They are not denying that their own lives can provide important resources for such projects, but they are arguing that other, different (and sometimes oppositional) women's lives also provide such resources. For example, women who are not prostitutes and have not been raped have argued that starting thought from women's experiences and activities in such events reveals that the state is male because it looks at women's lives here just as men (but not women) do. Dorothy Smith writes of the value of starting to think about a certain social situation she describes from the perspective of Native Canadian lives.[30] Bettina Aptheker has argued that starting thought from the everyday lives of women who are holocaust survivors, Chicana cannery workers, older lesbians, African-American women in slavery, Japanese-American concentration camp survivors, and others who have had lives different from hers increases our ability to understand a great deal about the distorted way the dominant groups conceptualize politics, resistance, community, and other key history and so-

cial science notions.[31] Patricia Hill Collins, an African-American so-
ciologist, has argued that starting thought from the lives of poor and
in some cases illiterate African-American women reveals important
truths about the lives of intellectuals, both African-American and Eu-
ropean-American, as well as about those women.[32] Many theorists who
are not mothers (as well as many who are) have argued that starting
thought in mother-work generates important questions about the social order. Of course some women no doubt do argue that their own
lives provide the one and only best starting point for all knowledge
projects, but this is not what standpoint theory holds. Thus, although
it is not an accident that so many women have argued for feminist
standpoint approaches, neither is it evidence that standpoint claims
are committed to ethnocentrism.

Second, and relatedly, thinkers with "center" identities have also
argued that marginalized lives are better places from which to start
asking causal and critical questions about the social order. After all,
Hegel was not a slave, though he argued that the master/slave relationship could better be understood from the perspective of slaves'
activities. Marx, Engels, and Lukacs were not engaged in the kind of
labor that they argued provided the starting point for developing their
theories about class society. There are men who have argued for the
scientific and epistemic advantages of starting thought from women's
lives, European-Americans who understand that much can be learned
about their lives as well as African-American lives if they start their
thought from the latter, and so on.[33]

Third, women's lives are shaped by the rules of femininity or womanliness; in this sense they "express feminine culture." Perhaps the
critic of standpoint theories thinks feminists are defending femininity
and thus "their own culture." But all feminist analyses, including
feminist standpoint writings, are in principle ambivalent about the
value of femininity and womanliness. Feminists criticize femininity
on the grounds that it is fundamentally defined by and therefore part
of the conceptual project of exalting masculinity; it is the "other"
against which men define themselves as admirably and uniquely human. Feminist thought does not try to substitute loyalty to femininity
for the loyalty to masculinity it criticizes in conventional thought.
Instead, it criticizes all gender loyalties as capable of producing only
partial and distorted results of research. However, it must do this while
also arguing that women's lives have been inappropriately devalued.
Feminist thought is forced to "speak as" and on behalf of the very
notion it criticizes and tries to dismantle—women. In the contradictory nature of this project lies both its greatest challenge and a source
of its great creativity. It is because the conditions of women's lives

are worse than their brothers' in so many cases that women's lives provide better places from which to start asking questions about a social order that tolerates and in so many respects even values highly the bad conditions for women's lives (women's double-day of work, the epidemic of violence against women, women's cultural obligation to be "beautiful," and so on).[34] Thus research processes that problematize how gender practices shape behavior and belief—that interrogate and criticize both masculinity and femininity—stand a better chance of avoiding such biasing gender loyalties.

Fourth, there are many feminisms, and these can be understood to be starting off their analyses from the lives of different historical groups of women. Liberal feminism initially started off its analyses from the lives of women in the eighteenth- and nineteenth-century European and U.S. educated classes; Marxist feminism, from the lives of wage-working women in the nineteenth- and early twentieth-century industrializing or "modernizing" societies; Third World feminism, from the lives of late twentieth-century women of Third World descent—and these different Third World lives produce different feminisms. Standpoint theory argues that each of these groups of women's lives is a good place to start in order to explain certain aspects of the social order. There is no single, ideal woman's life from which standpoint theories recommend that thought start. Instead, one must turn to all of the lives that are marginalized in different ways by the operative systems of social stratification. The different feminisms inform each other; we can learn from all of them and change our patterns of belief.

Last, one can note that from the perspective of marginalized lives, it is the dominant claims that we should in fact regard as ethnocentric. It is relatively easy to see that overtly racist, sexist, classist, and heterosexist claims have the effect of insisting that the dominant culture is superior. But it is also the case that claims to have produced universally valid beliefs—principles of ethics, of human nature, epistemologies, and philosophies of science—are ethnocentric. Only members of the powerful groups in societies stratified by race, ethnicity, class, gender, and sexuality could imagine that their standards for knowledge and the claims resulting from adherence to such standards should be found preferable by all rational creatures, past, present, and future. This is what the work of Smith, Hartsock, and the others discussed earlier shows. Moreover, standpoint theory itself is a historical emergent. There are good reasons why it has not emerged at other times in history; no doubt it will be replaced by more useful epistemologies in the future—the fate of all human products.[35]

*Standpoint Theory versus Relativism, Perspectivalism, and Pluralism*

If there is no single, transcendental standard for deciding between competing knowledge claims, then it is said that there can be only local historical ones, each valid in its own lights but having no claims against others. The literature on cognitive relativism is by now huge, and here is not the place to review it.[36] However, standpoint theory does not advocate—nor is it doomed to—relativism. It argues against the idea that all social situations provide equally useful resources for learning about the world and against the idea that they all set equally strong limits on knowledge. Contrary to what universalists think, standpoint theory is not committed to such a claim as a consequence of rejecting universalism. Standpoint theory provides arguments for the claim that some social situations are scientifically better than others as places from which to start off knowledge projects, and those arguments must be defeated if the charge of relativism is to gain plausibility.[37]

Judgmental (or epistemological) relativism is anathema to any scientific project, and feminist ones are no exception.[38] It is not equally true as its denial that women's uteruses wander around in their bodies when they take math courses, that only Man the Hunter made important contributions to distinctively human history, that women are biologically programmed to succeed at mothering and fail at equal participation in governing society, that women's preferred modes of moral reasoning are inferior to men's, that targets of rape and battering must bear the responsibility for what happens to them, that the sexual molestation and other physical abuses children report are only their fantasies, and so on—as various sexist and androcentric scientific theories have claimed. Feminist and prefeminist claims are usually not complementary but conflicting, just as the claim that the earth is flat conflicts with the claim that it is round. *Sociological* relativism permits us to acknowledge that different people hold different beliefs, but what is at issue in rethinking objectivity is the different matter of *judgmental* or epistemological relativism. Standpoint theories neither hold nor are doomed to it.

Both moral and cognitive forms of judgmental relativism have determinate histories; they appear as intellectual problems at certain times in history in only some cultures and only for certain groups of people. Relativism is not fundamentally a problem that emerges from feminist or any other thought that starts in marginalized lives; it is one that emerges from the thought of the dominant groups. Judgmental relativism is sometimes the most that dominant groups can stand to grant to their critics—"OK, your claims are valid for you, but mine are valid for me."[39] Recognizing the importance of thinking about who such a problem belongs to—identifying its social location—is one of the advantages of standpoint theory.

### Standpoint Theory versus the Unique Abilities of the Oppressed to Produce Knowledge

This is another way of formulating the charge that standpoint theories, in contrast to conventional theories of knowledge, are ethnocentric. However, in this form the position has tempted many feminists, as it has members of other liberatory knowledge projects.[40] We can think of this claim as supporting "identity science" projects—the knowledge projects that support and are supported by "identity politics." In the words of the Combahee River Collective's critique of liberal and marxist thought (feminist as well as prefeminist) that failed to socially situate anti-oppression claims: "Focusing upon our own oppression is embodied in the concept of identity politics. We believe that the most profound and potentially the most radical politics come directly out of our own identity, as opposed to working to end somebody else's oppression."[41] (They were tired of hearing about how they should be concerned to improve others' lives and how others were going to improve theirs.)

To pursue the issue further, we will turn to examine just who is the "subject of knowledge" for standpoint theories. But we can prepare for that discussion by recollecting yet again that Hegel was not a slave, though he grasped the critical understanding of the relations between master and slave that became available only if he started off his thought from the slave's activities, and that Marx, Engels and Lukacs were not proletarians. Two questions are raised by these examples: What is the role for marginalized experience in the standpoint projects of members of dominant groups? And what are the special resources, but also limits, that the lives of people in dominant groups provide in generating the more objective knowledge claims standpoint theories call for? We shall begin to address these issues in the next section.

To conclude this one, marginalized lives provide the scientific problems and the research agendas—not the solutions—for standpoint theories. Starting off thought from these lives provides fresh and more critical questions about how the social order works than does starting off thought from the unexamined lives of members of dominant groups. Most natural and social scientists (and philosophers!) are themselves members of these dominant groups, whether by birth or through upward mobility into scientific and professional/managerial careers. Those who are paid to teach and conduct research receive a disproportionate share of the benefits of that very nature and social order that they are trying to explain. Thinking from marginal lives leads one to question the adequacy of the conceptual frameworks that the natural and social sciences have designed to explain (for themselves) themselves and the world around them. This is the sense in which marginal lives ground knowledge for standpoint approaches.

## 4. New Subjects of Knowledge

For empiricist epistemology, the subject or agent of knowledge—that which "knows" the "best beliefs" of the day—is supposed to have a number of distinctive characteristics. First, this subject of knowledge is culturally and historically disembodied or invisible because knowledge is by definition universal. "Science says . . . ," we are told. Whose science, we can ask? The drug and cigarette companies? The Surgeon General's? The National Institute of Health's? The science of the critics of the NIH's racism and sexism? Empiricism insists that scientific knowledge has no particular historical subject. Second, in this respect, the subject of scientific knowledge is different in kind from the objects whose properties scientific knowledge describes and explains, because the latter are determinate in space and time. Third, though the subject of knowledge for empiricists is transhistorical, knowledge is initially produced ("discovered") by individuals and groups of individuals (reflected in the practice of scientific awards and honors), not by culturally specific societies or subgroups in a society such as a certain class or gender or race. Fourth, the subject is homogeneous and unitary, because knowledge must be consistent and coherent. If the subject of knowledge were permitted to be multiple and heterogeneous, then the knowledge produced by such subjects would be multiple and contradictory and thus inconsistent and incoherent.

The subjects of knowledge for standpoint theories contrast in all four respects. First, they are embodied and visible, because the lives from which thought has started are always present and visible in the results of that thought. This is true even though the way scientific method is operationalized usually succeeds in removing all personal or individual fingerprints from the results of research. But personal fingerprints are not the problem standpoint theory is intended to address. The thought of an age is *of an age*, and the delusion that one's thought can escape historical locatedness is just one of the thoughts that is typical of dominant groups in these and other ages. The "scientific world view" is, in fact, a view of (dominant groups in) modern, Western societies, as the histories of science proudly point out. Standpoint theories simply disagree with the further ahistorical and incoherent claim that the content of "modern and Western" scientific thought is also, paradoxically, not shaped by its historical location.

Second, the fact that subjects of knowledge are embodied and socially located has the consequence that they are not fundamentally different from objects of knowledge. We should assume causal symmetry in the sense that the same kinds of social forces that shape objects of knowledge also shape (but do not determine) knowers and their scientific projects.

This may appear to be true only for the objects of social science knowledge, not for the objects that the natural sciences study. After all, trees, rocks, planetary orbits, and electrons do not constitute themselves as historical actors. What they are does not depend on what they think they are; they do not think or carry on any of the other activities that distinguish human communities from other constituents of the world around us. However, this distinction turns out to be irrelevant to the point here because, in fact, scientists never can study the trees, rocks, planetary orbits, or electrons that are "out there" and untouched by human concerns. Instead, they are destined to study something different (but hopefully systematically related to what is "out there"): *nature as an object of knowledge*. Trees, rocks, planetary orbits, and electrons always appear to natural scientists only as they are already socially constituted in some of the ways that humans and their social groups are already socially constituted for the social scientist. Such objects are already effectively "removed from pure nature" into social life—they are social objects—by, first of all, the contemporary general cultural meanings that these objects have for everyone, including the entire scientific community.[42] They also become socially constituted objects of knowledge through the shapes and meanings these objects gain for scientists because of earlier generations of scientific discussion about them. Scientists never observe nature apart from such traditions; even when they criticize some aspects of them they must assume others in order to carry on the criticism. They could not do science if they did not both borrow from and also criticize these traditions. Their assumptions about what they see are always shaped by "conversations" they carry on with scientists of the past. Finally, their own interactions with such objects also culturally constitute them; to treat a piece of nature with respect, violence, degradation, curiosity, or indifference is to participate in culturally constituting such an object of knowledge. In these respects, nature as an object of knowledge simulates social life, and the processes of science themselves are a significant contributor to this phenomenon. Thus the subject and object of knowledge for the natural sciences are also not significantly different in kind. Whatever kinds of social forces shape the subjects are also thereby shaping their objects of knowledge.

Third, consequently, communities and not primarily individuals produce knowledge. For one thing, what I believe that I thought through all by myself (in my mind), which I know, only gets transformed from my personal belief to knowledge when it is socially legitimated. Just as importantly, my society ends up assuming all the claims I make that neither I nor my society critically interrogate. It assumes the eurocentric, androcentric, heterosexist, and bourgeois beliefs that I do not critically examine as part of my scientific research and that, consequently, shape my thought and appear as part of my knowledge claims. These are some of the kinds of features that subsequent ages (and Others today) will say make my thought characteristic of my age, or society, community, race, class, gender, or sexuality. The best scientific thought of today is no different in this respect from the thought of Galileo or Darwin; in all can be found not only brilliant thoughts first expressed by individuals and then legitimated by communities but also assumptions we now regard as false that were distinctive to a particular historical era and not identified as part of the "evidence" that scientists actually used to select the results of research.[43]

Fourth, the subjects/agents of knowledge for feminist standpoint theory are multiple, heterogeneous, and contradictory or incoherent, not unitary, homogeneous, and coherent as they are for empiricist epistemology.[44] Feminist knowledge has started off from women's lives, but it has started off from many different women's lives; there is no typical or essential woman's life from which feminisms start their thought. Moreover, these different women's lives are in important respects opposed to each other. Feminist knowledge has arisen from European and African women, from economically privileged and poor women, from lesbians and heterosexuals, from Protestant, Jewish, and Islamic women. Racism and imperialism, local and international structures of capitalist economies, institutionalized homophobia and compulsory heterosexuality, and the political conflicts between ethnic and religious cultures produce multiple, heterogeneous, and contradictory feminist accounts. Nevertheless, thought that starts off from each of these different kinds of lives can generate less partial and distorted accounts of nature and social life.

However, the subject/agent of feminist knowledge is multiple, heterogeneous, and frequently contradictory in a second way that mirrors the situation for women as a class. It is the thinker whose consciousness is bifurcated, the outsider within, the marginal person now located at the center,[45] the person who is committed to two agendas that are by their nature at least partially in conflict—the liberal feminist, socialist feminist, Sandinista feminist, Islamic feminist, or feminist scientist—who has generated feminist sciences and new knowledge. It is starting off thought from a contradictory social position that generates feminist knowledge. So the logic of the directive to "start thought from women's lives" requires that one start one's thought from multiple lives that are in many ways in conflict with each other, each of which itself has multiple and contradictory commitments. This may appear an overwhelming requirement—or even an impossible one—because Western thought has required the fiction that we have and thus think from unitary and coherent lives. But the challenge of learning to think from the perspective of more than one life when those lives are in conflict with each other is familiar to anthropologists, historians, conflict negotiators, domestic workers, wives, mothers—indeed, to most of us in many everyday contexts.

Both empiricist philosophy and marxism could maintain the fiction that unitary and coherent subjects of knowledge were to be preferred only by defining one socially distinctive group of people as the ideal knowers and arguing that all others lacked the characteristics that made this group ideal. Thus, the liberal philosophy associated with empiricism insisted that it was the possession of reason that enabled humans to know the world the way it is and then defined as not fully rational women, Africans, the working class, the Irish, Jews, other peoples from Mediterranean cultures, and so on. It was said that no individuals in these groups were capable of the dispassionate, disinterested exercise of individual moral and cognitive reason that was the necessary condition for becoming the ideal subject of knowledge. Similarly, traditional marxism argued that only the industrial proletariat possessed the characteristics for the ideal subject of marxist political economy. Peasants', slaves' and women's work, as well as bourgeois activities, made these people's lives inferior starting points for generating knowledge of the political economy.[46] In contrast, the logic of standpoint theory leads to the refusal to essentialize its subjects of knowledge.

This logic of multiple subjects leads to the recognition that the subject of liberatory feminist knowledge must also be, in an important if controversial sense, the subject of every other liberatory knowledge project. This is true in the collective sense of "subject of knowledge," because lesbian, poor, and racially marginalized women are all women, and therefore all feminists will have to grasp how gender, race, class, and sexuality are used to construct each other. It will have to do so if feminism is to be liberatory for marginalized women, but also if it is to avoid deluding dominant group women about their/our own situations. If this were not so, there would be no way to distinguish between feminism and the narrow self-interest of dominant group women—just as conventional androcentric thought permits no criterion for distinguishing between "best beliefs" and those that serve the self-interest of men as men. (Bourgeois thought permits no criterion for identifying specifically bourgeois self-interest; racist thought, for identifying racist self-interest; and so on.)

But the subject of every other liberatory movement must also learn how gender, race, class, and sexuality are used to construct each other in order to accomplish their goals. That is, analyses of class relations must look at their agendas from the perspective of women's lives, too. Women, too, hold class positions, and they are not identical to their brothers'. Moreover, as many critics have pointed out, agendas of the left need to deal with the fact that bosses regularly and all too successfully attempt to divide the working class against itself by manipulating gender hostilities. If women are forced to tolerate lower wages and double-days of work, employers can fire men and hire women to make more profit. Antiracist movements must look at their issues from the perspective of the lives of women of color, and so forth. Everything that feminist thought must know must also inform the thought of every other liberatory movement, and vice versa. It is not just the women in those other movements who must know the world from the perspective of women's lives. Everyone must do so if the movements are to succeed at their own goals. Most importantly, this requires that women be active directors of the agendas of these movements. But it also requires that men in those movements be able to generate original feminist knowledge from the perspective of women's lives as, for example, John Stuart Mill, Marx and Engels, Frederick Douglass, and later male feminists have done.[47]

However, if every other liberatory movement must generate feminist knowledge, it cannot be that women are the unique generators of feminist knowledge. Women can not claim this ability to be uniquely theirs, and men must not be permitted to claim that because they are not women, they are not obligated to produce fully feminist analyses. Men, too, must contribute distinctive forms of specifically feminist knowledge from their particular social situation. Men's thought, too, will begin first from women's lives in all the ways that feminist theory, with its rich and contradictory tendencies, has helped us all—women as well as men—to understand how to do. It will start there in order to gain the maximally objective theoretical frameworks within which men can begin to describe and explain their own and women's lives in less partial and distorted ways. This is necessary if men are to produce more than the male supremacist "folk belief" about themselves and the world they live in to which female feminists object. Women have had to learn how to substitute the generation of feminist thought for the "gender nativism" androcentric cultures encourage in them, too. Female feminists are made, not born. Men, too must learn to take historic responsibility for the social position from which they speak.

Patricia Hill Collins has stressed the importance to the development of Black feminist thought of genuine dialogue across differences, and of the importance of making coalitions with other groups if that dialogue is to happen.

> While Black feminist thought may originate with Black feminist intellectuals, it cannot flourish isolated from the experiences and ideas of other groups. The dilemma is that Black women intellectuals must place our own experiences and consciousness at the center of any serious efforts to develop Black feminist thought yet not have that thought become separatist and exclusionary. . . .
>
> By advocating, refining, and disseminating Black feminist thought, other groups—such as Black men, white women, white men, and other people of color—further its development. Black women can produce an attenuated version of Black feminist thought separated from other groups. Other groups cannot produce Black feminist thought without African-American women. Such groups can, however, develop self-defined knowledge reflecting their own standpoints. But the full actualization of Black feminist thought requires a collaborative enterprise with Black women at the center of a community based on coalitions among autonomous groups.[48]

It seems to me that Collins has provided a powerful analysis of the social relations necessary for the development of less partial and distorted belief by any knowledge community.

Far from licensing European-Americans to appropriate African-American thought or men to appropriate women's thought, this approach challenges members of dominant groups to make themselves "fit" to engage in collaborative, democratic, community enterprises with marginal peoples. Such a project requires learning to listen attentively to marginalized people; it requires educating oneself about their histories, achievements, preferred social relations, and hopes for the future; it requires putting one's body on the line for "their" causes until they feel like "our" causes; it requires critical examination of the dominant institutional beliefs and practices that systematically disadvantage them; it requires critical self-examination to discover how one unwittingly participates in generating disadvantage to them . . . and more. Fortunately, there are plenty of models available to us not only today but also through an examination of the history of members of dominant groups who learned to think from the lives of marginalized people and to act on what they learned. We can choose which historical lineage to claim as our own.

To conclude this section, we could say that since standpoint analyses explain how and why the subject of knowledge always appears in scientific accounts of nature and social life as part of the object of knowledge of those accounts, standpoint approaches have had to learn to use the social situatedness of subjects of knowledge systematically as a resource for maximizing objectivity. They have made the move from declaiming as a problem or acknowledging as an inevitable fact to theorizing as a *systematically accessible* resource for maximizing objectivity the inescapable social situatedness of knowledge claims.

## 5. Standards for Maximizing Objectivity

We are now in a position to draw out of this discussion of the innovative grounds and subject of knowledge for feminist standpoint theories the stronger standards for maximizing objectivity that such theories both require and generate. Strong objectivity requires that the subject of knowledge be placed on the same critical, causal plane as the objects of knowledge. Thus, strong objectivity requires what we can think of as "strong reflexivity." This is because culturewide (or nearly culturewide) beliefs function as evidence at every stage in scientific inquiry: in the selection of problems, the formation of hypotheses, the design of research (including the organization of research communities), the collection of data, the interpretation and sorting of data, decisions about when to stop research, the way results of research are reported, and so on. The subject of knowledge—the individual and the historically located social community whose unexamined beliefs its members are likely to hold "unknowingly," so to speak—must be considered as part of the object of knowledge from the perspective of scientific method. All of the kinds of objectivity-maximizing procedures focused on the nature and/or social relations that are the direct object of observation and reflection must also be focused on the observers and reflectors—scientists and the larger society whose assumptions they share. But a maximally critical study of scientists and their communities can be done only from the perspective of those whose lives have been marginalized by such communities. Thus, strong objectivity requires that scientists and their communities be integrated into democracy-advancing projects for scientific and epistemological reasons as well as moral and political ones.

From the perspective of such standpoint arguments, empiricism's standards appear weak; empiricism advances only the "objectivism" that has been so widely criticized from many quarters.[49] Objectivism impoverishes its attempts at maximizing objectivity when it turns away from the task of critically identifying all of those broad, historical social desires, interests, and values that have shaped the agendas, contents, and results of the sciences much as they shape the rest of human affairs.

Consider, first, how objectivism too narrowly operationalizes the notion of maximizing objectivity.[50] The conception of value-free, impartial, dispassionate research is supposed to direct the identification of all social values and their elimination from the results of research, yet it has been operationalized to identify and eliminate only those social values and interests that differ among the researchers and critics who are regarded by the scientific community as competent to make such judgments. If the community of "qualified" researchers and critics systematically excludes, for example, all African-Americans and women of all races and if the larger culture is stratified by race and gender and lacks powerful critiques of this stratification, it is not plausible to imagine that racist and sexist interests and values would be identified within a community of scientists composed entirely of people who benefit—intentionally or not—from institutionalized racism and sexism. This kind of blindness is advanced by the conventional belief that the truly scientific part of knowledge seeking—the part controlled by methods of research—occurs only in the context of justification. The context of discovery, in which problems are identified as appropriate for scientific investigation, hypotheses are formulated, key concepts are defined—this part of the scientific process is thought to be unexaminable within science by rational methods. Thus "real science" is restricted to those processes controllable by methodological rules. The methods of science—or rather, of the special sciences—are restricted to procedures for the testing of already formulated hypotheses. Untouched by these methods are those values and interests entrenched in the very statement of what problem is to be researched and in the concepts favored in the hypotheses that are to be tested. Recent histories of science are full of cases in which broad social assumptions stood little chance of identification or elimination through the very best research procedures of the day.[51] Thus objectivism operationalizes the notion of objectivity in much too narrow a way to permit the achievement of the value-free research that is supposed to be its outcome.

But objectivism also conceptualizes the desired value-neutrality of objectivity too broadly. Objectivists claim that objectivity requires the elimination of *all* social values and interests from the research process and the results of research. It is clear, however, that not all social values and interests have the same bad effects upon the results of research. Democracy-advancing values have systematically generated less partial and distorted beliefs than others.[52]

Objectivism's rather weak standards for maximizing objectivity make objectivity a mystifying notion, and its mystificatory character is largely responsible for its usefulness and its widespread appeal to dominant groups. It offers hope that scientists and science institutions, themselves admittedly historically located, can produce claims that will be regarded as objectively valid without having to examine critically their own historical commitments from which—intentionally or not—they actively construct their scientific research. It permits scientists and science institutions to be unconcerned with the origins or consequences of their problematics and practices or with the social values and interests that these problematics and practices support. It offers the false hope of enacting what Francis Bacon erroneously promised for the method of modern science: "The course I propose for the discovery of sciences is such as leaves but little to the acuteness and strength of wits, but places all wits and understandings nearly on a level." His "way of discovering science goes far to level men's wits, and leaves but little to individual excellence, because it performs everything by surest rules and demonstrations."[53] In contrast, standpoint approaches requires the strong objectivity that can take the subject as well as the object of knowledge to be a necessary object of critical, causal—scientific!—social explanations. This program of strong reflexivity is a resource for objectivity, in contrast to the obstacle that de facto reflexivity has posed to weak objectivity.

Some feminists and thinkers from other liberatory knowledge projects have thought that the very notion of objectivity should be abandoned. They say that it is hopelessly tainted by its use in racist, imperialist, bourgeois, homophobic, and androcentric scientific projects. Moreover, it is tied to a theory of representation and concept of the self or subject that insists on a rigid barrier between subject and object of knowledge—between self and Other—which feminism and other new social movements label as distinctively androcentric or eurocentric. Finally, the conventional notion of objectivity institutionalizes a certain kind of lawlessness at the heart of science, we could say, by refusing to theorize any criteria internal to scientific goals for distinguishing between scientific method, on the one hand, and such morally repugnant acts as torture or ecological destruction, on the other. Scientists and scientific institutions disapprove of, engage in political activism against, and set up special committees to screen scientific projects for such bad consequences, but these remain ad hoc measures, extrinsic to the conventional "logic" of scientific research.

However, there is not just one legitimate way to conceptualize objectivity, any more than there is only one way to conceptualize freedom, democracy, or science. The notion of objectivity has valuable political and intellectual histories; as it is transformed into "strong objectivity" by the logic of standpoint epistemologies, it retains central features of the older conception. In particular, might should not make right in the realm of knowledge production any more than in matters of ethics. Understanding ourselves and the world around us requires understanding what others think of us and our beliefs and actions, not just what we think of ourselves and them.[54] Finally, the appeal to objectivity is an issue not only between feminist and prefeminist science and knowledge projects but also within each feminist and other emancipatory research agenda. There are many feminisms, some of which result in claims that distort the racial, class, sexuality, and gender relationships in society. Which ones generate less or more partial and distorted accounts of nature and social life? The notion of objectivity is useful in providing a way to think about the gap that should exist between how any individual or group wants the world to be and how in fact it is.[55]

## 6. An Objection Considered

"Why not just keep the old notion of objectivity as requiring value-neutrality and argue instead that the problem feminism raises is how to get it, not that the concept itself should be changed? Why not argue that it is the notion of scientific method that should be transformed, not objectivity?"

This alternative position is attractive for several reasons. For one thing, clearly feminist standpoint theorists no less than other feminists want to root out sexist and androcentric bias from the results of research. They want results of research that are not "loyal to gender"—feminine or masculine. In this sense, don't they want to maximize value-neutrality—that is, old-fashioned objectivity—in the results of research?

Moreover, in important respects an epistemology and a method for doing research in the broadest sense of the term have the same consequences or, at least, are deeply implicated in each other. What would be the point of a theory of knowledge that did not make prescriptions for how to go about getting knowledge or of a prescription for getting knowledge that did not arise from a theory about how knowledge can be and has been produced? So why not appropriate and transform what the sciences think of as scientific method, but leave the notion of objectivity intact? Why not argue that the standpoint theories have finally completed the quest for a "logic of discovery" begun and then abandoned by philosophers some decades ago? They are calling for an "operationalization" of scientific method that includes the context of discovery and the social practices of justification in the appropriate domain of its rules and recommended procedures.[56] Scientific method must be understood to begin back in the context of discovery, in which scientific "problems" are identified and bold hypotheses conjectured. Then "starting from marginalized lives" becomes part of the method of maximizing value-neutral objectivity. This possibility could gain support from the fact that some standpoint theorists consistently talk about their work interchangeably as an epistemology and a method for doing research.[57]

Attractive as this alternative is, I think it is not attractive enough to convince that only method and not also the concept of objectivity should be reconceptualized. For one thing, this strategy makes it look reasonable to think it possible to gain value-neutrality in the results of research. It implies that human ideas can somehow escape their location in human history. But this no longer appears plausible in the new social studies of science.

Second, and relatedly, this strategy leads away from the project of analyzing how our beliefs regarded as true as well as those regarded as false have social causes and thus, once again, to the assumption of a crucial difference between subjects and objects of knowledge. It would leave those results of research that are judged by the scientific community to be maximally objective to appear to have no social causes, to be the result only of nature's impressions on our finally well-polished, glassy-mirror minds. Objects of knowledge then become, once again, dissimilar for the subjects of knowledge. Subjects of real knowledge, unlike subjects of mere opinion, are disembodied and socially invisible, whereas their natural and social objects of knowledge are firmly located in social history. Thus the "strong method" approach detached from "strong objectivity" leaves the opposition between subjects and objects firmly in place—an opposition that both distorts reality and has a long history of use in exploiting marginalized peoples. The "strong objectivity" approach locates this very assumed difference between subject and object of knowledge in social history; it calls for a scientific account of this assumption, too.

Third, this strategy leaves reflexivity merely a perpetual problem rather than also the resource into which standpoint theorists have transformed it. Observers do change the world that they observe, but refusing to strengthen the notion of objectivity leaves reflexivity always threatening objectivity rather than also as a resource for maximizing it.

Finally, it is at least paradoxical and most certainly likely to be confusing that the "strong method only" approach must activate in the process of producing knowledge those very values, interests, and politics that it regards as anathema in the results of research. It is at least odd to direct would-be knowers to go out and reorganize social life—as one must do to commit such forbidden (and difficult) acts as starting thought from marginal lives—in order to achieve value-neutrality in the results of research. Standpoint approaches want to eliminate dominant group interests and values from the results of research as well as the interests and values of *successfully colonized* minorities—loyalty to femininity as well as to masculinity is to be eliminated through feminist research. But that does not make the results of such research value-neutral. It will still be the thought of this era, making various distinctive assumptions that later generations and others today will point out to us.

On balance, these disadvantages outweigh the advantages of the "strong method only" approach.

Can the new social movements "have it both ways"? Can they have knowledge that is fully socially situated? We can conclude by putting the question another way: if they cannot, what hope is there for anyone else to maximize the objectivity of *their* beliefs?

## Notes

1. "Situated Knowledges: The Science Question in Feminism and the Privilege of Partial Perspective," *Feminist Studies* 14, 3 (1988): 581. Reprinted and revised in Donna J. Haraway, *Simians, Cyborgs, and Women* (New York: Routledge, 1991). I thank Linda Alcoff and Elizabeth Potter for helpful comments on an earlier draft.

2. Important works here include Susan Bordo, *The Flight to Objectivity: Essays on Cartesianism & Culture* (Albany: SUNY Press, 1987); Anne Fausto-Sterling, *Myths of Gender* (New York: Basic Books, 1985); Elizabeth Fee, "Women's Nature and Scientific Objectivity," in *Woman's Nature: Rationalizations of Inequality*, ed. Marion Lowe and Ruth Hubbard (New York: Pergamon Press, 1981); Donna Haraway, op. cit. and *Primate Visions: Gender*,

*Race and Nature in the World of Modern Science* (New York: Routledge, 1989); Ruth Hubbard, *The Politics of Women's Biology* (New Brunswick: Rutgers University Press, 1990); Evelyn Keller, *Reflections on Gender and Science* (New Haven: Yale University Press, 1984); Helen Longino, *Science as Social Knowledge* (Princeton, N.J.: Princeton University Press, 1990); and Lynn Hankinson Nelson, *Who Knows: From Quine to a Feminist Empiricism* (Philadelphia: Temple University Press, 1990). These are just *some* of the important works on the topic; many other authors have made contributions to the discussion. I have addressed these issues in *The Science Question in Feminism* (Ithaca: Cornell University Press, 1986) and *Whose Science? Whose Knowledge? Thinking From Women's Lives* (Ithaca: Cornell University Press, 1991); see also the essays in Sandra Harding and Merrill Hintikka, ed., *Discovering Reality: Feminist Perspectives on Epistemology, Metaphysics, Methodology and the Philosophy of Science* (Dordrecht: Reidel 1983). An interesting parallel discussion occurs in the feminist jurisprudence literature in the course of critiques of conventional conceptions of what "the rational man" would do, "the objective observer" would see, and "the impartial judge" would reason; see, for example many of the essays in the special issue of the *Journal of Legal Education* on *Women in Legal Education—Pedagogy, Law, Theory, and Practice* 39, 1–2 (1988), ed. Carrie Menkel-Meadow, Martha Minow, and David Vernon; and Katharine T. Bartlett, "Feminist Legal Methods," *Harvard Law Review* 103, 4 (1990).

3. This literature is by now huge. For a sampling of its concerns, see Richard Bernstein, *Beyond Objectivism and Relativism* (Philadelphia: University of Pennsylvania Press, 1983); Martin Hollis and Steven Lukes, eds., *Rationality and Relativism* (Cambridge, Mass.: Harvard University Press, 1982); Michael Krausz and Jack Meiland, eds., *Relativism: Cognitive and Moral* (Notre Dame, Ind.: University of Notre Dame Press, 1982); and Stanley Aronowitz, *Science and Power: Discourse and Ideology in Modern Society* (Minneapolis: University of Minnesota Press, 1988).

4. Haraway, "Situated Knowledges," loc. cit., 579. In the phrase "a critical practice for recognizing our own 'semiotic technologies' for making meanings," she also raises here the troubling issue of reflexivity, to which I shall return.

5. Dorothy Smith, *The Everyday World as Problematic: A Feminist Sociology,* (Boston: Northeastern University Press, 1987) and *The Conceptual Practices of Power: A Feminist Sociology of Knowledge,* (Boston: Northeastern University Press, 1990); Nancy Hartsock, "The Feminist Standpoint: Developing the Ground for a Specifically Feminist Historical Materialism," in Harding and Hintikka, eds., *Discovering Reality;* Hilary Rose, "Hand, Brain and Heart: A Feminist Epistemology of the Natural Sciences," *Signs* 9, 1 (1983); and my discussion of these writings in chapter 6 of *The Science Question in Feminism.* Alison Jaggar also developed an influential account of standpoint epistemology in chapter 11 of *Feminist Politics and Human Nature* (Totowa, N.J.: Rowman & Allenheld, 1983). For more recent developments of standpoint theory see Patricia Hill Collins, chapters 10 and 11 of *Black Feminist Thought: Knowl-*

*edge, Consciousness and the Politics of Empowerment* (Boston: Unwin Hyman, 1990) and chapters 5, 6, 7, and 11 of my *Whose Science? Whose Knowledge?*

6.   Chapter 6 of *Whose Science?*, " 'Strong Objectivity' and Socially Situated Knowledge," addresses some of the issues I raise here. However, here I develop further the differences between the "grounds" and the subject of knowledge for standpoint theory and for other epistemologies. This is partly an archeology of standpoint theory—bringing to full light the obscured aspects of its logic—and partly a reformulation of some of its claims.

7.   Scientists sometimes confuse the philosophy of science called "empiricism" with the idea that it is a good thing to collect information about the empirical world. All philosophies of science recommend the latter. Empiricism is that account of such practices associated paradigmatically with Locke, Berkeley and Hume and claiming that sensory experience is the only or fundamental source of knowledge. It contrasts with theological accounts that were characteristic of European science of the Middle Ages, with rationalism, and with Marxist philosophy of science. However, from the perspective of standpoint theory, it also shares key features with one or another of these three philosophies. For example, it borrows the monologic voice that seems proper if one assumes the necessity of a unitary and coherent subject of knowledge, as do all three.

8.   Roy Bhaskar writes that although positivism mystifies the processes of science, nevertheless it has a certain degree of necessity in that it reflects the spontaneous consciousness of the lab bench—the tenets of positivism reflect how it feels like science is done when one is actually gathering observations of nature. Similarly, from the perspective of standpoint approaches, the "spontaneous" feminist empiricism I discuss here mystifies the processes of feminist research, although it has a certain necessity in that it just felt to these feminist empirical workers like what it was that they were doing as their work overturned the results of supposedly value-free prefeminist research. See Roy Bhaskar, "Philosophies as Ideologies of Science: A Contribution to the Critique of Positivism," in *Reclaiming Reality* (New York: Verso, 1989). Not all forms of empiricism are reasonably thought of as positivist, of course, but the most prevalent contemporary forms are. The philosophical feminist empiricism noted below is not positivist.

9.   Longino, *Science as Social Knowledge*; Nelson, *Who Knows*.

10.   There are many standpoint theorists and many spontaneous feminist empiricists. I present here ideal types of these two theories of knowledge. I have contrasted these two theories in a number of earlier writings, most recently on p. 111–37 of *Whose Science: Whose Knowledge?* The following passage draws especially on pp. 111–20.

11.   Dorothy Smith was right, I now think, to insist (in effect) that standpoint theory appropriates and transforms the notion of scientific method, not just of epistemology; see her comments on a paper of mine in *American Philosophical Association Newsletter on Feminism* 88, 3 (1989). It is interesting to

note that by 1989, even the National Academy of Science—no rabble-rousing antiscience critic!—argues that the methods of science should be understood to include "the judgments scientists make about the interpretation or reliability of data . . . , the decisions scientists make about which problems to pursue or when to conclude an investigation," and even "the ways scientists work with each other and exchange information" [*On Being a Scientist* (Washington D.C.: National Academy Press, 1989), 5–6].

12. Marcia Millman and Rosabeth Moss Kanter, "Editor's Introduction" to *Another Voice: Feminist Perspectives on Social Life and Social Science* (New York: Anchor Books, 1975), vii. [Reprinted in S. Harding, ed., *Feminism and Methodology*, (Bloomington: Indiana University Press, 1987.)]

13. This description seems to imply that scientists are somehow outside of the history they are using—for example, capable of determining which are, in fact, the scientifically and epistemologically most favorable historical locations. This is not so, of course, and that is why the reflexivity project Haraway refers to is so important.

14. "Of course here and there will be found careless or poorly trained scientists, but no *real* scientist, no *good* scientist, would produce sexist or androcentric results of research." This line of argument has the consequence that there have been no real or good scientists except for feminists! See "What Is Feminist Science?," chapter 12 of *Whose Science? Whose Knowledge?*, for discussions of this and other attempts to resist the idea that feminist science is exactly good science but that refusing to acknowledge the feminist component in good science obscures what makes it good.

15. Frederic Jameson has argued that the feminist standpoint theorists are the only contemporary thinkers fully to appreciate the Marxist epistemology. See "History and Class Consciousness as an 'Unfinished Project,' " *Rethinking Marxism* 1 (1988): 49–72. It should be noted that empiricist explanations of Marxist accounts are common: "Marx had this puzzle. . . . He made a bold conjecture and then attempted to falsify it. . . . The facts supported his account and resolved the puzzle." These make the accounts plausible to empiricists but fail to engage both with Marx's own different epistemology and with the additional "puzzle" of the historical causes of the emergence of his account, to which Marxist epistemology draws attention.

16. See note 6.

17. Cf., for example, Edward Said, *Orientalism* (New York: Pantheon Books, 1978); Samir Amin, *Eurocentrism* (New York: Monthly Review Press, 1989); Monique Wittig, "The Straight Mind," *Feminist Issues* 1, 1 (1980); Marilyn Frye, *The Politics of Reality* (Trumansburg, N.Y.: The Crossing Press, 1983); and Charles Mills, "Alternative Epistemologies," *Social Theory and Practice* 14, 3 (1988).

18. Hartsock, "The Feminist Standpoint," 159. Hartsock's use of the term "real relations" may suggest to some readers that she and other standpoint theorists are hopelessly mired in an epistemology and metaphysics that have

been discredited by social constructionists. This judgment fails to appreciate the way standpoint theories reject *both* pure realist and pure social constructionist epistemologies and metaphysics. Donna Haraway is particularly good on this issue. (See her "Situated Knowledges," cited in note 1.)

19. We shall return later to the point that, for standpoint theorists, reports of marginalized experience or lives or phenomenologies of the "lived world" of marginalized peoples are not the *answers* to questions arising either inside or outside those lives, though they are necessary to asking the best questions.

20. For an exploration of a number of different ways in which marginal lives can generate more critical questions, see chapter 5, "What is Feminist Epistemology?" in *Whose Science? Whose Knowledge?*

21. See, for example, *The Conceptual Practices of Power: A Feminist Sociology of Knowledge*, 54.

22. The image of knowledge seeking as a journey—"starting off thought from women's lives"—is a useful corrective to misunderstandings that more easily arise from the visual metaphor—"thinking from the perspective of women's lives." The journey metaphor appears often in writings by Hartsock, Smith, and others.

23. Some women are assigned more of this work than others, but even wealthy and aristocratic women with plenty of servants are left significantly responsible for such work in ways their brothers are not.

24. Of course body work and emotional work also require head work—contrary to the long history of sexist, racist, and class-biased views. See, for example, Sara Ruddick, *Maternal Thinking* (New York: Beacon Press, 1989). And the kind of head work required in administrative and managerial work—what Smith means by "ruling"—also involves distinctive body and emotional work, though it is not acknowledged as such. Think of how much of early childhood education of middle-class children is really about internalizing a certain kind of (gender-specific) regulation of bodies and emotions.

25. This is Donna Haraway's phrase in "Situated Knowledges" cited in note 1.

26. Smith, "Women's Perspective as a Radical Critique of Sociology," in *Feminism and Methodology*, 91.

27. I idealize the history of science here as is indicated by recent studies of fraud, carelessness, and unconscious bias that is not detected. See, for example, Stephen Jay Gould, *The Mismeasure of Man* (New York: W. W. Norton, 1981); L. Kamin, *The Science and Politics of IQ* (Potomac, Md.: Erlbaum, 1974); and William Broad and Nicholas Wade, *Betrayers of the Truth* (New York: Simon & Schuster, 1982). The issue here can appear to be one about the sins of individuals, which it is. But far more importantly, it is an issue about both the unwillingness and impotence of scientific institutions to police their own practices. They *must* do so, for any other alternative is less effective. But science institutions will not want to or be competent to do so until they are more integrated into democratic social projects.

28. Richard Rorty is unusual in arguing that because social situatedness is indeed the lot of all human knowledge projects, we might as well embrace our ethnocentrism while pursuing the conversations of mankind. His defense of ethnocentrism is a defense of a kind of fatalism about the impossibility of people ever transcending their social situation; in a significant sense this comes down to and converges with the standard definition of ethnocentrism centered in my argument here. (I thank Linda Alcoff for helping me to clarify this point.) He does not imagine that one can effectively change one's "social situation" by, for example, participating in a feminist political movement, reading and producing feminist analyses, and so on. From the perspective of his argument, it is mysterious how any woman (or man) ever becomes a feminist because our "social situation" is initially to be constrained by patriarchal institutions, ideologies, and the like. How *did* John Stuart Mill or Simone de Beauvoir ever come to think such thoughts as they did? See his *Objectivity, Relativism and Truth* (New York: Cambridge University Press, 1991).

29. Of course a gender is not an ethnicity. Yet historians and anthropologists write of women's cultures, so perhaps it does not stretch the meaning of ethnicity too far to think of women's cultures this way. Certainly some of the critics of standpoint theory have done so.

30. "Women's Perspective," cited in note 26.

31. Bettina Aptheker, *Tapestries of Life: Women's Work, Women's Consciousness, and the Meaning of Daily Life* (Amherst: University of Massachusetts Press, 1989).

32. *Black Feminist Thought*, cited in note 6.,

33. The preceding citations contain many examples of such cases.

34. "So many," but not all. African-American and Latina writers have argued that in U.S. society, at least, a poor African-American and Latino man cannot be regarded as better off than his sister in many important respects.

35. What are the material limits of standpoint theories? Retroactively, we can see that they require the context of scientific culture; that is, they center claims about greater objectivity, the possibility and desirability of progress, the value of causal accounts for social projects, and so on. They also appear to require that the barriers between dominant and dominated be not absolutely rigid; there must be some degree of social mobility. Some marginal people must be able to observe what those at the center do, some marginal voices must be able to catch the attention of those at the center, and some people at the center must be intimate enough with the lives of the marginalized to be able to think how social life works from the perspective of their lives. A totalitarian system would be unlikely to breed standpoint theories. So a historical move to antiscientific or to totalitarian systems would make standpoint theories less useful. No doubt there are other historical changes that would limit the resources standpoint theories can provide.

36. See the citations in note 3.

37. All of the feminist standpoint theorists and science writers insist on distinguishing their positions from relativist ones. I have discussed the issue of relativism in several places, most recently in chapters 6 and 7 of *Whose Science? Whose Knowledge?*

38. See S. P. Mohanty, "Us and Them: On the Philosophical Bases of Political Criticism," *Yale Journal of Criticism*, 2, 2 (1989); and Donna Haraway's "Situated Knowledges" for especially illuminating discussions of why relativism can look attractive to many thinkers at this moment in history, but why it should nevertheless be resisted.

39. Mary G. Belenky and her colleagues point out that the phrase "It's my opinion . . . " has different meanings for the young men and women they have studied. For men this phrase means "I've got a right to my opinion," but for women it means "It's just my opinion." Mary G. Belenky, B. M. Clinchy, N. R. Goldeberger, and J. M. Tarule, *Women's Ways of Knowing: the Development of Self, Voice, and Mind* (New York: Basic Books, 1986).

40. Critics of standpoint theories usually attribute this position to standpoint theorists. Within the array of feminist theoretical approaches, the claim that only women can produce knowledge is most often made by Radical Feminists.

41. The Combahee River Collective, "A Black Feminist Statement," in *This Bridge Called My Back: Writings by Radical Women of Color*, ed. Cherríe Moraga and Gloria Anzaldúa (Latham, N.Y.: Kitchen Table: Women of Color Press, 1983), 212.

42. For example, mechanistic models of the universe had different meanings for Galileo's critics than they have had for modern astronomers or, later, for contemporary ecologists, as Carolyn Merchant and other historians of science point out. See Carolyn Merchant, *The Death of Nature: Women, Ecology and the Scientific Revolution* (New York: Harper & Row, 1980). To take another case, "wild animals" and, more generally, "nature" are defined differently by Japanese, Indian, and Anglo-American primatologists, as Donna Haraway points out in *Primate Visions* (cited in note 2). The cultural character of nature as an object of knowledge has been a consistent theme in Haraway's work.

43. Longino and Nelson's arguments are particularly telling against the individualism of empiricism. See Nelson's "Who Knows," chapter 6 in *Who Knows*, and Longino's discussion of how the underdetermination of theories by their evidence insures that "background beliefs" will function as if they were evidence in many chapters of *Science as Social Knowledge* (cited in note 2) but especially in chapters 8, 9, and 10.

44. See Elizabeth Spelman, *Inessential Woman: Problems of Exclusion in Feminist Thought* (Boston: Beacon Press, 1988) for a particularly pointed critique of essentialist tendencies in feminist writings. Most of the rest of this section appears also in "Subjectivity, Experience and Knowledge: An Epistemology from/for Rainbow Coalition Politics," forthcoming in *Questions of*

*Authority: The Politics of Discourse and Epistemology in Feminist Thought,* ed. Judith Roof and Robyn Weigman. I have also discussed these points in several other places.

45. These ways of describing this kind of subject of knowledge appear in the writings of, respectively, Smith ("Women's Perspective"), Collins (*Black Feminist Thought*) and Bell Hooks, *Feminist Theory From Margin to Center* (Boston: South End Press, 1983).

46. Consequently, a main strategy of the public agenda politics of the new social movements has been to insist that women, or peoples of African descent, or the poor, and so on do indeed possess the kinds of reason that qualify them as "rational men"; that women's, industrial, or peasant labor makes these groups also the "working men" from whose laboring lives can be generated less partial and distorted understandings of local and international economies.

47. I do not say these thinkers are perfect feminists—they are not, and no one is. But here and there one can see them generating original feminist knowledge as they think from the perspective of women's lives as women have taught them to do.

48. Collins, *Black Feminist Thought,* 35–36. Chapters 1, 2, 10, and 11 of this book offer a particular rich and stimulating development of standpoint theory.

49. See the citations in note 3. The term "objectivism" has been used to identify the objectionable notion by Bernstein, Keller, and Bordo (see earlier citations), among others.

50. The following arguments are excerpted from pp. 143–48 in my *Whose Science? Whose Knowledge?*

51. See note 27.

52. Many Americans—even (especially?) highly educated ones—hold fundamentally totalitarian notions of what democracy is, associating it with mob rule or some at least mildly irrelevant principle of representation but never with genuine community dialogue. (A physicist asked me if by democracy I really meant that national physics projects should be managed by, say, fifty-two people, one selected randomly from each state! This made me think of the wisdom of William Buckley, Jr.'s desire to be governed by the first 100 people in the Boston phone book rather than the governors we have.) A good starting point for thinking about how to advance democracy is John Dewey's proposal: those who will bear the consequence of a decision should have a proportionate share in making it.

53. Quoted in Werner Van den Daele, "The Social Construction of Science," in *The Social Production of Scientific Knowledge,* ed. E. Mendelsohn, P. Weingart, and R. Whitley (Dordrecht: Reidel, 1977), 34.

54. David Mura puts the point this way in "Strangers in the Village," in *The Graywolf Annual Five: Multi-cultural Literacy* ed. Rick Simonson and Scott Walker (St. Paul: Graywolf Press, 1988), 152.

55. These arguments for retaining the notion of objectivity draw on ones I have made several times before, most recently in *Whose Science? Whose Knowledge?* p. 157–61.

56. The National Academy of Sciences recommends such an expansion, as indicated earlier.

57. For example, Smith and Hartsock, cited in note. 5.

# 4

# Marginality and Epistemic Privilege

*Bat-Ami Bar On*

## I.

Since the early days of the current wave of the women's movement, feminists have claimed that experience is not gender-neutral in societies in which gender matters because it is the experience of gendered persons. Feminists have accumulated plenty of empirical data in support of this claim[1] and have deployed it strategically to legitimate demands for attention to what women, and feminists as their spokeswomen, have to say about discrimination against and oppression of women. The claim has served feminists especially well in the academy, where curricula and pedagogy alike have come under feminist scrutiny and have been found lacking because of the exclusion of women's voices.

The claim that experience is gender-specific implies that gender is a constitutive element of experience, and one of the tasks undertaken by feminist epistemologists has been to explore why and how gender constitutes experience.[2] In addition, feminist epistemologists have been investigating the epistemological significance of the constitution of experience by gender.[3]

The constitution of experience by gender is asserted to be epistemologically significant by most Western second-wave feminists, including ethnic feminists. Although for some feminists all that this assertion means is that knowledge claims based on the experience of one gender are partially true, for other feminists it means that not only is all knowledge perspectival but also that some perspectives are more revealing than others. These are the perspectives of members of groups that are socially marginalized in their relations to dominant groups—for example, women or subgroups thereof, such as African-American women or lesbians.[4]

One can find traces of this feminist position in early second-wave feminist essays. Thus in 1969, Mary Ann Weathers claimed in "An Argument for Black Women's Liberation as a Revolutionary Force" that Black women "are clearly the most oppressed minority in the world, let alone the [USA]" and are the best agents of their own liberation.[5] And in 1977, the Combahee River Collective reiterated and clarified this position in "A Black Feminist Statement":

> We believe that the most profound and potentially the most radical politics come directly out of our own identity, as opposed to working to end somebody else's oppression. . . . We believe that sexual politics under patriarchy is as pervasive in black women's lives as are the politics of race and class. . . . We know that there is such a thing as racial-sexual oppression which is neither solely racial nor solely sexual.[6]

In "Goodbye to All That," written in 1970, Robin Morgan stated that "it seems obvious that a legitimate revolution must be led by, *made* by those who have been most oppressed: black, brown and white *women*—with men relating to that the best they can."[7] And in 1971, Vivian Gornick wrote in "Woman as Outsider":

> In every real sense woman . . . is an outsider. . . . Only a brief look at the cultural and religious myths and the literary projections of woman that surround the female existence . . . will instantly reveal the essential outsiderness of woman: her distance from the center of self-realized life, the extremity of her responses to experience, her characteristic femaleness incorporating . . . a distillation of human behavior that grows directly out of the excluded nature of her destined life.[8]

Also in 1971, Sidney Abbott and Barbara Love made this observation in "Is Women's Liberation a Lesbian Plot?":

> Lesbians are the women who potentially can demonstrate life outside the male power structure that dominates marriage as well as every other aspect of our culture. Thus, the lesbian movement is not only related to women's liberation, it is at the very heart of it.[9]

Finally in 1975, Charlotte Bunch reiterated and clarified this position in "Not for Lesbians Only":

> [The] analysis of the function of heterosexuality in women's oppression is available to any woman, lesbian or straight. Lesbian-feminism is a political analysis not "for lesbians only." . . . Since lesbians are materially oppressed by heterosexuality daily, it is not surprising that we have seen and understood its impact first—not because we are more moral,

but because our reality is different—and it is a materially different reality.[10]

## II.

The attribution of epistemic privilege to socially marginalized subjects is not a feminist innovation. In the West, second-wave feminists appropriated the idea from the New Left who, although rejecting Marx's attribution of epistemic privilege to the proletariat alone, nonetheless continued to believe that subjects located at the social margins have an epistemic advantage over those located in the social center. The descent from Marx is most obvious in the writings of socialist-feminists like Ann Ferguson and Nancy Hartsock, who explicitly model their claims about women on Marx's claims about the proletariat.

In "Women as a New Revolutionary Class in the United States," Ann Ferguson relies on Marxist methodology and discussions of class to identify general criteria that allow her to show that women are not only a class but a revolutionary class, that "women are unlike Marx's characterization of peasants and like his characterization of the working class."[11] In Ferguson's essay the epistemic advantage conferred by occupying a certain class position is only implicit; in Hartsock's essay, "The Feminist Standpoint: Developing the Ground for a Specifically Feminist Historical Materialism," the epistemic advantage is brought into focus:

> I set off from Marx's proposal that a correct vision of class society is available from only one of the two major class positions in capitalist society. . . . By setting off from the Marxian meta-theory I am implicitly suggesting that this, rather than his critique of capitalism, can be most helpful to feminists. I will explore some of the epistemological consequences of claiming that women's lives differ structurally from those of men. In particular, I will suggest that like the lives of the proletarians according to Marxian theory, women's lives make available a particular and privileged vantage point on male supremacy, a vantage point which can ground a powerful critique of the phallocratic institutions and ideology which constitute the capitalist form of patriarchy.[12]

In the process of critically generalizing from the marxist models and then critically applying them to women, both Ferguson and Hartsock transform Marx's conceptualization of the relation of social marginality to epistemic privilege. For Marx, social marginality alone is not a necessary and sufficient condition for epistemic privilege; if it were, he could have not claimed exclusive epistemic privilege for the proletariat, which, though socially marginal, is not the only socially marginal group in a capitalist society. Thus, Marx declares in *The Communist Manifesto:*

> Of all the classes that stand face to face with the bourgeoisie today, the proletariat alone is a really revolutionary class. . . . The lower middle classes: the small manufacturer, the shopkeeper, the artisan, the peasant, all these fight against the bourgeoisie to save from extinction their existence as fractions of the middle class. . . . If by chance they are revolutionary . . . they desert their own standpoint to place themselves at that of the proletariat. The "dangerous class," the social scum, that passively rotting mass thrown off by the lowest layers of old society may, here and there, be swept into the movement by a proletarian revolution; its conditions of life, however, prepare it far more for the part of a bribed tool of revolutionary intrigue.[13]

Marx's proletariat differs from the lower middle classes in part by having no vested interests in capitalist society because it is a propertyless class. Yet the class that Marx refers to in the *Manifesto* as the "dangerous class," the class of the chronically unemployed, is also propertyless. The proletariat differs from this class by being usually employed in the exploitative ways that make it crucial to the capitalist mode of production.

Marx's proletariat occupies two places in capitalist society. It is socially marginal in relation to the capitalist class, which occupies center stage by virtue of an economic power that enables it to have enormous political and cultural influence and even control. At the same time it is the proletariat that is at the center stage of capitalist production because it is the living creative force of production that is appropriated by the capitalist class and transformed into the capital that gives the capitalists their power.

Indeed, in the case of Marx's proletariat, social marginality is a function of economic centrality. The economic relations between the capitalist class and the proletariat are exploitative, and this exploitation of the proletariat by the capitalist class is the cause of its alienation and material impoverishment, which maintain the power of the capitalist class over society.

Were one to model claims abut women's social marginality on Marx's claims about the proletariat's social marginality, one would have to identify some social system in which women are central as a gender or sex-class and are socially marginal due to this centrality. According to both Ferguson and Hartsock, the system in which women are socially marginal as a gender or sex-class is patriarchy;

the patriarchal division of labor is gender- or sex-based, and the kind of labor that women usually do (Ferguson calls it *sex/effective labor*) has unique characteristics and requires special skills, whether done for a wage or in a household. Moreover, according to Ferguson, women's sex/effective labor is exploited. Yet neither Ferguson nor Hartsock claim that women's social marginality is a function of women's centrality in a systemically organized relation with men taken as a gender or sex-class.

Because they sever the relation between social marginality and centrality, Ferguson and Hartsock have to conceptualize the relation between social marginality and epistemic privilege differently than Marx. What they share with him is a reliance on a class-based (in their case, a sex class–based) interest or disinterest in maintaining an oppressive system. But as Marx pointed out in the case of the chronically unemployed—the "dangerous class" of the capitalist system—social marginality alone does not assure the kind of disinterest needed for a revolutionary and thus liberatory vision. For Marx, the proletariat's disinterest is a function of its subjection to capital, a subjection that transforms the proletariat and the social relations among its members in such a way that proletarian social relations do not resemble capitalist ones and the proletariat has no loyalties to capitalist society.

## III.

Of course, one need not go Marx's way in conceptualizing the relation between social marginality and epistemic privilege. Bell Hooks presents marginality as the space of radical possibility and hence the center for the production of a counterhegemonic discourse. She makes the following point in "Choosing the Margin as a Space of Radical Openness":

> Understanding marginality as position and place of resistance is crucial for oppressed, exploited, colonized people. If we only view the margin as sign marking the despair, a deep nihilism penetrates in a destructive way the very ground of our being. It is there in that space of collective despair that one's creativity, one's imagination is at risk, there that one's mind is fully colonized, there that the freedom one longs for is lost.[14]

What Hooks offers as a response to Marx's suspicion of a marginality that is not at the same time a centrality is a different sense of marginality. What her claims imply is that conceiving of marginality in Marx's way denies marginal subjects agency. Although her claim is a move in a reverse discourse, she locates this move in what she takes as the empirical reality of lived oppression, which as a lived experience is not only an experience of powerlessness but also an experience of agency in the form of resistance to victimization.

Hooks's move echoes earlier feminist moves. Toward the end of the 1970s, Western second-wave feminists began to reconceive women's sociopolitical situation and retell it not as a story of victimization but as a story of survival.[15] Feminist historians in particular began recreating women's history along this line, realizing, as Hooks does, that an important form of a resistance that is at the same time the creation of a counterhegemonic discourse is a construction of the self through the creation of a memory of a past that either precedes oppression or is a memory of other resisting voices. Thus Hooks says in "On Self-Recovery":

> Social construction of the self in relation would mean . . . that we would know the voices that speak in and to us from the past. . . . Yet, it is precisely these voices that are silenced, suppressed, when we are dominated. . . . Domination and colonization attempt to destroy our capacity to know the self, to know who we are. We oppose this violation, this dehumanization, when we seek self-recovery, when we work to unite fragments of being, to recover our history.[16]

In addition, Hooks's move fits with the reconceptualization of power under the influence of and in critical response to postmodern critics. According to theoreticians like Foucault, power has multiple and not necessarily systemically related forms, all operating on individuals to inscribe and determine them. Feminists responding to this position reject the implication of overdetermination because it suggests the loss of agency. As Nancy Hartsock comments in "Foucault on Power: A Theory for Women?":

> [R]ather than getting rid of subjectivity or notions of the subject as Foucault does and substituting his notion of the individual as an effect of power-relations, we need to engage in the historical, political, and theoretical process of constituting ourselves as subjects as well as objects of history. We need to recognize that we can be the makers of history as well as the object of those who have made history.[17]

## IV.

The attribution of agency to a marginality that is not at the same time a centrality problematizes the attribution of epistemic privilege to the socially marginalized subjects. The source of the problem is the existence of multiple socially marginalized groups; is any one of these groups more epistemically privileged than the others, and if that is not so—if they are all equally epistemically privileged—does epistemic privilege matter?

When one among a multiplicity of socially marginalized groups is claimed to be epistemically more privileged than the others, the usual criterion for justifying such a claim is the extent to which the group in question is peripheralized. Epistemic privilege then becomes a function of the distance from the center. Presumably the more distant one is from the center, the more advantageous is one's point of view.

An example of a claim for an epistemic privilege based on distance is Marilyn Frye's claim for epistemic privilege for lesbians. In "To Be and Be Seen: The Politics of Reality," Frye first cites from a 1978 paper on lesbian epistemology by Sarah Hoagland:

> In the conceptual schemes of phallocracies . . . there is no such thing as a lesbian. This puts a lesbian in the interesting and peculiar position of being something that does not exist, and this position is a singular vantage point with respect to the reality which does not include her.[18]

She next goes on to show that the lesbian is excluded from phallocratic conceptual schemes in three different ways, whereas woman, though excluded in some ways, is generally included in these schemes.

Another example is Gayle Rubin's claim for epistemic privilege for women whose sexual practices are more transgressive than what Pat Califia calls "vanilla" lesbian-feminist practices. In "Thinking Sex: Notes for a Radical Theory of the Politics of Sexuality," Rubin describes the distance as a function of what she calls the "anti-sex" variant of feminism:

> Proponents of this viewpoint have condemned virtually every variant of sexual expression as anti-feminist. Within this framework, monogamous lesbianism that occurs within long-term, intimate relationships and which does not involve playing with polarized roles, has replaced married, procreative heterosexuality at the top of the value hierarchy. Heterosexuality has been demoted to somewhere in the middle. Apart from this change, everything else looks more or less familiar. The lower depths are occupied by the usual groups and behaviors: prostitution, transsexuality, sadomasochism, and cross-generational activities.[19]

While Frye and Rubin see distance in terms that are analogous to the conceptualization of physical distance, distance can also be conceptualized as a function of multiple oppression. Some individuals are subjected in more than one way and thus are members of more than one socially marginalized group. If the multiple ways in which a person can be socially marginalized can be seen as cumulative, then they can be seen as creating further distances from the center.

An example of a claim for epistemic privilege that is built on the notion of distance as a function of multiple oppressions can be found in statements like the following one by Barbara Smith:

> Third World women are forming the leadership in the feminist movement because we are not one dimensional, one-issued in our political understanding. Just by virtue of our identities we certainly define race and usually define class as being fundamental issues that we have to address. The more wide-ranged your politics, the more potentially profound and transformative they are.[20]

Consider a similar statement by her sister Beverly Smith:

> We are in the position to challenge the feminist movement as it stands to date and not out of any theoretical commitment. Our analysis of race and class oppression and our commitment to really dealing with those issues, including homophobia, is something we know we have to struggle with to insure our survival. It is organic to our very existence.[21]

Frye's, Rubin's, and Barbara and Beverly Smith's conceptions of distance and its relation to epistemic privilege suggest two different ways of conceiving epistemic privilege as a function of distance. According to one, which is a conception grounded in a single oppression and the identity and practices of those identified by it, epistemically privileged, socially marginalized subjects are horizontally distanced from the center and placed in a "liberated" space. The other, grounded in multiple oppressions and the identity and practices of those identified by them, locates epistemically privileged, socially marginalized subjects at a point distant from the center and intersected by many axes. This too is a sort of a "liberated" space.

Although they differ in their description of the space inhabited by epistemically privileged, socially marginalized subjects, both conceptions assume a single center and both ground the epistemic privilege of the specified group of socially marginalized subjects in their identity and practices. In the latter respect they resemble other feminist conceptions of epistemic privilege, such as those developed by some feminist philosophers of science. Thus, for example, Hilary Rose argues that a better science—a science responsive to the needs of the people—will be based in forms of practice derived from women's domestic practices.[22] Evelyn Fox-Keller suggests in her discussion of Barbara McClintock's work in genetics that it was because McClintock was not a man that she had to develop a nonmasculinist practice of science:

> In a science constructed around the naming of the object (nature) as female and the parallel naming of the subject (mind) as male, any scientist who happens to be a woman is confronted with an a priori contradiction in terms. This poses a critical problem of identity. . . . Only if she undergoes a radical disidentification from self can she share masculine pleasure in mastering nature cast in the image of woman as passive, inert, and blind. Her alternative is to attempt a radical redefinition of terms. . . . This is not to say that the male scientist cannot claim similar redefinition . . . but, by contrast to the woman scientist, his identity does not require it.[23]

## V.

Both the assumption of a single center from which the epistemically privileged, socially marginalized subjects are distanced and the grounding of their epistemic privilege in their identity and practices are problematic. Although the latter resonates with ideas of the New Left, the former was even then questionable. Since the 1960s and the dawn of a recognition that racism, sexism, and heterosexism are not merely individually held bad attitudes but rather institutionally and systemically entrenched structures, there has been a movement away from theorizing power as located in one center.

Western second-wave feminists, especially socialist-feminists, debated one aspect of this issue of power at length from the end of the 1970s through the beginning of the 1980s.[24] This debate seems to have resulted in a tacit theoretical agreement that there are multiple oppressive systems that interrelate in various ways that may either enhance or undermine each other. The question of power is currently debated among (and with) postmodern feminists.[25] This debate also seems to lead away from a theoretical positioning of a single, central power from which all the oppressed are similarly distanced through their social marginalization.

Iris Young's work on power, which combines socialist-feminist and postmodern-feminist insights, is quite instructive here.[26] Young begins with the brute fact of multiple social groups, each conceiving itself as oppressed in relation to some other privileged group. Instead of attempting to unify the oppressed by providing a theoretical framework that will explain each and every kind of oppression and order the different kinds of oppressive relations, she provides a theoretical framework that explains why one should resist the impulse to unify and how to go about politics in a heterogeneous world. While Young believes that historically situated and contextualized analyses may reveal some connections between forms of oppression, she does not assume an all-inclusive structure or system with a single, central power operating on all the oppressed in connected ways and thus unifying them. For Young, unity is possible only as a function of a political process in which, among other things, the possibility of unity is explored openly and sincerely.

The problem of grounding epistemic privilege in the identity and practices of socially marginalized subjects is not derivative to the problem of theorizing a single, central power from which these subjects are distanced. Such a theory does not merely recover the agency of socially marginalized subjects but valorizes it in such a way that even if the theory does not essentialize agency, it always idealizes it, abstracting from the actual lived practices and generalizing from normatively approved ones.

The kind of idealization that is entailed by valorization is problematic because rather than working from a conception of practices as heterogeneous, it includes some while excluding others, presupposing that there are practices that in one way or another are more authentically expressive of something about the oppressed group. Two kinds of practices have been identified by feminist authors as authentic—practices that are generally associated with the group (in the case of women, for example, nurturing, domestic practices) and practices of resistance.

The construal of women's agency in nurturing, domestic terms has led to the idealization of a certain set of women's dispositions, especially the disposition to care or love and in particular its manifestation in the mother–child relationship. The following examples of feminist writings about the mother–child relationship show the process of idealization at work.

Sara Ruddick, after noting that "maternal love is said to be gentle and unconditional when, in fact, it is erotic, inseparable from anger, fierce, and fraught with ambivalence,"[27] nonetheless appeals to maternal thinking as the source of a gender-based disposition to nonviolence and thus as a gendered kind of moral agency. Virginia Held, after noting that in actuality parents may not care for their children in just the right ways, similarly proceeds to use an idealized maternal care as a model for moral motivation in "Feminism and Moral Theory":

> We should not glamorize parental care. Many mothers and fathers dominate their children in harmful ways, or fail to care adequately for them.

But, when the relationship between "mother" and child is as it should be, the caretaker does not care for the child (nor the child for the caretaker) because of universal moral rules. The love and concern that one feels for the child already motivates much of what one does.[28]

Like Ruddick, Held recognizes that women's practices vary. Some women care for their children; some neglect and even harm them. She maintains that this recognition should restrain us from glamorizing parental care. Yet, this does not stop her from doing just what she has advised against by introducing the normative "should" once again, this time postulating care as what should be the case, a move that frees her to claim a moral agency based in and motivated by care.

By conceiving agency in relation to care, both Ruddick and Held link it to specific women's practices. These practices are related to women's identity as defined within the system that oppresses them. But agency has also been conceptualized as resistance, which seems to purge any oppressive content from agency because the equation of agency with resistance divides the practices of socially marginalized subjects into two groups. One is the group of practices that are acted upon by oppressive forces, like nurturing or domestic practices, which embody choices delimited by the values of one's oppressors. The other group of practices—practices of resistance—is free from the operation of oppressive forces.

Two kinds of practices have been suggested as candidates for practices of resistance. One kind consists of practices claimed to belong to a culture that either precedes the beginning of the marginalizing oppression, such as a matriarchal culture, or is produced in the context of oppression and yet is somehow untouched by oppressive forces, such as a women's culture.[29] The other kind consists of practices that respond to oppression and show that the socially marginalized subjects are not powerless, that they can set limits on or subvert the oppressive forces, and that they can be creative and go beyond the boundaries set for them by their oppression.[30]

The two kinds of practices of resistance are not necessarily separated from each other. Thus, for example, in "La conciencia de la mestiza: Toward a New Consciousness,"[31] Gloria Anzaldúa appeals to the possibility of both kinds of practices of resistance and in one place in her essay anticipates the reconstruction of a culture preceding and resisting oppression:

> Seeing the Chicana anew in light of her history, I seek an exoneration, a seeing through the fiction of white supremacy, a seeing of ourselves in our true guise and not as the false racial personality that has been given to us and that we have given to ourselves.[32]

Elsewhere in this essay Anzaldúa talks about practices through which she challenges oppression:

> I am cultureless, because as a feminist, I challenge the collective cultural/religious male-derived beliefs of Indo-Hispanics and Anglos; yet I am cultured because I am participating in the creation of yet another culture, a new story to explain the world and our participation in it, a new value system with images and symbols that connect us to each other and to the planet.[33]

Although oppression does not necessarily erase all the practices of a culture that precedes it, the traces of the practices that are left do not retain their original meaning but change through their interaction with the practices of the oppressive system.[34] They are, therefore, necessarily tainted by oppression. Also tainted are the practices that may be said to belong to something like a women's culture because they too acquire their meaning in the context of oppression. Practices of resistance are just as tainted, and to believe otherwise lacks irony as it is understood in postmodernism, an irony that stems from the recognition that even critique is complicitous because it is inevitably entangled with power and domination.[35]

In addition, the very division of the practices of socially marginalized subjects into submissively passive and resistant classifications through the equation of the latter with agency reproduces a normative dualism that Western second-wave feminists have tried to overcome. They have objected to this obviously masculinist dualism because submissive passivity and agency have been associated with women and men, respectively, and agency has been normatively prioritized.

## VI.

The theorized dispersion of power among multiple centers makes it hard to attribute epistemic privilege to just one of the many socially marginalized groups cohabitating in one society. And the problems of grounding epistemic privilege in the practices of socially marginalized subjects suggest to me that even if it were possible to identify one socially marginalized group as special, it would be hard to make an attribution of epistemic privilege to this group that does not idealize its practices.

What should follow from this is a recommendation to give up epistemic privilege. Yet the claim for epistemic privilege has served to empower movements of oppressed people in important ways.

Taken quite generally, the claim of epistemic privilege in the realm of sociopolitical theory mostly justifies claims for authority, specifically the authority of members of socially marginalized groups to speak for themselves, which is an authority they do not have if everyone is equally capable to know them and their situation. Through this justification they grant themselves the authority to produce their own self-defined description of themselves and the world. And they demand that their voices, voices that have been excluded through the process of social marginalization, be given the respectful attention given to the voices of socioculturally hegemonic experts.

The importance of the process of authorization can be seen, for example, in Patricia Hill Collins's discussion of the authority of African-American feminist knowledge:

> Black feminist thought, like all specialized thought, reflects the interests and standpoint of its creators. . . . Black feminist thought as specialized thought reflects the thematic content of African-American women's experiences. . . . While Black women can produce knowledge claims that contest those advanced by the white male community, this community does not grant that Black women scholars have competing knowledge claims based in another knowledge validation process.[36]

Given this understanding of the strategic uses of the claim to epistemic privilege, it seems that what members of socially marginalized groups do by claiming epistemic privilege is to constitute themselves as socially differentiated, rather than individuated, Enlightenment subjects. In the case of second-wave Western feminism, this self-constitution is problematic not merely due to the postmodern flight from subjectivity, which fractures identities so much so as to cast suspicions on the belief that there are genders and that their relations are systemic,[37] but also because the Enlightenment subject of various forms of feminism in the West tends to be not an Enlightenment rational being, but a neo-Romantic subject.[38] As such, it is an emotional subject whose rationality is not formulaic. It is a subject that is not separated from its objects in a dualistic relation that gives the subject the power to dominate the objects. It is also a subject in a special relation to nature and the production of use-values.

Put differently, Western second-wave feminist claims for epistemic privilege entangle feminists in the Enlightenment sociopolitical liberatory project of legitimizing the voices of the many, as narrowly as this might have been understood in specific historical times and places. Initially this project was based in the struggle against the authoritarianism of rulers and churches. With socialists, especially Marx, the project changed somewhat, and the struggle became a struggle of socially marginalized groups against the authority of socially dominant ones, in which marginality and dominance had material grounding in the workings of a political economy. In the West, feminists are among those who, since the 1960s, have been shifting this project a little more by multiplying the socially marginalized groups whose voices are legitimized.

But, the Enlightenment sociopolitical liberatory project is not the only project in which feminists are entangled. At least in the West, feminists are also entangled in the postmodern project, which is one of the contributors to what I called earlier a neo-Romantic subjectivity. The construction of this subjectivity is a project that, like the Romantic project, responds to the Enlightenment by emphasizing what the Enlightenment deemphasized, such as emotionality and the irrational, and seeking solutions to the problems created by the Enlightenment writ large, by its instrumental rationality, exclusionary practices, and modes of subjection.

Because feminists are entangled in both the Enlightenment project and the neo-Romantic project, the feminist situation seems contradictory—a situation in which contradictory forces push and pull feminist sociopolitical theorizing. Although I do not know how to disentangle feminist sociopolitical theorizing from this contradictory situation, in light of all the problems that I have raised and in light of a few to follow, I would like to recommend that we rethink the project of authorizing the speech of marginal subjects.

In "On Authority: Or Why Women Are Not Entitled to Speak," Kathleen B. Jones argues that the very concept of authority should be suspected by feminists because "the very institution of authority as a set of practices . . . lies at the root of the separation of women from the process of 'authorizing,' "[39] a process that she shows to be rather masculinist. Jones's point about the exclusion of women through the process of authorization can be generalized to say that authorization is an exclusionary practice, a practice designed to both silence and command obedience to the authorized voice.

A socially marginalized group does not have the power to exclude, silence, and command obedience from a dominant group. Its claims for epistemic privilege, lacking a social power on which to base them, cannot yield the same results as the self-authorizing claims of a dominant group and are, therefore, merely normative, compelling only for those who are theoretically persuaded by them, usually members of the socially marginalized group who find them empowering. Although the empowerment of its own members is an important goal for every marginalized social group, by claiming an authority based in epistemic privilege the group reinscribes the values and practices used to socially marginalize it by excluding its voice, silencing it and commanding its obedience to the voice of the dominant group.

Audre Lorde says in the title of one of her speeches that "the master's tools will never dismantle the master's house."[40] Although the claim to epistemic privilege as a tool may seem to be a claim of the oppressed, due to some of its history, it nonetheless reveals itself also as a master's tool. There are no tools that can replace it, nor are any needed, because when the oppressed feel a need to authorize speech, they are acting on feelings that are a function of their oppression. Speech needs to be authorized only where silence is the rule. This is an oppressive rule. It need not be obeyed, and the justification of disobedience in this case is not a special kind of expertise guaranteed by epistemic privilege but rather by the demands of justice.

## Notes

1. For an early example see Marcia Millman and Rosabeth Moss Kanter, eds., *Another Voice: Feminist Perspectives on Social Life and Social Science* (Garden City, N.Y.: Anchor Books, 1975). Later examples include Carol Gilligan, *In A Different Voice: Psychological Theory and Women's Development* (Cambridge, Mass.: Harvard University, 1982); and Mary Field Belenky, Blythe McVicker Clinchy, Nancy Rule Goldberger, and Jill Mattuck Tarule, *Women's Ways of Knowing: The Development of Self, Voice, and Mind* (New York: Basic Books, 1986).

2. The most commonly used explanatory schema of why and how gender constitutes experience is found in Nancy Chodorow, *The Reproduction of Mothering* (Berkeley: University of California Press, 1978). According to Chodorow, girls having to grow up and become women and mothers in a heterosexist, patriarchal society distance themselves from their mothers only partially and develop permeable ego boundaries, whereas boys having to grow up and become nonwomen and nonmothers distance themselves from women in ways that result in the formation of rigid ego boundaries. Some explanatory schemas, such as Nancy Hartsock's in *Money, Sex and Power: Toward a Feminist Historical Materialism* (Boston: Northeastern University Press, 1983), even when relying on Chodorow's work, place greater emphasis on certain aspects of women's labor in the context of the gender-based division of labor in a heterosexist, patriarchal society, such as its sensuality, than does Chodorow.

3. Among the recent contributions to this endeavor is Lorraine Code, *What Can She Know?: Feminist Theory and the Construction of Knowledge* (Ithaca: Cornell University Press, 1991).

4. In *The Science Question in Feminism* (Ithaca: Cornell University Press, 1986), Sandra Harding refers to feminists who merely assert the perspectival nature of experience as empiricists and classifies the feminists who not only assert the perspectival nature of experience but also valorize the perspectives of members of socially marginalized groups as standpoint theorists. According to her, at least some postmodern feminist theorists also valorize the perspectives of members of socially marginalized groups.

5. Mary Ann Weathers, "An Argument for Black Women's Liberation as a Revolutionary Force," in Leslie B. Tanner, ed., *Voices from Women's Liberation* (New York: New American Library, 1970), 303–7.

6. The Combahee River Collective, "A Black Feminist Statement," in Zillah R. Eisenstein, ed., *Capitalist Patriarchy and the Case for Socialist Feminism* (New York: Monthly Review, 1979), 365.

7. Robin Morgan, "Goodbye to All That," in Leslie B. Tanner, ed., *Voices from Women's Liberation* (New York: New American Library, 1970), 269.

8. Vivian Gornick, "Woman as Outsider," in Vivian Gornick and Barbara K. Moran, eds., *Woman in Sexist Society: Studies in Power and Powerlessness* (New York: New American Library, 1972), 128–29.

9. Sidney Abbot and Barbara Love, "Is Women's Liberation a Lesbian Plot?" in Gornick and Moran, *Woman in Sexist Society*, 620.

10. Charlotte Bunch, "Not for Lesbians Only," in *Passionate Politics: Feminist Theory in Action* (New York: St. Martin's Press, 1987), 178.

11. Ann Ferguson, "Women as a New Revolutionary Class," in Pat Walker, ed., *Between Labor and Capital* (Boston: South End, 1979), 279–309.

12. Nancy Hartsock, "The Feminist Standpoint: Developing the Ground for a Specifically Feminist Historical Materialism," in Sandra Harding and Merrill B. Hintikka, eds., *Discovering Reality: Feminist Perspectives on Epistemology, Metaphysics, Methodology, and Philosophy of Science* (Dordrecht, Holland: D. Reidel, 1983), 284.

13. Karl Marx and Frederick Engels, "Manifesto of the Communist Party," in *Collected Works*, 6 vols. (New York: International Publishers, 1976), 6:494–95.

14. Bell Hooks, "Choosing the Margin as a Space of Radical Openness," in *Yearning: Race, Gender, and Cultural Politics* (Boston: South End, 1990), 150–51.

15. An influential discussion of this is Kathleen Barry, "Victims and Survivors," chapter 3 in *Female Sexual Slavery* (Englewood Cliffs, N.J.: Prentice Hall, 1979), 33–42.

16. Bell Hooks, *Talking Back: Thinking Feminist, Thinking Black* (Boston: South End, 1989), 31.

17. Nancy Hartsock, "Foucault on Power: A Theory for Women?" in Linda Nicholson, ed., *Feminism/Postmodernism* (New York: Routledge, 1990), 170–71.

18. Marilyn Frye, "To Be and Be Seen: The Politics of Reality," in *The Politics of Reality: Essays in Feminist Theory* (Trumansberg, New York: Crossing, 1983), 152–53.

19. Gayle Rubin, "Thinking Sex: Notes for a Radical Theory of the Politics of Sexuality" in Carole S. Vance, ed., *Pleasure and Danger: Exploring Female Sexuality* (Boston: Routledge and Kegan Paul, 1984), 301.

20. Barbara Smith and Beverly Smith, "Across the Kitchen Table: A Sister-to-Sister Dialogue" in Cherrie Moraga and Gloria Anzaldúa, eds., *This Bridge Called My Back: Writings by Radical Women of Color* (Watertown, Mass.: Persephone, 1981), 127.

21. Ibid.

22. Hilary Rose, "Hand, Brain and Heart: A Feminist Epistemology for the Natural Sciences," in *Signs: Journal of Women in Culture and Society* 9(1) (1983): 73–90.

23. Evelyn Fox Keller, *Reflections on Gender and Science* (New Haven: Yale University Press, 1985), 174–75.

24. See, for example, the essay in Lydia Sargent, ed., *Women and Revolution: A Discussion of the Unhappy Marriage of Marxism and Feminism* (Boston: South End, 1981).

25. See, for example, essays in Irene Diamond and Lee Quinby, eds., *Feminism and Foucault: Reflections on Resistance* (Boston: Northeastern University Press, 1988); and Nicholson, *Feminism/Postmodernism*.

26. Iris Marion Young, *Justice and the Politics of Difference* (Princeton, N.J.: Princeton University, 1990).

27. Sara Ruddick, "Remarks on the Sexual Politics of Reason," in Eva Feder Kittay and Diana T. Meyers, eds., *Women and Moral Theory* (Totowa, N.J.: Rowman and Littlefield, 1987), 246.

28. Virginia Held, "Feminism and Moral Theory," in Kittay and Meyers, *Women and Moral Theory*, 118.

29. Cultural feminists tend to appeal to prepatriarchal practices and symbols more than other feminists. Two examples are Susan Griffin, *Woman and Nature: The Roaring Inside Her* (New York: Harper and Row, 1987); and Mary Daly, *Pure Lust: Elemental Feminist Philosophy* (Boston: Beacon Press, 1984). The idea of a women's culture, on the other hand, is quite widespread and is usually associated with gender-specific practices.

30. In this respect see, for example, Ann Ferguson, "Is There A Lesbian

Culture?" in Jeffner Allen, ed., *Lesbian Philosophies and Culture* (Albany N.Y.: State University of New York, 1990), 63–88.

31. Gloria Anzaldúa, "La conciencia de la mestiza: Toward a New Consciousness," in Gloria Anzaldúa, ed., *Making Face, Making Soul: Haciendo Caras: Creative and Critical Perspectives by Women of Color* (San Francisco: Aunt Lute, 1990), 377–89.

32. Ibid., 385–86.

33. Ibid., 380.

34. An example of a work that shows an awareness of this is Frantz Fanon, *The Wretched of the Earth* (New York: Grove, 1968).

35. The recognition of complicity as an element of postmodernism is emphasized by Linda Hutcheon in *The Politics of Postmodernism* (London: Routledge, 1989).

36. Patricia Hill Collins, *Black Feminist Thought: Knowledge, Consciousness, and the Politics of Empowerment* (Boston: Unwin Hyman, 1990), 201–4.

37. See, for example, Denise Riley, *"Am I That Name?" Feminism and the Category of 'Women' in History* (Minneapolis: University of Minnesota Press, 1988; Joan Wallach Scott, *Gender and the Politics of History* (New York: Columbia University Press, 1988); and Judith Butler, *Gender Trouble: Feminism and the Subversion of Identity* (New York: Routledge, 1990).

38. What I call here a neo-Romantic subjectivity is not a uniquely feminist subjectivity. Rather, feminists are among the contributors to a movement as widespread as Romanticism was. Some of the interesting examples of what I call here a feminist neo-Romantic subjectivity can be found in the writings of feminists of color. Two such examples are Gloria Anzaldúa, *Boarderlands/La Frontera: The New Mestiza* (San Francisco: Spinsters/Aunt Lute, 1987); and Trinh T. Minh-ha, *Woman, Native, Other* (Bloomington: Indiana University, 1989).

39. Kathleen B. Jones, "On Authority: Or, Why Women Are Not Entitled to Speak," in Irene Diamond and Lee Quinby, eds., *Feminism and Foucault: Reflections on Resistance* (Boston: Northeastern University, 1988), 120.

40. Audre Lorde, "The Master's Tools Will Never Dismantle the Master's House," in *Sister Outsider* (Freedom, Calif.: Crossing, 1984).

# 5

# Subjects, Power, and Knowledge: Description and Prescription in Feminist Philosophies of Science

*Helen E. Longino*

## I. Prologue

Feminists, faced with traditions in philosophy and in science that are deeply hostile to women, have had practically to invent new and more appropriate ways of knowing the world. These new ways have been less invention out of whole cloth than the revival or reevaluation of alternative or suppressed traditions. They range from the celebration of insight into nature through identification with it to specific strategies of survey research in the social sciences. Natural scientists and laypersons anxious to see the sciences change have celebrated Barbara McClintock's loving identification with various aspects of the plants she studied, whether whole organism or its chromosomal structure revealed under the microscope. Social scientists from Dorothy Smith to Karen Sacks have stressed designing research *for* rather than merely about women, a goal that requires attending to the specificities of women's lives and consulting research subjects themselves about the process of gathering information about them. Such new ways of approaching natural and social phenomena can be seen as methods of discovery, ways of getting information about the natural and social worlds not available via more traditional experimental or investigative methods.

Feminists have rightly pointed out the blinders imposed by the philosophical distinction between discovery and justification; a theory of scientific inquiry that focuses solely on the logic of justification neglects the selection processes occurring in the context of discovery that limit what we get to know about. Methods of discovery, or heuristics, are in effect selection processes that present for our consideration certain sorts of hypotheses and not other sorts. Feminists have

identified heuristic biases—androcentrism, sexism, and gender ideology—that limit the hypotheses in play in specific areas of inquiry
and have also pointed out that alternative heuristics put different hypotheses in play. However, a theory of scientific inquiry that focuses
solely on methods of discovery presents its own difficulties. In particular, a given heuristic method that puts certain hitherto suppressed
or invisible hypotheses into play is not ipso facto ratifiable as a pro-
ducer of knowledge, as distinct from interesting or even plausible
ideas. Something more is required before we can speak of knowledge
(or even confirmation) as opposed to plausibility. One way to articulate the distinctions I am urging is to treat analysis of the context of
discovery as a primarily descriptive analysis of how hypotheses are
generated and to treat analysis in the context of justification as involving a normative or prescriptive analysis regarding the appropriate
criteria for the acceptance of hypotheses. This is problematic because
philosophers in the past who made this distinction sometimes concluded that only the context of justification is worthy of philosophical
analysis. Nevertheless, ignoring the context of justification for the context of discovery is equally problematic. I wish in this essay to explore
some of the tensions between descriptivism and normativism (or pre-
scriptivism) in the theory of knowledge, arguing that although many
of the most familiar feminist accounts of science have helped us to
redescribe the process of knowledge (or belief) acquisition, they stop
short of an adequate normative theory. However, these accounts do
require a new approach in normative epistemology because of their
redescription.

Although this essay focuses on issues in the epistemology of science,
it bears on general issues in epistemology in two ways. First, to the
extent that "science" simply means knowledge, an analysis of scientific knowledge is an analysis of knowledge. Second, philosophy of
science to a large degree relies on general epistemological principles.
Critical discussion of their adequacy for the philosophy of science is
relevant to, although not conclusive regarding, their tenability in a
general theory of knowledge. To the extent that human knowledge is
not coextensive with scientific knowledge, however, remarks bearing
on science are only partially relevant to knowledge in general.

The relevance relations from general epistemology to scientific
knowledge are even less direct. In contemplating the problems of
developing new and more appropriate knowledge, it is tempting to
suppose that epistemology could provide the key that would unlock
the right door—that if we could just get the epistemology right, we
would get the science right, too. Surely one source of this belief is
the close relationship between the science and the philosophy done

at the beginning of the modern period. Does not the epistemology of Descartes and of Locke have something to do with the theories of nature that took hold during the Seventeenth Century? Another is reflection on the persistence of misogynist views in biological theories, from the various subfields of evolutionary theory to theories of development. If one hallmark of the modern period is the development of rule-based inquiry, something in the justification rules must account for this persistence. If getting the epistemology wrong accounts for harmful science, getting the epistemology right must be the key to better science. This is probably an oversimplification of the thinking that has underlain the attraction to epistemology for many feminist scholars outside of philosophy, but I do not think it is too far off the mark. And although I do think that new approaches in the theory of knowledge would alter some of our attitudes in and about science, I also think that the relationship between epistemology—the theory of what practices produce knowledge—and science—what counts as knowledge—in any given period is more complicated than the temptation allows. We cannot produce knowledge of the world on the strength of a general theory of knowledge.

Nor can we simply dismiss the accumulated knowledge of the natural world produced by the traditional methods of the natural sciences. These sciences have transformed conditions of life in industrialized portions of the world, both conceptually as models of knowledge and materially through science-based technologies. Why, then, do some of us feel so uneasy not only about the theories directly concerning females and gender but also about the very nature of scientific knowledge and the power it creates? After all, even feminists who wish to change the sciences are also, by that very ambition, expressing a hope for power. There are surely various sources for and locations of this uneasiness. Those of us who are feminists have been struck by the interlocking character of several aspects of knowledge and power in the sciences. Women have been excluded from the practice of science, even as scientific inquiry gets described both as a masculine activity and as demonstrating women's unsuitability to engage in it, whether because of our allegedly deficient mathematical abilities or our insufficient independence. Some of us notice the location of women in the production of the artifacts made possible by new knowledge: swift and nimble fingers on the microelectronics assembly line. Others notice the neglect of women's distinctive health issues by the biomedical sciences, even as new techniques for preserving the fetuses they carry are introduced into hospital delivery rooms. The sciences become even more suspect as analysis of their metaphors (for example, in cell biology and in microbiology) reveals an acceptance (and hence reinforcement) of the cultural identification of the male with activity and of the female with passivity. Finally, feminists have drawn a connection between the identification of nature as female and the scientific mind as male and the persistent privileging of explanatory models constructed around relations of unidirectional control over models constructed around relations of interdependence. Reflection on this connection has prompted feminist critics to question the very idea of a scientific method capable of adjudicating the truth or probability of theories in a value-neutral way.

Although the sciences have increased human power over natural processes, they have, according to this analysis, done so in a lop-sided way, systematically perpetuating women's cognitive and political disempowerment (as well as that of other groups marginalized in relation to the Euro-American drama). One obvious question, then, is whether this appropriation of power is an intrinsic feature of science or whether it is an incidental feature of the sciences as practiced in the modern period, a feature deriving from the social structures within which the sciences have developed. A second question is whether it is possible to seek and possess empowering knowledge without expropriating the power of others. Is seeking knowledge inevitably an attempt at domination? And are there criteria of knowledge other than the ability to control the phenomena about which one seeks knowledge? Feminists have answered these questions in a number of ways. I will review some of these before outlining my own answer.

## II. Feminist Epistemological Strategies 1: Changing the Subject

Most traditional philosophy of science (with the problematic exception of Descartes's) has adopted some form of empiricism. Empiricism's silent partner has been a theory of the subject, that is, of the knower.[1] The paradigmatic knower in Western epistemology is an individual—an individual who, in several classic instances, has struggled to free himself from the distortions in understanding and perception that result from attachment. Plato, for example, maintained that knowledge of the good is possible only for those whose reason is capable of controlling their appetites and passions, some of which have their source in bodily needs and pleasures and others of which have their source in our relations with others. The struggle for epistemic autonomy is even starker for Descartes, who suspends belief in all but his own existence in order to recreate a body of knowledge cleansed of faults, impurities, and uncertainties. For Descartes, only those grounds available to a single, unattached, disembodied mind are acceptable principles for the construction of a system of beliefs. Most subsequent epistemology has granted Descartes's conditions and disputed what those grounds are and whether any proposed grounds are sufficient grounds for knowledge. Descartes's creation of the radically and in principle isolated individual as the ideal epistemic agent has for the most part gone unremarked.[2] Locke, for example, adopts the Cartesian identification of the thinking subject with the disembodied soul without even remarking upon the individualism of the conception he inherits and then struggles with the problem of personal identity. Explicitly or implicitly in modern epistemology, whether rationalist or empiricist, the individual consciousness that is the subject of knowledge is transparent to itself, operates according to principles that are independent of embodied experience, and generates knowledge in a value-neutral way.

One set of feminist epistemological strategies, sometimes described as modifications or rejections of empiricism, can also, and perhaps better, be described as changing the subject. I will review three such strategies of replacement, arguing that although they enrich our understanding of how we come to have the beliefs we have and so are more descriptively adequate than the theories they challenge, they fall short of normative adequacy. The strategies identify the problems of contemporary science as resulting from male or masculinist bias. Each strategy understands both the bias and its remedy differently. One holds out the original ideal of uncontaminated or unconditioned subjectivity. A second identifies bias as a function of social location. A third identifies bias in the emotive substructure produced by the psychodynamics of individuation.

Feminist empiricism has by now taken a number of forms. That form discussed and criticized by Sandra Harding is most concerned with those fields of scientific research that have misdescribed or misanalyzed women's lives and bodies. It's not clear that any feminist scholars have totally conformed to the profile identified by Harding, but certain moments in the analyses offered by practicing scientists who are feminists do fit this model.[3] At any rate, feminist empiricism (*sub* Harding) identifies the problems in the scientific accounts of women and gender as the product of male bias. Typical examples of problematic views are the treatment of the male of the species as the locus of variation (and hence the basis of evolutionary change for a species), the persistent treatment of male difference as male superiority, the assumption of universal male dominance, and the treatment of sexual divisions of labor in industrialized societies as the product of biological species evolution. Each of these involves neglecting contradictory empirical information. It should be no surprise that a focus on these sorts of problems suggests their solution in replacing the androcentric subject of knowledge with an unbiased subject—one that would not ignore the empirical data already or easily available. From this perspective, certain areas of science having to do with sex and gender are deformed by gender ideology, but the methods of science are not themselves masculinist and can be used to correct the errors produced by ideology. The ideal knower is still the purified mind, and epistemic or cognitive authority inheres in this purity. This strategy, as Harding has observed, is not effective against those research programs that feminists find troublesome but that cannot be faulted by reference to the standard methodological precepts of scientific inquiry. I have argued, for example, that a critique of research on the influence of prenatal gonadal hormones on behavioral sex differences that is limited to methodological critique of the data fails to bring out the role of the explanatory model that both generates the research and gives evidential relevance to that data.[4]

Another approach is, therefore, the standpoint approach. There is no one position from which value-free knowledge can be developed, but some positions are better than others. Standpoint epistemologies notice systematic distortions in description and analysis produced by those occupying social positions of power. Traditional Marxists identified the standpoint of the bourgeoisie as producing such distortions, whereas feminists have identified the standpoint of men (of the dominant class and race) as equally distorting. Nancy Hartsock and other feminist standpoint theorists have argued that the activities of ruling-class men produce a knowledge of the world characterized by abstractness and impersonality, that their own politically structured freedom from the requirements of re/producing the necessities of daily life is reflected in the kind of understanding they produce of the social and natural world.[5] Women's work, by contrast, is characterized by greater interaction with material substances, by constant change, and by its requirement of emotional investment in the form of caring. Not only does women's characteristic activity and relation to the means of production/reproduction produce its own unique form of understanding, but also women who become self-conscious agents in this work are able to incorporate men's perspectives as well as their own and hence to develop a more accurate, more objective, set of beliefs about the world.

By valorizing the perspectives uniquely available to those who are socially disadvantaged, standpoint theorists turn the table on traditional epistemology; the ideal epistemic agent is not an unconditioned subject but the subject conditioned by the social experiences of oppression. The powerless are those with epistemic legitimacy, even if they lack the power that could turn that legitimacy into authority. One of the difficulties of the standpoint approach comes into high relief, however, when it is a women's or a feminist standpoint that is in question. Women occupy many social locations in a racially and economically stratified society. If genuine or better knowledge depends on the correct or a more correct standpoint, social theory is needed to ascertain which of these locations is the epistemologically privileged one. But in a standpoint epistemology, a standpoint is needed to justify such a theory. What is that standpoint and how do we identify *it*? If no single standpoint is privileged, then either the standpoint theorist must embrace multiple and incompatible knowledge positions or offer some means of transforming or integrating multiple perspectives into one. Both of these moves require either the abandonment or the supplementation of standpoint as an epistemic criterion.

Standpoint theory faces another problem as well. It is by now commonplace to note that standpoint theory was developed by and for social scientists. It has been difficult to see what its implications for the natural sciences might be. But another strategy has seemed more promising. Most standpoint theorists locate the epistemic advantage in the productive/reproductive experience of the oppressed whose perspective they champion. A different change of subject is proposed by those identifying the problems with science as a function of the psychodynamics of individuation. Evelyn Fox Keller has been asking, among other things, why the scientific community privileges one kind of explanation or theory over others. In particular she has asked why, when both linear reductionist and interactionist perspectives are available, the scientific community has preferred the linear or "master molecule" theory that understands a natural process as controlled by a single dominant factor. This question was made vivid by her discussion of her own research on slime mold aggregation and the fate of Barbara McClintock's work on genetic transposition.[6]

Keller's original response, spelled out in *Reflections on Gender and Science*, involved an analysis of the traditional ideal of scientific objectivity, which she understood as the ideal of the scientist's detachment from the object of study.[7] In her view, epistemic and affective ideals are intermingled, and from the psychoanalytic perspective she adopted, distorted affective development—autonomy as exaggerated separateness—was expressed in a distorted epistemic ideal—objectivity as radical detachment. Drawing on and developing object relations theory, she attributed this "static autonomy" to the conditions under which boys develop psychologically: exaggerated separateness is a solution to the anxieties provoked by those conditions. Keller analyzed the consequent ideal of static objectivity as generating and satisfied by accounts of natural processes that foreground controlling relationships—for example, accounts of organismic development as determined by the individual's genetic program. She, therefore, proposed an alternative conceptualization of autonomy, contrasting static autonomy with what she called dynamic autonomy, an ability to move in and out of intimate connection with the world. Dynamic autonomy provides the emotional substructure for an alternative conception of objectivity: dynamic objectivity. The knower characterized by dynamic objectivity, in contrast to the knower characterized by static objectivity, does not seek power over phenomena but acknowledges instead the ways in which knower and phenomena are in relationship as well as the ways in which phenomena themselves are complexly interdependent. Barbara McClintock's work has offered one of the most striking examples of the effectiveness of such an approach, although interactionist approaches have also been applied in areas besides developmental biology. McClintock's work, long ignored, was finally vindicated by developments in molecular biology of the 1970s—the acknowledgment of genetic transposition in the prokaryotes that had been the model organisms for contemporary molecular genetics. Dynamic objectivity is not presented as a typically feminine epistemological orientation but as an alternative to an epistemological orientation associated with both masculine psychological development and masculinist gender ideology. But however much interactionist approaches might appeal to us, and however much dynamic objectivity might appeal to us, there isn't a general argument to the truth of interactionism or to the epistemological superiority of dynamic objectivity.

Both standpoint theory and the psychodynamic perspective suggest the inadequacy of an ideal of a pure transparent subjectivity that registers the world as it is in itself (or, for Kantians, as structured by universal conditions of apperception or categories of understanding). I find it most useful to read them as articulating special instances of more general descriptive claims that subjectivity is conditioned by social and historical location and that our cognitive efforts have an ineluctably affective dimension. Classical standpoint theory identifies relation to production/reproduction as the key, but there are multiple, potentially oppositional relations to production/reproduction in a complex society, and there are other kinds of social relation and location that condition subjectivity. For example, one of the structural features of a male-dominant society is asymmetry of sexual access. Men occupy a position of entitlement to women's bodies, whereas women, correspondingly, occupy the position of that to which men are entitled. Complications of the asymmetry arise in class- and race-stratified societies. There may be other structural features as well, such as those related to the institutions of heterosexuality, that condition subjectivity. Because each individual occupies a location in a multidimensional grid marked by numerous interacting structures of power asymmetry, the analytical task is not to determine which is epistemically most adequate. Rather, the task is to understand how these complexly conditioned subjectivities are expressed in action and belief. I would expect that comparable complexity can be introduced into the psychodynamic account.

Treating subjectivity as variably conditioned and cognition as affectively modulated opens both opportunities and problems. The opportunities are the possibilities of understanding phenomena in new ways; by recognizing that mainstream accounts of natural processes have been developed from particular locations and reflect particular affective orientations, we can entertain the possibility that quite different accounts might emerge from other locations with the benefit of different emotional orientations. Although either transferring or diffusing power, the strategies discussed so far have in common a focus on the individual epistemic agent, on the autonomous subject. (The subject in the second and third approaches comes to be in a social context and as a consequence of social interactions, but its knowledge is still a matter of some relation between it and the subject matter.) The standpoint and psychodynamically based theories recommend certain new positions and orientations as superior to others but fail to explain how we are to decide or to justify decisions between what seem to be conflicting claims about the character of some set of natural processes. On what grounds can one social location or affective orientation be judged epistemically superior to another? Normative epistemology arises in the context of conflicting knowledge claims. Naturalism, or descriptivism, in epistemology presupposes that we know what we think we know and asks how. But the existence of comparably persuasive incompatible claims calls into question whether we know at all, requires that we reexamine what we take to be adequate justification, and may even call into question our very concept of knowledge.

Feminist science critics have provided analyses of the context of discovery that enable us to see how social values, including gender ideology in various guises, could be introduced into science. Some theories that have done so go on to recommend an alternate subject position as epistemically superior. But arguments are missing—and it's not clear that any particular subject position could be adequate to generate knowledge. Can a particular subject position be supported by an a priori argument? It can, but only by an argument that claims a particular structure for the world and then identifies a particular subjectivity as uniquely capable of knowing that structure. The problem with such arguments is that they beg the question. The one subject position that could be advanced as epistemically superior to others without presupposing something about the structure of the world is the unconditioned position, the position of no position that provides a view from nowhere. Attractive as this ideal might seem, arguments in the philosophy of science suggest that this is a chimera. Let me turn to them.

### III.  Feminist Epistemological Strategies 2: Multiplying Subjects

The ideal of the unconditioned (or universally conditioned) subject is the traditional proposal for escaping the particularity of subjectivity. Granting the truth of the claim that individual subjectivities are conditioned, unconditioned subjectivity is treated as an achievement rather than a natural endowment. The methods of the natural sciences constitute means to that achievement. Some well-known arguments in the philosophy of science challenge this presumption. As they have received a great deal of attention in the philosophical literature, I shall only mention them here in order to bring out their relevance to the general point. The methods of the natural sciences, in particular, have been thought to constitute the escape route from conditioned subjectivity. The difficulty just outlined for the feminist epistemological strategy of changing the subject, however, has a parallel in developments in the philosophy of science. Both dilemmas suggest the individual knower is an inappropriate focus for the purpose of understanding (and changing) science.

In the traditional view, the natural sciences are characterized by a methodology that purifies scientific knowledge of distortions produced by scientists' social and personal allegiances. The essential features of this methodology—explored in great detail by positivist philosophers of science—are observation and logic. Much philosophy of science in the last twenty-five years has been preoccupied with two potential challenges to this picture of scientific methodology—the claim of Kuhn, Feyerabend, and Hanson that observation is theory laden and the claim of Pierre Duhem that theories are underdetermined by data. One claim challenges the stability of observations themselves, the other the stability of evidential relations. Both accounts have seemed (at least to their critics and to some of their proponents) to permit the unrestrained expression of scientists' subjective preferences in the content of science. If observation is theory laden, then observation cannot serve as an independent constraint on theories, thus permitting subjective elements to constrain theory choice. Similarly, if observations acquire evidential relevance only in the context of a set of assumptions, a relevance that changes with a suitable change in assumptions, then it's not clear what protects theory choice from subjective elements hidden in background assumptions. Although empirical adequacy serves as a constraint on theory acceptance, it is not sufficient to pick out one theory from all contenders as the true theory about a domain of the natural world. These analyses of the relation between observation, data, and theory are often thought to constitute arguments against empiricism, but, like the feminist epistemological strategies, they are more effective as arguments against empiricism's silent partner, the theory of the unconditioned subject. The conclusion to be drawn from them is that what has been labeled scientific method does not succeed as a means to the attainment of unconditioned subjectivity on the part of individual knowers. And as long as the scientific knower is conceived of as an individual, knowing best when freed from external influences and attachment (that is, when detached or free from her/his context), the puzzles introduced by the theory-laden nature of observation and the dependence of evidential relations on background assumptions will remain unsolved.

It need not follow from these considerations, however, that scientific knowledge is impossible of attainment. Applying what I take to be a feminist insight—that we are all in relations of interdependence—I have suggested that scientific knowledge is constructed not by individuals applying a method to the material to be known but by individuals in interaction with one another in ways that modify their observations, theories and hypotheses, and patterns of reasoning. Thus scientific method includes more than just the complex of activities that constitutes hypothesis testing through comparison of hypothesis statements with (reports of) experiential data, in principle an activity of individuals. Hypothesis testing itself consists of more than the comparison of statements but involves equally centrally the subjection of putative data, of hypotheses, and of the background assumptions in light of which they seem to be supported by those data to varieties of conceptual and evidential scrutiny and criticism.[8] Conceptual criticism can include investigation into the internal and external consistency of a hypothesis and investigation of the factual, moral, and social implications of background assumptions; evidential criticism includes not only investigation of the quality of the data but of its organization, structuring, and so on. Because background assumptions can be and most frequently are invisible to the members of the

scientific community for which they are background and because unreflective acceptance of such assumptions can come to define what
it is to be a member of such a community (thus making criticism
impossible), effective criticism of background assumptions requires
the presence and expression of alternative points of view. This sort
of account allows us to see how social values and interests can become
enshrined in otherwise acceptable research programs (i.e., research
programs that strive for empirical adequacy and engage in criticism).
As long as representatives of alternative points of view are not included in the community, shared values will not be identified as shaping observation or reasoning.

Scientific knowledge, on this view, is an outcome of the critical
dialogue in which individuals and groups holding different points of
view engage with each other. It is constructed not by individuals but
by an interactive dialogic community. A community's practice of inquiry is productive of knowledge to the extent that it facilitates transformative criticism. The constitution of the scientific community is
crucial to this end as are the interrelations among its members. Community level criteria can, therefore, be invoked to discriminate among
the products of scientific communities, even though context-independent standards of justification are not attainable. At least four criteria
can be identified as necessary to achieve the transformative dimension
of critical discourse:

1. There must be publicly recognized forums for the criticism of
   evidence, of methods, and of assumptions and reasoning.

2. The community must not merely tolerate dissent, but its beliefs
   and theories must change over time in response to the critical
   discourse taking place within it.

3. There must be publicly recognized standards by reference to
   which theories, hypotheses, and observational practices are evaluated and by appeal to which criticism is made relevant to the
   goals of the inquiring community. With the possible exception
   of empirical adequacy, there needn't be (and probably isn't) a
   set of standards common to all communities. The general family
   of standards from which those locally adopted might be drawn
   would include such cognitive virtues as accuracy, coherence,
   and breadth of scope, and such social virtues as fulfilling technical or material needs or facilitating certain kinds of interactions between a society and its material environment or among
   the society's members.

4. Finally, communities must be characterized by equality of in-

tellectual authority. What consensus exists must not be the result of the exercise of political or economic power or of the exclusion of dissenting perspectives; it must be the result of critical dialogue in which all relevant perspectives are represented.

Although requiring diversity in the community, this is not a relativist position. True relativism, as I understand it, holds that there are no legitimate constraints on what counts as reasonable to believe apart from the individual's own beliefs. Equality of intellectual authority does not mean that anything goes but that everyone is regarded as equally capable of providing arguments germane to the construction of scientific knowledge. The position outlined here holds that both nature and logic impose constraints. It fails, however, to narrow reasonable belief to a single one among all contenders, in part because it does not constrain belief in a wholly unmediated way. Nevertheless, communities are constrained by the standards operating within them, and individual members of communities are further constrained by the requirement of critical interaction relative to those standards. To say that there may be irreconcilable but coherent and empirically adequate systems for accounting for some portion of the world is not to endorse relativism but to acknowledge that cognitive needs can vary and that this variation generates cognitive diversity.

Unlike the view from nowhere achievable by unconditioned subjectivity or the view from that somewhere identified as maximizing knowledge, this notion of knowledge through interactive intersubjectivity idealizes the view from everywhere (perhaps better thought of as *views* from *many wheres*). These criteria for objective communities represent not a description of actual scientific communities but a set of prescriptions that are probably not anywhere satisfied. Nevertheless, they provide a measure against which actual communities and, indirectly, criteria for the comparison of theories can be evaluated. For example, theories accepted in different communities can be compared with respect to the conditions under which the critical dialogue concerning a given theory has occurred. Although there are any number of objections that advocates of such a notion must address, I will confine myself here to one major problem, the answer to which opens up some future directions for feminist analysis and scientific practice.

## IV. Dilemmas of Pluralism

This sort of account is subject to the following dilemma.[9] What gets produced as knowledge depends on the consensus reached in the scientific community. For knowledge to count as genuine, the community must be adequately diverse. But the development of a theoretical idea or hypothesis into something elaborate enough to be called knowledge requires a consensus. The questions must stop somewhere, at some point, so that a given theory can be developed sufficiently to be applied to concrete problems. How is scientific knowledge possible while pursuing socially constituted objectivity? That is, if objectivity requires pluralism in the community, then scientific knowledge becomes elusive, but if consensus is pursued, it will be at the cost of quieting critical oppositional positions.

My strategy for avoiding this dilemma is to detach scientific knowledge from consensus, if consensus means agreement of the entire scientific community regarding the truth or acceptability of a given theory. This strategy also means detaching knowledge from an ideal of absolute and unitary truth. I suggest that we look at the aims of inquiry (at least some) as satisfied by embracing multiple and, in some cases, incompatible theories that satisfy local standards. This detachment of knowledge from universal consensus and absolute truth can be made more palatable than it might first appear by two moves. One of these is implicit in treating science as a practice or set of practices; the other involves taking up some version of a semantic or model-theoretic theory of theories.

Beginning with the second of these, let me sketch what I take to be the relevant aspects and implications of the semantic view.[10] This view is proposed as an alternative to the view of theories as sets of propositions (whether axiomatized or not). If we take the semantic view, we understand a theory as a specification of a set of relations among objects or processes characterized in a fairly abstract way. Another characterization would be that on the semantic view, a theory is the specification of a structure. The structure as specified is neither true nor false; it is just a structure. The theoretical claim is that the structure is realized in some actual system. As Mary Hesse has shown, models are proposed as models of some real world system on the basis of an analogy between the model and the system, that is, the supposition that the model and the system share some significant features in common.[11] Models often have their start as metaphors. Examples of such metaphoric models are typical philosophers' examples like the billiard ball model of particle interactions or the solar system model of the atom. What many feminists have pointed out (or can be understood as having pointed out) is the use of elements of gender ideology and social relations as metaphors for natural processes and relations. Varieties of heterosexual marriage have served as the metaphoric basis for models of the relation between nucleus and cytoplasm in the cell, for example.[12] The master molecule approach to

gene action, characterized by unidirectional control exerted on or-
ganismal processes by the gene, reflects relations of authority in the
patriarchal household. Evelyn Fox Keller has recently been investigating the basis of models in molecular biology in androcentric metaphors of sexuality and procreation.[13] When Donna Haraway says that
during and after the Second World War the organism changed from
a factory to a cybernetic system, she can be understood as saying that
the metaphor generating models of organismic structure and function
shifted from a productive system organized by a hierarchical division
of labor to a system for generating and processing information.[14] Alternatively put, cells, gene action, and organisms have been modelled
as marriage, families, and factories and cybernetic networks, respectively. Supporting such analysis of particular theories or models requires not merely noticing the analogies of structure but also tracing
the seepage of language and meaning from one domain to another as
well as studying the uses to which the models are put.[15]

The adequacy of a theory conceived as a model is determined by
our being able to map some subset of the relations/structures posited
in the model onto some portion of the experienced world. (Now the
portions of the world stand in many relations to many other portions.)
Any given model or schema will necessarily select among those relations. So its adequacy is not just a function of isomorphism of one
of the interpretations of the theory with a portion of the world but of
the fact that the relations it picks out are ones in which we are interested. A model guides our interactions with and interventions in
the world. We want models that guide the interactions and interventions we seek. Given that different subcommunities within the larger
scientific community may be interested in different relations or that
they may be interested in objects under different descriptions, different models (that if taken as claims about an underlying reality would
be incompatible) may well be equally adequate and provide knowledge, in the sense of an ability to direct our interactions and interventions, even in the absence of a general consensus as to what's
important. Knowledge is not detached from knowers in a set of propositions but consists in our ability to understand the structural features
of a model and to apply it to some particular portion of the world; it
is knowledge of that portion of the world through its structuring by
the model we use. The notion of theories as sets of propositions requires that we view the adequacy of a theory as a matter of correspondence of the objects, processes, and relations described in the
propositions of the theory with the objects, processes, and relations
in the domain of the natural world that the theory purports to explain;
that is, it requires that adequacy be conceptualized as truth. The

model-theoretic approach allows us to evaluate theories in relation to our aims as well as in relation to the model's isomorphism with elements of the modeled domain and permits the adequacy of different and incompatible models serving different and incompatible aims. Knowledge is not contemplative but active.

The second move to escape the dilemma develops some consequences of treating science as practice. There are two worth mentioning. If we understand science as practice, then we understand inquiry as ongoing, that is, we give up the idea that there is a terminus of inquiry that just is the set of truths about the world. (What LaPlace's demon knew, for example.) Scientific knowledge from this perspective is not the static end point of inquiry but a cognitive or intellectual expression of an ongoing interaction with our natural and social environments. Indeed, when we attempt to identify the goals of inquiry that organize scientific cognitive practices, it becomes clear that there are several, not all of which can be simultaneously pursued.[16] Scientific knowledge, then, is a body of diverse theories and their articulations onto the world that changes over time in response to the changing cognitive needs of those who develop and use the theories, in response to the new questions and anomalous empirical data revealed by applying theories, and in response to changes in associated theories. Both linear-reductionist and interactionist models reveal aspects of natural processes, some common to both and some uniquely describable with the terms proper to one but not both sorts of model. If we recognize the partiality of theories, as we can when we treat them as models, we can recognize pluralism in the community as one of the conditions for the continued development of scientific knowledge in this sense.

In particular, the models developed by feminists and others dissatisfied with the valuative and affective dimensions of models in use must at the very least (given that they meet the test of empirical adequacy) be recognized as both revealing the partiality of those models in use and as revealing some aspects of natural phenomena and processes that the latter conceal. These alternative models may have a variety of forms and a variety of motivations, and they need not repudiate the aim of control. We engage in scientific inquiry to direct our interactions with and interventions in the world. Barbara McClintock was not a feminist, but she was in part reacting against the gendered meanings in natural philosophy, meanings which shut her out of inquiry; Ruth Hubbard advocates interactionist perspectives out of more explicitly political commitments; feminists and others concerned with the environment reject the control orientation of technocrats effective in the short term for more complex models that can address long-term change and stasis in the ecosystem. If we aim for effective action in the natural world, something is to be controlled. The issue should be not whether but what and how. Rather than repudiate it, we can set the aim of control within the larger context of overall purposes and develop a more refined sense of the varieties of control made possible through scientific inquiry.

A second consequence for feminist and other oppositional scientists of adopting both the social knowledge thesis and a model-theoretic analysis of theories is that the constructive task does not consist in finding the one best or correct feminist model. Rather, the many models that can be generated from the different subject positions ought to be articulated and elaborated. Very few will be exclusively feminist if that means exclusively gender-based or developed only by feminists. Some will be more appropriate for some domains, others for others, and some for none. We can't know this unless models get sufficiently elaborated to be used as guides for interactions. Thus, this joint perspective implies the advocacy of subcommunities characterized by local standards. To the extent that they address a common domain and to the extent that they share some standards in common, these subcommunities must be in critical dialogue with each other as well as with those subcommunities identified with more mainstream science. The point of dialogue from this point of view is not to produce a general and universal consensus but to make possible the refinement, correction, rejection, and sharing of models. Alliances, mergers, and revisions of standards as well as of models are all possible consequences of this dialogic interaction.

## V. Conclusions

Understanding scientific knowledge in this way supports at least two further reflections on knowledge and power. First of all, the need for models within which we can situate ourselves and the interactions we desire with the natural world will militate against the inclusiveness required for an adequate critical practice, if only because the elaboration of any model requires a substantial commitment of material and intellectual resources on the part of a community.[17] This means that, in a power-stratified society, the inclusion of the less powerful and hence of models that could serve as a resource for criticism of the received wisdom in the community of science will always be a matter of conflict. At the same time, the demand for inclusiveness should not be taken to mean that every alternative view is equally deserving of attention. Discussion must be conducted in reference to public standards, standards which, as noted above, do not provide timeless criteria, but which change in response to changes in cognitive and social needs. Nevertheless, by appeal to standards adopted and legitimated through processes of public scrutiny and criticism, it is possible to set aside as irrelevant positions such as New Age "crystalology" or creationism. To the extent that these satisfy none of the central standards operative in the scientific communities of their cultures, they indeed qualify as crackpot. Programs for low-tech science appropriate to settings and problems in developing nations may, by contrast, be equally irritating to or against the grain of some of the institutionalized aspects of science in the industrialized nations, but as long as they do satisfy some of the central standards of those communities, then the perspectives they embody must be included in the critical knowledge-constructive dialogue. Although there is always a danger that the politically marginal will be conflated with the crackpot, one function of public and common standards is to remind us of that distinction and to help us draw it in particular cases. I do not know of any simple or formulaic solution to this problem.

Second, those critiques of scientific epistemology that urge a change of subject preserve the structures of cognitive authority but propose replacing those currently wielding authority with others: a genuinely unbiased subject in one case, a differently located or a differently formed subject in the other. Either no assumptions or different assumptions will be engaged in the knowledge-constructive process. In the position I am advocating, which makes salient those features of knowledge construction made invisible by more traditional accounts, the structures of cognitive authority themselves must change. No segment of the community, whether powerful or powerless, can claim epistemic privilege. If we can see our way to the dissolution of those structures, then we need not understand the appropriation of power in the form of cognitive authority as intrinsic to science. Nevertheless, the creation of cognitive democracy, of democratic science, is as much a matter of conflict and hope as is the creation of political democracy.

## Notes

I wish to thank the members of the Centre for Women's Research at the University of Oslo for their hospitality and for the stimulating discussions that shaped the final draft of this essay. I am grateful also for the editorial suggestions of Elizabeth Potter and Linda Alcoff. An earlier and much abbreviated version was prepared for the December 1991 meetings of the Eastern Division of the American Philosophical Association and published as "Multiplying Subjects and Diffusing Power" in the *Journal of Philosophy*, LXXXVIII, II (December, 1991).

1. Empiricist philosophers have found themselves in great difficulty when confronting the necessity to make their theory of the knower explicit, a difficulty most eloquently expressed in David Hume's Appendix to *A Treatise of Human Nature*, ed. L. A. Selby-Bigge (Oxford, UK: Clarendon Press, 1960).

2. The later philosophy of Wittgenstein does challenge the individualist ideal. Until recently few commentators have developed the anti-individualist implications of his work. See Naomi Scheman, "Individualism and the Objects of Psychology" in *Discovering Reality*, ed. Sandra Harding and Merrill Hintikka (Boston: Reidel, 1983), 225–44.

3. Harding has treated Marcia Millman and Rosabeth Kantor's Introduction to their collection, *Another Voice* (New York: Doubleday, 1975) and my essay with Ruth Doell, "Body, Bias and Behavior," from *Signs* 9, 2 (Winter 1983) as exemplars of feminist empiricism. The latter is discussed extensively in Harding's *The Science Question in Feminism* (Ithaca: Cornell University Press, 1986). Because the article nowhere claims that masculinist bias can be corrected by application of current methodologies in the sciences, I have always found the discussion in *The Science Question* a puzzlingly perverse misreading.

4. Cf. Longino, "Can There Be A Feminist Science?" in *Hypatia* 2, 3 (Fall 1987); and chapter 7 of Longino, *Science as Social Knowledge* (Princeton: Princeton University Press, 1990).

5. Cf. Nancy Hartsock, "The Feminist Standpoint: Developing the Ground for a Specifically Feminist Historical Materialism," in Harding and Hintikka, *Discovering Reality*, 283–310.

6. Cf. Evelyn F. Keller, "The Force of the Pacemaker Concept in Theories of Slime Mold Aggregation," in *Perspectives in Biology and Medicine* 26 (1983): 515–21; and *A Feeling for the Organism* (San Francisco: W. H. Freeman, 1983).

7. Evelyn F. Keller, *Reflections on Gender and Science* (New Haven: Yale University Press, 1984).

8. For argument for and exposition of these points, see Longino, *Science as Social Knowledge*, especially chapter 4.

9. Thanks to Sandra Mitchell for this formulation.

10. My understanding of the semantic view is shaped by its presentations in Bas van Fraassen, *The Scientific Image* (New York: Oxford University Press, 1980); and Ronald Giere, *Explaining Science* (Chicago: University of Chicago Press, 1988); as well as by conversations with Richard Grandy and Elisabeth Lloyd. Nancy Cartwright's views on explanation, as developed in *How the*

*Laws of Physics Lie* (New York: Oxford University Press, 1983) have deeply influenced my thinking.

11.  Mary Hesse, *Models and Analogies in Science* (Notre Dame: Notre Dame University Press, 1966).

12.  The Gender and Biology Study Group, "The Importance of Feminist Critique for Contemporary Cell Biology," in *Hypatia* 3, 1 (1988).

13.  Evelyn Fox Keller, "Making Gender Visible in the Pursuit of Nature's Secrets," in *Feminist Studies/Critical Studies*, Teresa de Lauretis, ed., (Bloomington: Indiana University Press, 1986), 67–77; and "Gender and Science," in *The Great Ideas Today* (Chicago: Encyclopedia Britannica, 1990).

14.  Donna Haraway, "The Biological Enterprise: Sex, Mind, and Profit from Human Engineering to Sociobiology," in *Radical History Review* 20 (1979): 206–37.

15.  This is the strategy adopted in chapter 8 of *Science as Social Knowledge*.

16.  This point is developed further in *Science as Social Knowledge*, chapter 2.

17.  For a somewhat different approach to a similar question, see Philip Kitcher, "The Division of Cognitive Labor," in *Journal of Philosophy* LXXXVII, 1 (January 1990): 5–23.

# 6

# Epistemological Communities

*Lynn Hankinson Nelson*

## The Agents of Epistemology

I begin a discussion of the agents or subjects of epistemology from the assumption that the category has no fixed or historic content, i.e., that it was not fixed once and for all by Cartesian (or any other) epistemology. By current lights it is persons, embodied and situated in specific social and historical contexts, who know, with both their embodiment and "situations" relevant to their knowing. According to feminist epistemologies, such situations need to be specified using the analytic category gender, a category whose "content" and meaning are dynamic and multileveled and one whose relationship to other categories and social relations (e.g., class, culture, and race), as well as to knowledge, remains both contested and central to feminist theory.[1]

The current views I have noted are evidence for the assumption I shared at the outset, for in being situated (as well as contested), the agents of feminist epistemologies, of sociology of knowledge, and of some empiricist frameworks,[2] differ significantly from the abstract (context-independent and disembodied) "individuals" of foundationalist epistemologies.[3] These agents also differ from their predecessors in foundationalist epistemologies in that they shape, as well as undergo and absorb, experience; they construct meaning and knowledge—even, some say, negotiate and decide these.[4] "The knower" of the frameworks developed by Descartes, Hume, and the early and later formulations of positivism was basically passive, a recipient or collector of knowledge.

A second assumption underlying my discussion is that views of the agents of epistemology are not isolated or isolatable, or "starting points," but deeply related to other features of an epistemology, particularly assumptions about the nature and role of evidence—another category whose content is historically dynamic. The view in foundationalist frameworks of knowers as passive recipients of knowledge, subjects whose situations within specific social relations and contexts are irrelevant to their knowing, was interdependent with a view that, at some level, evidence is definitive and "self-announcing." The demise of foundationalism engendered deep disagreements about whether there are constraints on knowledge and the nature of those constraints; but among the current frameworks that continue to talk of evidence, there is recognition that standards of evidence are historically relative and dynamic, emerging concomitantly with the processes through which knowledge is generated, rather than having been laid down prior to these processes.[5] Far-reaching disagreements remain, of course, concerning the implications of this view of evidence—including the implications for the future of epistemology; my point here is (only) that the change to viewing evidence as dynamic is related to the active role now attributed to knowers in feminist and other epistemologies and to the insistence within various frameworks that knowers are situated.

Many of us are also more likely to speak of "knowers" and "scientists" than of "a (or the) knower" or "the scientist," phrases that figured prominently in foundationalist frameworks. For many feminists, the adoption of plural terms has been deliberate, reflecting the changes I have outlined and developments specific to feminist theory. Particularly important have been feminist arguments that point to the deep implausibility of "epistemological individualism": the view of knowledge as "an individual affair . . . the mental activity of individual knowers grasping the one objective truth" (Addelson and Potter 1991, 12). Feminists have argued that a solipsistic knower is implausible in light of human biology, including neurobiology (Jaggar 1983; Longino 1990; Nelson 1990); some have challenged the view that beliefs and knowledge are "properties" of individuals (Scheman 1983); and many have argued that interpersonal experience is necessary for individuals to have beliefs and to know (Bleier 1984; Code 1991; Jaggar 1983; Longino 1990; Nelson 1990; Scheman 1983). And for more than a decade feminists have argued that a commitment to epistemological individualism would preclude reasonable explanations of feminist knowledge; such explanations (or, on some accounts, justifications of that knowledge) would need to incorporate the historically specific social and political relationships and situations, including gender and political advocacy, that have made feminist knowledge possible (Harding 1986; Harstock 1983; Jaggar 1983; Smith 1987).

The arguments against individualism I have mentioned appeal to the implications of feminist scholarship and activism (e.g., that these indicate that social relations, including gender, and political advocacy have a bearing on what we know (and could know) and that human biology dictates an interdependency that undermines the self-sufficiency implicit in the modernist view of "selves"); they also appeal to other aspects of current knowledge (models of higher brain function in neurobiology and of postnatal neurobiological development, for example, that render epistemological individualism implausible). Such appeals illuminate another and broader relationship: that between views of evidence and of agents of epistemology, on the one hand, and other things known and undertaken, on the other hand. The third assumption I bring to this discussion is that epistemology is radically interdependent with other knowledge and undertakings, a view I defend in more detail below.

Elsewhere I have suggested a deeper change in our view of the agents of epistemology than that reflected in the use of plural terms (Nelson 1990). Building on the assumptions and developments I have outlined, I argued that it is communities that construct and acquire knowledge and recommended that feminists recognize "epistemological communities" as the agents of epistemology.[6] My arguments were based in large part on the implausibility of the solipsistic knower of foundationalist epistemology. They made use of the necessity of environmental stimuli and membership in a sociolinguistic community for the postnatal neurobiological development that permits cognitive functioning; Quine's challenges to positivist versions of foundationalism, particularly his arguments that public conceptual schemes make possible and shape coherent and recoverable experience; and the inherently social and historically relative nature of current androcentric and feminist assumptions, theories, and standards.[7] All three, I argued, indicate that communities are the generators of knowledge.

But communities are not the only alternative to the solipsistic knower that figured in foundationalist epistemologies. Persons who are situated or located in ways earlier noted are another (see, for example, Haraway 1988; Harding 1991, and in this volume). And, according to recent postmodern arguments, there are no candidates for the subjects or agents of epistemology—hence, some conclude, no future for epistemology (Hekman 1990). It is within the context of postmodern arguments that appear to mitigate against the plausibility of agents of epistemology that I develop my earlier proposal that communities are the primary epistemological agents.[8]

My arguments here build on an account of evidence that recognizes it to be fundamentally communal. The account, I will argue, is compatible with and supported by feminist experience and knowledge. It indicates that communities are the primary loci—the primary generators, repositories, holders, and acquirers—of knowledge. I outline and defend the account of evidence in the next section; in a third, I relate it and the view that communities are the primary epistemological agents to issues raised in and by feminist science criticism.

In suggesting that it is communities that construct and acquire knowledge, I do not mean (or "merely" mean) that what comes to be recognized or "certified" as knowledge is the result of collaborations between, consensus achieved by, political struggles engaged in, negotiations undertaken among, or other activities engaged in by individuals who, *as individuals, know* in some logically or empirically "prior" sense. Work in sociology of knowledge, feminist epistemology and philosophy of science, and social studies of science indicates that it is in and through a variety of such activities that knowledge is generated.[9] The change I am proposing involves what we should construe as the *agents* of these activities. My arguments suggest that the collaborators, the consensus achievers, and, in more general terms, the agents who generate knowledge are communities and subcommunities, not individuals.

But although I do not think individuals are the primary epistemological agents (even individuals who are embodied, gendered, and in other ways situated historically and culturally), I do not deny that individuals know. My claim is that the knowing we do as individuals is derivative, that your knowing or mine depends on *our* knowing, for some "we." More to the point, I will argue that you or I *can* only know what *we know* (or could know), for some "we." The sense of "can" will emerge in the discussion of evidence. The "we," as I understand things, is a group or community that constructs and shares knowledge and standards of evidence—a group, in short, that is an "epistemological community." Hence, on the view I am advocating, communities that construct and acquire knowledge are not collections of independently knowing individuals; such communities are epistemologically prior to individuals who know.

There are important differences between the role I propose for epistemological communities and that accorded abstract individuals in foundationalist epistemologies. First, the arguments I draw on indicate that the epistemological priority of communities is not a self-evident truth (and that I do not pretend that it is); it depends, rather, on our best current theories in a variety of areas, including philosophy and sociology of science and feminist science criticism, particularly on developments within these fields that indicate that evidence is communal.[10] Hence, the arguments reflect the three assumptions that I shared at the outset: that the category "agents of epistemology" is dynamic; that our views of such agents are interdependent with our understandings of evidence; and that epistemology is radically interdependent with other knowledge and projects.

The agents I am proposing will also have a more obviously empirical role than the "abstract individuals" of foundationalist epistemologies, the empirical study of which was, arguably at least, never envisioned. As I see them, epistemological communities are multiple, historically contingent, and dynamic: they have fuzzy, often overlapping boundaries; they evolve, dissolve, and recombine; and they have a variety of "purposes" and projects which may include (as in the case of science communities) but frequently do not include (as a priority) the production of knowledge. Hence, communities that generate knowledge can not be accorded the "deep background status" that, as Kathryn Pyne Addelson notes, came eventually to characterize "selves" or persons in modernist frameworks (Addelson, this volume). They cannot, that is, be assumed to be without need of empirical study and specification. On my view, a feminist epistemology that recognizes communities as the primary epistemological agents must be a naturalized epistemology (see Addelson, in this volume; Duran 1991).

The rationale for naturalizing epistemology is, in fact, multileveled.[11] As reflected in the arguments offered by some who proposed the project three decades ago, the demise of foundationalism and, thus, the impossibility of a "first" science or basic knowledge forced a change in the way epistemology is to be understood and pursued.[12] A naturalized epistemology, as Quine advocated the project, would be pursued as an empirical science; it would involve constructing accounts of how we go about building knowledge and of the evidence we have for doing so, drawing on the methods and knowledge of other areas of science. The reference to epistemology as a science reflects the view that epistemology is radically interdependent with bodies of things we know (for Quine defined science broadly, as inclusive of "everything we say about the world"[13]), that it does not (and could not) provide the justification for our knowledge. So understood, naturalized epistemology is clearly distinct from foundationalist epistemology; it begins from the assumption that we do in fact know (an assumption implied in various things I have said in this section) and that such knowledge will be justified (if it is) by its ability to make sense of and explain experience.

But a naturalized epistemology is also distinguishable from some other projects in "postfoundationalist" epistemology (e.g., from the strong program in sociology of knowledge) in that it is not simply a descriptive enterprise. Providing accounts of how knowledge is constructed and of the evidence available and used in such constructions may involve—indeed, may require—recasting the experiences of those involved so as to make the most overall sense. In a naturalized epistemology, such reconstructions appeal to and are recognized as interdependent with a larger body of experience and knowledge (also historically relative and dynamic) rather than any alleged ahistoric or extratheoretical foundations or standards. Hence, unlike sociology of knowledge, a naturalized epistemology recognizes that evaluations of knowledge claims and of the processes and arrangements through which knowledge is generated are appropriate.

In constructing accounts of how knowledge is generated, a feminist naturalized epistemology would appeal, among other things, to feminist experience and knowledge—thus reflecting the inherent circularity, or what I have called the radical interdependence, between an epistemology and other knowledge and undertakings. [As I have argued elsewhere, we view the circularity here as vicious only if we assume (or demand) that epistemology justify what we know; a naturalized epistemology makes no pretense to be doing this (Nelson 1990).] The interdependence referred to is real, for in undertaking a project to understand the knowledge and standards accepted by another community or those of our own communities (and many of us belong to more than one), we may find that we need to alter the assumptions with which we began—to abandon some of the standards of evidence and/or revise our views about what we know. And as I explore in later sections, such projects may result in shifts in the membership of our epistemological communities.

The change I propose in terms of our understanding of the agents of epistemology will mean that studies of how knowledge is generated will begin from the histories, social relations, and practices of communities: from the contexts and activities in and through which ontologies are developed, standards of evidence and methodologies are adopted, theories are constructed, and others are abandoned or excluded. There is, I will argue, no more basic agent to study; there are also, of course, no extratheoretic standards to bring to bear. But I expect a feminist naturalized epistemology to recast or reconstruct the experiences and activities of many communities, drawing on other aspects of feminist knowledge as well as other current knowledge; I expect that such projects will result in (or, more aptly, further) the revision or abandonment of some of the assumptions and knowledge with which those engaged in feminist epistemology begin. (Both kinds of reconstruction have, of course, characterized feminist epistemology to date.) The focus on communities further suggests that a feminist naturalized epistemology will draw heavily on sociology (but not, on my view, exclusively[14]), but I am not suggesting that the models and methodologies that currently characterize sociology (or any other science or framework on which feminists might draw) will prove adequate in their present form to feminist epistemology. It seems far more likely, in light of feminist science criticism, that both the sciences drawn on by those doing epistemology, and feminist epistemology itself will evolve.

The foregoing has implications for the kind of project I undertake here. It indicates that discussions at the level of this one are aptly regarded as research proposals and that, in the main, the *doing* of epistemology—the constructing of accounts of how knowledge is produced and of what constitutes evidence for that knowledge—will require more obviously empirical studies, with these having, in turn, implications for how we understand and undertake feminist epistemology. The qualifications in the last sentence ("in the main" and "more obviously") reflect the lack of real or interesting boundaries between such studies and proposals that they be undertaken and the interdependence between epistemology and other knowledge.

Articulating the general outlines of a nonfoundationalist view of experience and evidence, and a communal view of both and of "knowers," involves issues that are a matter of some controversy in feminist theory as well as within a larger intellectual arena, controversy which has been sharpened by recent postmodern arguments against epistemology.[15] Relatedly, recent postmodern (and other) arguments have drawn attention to the dangers of replacing "old" foundations with new ones (however inadvertently) in insisting on the instability and nonfoundational nature of categories central to feminist epistemologies—including, if not especially, gender and evidence (Flax 1987; Harding 1986, 1991; Hekman 1990).

But to return to earlier remarks about some of what motivates this discussion, the abandonment of epistemology heralded by postmoderns seems less inevitable if we are not compelled to grant the terms of Cartesian epistemology (or Enlightenment or modernist epistemology, and none of these are synonyms)—and, more specifically, if views of the agents of epistemology and of evidence are both dynamic and interdependent as well as relative to other things we know and undertake.[16] That is, it is at least an open question whether the only candidates for the agents of epistemology are individuals (an assumption common to both Cartesian epistemology and some postmodern arguments against epistemology); thus, as Nancy Tuana points out, it is an open question whether some alleged dichotomies are real: that, for example, we must either construe the subjects or agents of feminist epistemology as "abstract, constituting subjects" (or, in some way, as discrete and basic units—e.g., as "essential, gendered, and enduring selves"); or we must reconcile ourselves to the fact that, as "subjects in process," constituted by "the discourses and practices of their culture," persons cannot be subjects or agents in the sense (it is argued) that epistemology "requires" (Hekman 1990; Tuana 1992).[17] The dichotomy recent postmodern arguments present does not bode well for a feminist epistemology (or any other); the first option would commit us to either a Cartesian self or (it has been argued) essentialism, and the second has been taken to indicate there can be no epistemology (Tuana 1992).[18] The arguments I offer for the epistemological priority of communities are intended, in one sense, to suggest that these options are not exhaustive—in part by revealing how this particular dichotomy presumes individualism.

Some postmodern arguments also suggest a dichotomy concerning evidence: that either there are extrahistoric and "pre-social" standards for judging beliefs and knowledge or such judgments are (ultimately) vacuous (see, for example, Harding 1991; Hekman 1990; and the collection in Nicholson 1990). Actually, another dichotomy is frequently worked into this dichotomy concerning evidence and is deeply related to it: that either there is "One Truth" or there is a multiplicity of "truths" *and, hence,* no truths are privileged in the sense of being "more true" or more warranted (Hekman 1990). Neither dichotomy is original to postmodernism (something like each has been maintained, for example, by objectivists); nor, as Sandra Harding notes, is the general assumption (also common to versions of objectivism and relativism) that historical relativism entails judgmental relativism (Harding 1991).[19] The arguments I offer in the next section indicate that it also remains an open question whether these dichotomies are real, in part by showing that it remains an open question whether evidence is something only individuals can gather or have and, relatedly, an open question whether the historically specific nature of evidence entails relativism of the sorts that the dichotomies present as the only alternative to objectivism. Alternatively said, if we grant the three dichotomies I have mentioned, we should at least be clear that we are committing ourselves to the *terms* of Cartesian epistemology—terms the contemporary advocates of such dichotomies claim, correctly, are bankrupt (see also Harding 1990, 1991; Tuana 1992).

The positions I will advocate in terms of the agents of epistemology and evidence are an attempt, then, to negotiate between what Evelyn Fox Keller describes as "the polarizing pressures . . . [propelling us] either towards objectivism; or towards relativism," pressures she notes that are "peculiarly insistent" and "make it difficult to occupy, let alone articulate, a middle ground" (Keller 1989, 34). The positions are not a middle ground in the following sense: in arguing for communal accounts of agents and evidence, I am suggesting that we abandon the individualism and demands for archimedean points that underlie both objectivism and some contemporary versions of judgmental relativism. In this section, I have used as counterpoint some of the assumptions underlying the view that what Susan Hekman calls "the postmodern attack on the subject" (Hekman 1990, 62) sounds the death knell of the category "agents of epistemology." I have argued that the category is neither fixed nor isolatable from other things we know and undertake and that it is an open question whether epistemology has been defined for all time. In the balance of the discussion, my arguments against what Linda Alcoff has called "the postmodern erasure of the subject" are indirect.[20] In articulating a communal account of evidence in the next section as support for the view that communities are the primary subjects or agents of epistemology, I use an objectivist position as counterpoint.

## Evidence

> The conviction persists—though history shows it to be a hallucination—that all the questions that the human mind has asked are questions that can be answered in terms of the alternatives that the questions themselves present. But, in fact, intellectual progress usually occurs through sheer abandonment of questions together with both of the alternatives they assume—an abandonment that results from their decreasing vitality and a change of urgent interest. We do not solve them: we get over them.[21] (Dewey 1910, 313)

At a recent Nobel conference, Harvard physicist Sheldon Glashow outlined his commitments as a scientist and attributed these to other scientists. I use his position as counterpoint in articulating a communal account of evidence, an account compatible with the view that knowledge is socially constructed *and* constrained by evidence—a view, I have argued elsewhere, that is compelling in light of feminist scholarship (Nelson 1990) and that I believe bridges various feminist epistemologies (Tuana 1992).[22] Using science to articulate the account reflects the view that included in the "experience" with which we need to contend, with which feminist accounts of evidence need either to be compatible or to provide a reasonable reconstruction, is the success science has in explaining and predicting experience, including feminist science. It will become clear that the account of evidence gives science its just due and that it is not appropriate only to science.

Glashow's self-described article of "faith" is this:

We [scientists] believe that the world is knowable, that there are simple rules governing the behavior of matter and the evolution of the universe. We affirm that there are eternal, objective, extrahistorical, socially neutral, external and universal truths, and that the assemblage of these truths is what we call physical science. Natural laws can be discovered that are universal, invariable, inviolate, genderless and verifiable.

They may be found by men or by women or by mixed collaborations of any obscene proportions. Any intelligent alien anywhere would have come upon the same logical system as we have to explain the structure of protons and the nature of supernovae.

This statement I cannot prove. This statement I cannot justify. This is my faith (Glashow 1989).[23]

But Glashow is surely being disingenuous when he says, "This statement I cannot prove. This statement I cannot justify. This is my faith." Suppose someone in the audience interrupted or followed Glashow to the podium and announced that her "faith" was that the correct (the *only* correct) understanding of the universe, the only access to the true and immutable laws of nature, is to be had through crystal ball gazing or divine revelation. What would Glashow's reaction be? Would he embrace the interloper as a "fellow" traveler who has come to Glashow's own view of proof and justification but simply come to a different though equally viable and equally reasonable view about gaining knowledge?

Of course not. It is far more likely that Glashow would be amazed and offended and that he would dismiss the interloper's claims as unworthy of response. Surely Glashow "really" believes that his own position is obviously a (or *the*) reasonable one and that the interloper's is unreasonable and not worthy of discussion. Why? Clearly because he thinks his position, his "faith," *makes sense of and explains* the success of science, whereas the interloper's position does not.

The paradox in Glashow's position is this: he clearly does not think anything goes in the realm of intellectual commitments. Yet he is locked into a view that does not give him the intellectual space within which he can defend that view. The lock is that imposed by the positivist (or perhaps more fundamentally Humean) tenet that every meaningful claim must either be derivable from sense experience (or statements about sense experience) or must be a claim about the meanings of words (a matter of definition). Glashow's article of faith does not follow directly from sensory experience; nor is it (nor does he want it to be) true by definition. Hence there can be no evidence for it. Hence it is not provable (and Glashow believes proof is possible). Hence, it is "just" an article faith . . .

But there is an alternative to Glashow's implicit view about evidence: a view that allows for evidence and reasonable belief without certitude, without derivability from unshakable foundations. This view allows for a discussion of Glashow's position, explains why it is *worth discussing*, and why it is more reasonable than the interloper's view. In the end, Glashow's view is less reasonable than this alternative, an alternative for which Glashow does not allow but which is needed to show that his own view is at least discussible, that it is a player in the field of epistemological theories.[24]

The view of evidence I am alluding to is very different from Glashow's (and from any theory that places similar demands on "knowledge") in at least three ways. First, it construes evidence as communal; second, it accepts coherence (and with it explanatory power) as a measure of reasonableness; and third, it holds that communities, not individuals, are the primary loci of knowledge. I develop my arguments for this view by focusing on three assumptions implicit in Glashow's article of faith:

- There is one full and unique truth about the world.
- Our sensory organs are sufficiently refined to discriminate that truth from other candidates for truth.
- Scientific investigation is such that, at some finite point, the evidence we acquire for a view finally and decisively rules out all alternative views.

In other words, there is one world to discover, our sense organs can uniquely discriminate that world, and science is a process which will lead, in a finite amount of time, to a single view about what that reality is.

Arguments against the third assumption are widely accepted,[25] and there have been arguments against assumptions related to the first and second. The arguments I outline here are not original. Their importance lies in the fact that they suggest that although all of the assumptions implicit in Glashow's position should be rejected, *nonetheless* the notion of a "reasonable" claim or theory makes sense and that adopting a particular view of knowledge acquisition (including science) need not be an act of faith.

There is no single way to make these points, for the threads are many and intertwined. I start with Glashow's commitment to the view that "any intelligent being anywhere" would have "come upon" the structure of protons. The commitment presumes a universality of experience (at least the potential for such universality), which presumes, in turn, both a view of evidence and a view of knowers: specifically, that individuals have unmediated or at least unfiltered access to a reality that itself admits of only one systemization. Now, one's faith in such universality might be partly underwritten by similarities in sense organs (which might not, of course, be duplicated in an "alien" species). But it *also* requires that there is a unique, true theory of nature and that our sense organs are sufficiently refined to discover it and discriminate it from possible alternatives. Only then (in the absence of innate ideas) could it be inevitable (even possible) that any human being anywhere (let alone any "being" anywhere) would discover proton structure. The third of the assumptions I earlier attributed to Glashow is also implicit in the commitment: that scientific investigation is such that, at some finite point, we acquire evidence for a view that finally and decisively rules out all alternative views. If this were not so, Glashow's "any being" might never reach the (one) truth about protons.

I have suggested that Glashow does not really view his position as an article of faith (that he would not grant faith in, say, crystal ball gazing the status of an equally reasonable view of how to discover truths). His position is more aptly viewed as an inference to the best explanation: as the best (if not only) explanation for science's success in explaining and predicting experience and features of the world. But as an explanation, Glashow's position faces immediate problems.

Perhaps the most obvious are posed by the history of science. The problem is not (most interestingly at least) that its history includes discarded theories and abandoned projects and that we would need to find some way of accommodating these that did not undermine the position itself (we would need, perhaps, to look for some general fault in past scientific practice—although not, of course, a problem with scientists' sense organs). A deeper problem for the view that evidence is definitive and self-announcing is that many theories and assumptions eventually abandoned were, in fact, well supported within the context of then current knowledge and accepted practice.

A purported explanation either needs to be compatible with our prior understandings of what is to be explained (in this case, the history of science, which many of us no longer approach using the notion of verisimilitude), or it should point to a reconstruction that offers a different but coherent understanding of that which is being explained. As an explanation of the history of science, Glashow's position does neither.

Using the above criteria, the three assumptions I earlier identified as implicit in Glashow's position are also deeply problematic. Many of us have come to see that we have no reason to take the third assumption I have attributed to Glashow seriously. Consider, for example, his second example of "certain" knowledge, the nature of supernovae. However much evidence we have for that account and however much we could have, we are not in a position (and never will be) to know that future experience will not cause us to abandon it or to organize things in ways that no longer include it. (The point of the last remark is that we do not have to assume we would come to reject our current theory as "false.") There is nothing in our experience to rule out the possibility of a future theory, commensurate with all of our experiences to date but incompatible with our current theory about supernovae, for what is currently claimed about supernovae far exceeds the evidence we have or ever will have.

The point, made decades ago by Quine among others, is that our theories are and will forever remain underdetermined by all the evidence we have or ever will have for them (Quine 1960).[26] There is, for example, nothing in our collective experience to date to preclude our abandoning our common-sense way of organizing things in terms of physical objects for a theory that makes equally good sense of our collective experience but is incompatible with physical object theory (Quine 1969).

There is also nothing in our collective experience to warrant the assumption about our sense organs implicit in Glashow's article of faith. It is commensurate with that experience that our sense organs are refined to such a degree that, so far at least, they enable us to survive by organizing and predicting relevant future experience. (Interpersonal experience figures largely in our survival. It is also, of course, dependent on our sense organs.) But there is nothing in our experience or in what we currently know about our sense organs to warrant the inference that they are able to discriminate a "best" theory of nature (if, indeed, there is such a thing) from multiple candidates. In light of current evolutionary theory, our sense organs represent a "jury rigging" of available parts, useful in the sense that they have enabled the species to survive (so far), but probably only one of the possible, functional combinations of available parts (Gould 1982). There is nothing to indicate that they are adequate to the task of encompassing *all* that goes on, all of the rhythms and order (or, perhaps, an inherent and even more basic disorder) of nature.[27]

This brings us to the first of the assumptions implicit in Glashow's statement: that there is one (and only one) true account of the world. It is commensurate with our collective experience, as well as developments in philosophy of science, that there are indefinitely many theories that would enable us to successfully explain and predict experience, that no single system would be better than all others and, hence, that we have no reason to think there is one unique and full account to be discovered (see, for example, Quine 1960). It is commensurate with what we know and have experienced, for example, that an alternative theory of nature that did not include "Boyle's Law" (or, for that matter, any "law"), that organized things differently, might equally well explain and predict what we experience (Nelson 1990; Potter, this volume). So, minimally, there is no one "most probable" account of the world. Given this, we need some further argument for the view that there is, nonetheless, one and only one *true* account. Glashow provides none, and I can provide more for him.

None of what I have said by way of criticizing the three assumptions implicit in Glashow's position suggests that any or all alternatives will do or that because we do not have evidence warranting these assumptions, all alternatives are equally viable. The bases for each of the points made so far have been our collective experience and other aspects of current knowledge (evolutionary theory, empirical psychology, and philosophy of science), and it is not compatible with either our experience or knowledge, including feminist experience and knowledge, that any theory, any belief, or any way of organizing things will do or that all are equally warranted. That there is a world that constrains what it is reasonable to believe makes the most sense of what we experience—predictions misfire, theories fail, we can and do get things wrong—or, as Evelyn Keller makes the point, "The constraints imposed by the recalcitrance of nature are reminders . . . that, despite its ultimate unrepresentability, nature does exist" (Keller 1989, 43). What we are not warranted in assuming is that only one system could organize the world or that the world is of a determinate nature, specifiable in categories our sense organs will lead us to discover.

Now, an appeal to faith would be a reasonable resort (if not the only resort) if individuals were the primary epistemological agents, if evidence were something only individuals could gather or have. If knowledge is acquired by individuals, if all that we know, including the knowledge that emerges in our everyday interactions with nature and one another as well as in highly focused endeavors like science, has been derived from the "immediate" and unfiltered sensory experience of individuals, then, unless there is one true theory and the evidence for it is unequivocal, our allegedly individual successes in explaining and predicting experience, and the match between your experiences and theories and mine, are mysteries. That is, only a determinate reality together with fully adequate sense organs *could* explain how each individual, working on an individual basis, does (or could) come, in the end, to exactly the same theories. Hence, I am suggesting that there is a deep connection between objectivism and epistemological individualism.

The alternative account of evidence I next articulate is also compatible with our success in organizing and predicting experience and features of the world, including science's success. But it avoids the paradox inherent in Glashow's position and, unlike the latter, it is compatible with feminist experience and knowledge. I begin by telling (in very broad strokes) a different story about the discovery of proton structure. The contextual aspects of the story, the historical relativity of any such discovery and its relationship to a going context of knowledge and practices, build on the implications of feminist science criticism and epistemology. In arguing that science is an ongoing, historically relative concern, I also draw on various of Quine's arguments against positivism. My arguments relating the context for the discovery directly to evidence draw on Quine's arguments for "holism," but I extend Quine's positions in ways called for by feminist science criticism.[28] At various points in the story, I use the insights that emerge about evidence to support the view that communities are the primary epistemological agents.

The discovery of proton structure became possible *within a going system or context* of theories and practices. That context included, minimally, a theory in which proton figured; methodologies, projects, and standards of evidence that emerged concomitantly in the process of building that theory (and possibly others); and a science community (or communities) that constructed or adopted these and rejected possible alternatives. The context permitting the discovery also included some extensive part of physics as well as knowledge and standards in other fields (mathematics, chemistry, and technology, for example) that underwrite—that is, permit and support—what is currently known about protons. The context also included some of the history of science—at least those aspects on which that current body of knowledge (including, again, physics, mathematics, and technology) builds or that led eventually to it. And it encompassed broader metaphysical commitments incorporated in theories, projects, standards of evidence, and methodologies in physics and other fields,[29] including, for example, that macroscopic objects are "made up" of smaller, "unobservable" objects; that the actions of subatomic particles underwrite events at the macroscopic level; and perhaps even that there are laws of nature (that natural relationships are linear, hierarchical, and universal). Without something like these commitments, it is difficult to know how physicists (or anyone else) would have "stumbled upon" protons or their structure.

In fact, the story so far is too simple and, without qualification, it is deeply misleading. I have phrased the above points as if the history of science is a "history of ideas." But the history of "scientific ideas" (by which strange locution I mean the adoption and abandonment of theories as well as methodologies, standards of evidence, fields, research projects, models, ontologies, hypotheses, and so on), is inseparable from a social context: from a context of social relations, practices, puzzles, pressures, conflicts, and undertakings.[30] Even if we construe that history and context narrowly so as to include only the "internal" context of science communities (excluding, that is, economic, political, and other features of a broader social context that permit the existence and functioning of communities that are both self-defined and socially recognized in terms of the "pursuit of knowledge"), any such discovery occurred, and could only occur, within a context of social relations and practices.[31] Moreover, limiting the relevant social context to science communities would rely on an assumption that the directions of research and the content of science are determined solely by a logic of scientific inquiry and that such inquiry is an autonomous process, assumptions no longer plausible in light of feminist science criticism and recent historical and social studies of science.[32]

To return to the commitment with which we began, the story I have sketched suggests that any community with an appropriate history, knowledge base, and system of accepted practices, interests, methods, and questions (as well as the time and funding to permit such undertakings) might well have come upon protons and their structure—but this is *hardly* "any intelligent being anywhere." (Indeed, I have not mentioned an "individual" or individual "discoverer" for reasons that are probably clear by now and that I address explicitly below.) The point is in keeping with insights that have emerged in and through feminist science criticism and epistemology, but it is not itself an account of evidence—let alone a viable alternative to an objectivist account. To recognize the discovery of proton structure as relative to a particular historical, social, and scientific context is compatible with judgmental relativism, and I do not believe such a view of evidence is empirically viable any more than it is politically viable.

I now suggest that much of the "context" I have noted has a direct bearing on what constitutes the evidence for current knowledge of proton structure—more to the point, that many of the factors that I have described as "underwriting" that knowledge constitute, in fact, *part of the evidence for it*. Hence, I include as evidence for proton structure a large body of current knowledge within which protons figure directly and theories and practices in other sciences which underwrite or support these. I am using the terms "underwrite" and "support" in a strong sense, in an *evidential* sense, arguing that a body of accepted knowledge and practices (methodologies, ontologies, and so on) that includes a theory about proton structure is akin to an arch; each "piece" supports and is supported by the other pieces (Quine 1960, 11).[33] Given this interdependence, the evidence for proton structure obviously includes theories, methodologies, and standards already noted (other aspects of physics, mathematics, and technology). And the evidence includes "common-sense" knowledge and experience of macroscopic objects and events and the standards we use to identify these, for it is terms of our experiences and knowledge of such objects and events that the evidence for—including the explanatory power of—theories in which protons figure becomes apparent and that such theories have empirical significance (Quine 1966).[34] Finally, broader metaphysical and methodological commitments incorporated in current scientific practices also constitute part of the evidence for proton structure: that there are objects and events that are not "directly" observable that explain, more systematically, what happens on the macroscopic level and that particular macroscopic events (instrument readings, for example) are evidence of these. These commitments are incorporated in theories that include protons, as well as in related methodologies and standards, and are among the things a physicist would appeal to in responding to (at least more than superficial) queries about how and why physicists came to determine proton structure and what warrants their claims about that structure.

In short, knowledge about protons is not discrete or free floating. It is not isolatable from a larger system of theories, practices, and standards of evidence, a system that includes other aspects of scientific knowledge and practices as well as those of common sense (although, obviously, some parts of the system are more closely connected to knowledge of proton structure than others). Sentences about protons do not have empirical content—a list of sensory stimulations associated with them—in isolation from the larger system within which they figure (theoretical statements, methodologies, views about what constitutes evidence, principles for individuating objects, broader metaphysical commitments). Consequently, there is no discrete piece of evidence that warrants (or could) a claim about protons, no isolated experience against which such claims are or could be tested.

I have so far stressed a going system of knowledge and practices as evidence for particular theories and claims—a point which suggests that, in a fundamental sense, evidence is communal. No individual invented the "system" or context that underwrites knowledge of proton structure, a theoretical system the latter systematizes in turn. Moreover, without reason to think there is a unique theory of nature (and that our sensory organs could discriminate such a theory), there is no reason to assume that "any individual anywhere" *would* have recapitulated that system. But internal consistency is not the sole criterion (or an adequate one) for reasonable beliefs and explanations. Part of the evidence for protons is experience. Protons both organize and are compatible with our experiences and they have explanatory power: they allow us to explain and predict some of what happens. Here, the account of evidence I am advocating diverges from judgmental relativism (as well as coherence theories of truth), for not all theories or claims will be equally compatible with experience (as an attempt, for example, to suspend one's belief in the existence of something akin to gravity will quickly attest).

This aspect of the account of evidence also diverges from individualistic accounts. Although "experience" may seem to lend itself to an individualistic account of evidence—although it may seem (and certainly has seemed) appropriately ascribed to individuals, something individuals, as individuals, "have" (either in a phenomenological sense or in the sense of physical states)—the discussion of the discovery of proton structure suggests that experience is fundamentally social. There are no "immediate" experiences of protons, nor any determinate list of sensory stimulations from which what is known about protons is derived (or derivable). Rather, the sensory experiences currently recognized as relevant to such knowledge are themselves shaped and mediated by a larger system of historically and culturally specific theory and practice (for a historically and culturally specific community or communities), a system which not only constitutes part of the evidence for current knowledge about protons but also shapes the experiences of individuals into coherent and relevant accounts. Put another way, experiences of protons were *not possible* until relatively recently, and this did not just reflect, at least not in any simple way, a lack of technological sophistication, for the latter emerged apace with projects and knowledge. Hence, in terms of the case we are considering, the epistemological burden is appropriately attributed to communities. Individuals can in fact use such systems, but the systems themselves are communal enterprises; it is these that make possible and shape relevant experience and these by which an individual and her community will judge her claims.

To view the evidence for proton structure as relative to a larger system of theories and practices in the two ways I have outlined (and, hence, as communal) may seem unproblematic (proton structure, after all, represents "high" theoretical ground) but not generalizable. But the view is no less appropriate for "common-sense" objects and events.[35] Our knowledge of rabbits and social movements is also not isolatable from larger systems and historical and cultural contexts and undertakings; our evidence for these is, in general terms, not different in kind from that for protons. Part of the evidence for rabbits and social movements is a larger system of organizing things (a conceptual scheme and set of practices that has long included physical objects and has, for some time, included the category "social movements" and standards for identifying them and analyzing their consequences); part of the evidence is that rabbits and social movements (or, more correctly, theories that include them) help us to organize, explain, and predict some of what happens—a point, again, about the world. (I am not endorsing a theory/world, or language/world, dichotomy here. The relationship at issue is one between *experience of* the world, experience that is shaped and made possible by communal ways of organizing things, and *systems* of connected theories, methodologies, and practices). There is no determinate list of sensory stimulations from which what we know about rabbits or social movements is derived (or derivable), nor are our abilities to recognize these different in kind from the ability of some of us to recognize protons; these, too, depend on public theories and practices that allow individuals to enjoy coherent and recoverable sensory experience and to organize the latter into coherent accounts.[36]

Hence, an answer to the question "what is the evidence for protons?" (as well as to a question about the evidence for rabbits or social movements) has three inseparable aspects: their compatibility with other things known, their explanatory power, and their coherence with experience. On the account I have outlined, evidence for protons is neither definitive nor "self-announcing." Nor does the account (or the usefulness of positing protons) support (let alone force) the views that the theories and practices that led to the positing of protons are the only (or even best) way that things might have been organized (or will come to be organized); that the body of knowledge and practice that underwrote the discovery of proton structure could not have underwritten alternative (even incompatible) discoveries; or that different social and political relations and practices might not have resulted in different sciences in terms of interests, status, questions, and participants—differences that might well have resulted in different projects, standards, methodologies, and bodies of knowledge. Indeed, the account indicates that such possibilities are real, for it assumes no "subbasement" in terms either of "pre-social" experience or a determinate reality specifiable in only one way (or any best way); it broadens the scope of the evidence that is relevant to specific theories to include theories and practices of a broader reach than those generated in science; and it insists on a slippage between all the evidence we have and the knowledge we construct—hence, that there is "room" for alternative constructions. But the account also does not lend credence to judgmental relativism. There are two general constraints on the knowledge we construct: experience and other things known and undertaken.

This view of evidence points to communities as the primary generators and repositories of knowledge. It suggests two things of individual who came upon the structure of protons: first, that such an individual would have been working within an ongoing context of public theory, practices, and standards that not only made it possible to discover proton structure and shaped that knowledge but constitute part of the evidence for it; second, that the standards (theoretical, practical, methodological) by which *that* person as well as her community would have determined that she *did know* proton structure would be communal standards (for some community or communities)—standards that emerged concomitantly with the processes (intellectual, social, and political) through which a theory about protons was generated. If an individual claimed to know something that was not in keeping with the knowledge and standards of her community (or any other), it would require a change in such standards and knowledge for the individual to know—and, then, of course, some community would know. To assume an individual could know something no one else knew *or could know* would require that there is one true theory "awaiting" discovery; that our sense organs provide immediate access to a reality that is, itself, specifiable in only one way; and that our sense organs are able to discriminate a unique true theory from multiple alternatives—assumptions that are not warranted.

Recall now the hypothetical interloper who offered her or his faith in crystal ball gazing as (at least as) viable an explanation of how to get to warranted beliefs as Glashow's self-described "faith" in science. The alternative account of evidence explored here provides a way of responding to the interloper that does not involve paradox, for it allows the room and provides the grounds to say of a view that it is not warranted (or not as warranted as another) without appeal to assumptions that are themselves unwarranted. When the interloper says (as interlopers frequently do), "you cannot prove I am wrong!"—thus, however inadvertently and illogically, exposing the weakness in Glashow's present position (its reliance on assumptions that he cannot prove in the way he demands proof)—those of us who share Glashow's doubts about crystal ball gazing as a method of arriving at warranted beliefs and theories could say that the interloper's explanation is not compatible with "our" experience or current understandings of how things are (the first-person plurals here would need to be carefully and self-consciously attended to, as I address in the next section). We could go on to explain that our current understandings of how things work do not include anything to suggest (or to enable us to account for) a connection between crystal ball gazing and reasonable theories. We could not insist that no future experience will lead us to revise our views about crystal ball gazing but we could say that, by current lights, research into crystal ball gazing is not promising or warranted (and we might, if we are in the position, decline funding for such research).

What lies behind my earlier statement that "communities construct and acquire knowledge" has emerged, and with it some features of an alternative to objectivism and relativism. The term *construct* reflects the view that knowledge, standards of evidence, and methodologies, are "of our own making" rather than pieces passively discovered and added incrementally to a unique, true theory of nature and that these are constructed in the contexts of our various projects and practices and evolve in response to the latter and experience. The "social construction of knowledge" runs deep on the view, for the knowledge we build both shapes our experience as individuals into coherent and recoverable accounts and determines what we will count as evidence. Moreover, as pieces of that knowledge become more general, they bridge and systematize other knowledge and practices—hence, I have spoken of "underwriting" and of a dynamic and broad system of evidential relations. And finally, experience itself is not, on the view, unproblematic, a "natural" resting place without need of evaluation.[37] Made possible and shaped by systems of theories and standards, not all experiences will be equal, for some theories and practices will enable more veridical experience and more viable knowledge (see also Harding 1991, and in this volume).[38] Hence, I have spoken of reconstructing experience and knowledge on the basis of what feminists know and come to know.

But the term *acquire* is equally deliberate, reflecting the fact that there are *constraints* on knowledge. The standards of evidence, ontologies, and methodologies we adopt and the knowledge we build are communal, interconnected, interdependent, and relative to larger blocks of things known and projects undertaken: beliefs and knowledge claims are constrained by these things and experience.

It is a consequence of the arguments advanced here that communities are the primary epistemological agents. Standards of evidence and knowledge are historically relative and dynamic and of our own making. They are inherently and necessarily communal. Experience remains the heart of the matter, but it is inherently social rather than individualistic, for we experience the world through the lens of going projects, categories, theories, and standards, and all of these are generated by communities. Experience is also not the only criterion. What constitutes evidence for specific claims and theories includes the knowledge and standards constructed and adopted by epistemological communities. Based on our experiences, we can each contribute uniquely to what we know—but none of us knows what no one else could.[39]

## Epistemological Communities

I stated earlier that the views of agents and evidence I would advocate are compatible with and supported by feminist experience and knowledge. To show this and to give more content to the notion of an epistemological community, I briefly consider some issues raised in and by feminist science criticism. I use one aspect of feminist criticism of "man-the-hunter theory" because the theory has received extensive attention in feminist science criticism and epistemology, and this will allow comparison between an analysis incorporating the view of evidence I have outlined and those in which evidence is construed narrowly and theories (or research programs) are considered in isolation.[40] My claim is that the reconstruction I will sketch can be generalized to other theories feminists criticize and advocate, and that such reconstructions carry significant benefits.

One aspect of the criticism feminists have offered of man-the-hunter theory is directed at an organizing principle the theory incorporates: that males are socially oriented—their activities and behaviors central to and determining of social dynamics; and that females are biologically oriented—their activities and behaviors primarily reproductive, with reproductive activities assumed to be "natural," unskilled, and without consequence for social dynamics (or culture). As evidence of the organizing principle, feminist critics point out that man-the-hunter theory credits the evolution of *Homo sapiens* to behaviors and activities its advocates attribute to our male ancestors. According to the theory, the invention of tools and the development of social organization led to the evolution of bipedalist and speaking "man," and both were the achievements of our male ancestors to facilitate the hunting of large animals (Bleier 1984; Harding 1986; Hubbard 1983).[41] Our female ancestors, on the other hand, appear to have gotten a free evolutionary ride; according to the theory, they were dependent on male providers, and their behavior and activities were primarily reproductive (again, at least by implication, "natural" and unskilled) and without consequence for human evolution. As feminist critics point out, the organizing principle has far-reaching consequences; in addition to shaping the general outlines of an androcentric recon-struction of human evolution, it shapes the interpretation of fossil and archeological data and underwrites contemporary arguments (by so-ciobiologists, for example) that a sexual division of labor and male dominance are genetically determined and the product of natural selection (Bleier 1984; Longino and Doell 1983).

Much of the criticism directed at the organizing principle has cen-tered on questions of theoretical warrant. Ruth Hubbard argues, for example, that without androcentric bias there is no reason to assume a sexual division of labor in early hominid and human groups (Hub-bard 1983). In her extensive and detailed criticism of the theory, Ruth Bleier argued that the theory "starts with a set of assumptions con-cerning the eternal nature of the characteristics . . . of women and men" (Bleier 1984, 123). Other feminist critics have argued similarly, citing androcentrism as shaping both the general outlines and details of the man-the-hunter account.[42]

Considered on their own terms, that is, in isolation from other theories and knowledge and, hence, in relation only to available ar-cheological and fossil evidence, both the organizing principle and the man-the-hunter account seem without warrant. Helen Longino and Ruth Doell argue that in the case of man-the-hunter theory (and, they argue, in the case of woman-the-gatherer theory as well), the "gap" between theory and the "data" is filled in—indeed, Longino and Doell argue, given the relative lack of physical evidence, the gap could *only* be filled in—by "preconceived and culturally determined ideas" (Lon-gino and Doell 1983, 175).

Few of us, I suspect, would deny that androcentrism and gyno-centrism have been factors in the development and advocacy of the man-the-hunter and woman-the-gatherer theories or that feminist crit-icism of the former has been prompted and shaped by feminist politics and scholarship.[43] It seems no less clear that there is a gap between these accounts of evolution and the fossil and archeological evidence and that problems attendant to historical explanations are at work, including the role of current context in shaping these and, in the present case, the relative lack and unevenness of "data."[44]

But my arguments of the last section suggest an alternative to two assumptions at least implicit in the criticism I have summarized: one, that there was (or is) little or no theoretical warrant for the organizing principle or man-the-hunter theory; the other, that "culturally deter-mined beliefs" (I am assuming these include androcentric and gynocentric beliefs) are either unable to function as evidence or are inappropriate when they do so function.

Consider a matter of debate between advocates of man-the-hunter theory and woman-the-gatherer theory: the significance of chipped stones found near fossil remains of *Homo erectus* (Longino and Doell 1983). Are they evidence that our male ancestors made tools to facilitate the hunting of large animals, as man-the-hunter theorists assume; evidence that women were making tools to assist them in gathering, as those advocating woman-the-gatherer theory argue; or evidence of some other activity that a future theory might posit (Longino and Doell 1983)? If we consider the stones and other artifacts to be the only relevant evidence, then any answer to the question of the stones' significance will be based, to use Longino's and Doell's phrase, on considerations other than "direct evidence" (175). Hence, on a narrow construal of evidence, any such answer will be supplied by beliefs and assumptions that are inappropriate, that cannot (at least should not) function as evidence. Our concerns about such answers would be deeper, of course, if we also assume or demand a values/science or politics/science dichotomy.

The view of evidence I have advocated suggests that the evidence we actually bring to bear, and that we should bring to bear on the question of the significance of these stones, is vast: that current work in fields related to human evolution (primate anatomy, geology, and primatology, for example) and theories that underwrite our assumptions about how such fields are relevant (or are not) will constitute part of the evidence for an explanation of the stones. And, in fact, feminist attention to man-the-hunter theory has revealed a substantial feedback system supporting the theory and the organizing principle it incorporates.

Far from being developed in isolation, man-the-hunter theory represented a synthesis of theories, models, and observations from a number of sciences. Primate anatomy, neurobiology, evolutionary biology, geology, paleontology, and population genetics were drawn on to develop and support the view that tool use was a fundamental factor in the evolution of the brain and the move to upright posture. Connections to other current models, theories, and research are no less apparent in terms of the organizing principle feminists have criticized. Both the theory's advocates and its feminist critics note that in reconstructing the social dynamics of early hominid and human groups, man-the-hunter theorists have drawn on accounts of behavior and social dynamics in contemporary hunter-gatherer societies and models and observations in primatology and the biobehavioral sciences.[45] And in each of these fields, in anthropology, animal sociology, and the biobehavioral sciences, and specifically in terms of the observations and models drawn on by man-the-hunter theorists, feminist scientists and science critics have documented similar, androcentric methods of organizing data and observations. Finally, feminist critics of the theory have noted the deep convergence between the man-the-hunter account of early hominid social organization and behavior and contemporary Western gender relations.

When we construe evidence broadly, we are in a position to recognize that, far from being theoretically *unwarranted*, both the theory and the organizing principle enjoyed *substantial* evidential support, that the evidence for the organizing principle and the theory lay in great measure in just such connections. These points hold even if we have our doubts about, say, the relevance of primatology to a reconstruction of human evolution or to contemporary human behavior, about the extent and nature of the evidence primatology can provide, or about the models and theories that have, to date, characterized animal sociology, the biobehavioral sciences, or anthropology.

Equally important, recognizing such evidential relations is necessary to an accurate account of the evidence that supports feminist criticism of man-the-hunter theory and of that which supports woman-the-gatherer theory. In both cases, scientists and science critics are synthesizing research in primatology, anthropology, and the biobehavioral sciences—specifically, research that was not shaped by androcentric organizing principles and assumptions and, in some cases, that indicates the limits to which primate behavior or hunter/gatherer societies can provide insight into early human behavior (Longino and Doell 1983, among others). The evidence for these projects also includes knowledge of androcentrism in other sciences and of the deep relationships between gender and science that have become visible in the last three decades, as well as the more general reconstructions of women's and men's experiences that have become possible due to feminist politics.

I am not suggesting that when we construe evidence broadly, the "gap" between reconstructions of human evolution and evidence will be closed. That gap will always remain, a consequence of the more general underdetermination of theories, of the specific problems faced by historical reconstructions, and of the relative lack of artifacts in this particular case. My point has been, rather, that individual theories neither develop nor face experience in isolation, that the evidence available, relevant, and appropriate is broader than the "data," and that such evidence is not (at least when it is interesting) arbitrary or unable to be evaluated. These points are, in fact, an implication of feminist science criticism, including the three critiques I have discussed. There *is* evidence indicating that the organizing principle incorporated in man-the-hunter theory and shaping research in primatology and anthropology leads to partial and distorted accounts of social dynamics. And there is evidence that reproductive activities have never exhausted women's activities and that the latter are variable and integral aspects of social dynamics.

Acknowledging the evidential relations I have identified has important benefits. First, judgments of theories, research programs, methodologies, and ontologies are more sophisticated, for they are inclusive of the actual evidential support underlying these. Hence, the judgments "good science" and "bad science" can be recognized as more complex than a focus on individual theories (or methods or ontologies) permits. In terms of the present example, it becomes apparent that far from there being "no reason" (or only "bad" reasons) for the man-the-hunter account, the evidence *was substantial* and that both those advocating and criticizing the theory need to acknowledge and evaluate more than the available data. Second, we are in a position to insist that the so-called common-sense assumptions and experiences of gender relations and dominance hierarchies that are functioning as evidence for man-the-hunter theory (and for other current theories and research) can and should be evaluated, that acknowledging these and subjecting them to evaluation is part and parcel of doing *good* science. Given the last three decades, we have perhaps never been in a better position to recognize that such beliefs can and should be evaluated. Third, without artificial boundaries, we avoid the potential paradox of arguing (or implying) that science influenced by politics and gender is, by virtue of the fact, bad science—a position which feminist science criticism undermines (or which, if we insist on it or allow it to be smuggled in to our analyses of androcentric science, leads to convoluted accounts of that criticism).[46] Finally, recognizing the breadth of the evidence that supports man-the-hunter theory reveals the depth, the pervasiveness, and the significance of androcentrism in science. This makes it far less plausible for examples like man-the-hunter theory to be dismissed as "idiosyncratic" or isolatable instances that have little import for "science itself" (whatever that is, if it does not include evolutionary theory, primatology, or anthropology) or as "just models" without the potential to underwrite other theories and research or to reinforce social relations.

Philosophical legend credits Hobbes with the line, "The Inn of Evidence has no signpost." I don't know if the legend is true, but I like to cite it. Viable theories, like evidence, are not self-announcing. When we judge a theory as viable or not, when we judge a research project, a model, a methodological principle, or a theory as an example of "good" or "bad" science or judge a particular claim or belief as warranted or unwarranted, it can not be on the basis of some simple test or criterion. These judgments require attention to as much evidence as we can (or find it necessary to) accommodate. After such evaluation, we may find that rather than pointing to a theory like man-the-hunter as an example of "bad science," we will want to say that "it was once promising in the context of then current knowledge and standards, but we are now in a position—(although certainly not ever in a position to say that "all the evidence is in")—to see that it is not viable."

Our analyses would also need to focus on communities (in the present case, these include primatologists, evolutionary biologists, and feminist communities, among others). We cannot credit individual scientists with the assumptions, ontologies, organizing principles, and theories that constitute evidence for man-the-hunter theory or with choosing and synthesizing these. For one thing, the assumptions and models were common to various sciences; for another, androcentric assumptions and methodologies, like feminist assumptions and methodologies, have been generated within social experiences, relations, traditions, and historically and culturally specific ways of organizing social life. Nor, of course, can we credit any individual with the recognition that male dominance is not an inevitable feature of social groups or that organizing principles like the one at issue in man-the-hunter theory distort observations and theories. The interests, standards, and knowledge generated and shared by feminist communities made that knowledge possible. Alternatively said, it was not the *gender of* individual scientists, or any "attribute" of individual scientists, that enabled such recognition—any more than it was an "attribute" of individual scientists that led to or furthered androcentric assumptions. The standards and knowledge that underwrite the acceptability of androcentric and feminist assumptions are communal.

There is an additional and important benefit to construing evidence broadly and focusing on communities: namely, that these preclude the claim that cases like that which we have considered are examples of incommensurability—or, in some other way, constitute "evidence for" judgmental relativism. Advocates of man-the-hunter theory and feminist critics disagree about many things, including models and observations in sciences currently viewed as relevant to human evolution (even whether some sciences are relevant) and, perhaps, so-called common-sense assumptions and knowledge about gender. But they do not disagree about everything; they share a larger body of knowledge and standards that includes physical object theory, a heliocentric view of the solar system, and the view that humans evolved and that their activities were factors in that process. Hence, members of these groups can discuss (and disagree about) the significance of "chipped stones" without any lapse in conversation and use other aspects of the knowledge and standards they share to evaluate the conflicting claims. The flip side of the point is this: although the knowledge and standards currently at issue are community specific, feminist communities and science communities both overlap (consider feminist primatologists) and are themselves subcommunities of larger communities—a fact that, along with the changing social relations that made it possible, has enabled feminist science criticism and feminist knowledge more broadly.

The discussion of this and the last section suggests that epistemological communities can be identified in terms of shared knowledge, standards, and practices. Science communities serve as obvious examples of epistemological communities, with bodies of theory, accepted procedures, questions, and projects defining such communities; and membership being a function of education in and allegiance to community-specific knowledge, standards, and practices. Moreover, science communities are both self-defined and socially recognized in terms of knowledge and, relatedly, are granted and exercise what Kathryn Pyne Addelson calls a "cognitive authority" to name and explain those features of the world that fall within their disciplinary boundaries—and, of course, beyond these (Addelson 1983).

But science communities are not the only epistemological communities, nor have they a lock on generating knowledge. In terms of their very existence and authority, and the knowledge and standards they generate, science communities are interdependent with the larger communities within which they function. More to the point, there are, in fact, *many* communities that develop and share knowledge and standards, including our larger world community and its multiple and evolving subcommunities.

As our consideration of man-the-hunter theory indicates, the boundaries of epistemological communities overlap with some aptly considered subcommunities of larger communities (e.g., part of the community of primatology falls within feminist communities), and such communities are dynamic and unstable. They evolve, disband, realign, and cohere as interests and undertakings evolve and are abandoned, as new experiences, standards, and knowledges become possible (when, for example, feminists come to be primatologists, and vice versa). There are subcommunities that have developed categories, methods, projects, knowledge, and standards in addition to those they share with larger communities (e.g., the physics community is a sub-community of a larger community with which it shares knowledge and standards: a community on which it is, in several senses, dependent).

There are also subcommunities that have generated knowledge and standards that challenge aspects of a larger body of shared knowledge and standards. Some examples of these are the various subcommunities of feminist philosophers, communities that share some (but not all) of the knowledge and standards of the community of philosophers, an epistemological community by virtue of its "canon," professional associations, and recognition as an academic discipline. Of as much importance, feminist philosophers share knowledge and standards generated and shared by feminist communities, communities whose political goals have led, among other things, to the rethinking of the categories and assumptions of the academic disciplines (including philosophy) and sciences, and to the development of categories and ontologies, theories, and methodologies that are enabling us to uncover women's experiences and to reconstruct and reevaluate the experiences of men and women.

There are, of course, no litmus tests for identifying epistemological communities. Not only are such communities dynamic, but there is no simple criterion for determining their boundaries. Where we recognize such communities and their parameters will be a function of the nature of our projects and purposes (e.g., in doing epistemology or in forming academic subcommunities, political action groups, or a neighborhood group to deal with local issues); of the definitions communities give to themselves and the projects they undertake; and of the importance such communities (or those engaged in epistemology or other projects) attribute to the standards and knowledge they share with larger groups and those they do not—decisions which will also be relative to specific purposes and interests. It currently seems both useful and important to recognize feminist subcommunities within the larger community of philosophy (a community within which other subcommunities can also be identified) and to recognize that these communities are subcommunities of larger feminist communities. On the other hand, it may seem appropriate to recognize a group of feminists and fundamentalists developing a policy against pornography as a coalition of communities, on the grounds that the nature and extent of the knowledge shared by the two groups is not extensive enough to outweigh the significant differences in interests, starting points, and knowledge.

There are other considerations that mitigate against the possibility and desirability of a litmus test for epistemological communities. One is that in undertaking a project focusing on community knowledge and standards, we may come to find that some of the standards of evidence or knowledge with which we begin do not withstand scrutiny (these might be our own standards or those of some community we are studying). Our community standards and knowledge will evolve in response to such results, and so, of course, might its membership. (We might, for example, decide to "throw out" the astrologers or anyone unwilling to abandon astrology.)

And, finally, epistemological communities are not monolithic. It is currently appropriate and useful to recognize feminist communities as epistemological communities, to recognize that such communities have generated bodies of knowledge, adopted standards, and developed categories of which each member of these communities accepts some—while recognizing that not all members of feminist communities agree on all things and that there may be no single belief that is held by all feminists. The point holds for any epistemological community, for we are each members of a number of such communities, a point, as I noted earlier, that is particularly relevant to feminist scholarship and politics of the last three decades, a period in which changing social relations have enabled feminists to become scientists (and vice versa) and hence have enabled experiences, knowledge, and standards that, prior to such changes, were not possible.

But although epistemological communities are not monolithic or stable, such communities also do not "dissolve" into "collections" of knowing individuals. By virtue of our membership in a number of such communities, as well as by virtue of our experiences as individuals, we can each contribute, and uniquely, to the knowledge generated by our various communities. But as I noted earlier, none of us knows (or could) what no one else could. However singular an experience may be, what we know on the basis of that experience has been made possible and is compatible with the standards and knowledge of one or more communities of which we are members: standards and knowledge that enable us to organize our experiences into coherent accounts, underwrite the specific contributions that we make as individuals, and determine what we and our communities will recognize as knowledge. It is that priority that makes it appropriate to extend the notion of an epistemological community beyond science communities—indeed, to see science communities as only special cases of a much broader category—and to recognize a multiplicity of communities as the primary knowers. This understanding of the agents of epistemology is in keeping with a long-standing feminist insight into the "collective" nature of feminist politics and knowing and the deep relationships between the latter and changing social and political relations, an insight that bridges various feminist epistemologies.

**Conclusion**

The unwillingness of some of us to abandon epistemology stems from considerations that are simultaneously empirical and political. Our reasons for exploring the implications of feminist knowledge for evidence and working to develop a viable account of the latter may include the view that arguments that purportedly reveal the bankruptcy or vacuousness of evidence presume, in fact, some account of evidence. Less abstractly (and without recourse to a *reductio*), we do manage to make sense of, to organize and attribute meaning to, and to predict and control events in multiple and meaningful ways and contexts, including but by no means limited to specialized contexts like science. Our successes and failures at these things indicate a reliance, and the appropriateness of that reliance, on evidence.

A second consideration underwriting such efforts is one of the central implications of feminist politics and scholarship: beliefs and knowledge claims have consequences. Although experience and evidence are inherently unstable and knowledge will never be "complete," the experiences and stories that have been the center of focus to date have been, in fact and at best, only partial; in their claims to "universality," they have simultaneously excluded and mystified other experiences and knowledges; and in their denial of their situatedness, they have been distorted.

To claim such, as well as to demand more empirically adequate knowledge, does not depend on the existence of one timeless truth in relation to which theories are partial or distorting. In reflecting the experiences of privileged men, the experiences and knowledge that have been generalized to date have been partial in terms of what it was or is possible to know in given historical, social, and cultural contexts and further qualified in terms of divisions in experience brought about by social relations (e.g., gender, race, and culture)—a point that alludes both to how things are and our ability to know it.

My arguments here indicate that identifying and explaining that partiality (and explaining why such partiality and the recognition of it are not equally warranted) require that we abandon individualism in all of its guises. They require a communal and more inclusive understanding of evidence than objectivist and relativist positions allow and, deeply related to this, the recognition of communities as the primary agents of epistemology: the primary generators and repositories of knowledge.

## Notes

Research for this paper was supported by a Glassboro State College Faculty Research Grant. Its central argument, which uses a communal account of evidence to support the view that the agents of epistemology are communities, was prompted by Nancy Tuana's review of my *Who Knows* at the APA Pacific Division Meeting in March 1991 (see Tuana 1992). Some of the arguments advanced here for the view that knowing is fundamentally social were prompted by questions by Lawrence Mirachi of Hartwick College (private correspondence) and Caraway (1991), both of which suggested ways to develop arguments I advanced in Nelson (1990). Kathryn Pyne Addelson, Linda Alcoff, Elizabeth Potter, and Jack Nelson provided invaluable criticisms of earlier drafts.

1. See, for example, Collins (1986), Haraway (1988), and Harding (1991) and in this volume, and the collection in Nicholson (1990). The notion of "situation" or "location" is increasingly complex and fertile in feminist theory (and certainly more complex than prefeminist empiricist and Marxist epistemologies were capable of conceptualizing), and I view it as bridging recent feminist empiricist epistemologies, standpoint epistemologies, and some postmodern arguments. See also Code (1991), Hekman (1990), Longino (1990), Nelson (1990), and Tuana (1992).

2. Representative works in feminist epistemology include those cited in note 1 and Addelson and Potter (1991), Duran (1991), Harding (1986), Harstock (1983), and Smith (1987). In contemporary empiricism, they include Quine (1960) and van Fraassen (1980); in sociology of knowledge, Bloor (1977); and in sociology of science, Latour and Woolgar (1986). The "divisions" I have used here are somewhat artificial. Three of the works listed under feminist epistemology, Duran (1991), Longino (1990), and Nelson (1990), develop empiricist approaches, although each is different from the view frequently described as "feminist empiricism" (see also Harding and Longino, in this volume). Moreover, feminist epistemologies have consistently challenged the alleged distinction between sociology of knowledge and science, and epistemology—a distinction many (nonfeminist) empiricists and sociologists of knowledge still maintain. See Harding (1991) for extended discussion.

3. I use "foundationalist" to describe these frameworks to avoid the classification schema that currently defines the "modernism/postmodernism" dichotomy. The work of many feminists, including some in this volume and cited in notes 1 and 2, is not appropriately described as "modernist" or "postmodernist," as many currently understand these classifications. I also use the terms *foundationalist* and *nonfoundationalist* to underscore the relationship between views of the agents of epistemology and views about evidence, a relationship explored throughout this discussion. Harding (1991) distinguishes between "Postmodernism" as "a specific set of claims and practices that have

been self- or otherwise identified as Postmodernism" and "postmodernism" as the "work of many different social groups . . . to think their way out of the hegemony of modern Western political philosophy, and the worlds it has constructed" (183–84). My references to postmodernism in this discussion are to some aspects of the former.

4. See works cited in notes 1 and 2.

5. The assumption is common to the work of Kuhn, Quine, and van Fraassen in philosophy of science as well as to recent feminist studies of science. See, for example, Harding (1991); Longino (1990); Nelson (1990); and Potter, in this volume.

6. My use of both "construct" and "acquire" is deliberate, as my arguments in the next section make clear. It reflects the view that knowledge is socially constructed and subject to evidential constraint.

7. My arguments for the priority of communities in Nelson (1990) did not rely solely on the fact that language is public, although the emphasis on Quine's arguments against positivism in early chapters apparently led some to so construe my arguments (Caraway 1991). Later chapters used research in neurobiology; the under-determination of theories; the lack of evidence to suggest there is a unique, true theory of nature waiting to be discovered; and the historically specific nature of current androcentric and feminist assumptions to support a communal view of knowers. Some of these arguments are expanded, and their implications for evidence are explored, in the next section of this article. The view that language is necessary for "recoverable" experience is also a consequence of arguments against private language. See Scheman (1983) for a discussion of the implications of Wittgenstein's arguments.

8. Both the approach and the project were prompted by Tuana (1992). Hekman (1990) provides a comprehensive analysis and defense of what she calls "the postmodern attack on the subject." My consideration of "postmodernism" is limited to some features of that attack and to Hekman's construal of its implications for epistemology. Alcoff (1988), Flax (1987), Harding (1986), (1991), Tuana (1992), and the collection in Nicholson (1990), provide detailed analyses of the implications of postmodernism for feminist epistemology and politics.

9. See works cited in notes 1 and 2.

10. Elsewhere I also appeal to research in postnatal neurobiological development and to Quine's arguments against empiricist versions of foundationalism (Nelson 1990).

11. The rationale for naturalizing epistemology I outline here builds on Quine's proposal (Quine 1969), a proposal prompted by the demise of foundationalism. But the naturalized epistemology I envision diverges significantly from Quine's. Quine proposed that epistemology be pursued in empirical psychology; I have argued that this proposal reflects a lingering commitment to individualism, although as I also point out, epistemological individualism is deeply inconsistent with other of Quine's positions (Nelson 1990). See also

Addelson (this volume) and Duran (1991) for arguments in support of a feminist naturalized epistemology and (perhaps different) views about what such an epistemology will be like.

12. I am referring to Quine (1969). See also note 11.

13. It turns out that Quine didn't actually mean that science, broadly construed, encompasses everything we say or that science narrowly construed, is interdependent with all of our ways of organizing and attributing meaning to experience. Although he did intend to encompass "common sense" and "philosophy," the former, on his view, is virtually exhausted by "physical object theory," and he argues for a boundary between science (broadly construed) and values (Nelson [1990]).

14. I assume a feminist naturalized epistemology would also draw on the neurosciences, on which, in fact, feminists have drawn (see Duran [1991] and Longino [1990]), as well as gender theory and political theory.

15. See, for example, Harding (1986, 1991), Hekman (1990), Tuana (1992), and the collection in Nicholson (1990).

16. These points are made clearly in Tuana (1992). In Hekman (1990), the terms *Cartesian, modernist,* and *enlightenment* are sometimes used as if they are synonyms.

17. Hekman adopts the phrase "subjects in process" from Kristeva (1984).

18. See works cited in note 15.

19. Harding outlines the important differences between "judgmental relativism" and historical, sociological, or cultural relativism. My discussion of the next and third section supports this distinction and Harding's claim that historical (or sociological) relativism does not entail judgmental relativism.

But my arguments embrace a deeper relativism; I argue that we are not warranted in assuming there is one unique theory to be discovered (or that our sense organs are sufficiently refined to encompass "all that goes on"): that indefinitely many theories might work equally well, but not all or any.

20. Private correspondence.

21. Dewey, 1910.

22. See also Harding (1991); Longino (1990); and Potter, in this volume.

23. Sheldon Glashow. Quoted in New York Times, Sec. 4, Oct. 22, 1989, 24.

24. Although I cannot pursue the point here, I believe that a parallel argument can be constructed in response to some recent postmodern arguments against epistemology; the grounds on which these anti-epistemological arguments are advanced undermine the plausibility of the arguments themselves. See Alcoff (1988); Harding (1990, 1991); Tuana (1992); and the collection in Nicholson (1990), especially the contributions by Bordo, Flax, and Di Stefano.

25. Ironically, given Glashow's claim to speak for scientists, arguments against the third assumption are clearly articulated in "On Being a Scientist," a booklet prepared by the Committee on the Conduct of Science of the National Academy of Sciences for students beginning graduate work in science.

26. The point is also drawn on by feminist empiricists. See Longino (1990); Nelson (1990); and Potter, in this volume. See also note 25.

27. Providing an evolutionary explanation of physical object theory in no way establishes that our sense organs are capable of discriminating a best theory or an allegedly unique, true theory of nature.

28. See note 13.

29. I defend the view that metaphysical commitments are not "free floating" or pernicious but incorporated within theories and methodologies, able to be subjected to evaluation, and that they constitute part of the evidence for specific theories and methods, in Nelson (1990).

30. As I note below, I am not here assuming a theory/world or language/world dichotomy. On the view of evidence I will outline, there is no distinction to be made out between that which we talk about and organize (e.g., "a world") and our ways of organizing and attributing meaning to our experience (e.g., theories).

31. See Addelson (1983) for an important discussion of the divisions in what she calls "cognitive authority and labor" that characterize Western societies and sciences.

32. See the works cited in notes 1 and 2 and other articles in this volume that explore deep relationships between scientific research and theories and social and political context.

33. Implicit in the foregoing is that "meaning" should be construed as empirical content, a view that is, of course, controversial. I explore and defend the view in detail in Nelson (1990). There I also describe an earlier version of the account of evidence outlined here as empiricist and holist. For an alternative and comprehensive account of empiricism as well as arguments against holism, see Longino (1990).

34. I use quotes to indicate that "common sense" cannot be granted a default status; that it, too, is dynamic, theoretical, and historically and culturally specific; and that so-called common-sense views are by no means unproblematic.

35. I have been asked if the points made about protons only obtain to "theoretical entities." As the next argument indicates, I do not believe there are any *non*-theoretical entities. See also Nelson (1990), especially chapter 3.

36. See note 7.

37. Appeals to experience can become vacuous unless the notion of what constitutes experience is further specified. As I argue in Nelson (1990), experience, at its most basic level, is the firings of sensory receptors but we do

not, of course, experience such firings. We experience the world through the lens of theories generated and shared by the communities of which we are members.

38. One of the more far-reaching implications of feminism is that what Sandra Harding calls "spontaneous experience" is itself shaped and mediated by social relations and ideology (Harding 1991). In developing a feminist empiricist view of evidence, I am suggesting that such considerations do not require anti-empiricist solutions but certainly require more sophisticated accounts of evidence and experience than traditional and foundationalist empiricist accounts were and are capable of providing. See Harding (in this volume) for a discussion of these issues from the perspective of feminist standpoint epistemology.

39. Linda Alcoff points out that, so stated, the claim is also a consequence of the repeatability criterion (private correspondence). The sense of the claim made within a framework that assumes the initial results are an individual achievement with repeatability ensuring the results because other individuals can, in fact, also (individually) achieve them, is different than the sense of my claim that even the initial results are not (in any interesting way) an individual achievement.

40. Bleier (1984), Harding (1986), Hubbard (1983), Longino and Doell (1983), and Longino (1990) include extensive analyses of man-the-hunter theory. In Nelson (1990), I use holism and an earlier version of the view of evidence I have outlined to analyze aspects of this theory, as well as feminist criticism of research in neuroendocrinology and reproductive endocrinology into sex differences, of "master molecule" theories, and commitments to linear, hierarchical models.

41. Some advocates of the theory construe the implications of hunting more broadly, arguing that what they call the "hunting adaptation" underlies human psychology, biology, emotions, and divisions of labor by sex (see the discussion in Bleier [1984]). Hence, the implications of the theory are broader than the discussion here suggests. See the works cited in note 40.

42. See works cited in note 40.

43. Those who maintain a position long described as "feminist empiricism" in Harding (1986), a position Harding and others have noted is not uncommon among scientists, may find the claim difficult as stated. But as Harding explores and I address here and in *Who Knows*, to argue that feminists are (in some straightforward way) "less biased" seems strained at the very least. I am also not convinced that androcentric and gynocentric approaches should be viewed as comparable (as equally "biased," for example). For one thing, the former were not recognized as such and viewed as "value-neutral"; the latter are often conscious and make no claim to value-neutrality. Moreover, the latter are corrective, not only in the sense that they "add to" prior knowledge but also because they change much of what counted as knowledge and our views of epistemology and of science.

44. Bleier (1984), Harding (1986), Longino and Doell (1983), and Longino (1990) include extensive consideration of these problems.

45. See works cited in note 40.

46. In her criticism of earlier versions of "feminist empiricism" (which she distinguishes from "philosophical feminist empiricisms" currently being developed), Sandra Harding has made this point clearly. See Harding (1986, 1991), and in this volume.

# References

Addelson, K.P. 1983. "The Man of Professional Wisdom." In *Discovering Reality: Feminist Perspectives on Epistemology, Metaphysics, Methodology, and Philosophy of Science*. Edited by S. Harding and M. Hintikka. Dordrecht: D. Reidel.

Addelson, K.P., and E. Potter. 1991. "Making Knowledge." In *Engendering Knowledge: Feminists in Academe*. Edited by Ellen Messer-Davidow and Joan E. Hartmann. Knoxville, Tenn.: Univ. of Tenn. Press.

Alcoff, L. 1988. "Cultural Feminism versus Post-structuralism: The Identity Crisis in Feminist Theory." Signs 13 (3): 405–36.

Bleier, R. 1984. *Science and Gender: A Critique of Biology and Its Theories on Women*. New York: Pergamon Press.

Bloor, D. 1977. *Knowledge and Social Imagery*. London: Routledge & Kegan Paul.

Caraway, C. 1991. "Review of Who Knows: From Quine to a Feminist Empiricism." *Teaching Philosophy* 14:2. June 1991, 221–224.

Code, L. 1991. *What Can She Know? Feminist Theory and the Construction of Knowledge*. Ithaca and London: Cornell University Press.

Collins, P.H. 1986. "Learning from the Outsider Within: The Sociological Significance of Black Feminist Thought." *Social Problems* 33 (6): 14–32.

Committee on the Conduct of Science, the National Academy of Sciences. 1989. "On Being a Scientist," Washington, D.C.: National Academy Press.

Dewey, J. 1910. "The Influence of Darwin on Philosophy." Reprinted in *Darwin: A Norton Critical Edition*. Edited by Philip Appleman. New York and London: W. W. Norton & Co., 1970, 305–314.

Duran, J. 1991. *Toward a Feminist Epistemology.* Totowa, N.J.: Rowman & Littlefield.

Flax, J. 1987 (1990). "Postmodernism and Gender Relations in Feminist Theory." *Signs* 12 (4):621–643. Reprinted in Feminism/Postmodernism. Edited by L. Nicholson. New York and London: Routledge: 39–62.

Gould, S.J. 1982. *The Panda's Thumb.* New York and London: W.W. Norton & Company.

Haraway, D. 1988. "Situated Knowledges: The Science Question in Feminism and the Privilege of Partial Perspective." *Feminist Studies* 14:3 575–599.

Harding, S. 1984. "Is Gender a Variable in Conceptions of Rationality?" In *Beyond Domination: New Perspectives on Women and Philosophy.* Edited by C. Gould. Totowa, N.J.: Rowman & Allenheld.

———. 1986. *The Science Question in Feminism.* Ithaca: Cornell University Press.

———. 1990. "Feminism, Science, and the Anti-Enlightenment Critiques." In *Feminism/Postmodernism.* Edited by L. Nicholson.

———. 1991. *Whose Science? Whose Knowledge? Thinking from Women's Lives.* Ithaca: Cornell University Press.

Harstock, N. 1983. "The Feminist Standpoint: Developing the Grounds for a Specifically Feminist Historical Materialism." In *Discovering Reality.* Edited by S. Harding and M. Hintikka.

Hekman, S. 1990. *Gender and Knowledge: Elements of a Postmodern Feminism.* Boston: Northeastern University Press.

Hubbard, R. 1983. "Have Only Men Evolved?" In *Discovering Reality.* Edited by S. Harding and M. Hintikka.

Jaggar, A.M. 1983. *Feminist Politics and Human Nature.* Totowa, NJ: Rowman & Allenheld.

Keller, E.F. 1989. "The Gender/Science System: or, Is Sex to Gender as Nature Is to Science." In *Feminism and Science.* Edited by N. Tuana. Bloomington and Indianapolis: Indiana University Press.

Kristeva, J. 1984. *Revolution in Poetic Language.* Translated by M. Waller. New York: Columbia University Press.

Latour, B., and S. Woolgar. 1986. *Laboratory Life: The Social Construction of Scientific Facts.* Princeton: Princeton University Press.

Longino, H. 1990. *Science as Social Knowledge: Values and Objectivity in Scientific Inquiry.* Princeton: Princeton University Press.

Longino, H., and R. Doell. 1983. "Body, Bias, and Behavior: A Comparative Analysis of Reasoning in Two Areas of Biological Science." *Signs* 9, no. 2: 206–227.

Nelson, L.H. 1990. *Who Knows: From Quine to a Feminist Empiricism.* Philadelphia: Temple University Press.

Nicholson, L., ed. 1990. *Feminism/Postmodernism*. New York and London: Routledge.

Quine, W.V. 1960. *Word and Object*. Cambridge, Mass.: MIT Press.

———. 1966. "The Scope and Language of Science." In *The Ways of Paradox and Other Essays*. New York: Random House.

———. 1969. "Epistemology Naturalized." In *Ontological Relativity and Other Essays*. New York: Columbia University Press.

Scheman, N. 1983. "Individualism and the Objects of Psychology." In *Discovering Reality*. Edited by S. Harding and M. Hintikka.

Smith, D. 1987. *The Everyday World as Problematic: A Feminist Sociology*. Boston: Northeastern University Press.

Tuana, N. 1992. "The Radical Future of Feminist Empiricism." *Hypatia* Winter 1992, 7 (1):100–114.

van Fraassen, B. 1980. *The Scientific Image*. New York: Oxford University Press.

# 7

# Gender and Epistemic Negotiation

*Elizabeth Potter*

---

> *In the beginning, God and Lilith and Adam sat in the garden negotiating the construction of nature. Lilith, who was farsighted, quick and strong of mind, negotiated well and the world began to be pleasing to women. But God and Adam were not pleased; they muttered together; and they banished Lilith from the garden and they made a pact. It was agreed that Adam could decide what was what if God could be constructed as almighty; they both vowed to claim that nature was a given and that Adam could know it and name it. The next day, Adam and almighty God constructed Eve and told her it was all over before she got there and women just were second rate by nature. Now Eve and her daughters doubted this in their hearts, but many years passed before the daughters of Eve—moved by the power and desire of Lilith, a living spirit in the root of their minds—reopened negotiations and reshaped the world.*

## Epistemological Individualism and the Private Language Argument

Modern philosophy has been deeply committed to epistemological individualism, the assumption that the individual is the source of and principle agent in the production of knowledge. Thus, Descartes invites us in the *Meditations* to conceive of an isolated individual who wants to know whether his sensory ideas allow him to know the world beyond his own mind. The isolation of the individual mind, alone with its sensory ideas, is the fundamental situation of the epistemic agent in the Cartesian project, and the fundamental epistemological project is to show that the isolated, individual mind can be sure that he has knowledge of the external world.

161

And most empiricists from Locke through Russell to the present have also taken it for granted that knowledge begins with the sensory ideas, impressions, data, or other mental content of a single individual. Here the project is to show how, using only an economical number of innate mental abilities, an individual can generate the structure of knowledge with which we are all familiar. Thus, Locke argues in Book II of the *Essay Concerning Human Understanding* that the individual has simple sensory impressions, forms simple ideas based upon them, and manipulates these ideas—compounding them, abstracting them, and so on—to generate complex ideas. Not until he sets out his philosophy of language in Book III does the society or community of speakers of English appear. But when he turns, in Book IV, to explain the various ways an individual connects his ideas in order to produce knowledge, the community disappears again.

Even Quine, who rejects "old epistemology," assumes that the individual is the proper object of attention for the new naturalized epistemology:

> The old epistemology aspired to contain, in a sense, natural science; it would construct it somehow from sense data. Epistemology in its new setting, conversely, is contained in natural science, as a chapter of psychology. . . . We are studying how the human subject . . . posits bodies and projects his physics from his data, and we appreciate that our position in the world is just like his. Our very epistemological enterprise, and the psychology wherein it is a component chapter, and the whole of natural science wherein psychology is a component—all this is our own construction or projection from stimulations *like* those we are meting out to our epistemological subject.[1]

The psychology Quine has in mind here is not social psychology but the neuropsychological science of the individual brain.

These epistemologies begin as if solipsism characterized the orginary human epistemic scene. And they are often criticized for their failure to get out of the solipsistic moment. But they do not intend to be solipsistic epistemologies; instead, as Hilary Putnam has said of Carnap, he understood himself to be arguing for methodological solipsism, not real solipsism: the methodological solipsist is an individual who "holds that everything he can conceive of is identical (in the ultimate logical analyses of his language) with one or another complex of his own experiences. What makes him a *methodological* solipsist as opposed to a real solipsist is that . . . *everybody* is a (methodological) solipsist."[2] Thus, methodological solipsism is distinguished from real solipsism in that the *real* solipsist believes himself or herself to be the only person (or mind) in the universe; methodological solipsism, however, suggests that when each individual learns language and produces knowledge, each does so, for all intents and purposes, alone, in the same way that he or she would if he or she were the only person in the universe. Epistemological individualism is marked by this assumption that, although other people exist (so real solipsism does not obtain), knowledge is produced by each person alone from his or her own experiences; epistemologically, each is a methodological solipsist.

Individualist epistemologies set up the agent of knowledge as a methodological solipsist. And inasmuch as the methodological solipsist learns language and produces knowledge privately, these epistemologies presume that private languages are possible. This presumption is found not in explicit claims that there exists only one person or one mind in the world but in analyses according to which language and the knowledge embodied in it are produced as if there were. The new-born field linguist brings order out of his or her sense data, sensations, or experiences. Experiences that we would describe as "mother pointing" or "saying 'red' " are just more sense data, more experiences, more sensory input to be ordered and conceptualized. From such private experiences the epistemologically independent individual is supposed to produce all the important distinctions and concepts we take for granted every day. The private language turns out to be our language after all.

It is this feature of a private language—that it is essentially our language, containing the fundamental distinctions of the language we speak now—that gave rise to Wittgenstein's attack on the very possibility of a private language. Thus, Wittgenstein pointed out that the individual who speaks our language knows, inter alia, the difference between true and false statements and so can make a distinction between truth and falsehood, truth and illusion, or truth and any number of other "infelicities," but Wittgenstein argued that the speaker of a private language cannot make such distinctions.[3] He is unable to do so because making the distinction between truth and falsehood requires an ability to distinguish true statements from those that seem true (and false statements from those that seem false). Against the possibility of any private language, Wittgenstin argued that there is no way for the isolated individual—who doesn't yet have any concepts including especially concepts of "same" and "different," the concept of pointing to something and naming it, or the concept of reference—to make this distinction between statements that are true and those that seem to him true.[4] Appeals to his memory are no help because he must be able to distinguish veridical memories from those that merely seem veridical in order to use them to correct his statements.

Therefore, the isolated individual cannot produce language—much less the knowledge it emobodies; language must be public, and this means that two or more people are necessary for concepts like truth and reference to work. Alone, one person cannot make the distinction between how things are and how they seem, but two or more can make it—though their agreement doesn't guarantee truth or successful reference; rather, Wittgenstein points out, one checks his belief that *a* and *b* are the same against the beliefs of other people. The possibility of "checking" how it seems to me by asking another person allows, because it entails, the possibility of correcting my belief; and this possibility is just the possibility that I might be correct or mistaken, that my belief might be true or false.

In defense of private languages, philosophers have had recourse to innate ideas (no longer implanted by God in the mind but by evolutionary forces in the brain), to the self-identifying nature of private experiences, or to innate "abilities" to make certain distinctions. These "black box" defenses insist that early on in the life of language someone must "just know" when two things are the same and must "just remember" them and so have made the distinction between true and false statements about those things. But these arguments reveal just how deep-seated epistemological individualism is. Philosophers like Carnap did not intend methodological solipsism to collapse into real solipsism;[5] instead, Carnap assumed there to be other minds and a natural world available to science, but he wanted knowledge to be produced (in principle) by each man alone. The originary alternative— that a community of individuals together decided (and continues to decide) when two things are similar enough to treat in the same way— is not taken up. But this alternative is made requisite by Wittgenstein's attack on the possibility of a private language. Any general concept allows or enables users to classify together or pick out two instances of that concept as similar; general concepts have, therefore, sometimes been thought of as rules or as rule-governed. But Wittgenstein argued that rules do not wear on their sleeves directions for following them or even criteria for what counts as following them. And from the fact that classifications change over time with changing human needs and interests, we can see that people sometimes decide, for good reasons (or for bad ones), to change what counts as "similar to x." We might say that they decide to change the rules. Wittgenstein's argument against the possibility of a private language can be read as showing why it is meaningless for a person who is in principle alone to try to make such decisions. These decisions, then, must be made by two or more people. And these are not just decisions about how to use words but about which things are similar and so belong in the same class; they are, then, decisions about classificatory beliefs. The impossibility of a private language means that private beliefs are not possible in the way that empiricists from Locke to Carnap thought. And the proper inference to draw from this impossibility is that two or more epistemic agents are required for the possibility of language and, hence, for the possibility of belief in general and, because knowledge is a species of belief, for the possibility of knowledge in particular.

If Wittgenstein is right and the individual is not linguistically prior to the community, then the individual cannot be epistemically prior either. And it follows that the epistemic community cannot be comprised of a set of epistemically independent individuals; we must, therefore, begin to view the community as comprised of epistemically interdependent individuals. Moreover, any adequate epistemology must analyze knowledge first in terms of the community and only then attend to the individual. Idealized models of epistemic agency proceeding as though the individual were, if not the source, then certainly the principle agent of knowledge, are at worst mistaken and at best put the epistemological cart before the horse. We will take it as an axiom, therefore, that the epistemological community is the primary agent for the production of knowledge and that any adequate epistemology must account for knowledge in social terms. Whatever else we may wish to say about knowledge, we must recognize that it is a social affair.[6] This in turn will allow us to see what cannot be seen by individualist epistemologies: the communal nature of knowledge production and the ways in which the politics of gender, class, and other axes of oppression are negotiated in the production of knowledge.[7]

## Epistemological Decisions

Epistemic decisions provide one important site for the intersection of gender politics with the productions of knowledge that may appear impervious to such influences. In this section, we will see how this is so even on an empiricist understanding of knowledge inasmuch as philosophers working in empiricist traditions have developed models of knowledge to which we can turn for an initial understanding of epistemic decisions. Mary Hesse's Network Model of scientific theories is empiricist in the broad sense that it insists upon empirical adequacy as the primary aim of any scientific theory of the natural world. Although her model is offered as an account of scientific knowledge and has been taken by many philosophers to capture the production of knowledge by an individual, we can use it as a first approximation of knowledge produced by an epistemic community. The

Network Model is particularly useful for making it clear that epistemological decisions are necessary even when our first commitment is to empirical adequacy.

Hesse reminds us that physical situations have indefinitely many aspects and at any given time we notice only some of these; it follows that every time we notice things in the world or observe things, we drop out information that could be taken up at other times or by other people. The information that is dropped includes, of course, all the ways in which the phenomena we observe are similar to other phenomena. Hesse understands scientific laws to classify phenomena on the basis of resemblances among them. Thus, when the scientist establishes a law, she picks out some of the respects in which phenomena resemble one another and ignores their differences and the different ways in which they resemble yet other phenomena. Any scientist is, then, constantly faced with decisions as to whether two things are similar in some respects and different in others, the question becomes, "Which respects are more important, the similar ones or the dissimilar ones?" When the data are all in—here observations of the repects in which phenomena do and do not resemble on another—decisions must be made about which data are significant. This is a fundamental case of "interpreting the data." Data alone, observations alone, do not determine a law or generalization; for example, we observe that whales swim in the water and so are like fish, but we also observe that they are viviparous like mammals. Are they fish or mammals? Because similarity is not transitive, a decision must be made on grounds other than observed similarity. That is, $b$ may resemble $a$ and $b$ may resemble $c$, but $a$ and $c$ do not therefore resemble one another; how, then, should we classify $b$? As an $a$ or as a $c$? Because any decision here is underdetermined by the data, it has to be determined on other grounds.

One criterion at work in such a case is logical coherence throughout the system; however, we cannot claim that this criterion alone is sufficient to account for theory production. Scientists do not always decide between conflicting observations on the grounds that one generalization provides coherence with the greatest number of other generalizations. The problematic generalization may instead be the occasion to decide that most of the generalizations in the theory are wrong.

At this point, the mainstream philosphers who adopt a network model argue that scientists either do or should have recourse to cognitive virtues. Scentists hold or should hold certain assumptions about what constitutes good systems of laws or "good theories." Just so, Quine has argued, the assumptions that good theories are "conservative" or are "simple" guide the scientist to make the decision that conserves most of what has been held true in the past or the one that makes the system simpler.[8] Hesse refers to the virtues as "coherence conditions" and argues that they also include assumptions such as the goodness of symmetry and of certain analogies, models, and so on.[9] However, feminists, as critical science scholars, argue that we need to *look and see* what assumptions scientists actually hold to when they decide between conflicting generalizations. The feminist working hypothesis is that the assumptions guiding classificatory decisions may be androcentric or sexist.

The assumption of some cognitive virtue(s) can determine which system of beliefs is desireable, but so can the assumption of some other principle—for instance, that male behavior is the norm, that male behavior is crucial to evolution, that hierarchies are functional, that hierarchical models are better than nonhierarchical ones, and so on. The suggestion here is that feminist studies of knowledge production in the sciences and in other areas of life should look carefully at the constraints affecting the choices people make between conflicting generalizations. On a network model, each belief in the system is—at any given time, though not at all times—corrigible, so there is nothing theoretically to prevent us from discovering that even the most innocent choice is constrained ultimately by an androcentric or sexist assumption.

The flexibility of any system of beliefs means that choices among beliefs can be made that allow at once some degree of empirical adequacy, of coherence, of fruitfulness, simplicity, and faithfulness to preferred analogies or models *and* the maintenance of androcentric or sexist assumptions. Thus, the model makes it clear that even good scientific theories, by all the traditional criteria, can be androcentric or sexist in the sense that a sexist or androcentric assumption constrains the distribution of truth values throughout the system.

We can see from this model that although at any one time we must hold most of our beliefs beyond question, there are still times when we must make epistemic decisions. And although the underdetermination of scientific and other beliefs by evidence does not entail that social assumptions influence the agents' choice of beliefs, nevertheless we can no longer assume that all decisions are based solely on technical grounds and are politically innocent. Instead, we must look at each case to see what constrains the choice.

## Micronegotiations

Sociologists who have looked at the production of scientific knowledge to see how scientists decide which beliefs to adopt have found that such decisions are usually negotiated. Based upon extended participant observation of scientists' daily laboratory work, Karen Knorr-Cetina notes that knowledge is produced, not by the lone scientist, but through social interaction:

> All laboratory studies of which substantial results are available demonstrate the interactive basis of scientific work, whether they address the phenomenon explicitly or not.[10]

And these interactions usually take the form of negotiation:

> Studies of scientific "reasoning" in the laboratory, during controversies, and generally on occasions when scientists communicate with eachother, tend to document the negotiated or socially accomplished character of technical outcomes. Whether it is the nature of the things one "sees" in scientific observation, the proper conduct of an experiment, or the adequacy of a theoretical interpretation, scientific agreement appears to be open to contestation and modification, a process often referred to as "negotiation." Through contestation and modification, the meaning of scientific observations as well as of theoretical interpretations tends to get selectively constructed and reconstructed in scientific practice.[11]

Through participant observation, these sociologists capture for us the everyday, mundane interactions in which scientific beliefs are contested, modified, accepted, or disregarded.

For example, from their two-year study of a laboratory at the Salk Institute, Latour and Woolgar give the following description of two scientists negotiating, among other things, over what counts as sufficient evidence:

> Wilson: Anyway, the question for this paper is what I said in one of the versions that there was *no evidence* that there was any psychobehavioural effect of these peptides injected I.V. . . . Can we write that down?
>     Flower: That's a *practical* question . . . what do *we accept* as a negative answer? [Flower mentioned a paper which reported the use of an "enormous" amount of peptides with a positive result.]
>     Wilson: That *much*?
>     Flower: Yes, so it depends on the peptides . . . but it is very important to do . . .
>     Wilson: I will give you the peptides, yes we have to do it . . . but I'd like to read the paper . . .
>     Flower: You know it's the one where . . .
>     Wilson: Oh, I have it, OK.
>     Flower: The threshold is one ug. . . . OK, if we want to inject 100 rats (we need at least a few micrograms) . . . it's a practical issue (XII, 85).[12]

Latour and Woolgar point out that this exchange "entails a complex negotiation about what constitutes a legitimate quantity of peptides." Is there evidence to support the claim that the peptides under analysis have a psychobehavioral effect when injected intravenously? How much or how little can be used on the test rats before a claim that the peptides have no effect is properly supported? Flower persuades Wilson that an "enormous amount" is necessary to support the claim.

This example shows us that although negotiations can be heated and can amount to controversy, they can also be short and cool. They need not be extensive, need not take long, and need not be bitter or agonistic; but this example also shows us that agreement is not automatic. Contrary to many of the pictures of science preferred by philosophers, this example reveals that there is no algorithm for sufficient evidence (or indeed, for what *counts* as evidence).

For that matter, sometimes even seeing the data must be negotiated, as Knorr-Cetina argues based on the following discussion between two scientists:

> V: How do you know they're microglia?
> H: Uhh
> V: I *mean*, uh, you know there's a big question of what is microglia, what isn't micrglia and where does microglia come from and . . .
> H: It *fuckin'* doesn't make any difference to me . . .
> V: Oh, it's a big . . . big d——d question and . . .
> ( ): hah hah hah hah hah
> H: I don't worry about—you know *that*—ah, you know you can use whatever *word* you want to use.
> V: Uh huh.
> H: Say, uh, Del Rio Hortega positive cells for all I care, *right?* . . . You see these little things? . . . Del Rio Hortega positive cells.[13]

Here V challenges H's claim that he is looking at microglia (through a very complex microscope); in the end, H falls back to the position that they are "Del Rio Hortega positive cells" because they have absorbed the Del Rio Hortega stain. We may surmise that one of the issues here is whether the Del Rio Hortega stain "marks" all and only microglia. That, too, must be negotiated.[14]

These microstudies show us only some of the many ways that negotiations take place; others include micro-interchanges at seminars and conference talks as well as church, political or business meetings. But as we shall see below, knowledge is also produced in very different interchanges.

*Macronegotiations*

Though most of our ordinary beliefs are not subject to negotiation, nevertheless, all are in principle negotiable, and when there are social stakes, they are contested. As Hobbes remarked, if anything hung on the theorems of Euclidian geometry, they would be as hotly disputed as the theorems of politics. When I was in graduate seminars, professors pointed to the white styrofoam cups and red Coca-Cola cans as paradigm examples of items with stable, universally agreed upon color properties. But the examples worked because usually no one much cares whether a soda can is red. But in fact, people have done legal battle over whether a soda can was "Coca-Cola red," or a T-shirt, "Yale blue." Arguments over these beliefs are constrained not only by legal precedent but by cognitive virtues as well: by conservatism, consistency, and generality, among others. In this case, we can see that socio-economic factors such as gender, race, and class might play a part in arguments for a belief such as "this can is Coca-Cola red."

As we can see from this example, not all negotiations are micronegotiations like those described by participant observers in scientific laboratories. There may be only two parties to a negotiation, but there may be more; there may be hundreds of interested people. Moreover, many interchanges—for example, those occurring through the pages of academic journals or books—take a long time: months and sometimes years. And in many arenas, negotiators do not explicitly recognize one another or even know one another; indeed, they may not acknowledge that there is an interchange at all. Let us examine briefly two illustrations of these points.

1. Philosphers, among others, participate in social neogiations over epistemic decisions, but we do not think of ourselves as doing so. Nevertheless, giving a conceptual analysis, a phenomenology, an archaelology, an account, a philosophy, or a theory can be part of a negotiation among many parties over what will be accepted as authoritative knowledge. I suspect that it is the failure to pay attention to the distinction between a descriptive and a prescriptive analysis that allows philosophers to negotiate without owning up to it. Quine's presentation of the cognitive virtues in *The Web of Belief* provides a simple case in point; there we get prescription disguised as description:

Virtue I is *conservatism*. In order to explain the happenings that we are inventing it to explain, the hypothesis may have to conflict with some of our previous beliefs; but the fewer the better. Acceptance of a hypothesis is of couse like acceptance of any belief in that it demands rejection of whatever conflicts with it. The less rejection of prior beliefs required, the more plausible the hypothesis—other things being equal.[15]

This "description" tacitly presupposes that everyone is consistent in their beliefs. Since Quine knows this is false even for scientists, he cannot really take himself to be describing practices but prescribing practices—we *should* be consistent. But *there is no point in prescribing anything unless we can choose to follow, decide to follow the prescription*. Thus, prescriptive philosophical theories presuppose, whether they admit it or not, that social decisions are being made about which beliefs to accept. And to encourage one decision over another is ipso facto to engage in social negotiation over the decision.

2. Even when parties to the production of knowledge acknowledge that they are engaged in a debate, they may not acknowledge their opponents or other significant parties to the negotiation. Feminist philosophers will recognize this phenomenon as it occurs in seminars, conference talks and professional publications; thus, for example, the 1970s saw the first articles on ethical issues raised by the civil rights and women's movements, though if one did not already know that the issues had been raised by African-Americans and by feminists, one would not learn that fact from those articles. On the issue of gender equality, for example, J.R. Lucas argues that being a woman in itself provides grounds for denying women equal opportunities for education, military service, and other benefits and employment traditionally open only to men. He does not mention the arguments of contemporary feminists who raised the issue either in the popular or the academic press; the only feminist he acknowledges is Plato, who, he says, "was the first feminist."[16] Unfortunately, proponents of race and gender equality may also fail to acknowledge other parties to the negotiations over equality; Thomas E. Hill argued that moral respect for equality among people demands self-respect and an end of servility without mentioning anyone on any side of the current debate.[17] Nevertheless, we can be reasonably certain that these authors were familiar with and responding to the current popular and academic debate because we are ourselves familiar with current arguments and recognize their work as contributions to the debate. But it is just this lack of familiarity that makes it difficult to recognize the negotiations of living people (from scientists to ordinary folk) in areas unfamiliar to us or of dead people from times and places that we know little about. Unless we make an effort to find out, we will not know whether, let alone with whom, these people were negotiating.

## The Spring and Weight of the Air

Against claims put forward by feminist scholars that gender strongly intersects the production of much of our knowledge, the laws of science are offered as counterexamples. Boyle's Ideal Gas Law is a favorite among these counterexamples. In this section, we will trace the intersection of gender with a technical hypothesis in early modern physics, the belief that the air has spring and weight.[18] This belief, later understood as the belief that the air has pressure, along with other beliefs such as the possibility of a vacuum, was necessary for the truth of the Ideal Gas Law. This example provides a case in point of why it is so difficult to see the social negotiations through which an important bit of knowledge was produced, and we will see that despite the failure of the men who are credited with discovering these facts to acknowledge all the parties to the negotiations over their production, the knowledge that the air has spring and weight was influenced by class and gender considerations. To see this, we must uncover the negotiations that took place among representatives of broad social groups in mid-seventeenth–century England, groups with strong interests in the social position of women.

The hypothesis that the air has spring and weight was part of the new paradigm unfolding in seventeenth-century science, a paradigm often referred to as the mechanical philosophy.[19] Here we will examine the interest in and work on this hypothesis by the English virtuoso, Robert Boyle.[20] Boyle (1627–1691) is remembered by Anglophone students of science primarily because he is credited with discovering the scientific law that bears his name, Boyle's Law of Gases, also referred to as the Ideal Gas Law. Boyle was a man of extensive property in England and Ireland, the only untitled son of the infamously wealthy Earl of Cork. His immediate family were, therefore, members of the aristocracy, but although some of the virtuosi with whom he worked out the mechanical philosophy were aristocrats, many were not. All were, however, from the upper or upper middle classes.

Seventeenth-century virtuosi were fascinated with an experiment performed in Italy by Evangelista Torricelli and with the apparatus he used to perform it, the Torricellian Tube. Torricelli filled a three-foot glass tube with mercury and, covering the open end with his finger, he inverted the tube and immersed the open end in a dish of mercury. As Conant tells us, "When he removed his finger from the open end, the mercury in the tube fell until the top of the mercury column was about 30 inches above the level of the mercury in the open dish. Between the top of the mercury column and the upper end of the tube was an empty space, which became known as a Torricellian vacuum. Twentieth century historians of science have interpreted Torricelli's experiment as a test of the hypothesis that 'the earth is surrounded by a sea of air that exerts pressure.' "[21] And in the same way, Pascal is understood to have deduced from Torricelli's hypothesis that the earth is surrounded by a sea of air the further hypothesis that the pressure exerted by the air should decrease as one ascends from sea level. And, indeed, the deduction was confirmed in 1648 when Pascal's brother-in-law, Perier, performed the experiment at the base of the Puy-de-Dome (a mountain in central France) and at several points on the way to the top.[22]

One of the earliest objections raised against Torricelli's experimental results was that if the air exerted pressure in the dish of mercury sufficient to force the mercury in the column up to 30 inches, then enclosing the dish and thereby sealing it off from the pressure exerted on it should cause the mercury in the column to fall; but it does not in fact. Therefore, Torricelli's broad working hypothesis was wrong. Boyle answered this objection, as did Torricelli, by arguing that when the dish was enclosed, the pressure on the enclosed mercury remained the same as it was before. But Boyle himself wished to test Torricelli's hypothesis by finding a way to remove the air from the enclosed space around the dish of mercury. To this end, he made use of one of the first vacuum pumps, then called an "air pump" or "pneumatical engine."

The piston of the air pump upon which Boyle's experiment was performed worked on a rack and pinion moved by turning the handle of a crank. The cylinder containing the pumping mechanism rested in a wooden frame and itself supported a glass globe or "receiver" from which the air was to be removed. This receiver had a small opening in the bottom through which the air passed and a larger opening in the top, sufficient to admit experimental apparatus. And between the receiver and the pump cylinder was a brass stopcock or key, which could be turned to open or close off the receiver from the pump.

We can summarize Boyle's experiment as follows. A glass tube about a yard long and sealed at one end was filled with mercury and inverted into a small cylindrical container half filled with mercury. After the mercury had settled, the height of the column of mercury was marked (by pasting a piece of paper to the tube), and the cylinder and tube were let down into the receiver. The cover of the receiver, with a hole in the middle to pass over the tube, was put in place, and all the leaks were stopped with melted wax. Boyle remarks that upon closing the receiver "there appeared not any change in the height of the mercurial cylinder, no more than if the interposed glass-receiver did not hinder the immediate pressure of the ambient atmosphere upon the inclosed air; which hereby appears to bear upon the mercury, rather by virtue of its spring than of its weight. . . ." The piston was drawn down (by turning the crank) and, Boyle says, "immediately upon the egress of a cylinder of air out of the receiver, the quicksilver in the tube did, according to expectation, subside: and notice being carefully taken (by a mark fastened to the outside) of the place where it stopt, we caused him that managed the pump to pump again, and marked how low the quicksilver fell at the second exsuction. . . ." Even after pumping for a quarter of an hour, the mercury did not descend to the level of the mercury in the cylinder because, Boyle says, enough air leaked into the receiver to keep the level of mercury up somewhat. Finally, the stopcock was opened, some air was let in, and the mercury began to ascend until the stopcock was closed and the mercury "immediately rested at the height which it had then attained. . . ." Boyle describes further steps in the experiment, but this step served, he says, "to satisfy ourselves farther, that the falling of the quicksilver in the tube to a determinate height, proceedeth from the aequilibrium, wherein it is at that height with the external air, the one gravitating, the other pressing with equal force upon the subjacent mercury. . . ." In other words, the mercury falls until it reaches a state of equilibrium with the external air, the equilibrium being a function of the weight of the mercury and the pressure of the air.[23]

What part do gender politics play in the production of the knowledge that the "ambient atmosphere" has pressure? Boyle's report of his experimental work certainly doesn't mention women. The report fits traditional accounts of scientific knowledge fairly well: Boyle argues that the experimental data are well accounted for by his hypothesis. It appears, then, that his choice of this hypothesis is constrained by experimental observations; the hypothesis is justified by observation. But there were competing hypotheses that also claimed to explain the same data, notably the Aristotelian hypothesis put forward by Franciscus Linus, that the mercury in a glass tube stands at 29½ inches because it is held up by a funiculus, an invisible cord connecting the surface of the mercury with the top and sides of the glass tube. The experimental evidence in support of his hypothesis is that when one closes the open end of a Torricellian tube with one's finger, one can feel the flesh being drawn into the tube by the funiculus. Against this interpretation of the evidence, Boyle argued for the alternate hypothesis that the pressure of the air forced the flesh of one's finger into the tube. (One's finger is being pushed not pulled, into the tube.) Linus' hypothesis belonged to the Aristotelian paradigm and with Aristotelian explanations that had a good deal of empirical adequacy. Immersed as we are in a postmechanistic paradigm, we find explanations of air and water pumps in terms of funiculi or nature's abhorrence of a vacuum to be ludicrous. But in the mid-seventeenth century, pumping phenomena did not determine among their competing explanations. Nevertheless, despite the underdetermination of his belief in the pressure of the air, Boyle argued strongly against the Aristotelian explanation on the grounds that the experimental phenomena observed in the air pump are adequately explained by his hypothesis. Why did he do so? Hesse's Network Model encourages us to look for further constraints leading Boyle to adopt the belief that the air has pressure. What further beliefs are conserved if the air has pressure? The air pump worked by partially or almost completely removing the air from an enclosed glass receiver. (The evacuation of air from such a space was referred to as the "Boylean Vacuum" to distinguish it from what we might call a "complete vacuum.") But if air can be evacuated from a receiver, the Aristotelian hypothesis that the world is a plenum is false. Moreover, if the (at least Boylean) vacuum exists and is best explained by the mechanistic principle that the air has pressure, then the entire paradigm, according to which nature is a living being with psychological traits like abhorrence, collapses.

In fact, Renaissance and seventeenth-century thinkers held a wide range of views on these issues. Here we will follow Carolyn Merchant's suggestion that we distinguish fundamentally between organicists and mechanists. Briefly, mechanists held that matter is passive, brute or dead; that change is ultimately due to an external, nonmaterial entity: God; and that all the properties of matter can be explained, as Boyle put it, by the "shape, size, motion, and other primary affections of the smallest parts of matter."[24] Mechanists included Gassendi and Descartes in France, and in England, Boyle and many others who were later members of the Royal Society. Early modern organicists, following medieval interpretations of Aristotle, held that the world is an organic system of interdependent parts whose growth is the result of an inherent principle(s). (Aristotle himself had argued that growth and change occur when an enitity moves from a potential state to actualize some form.) In the orthodox view, the cosmos is hierachically constituted by a great chain of being extending from the four inanimate elements, through living beings, to the First Mover, and up to the Empyrean Heaven. The early modern period, however, saw many variations of this view: neo-platonic natural magicians, including Ficino, Pico della Mirandola, Agrippa, Della Porta, and Thomas Vaughn; naturalists, among whom we may include Telesio, Campanella, and Bruno; and hylozooists such as Paracelsus; J.B. Van Helmont and his son, F.M. Van Helmont; and the protestant sectarians (including the Quaker, Anne Conway).[25] Of interest to us here are the naturalists and hylozooists who believed in a World Soul or universal spirit that enlivens the world, provides for all the activity in it, and guides that activity or, in the case of the hylozooists, held that matter is alive and inspirited because matter and spirit are one. For these thinkers (as well as others) nature or the World Soul (understood as female) provide the ultimate explanation for natural phenomena.

Moreover, although the mechanists were atomists—they thought of matter as constituted of small bits—not all mechanists thought that a vacuum is possible; some were plenists. But mechanists were not the only ones who adopted atomism. Telesio and Bruno were atomists, as was Thommaso Campanella, who held that the earth is alive and sentient and that matter is comprised of atoms, which are alive and love one another so much that they refuse to be separated from one another with the result that a vacuum is impossible. On the other hand, Descartes argued that matter is not alive or conscious, that atoms are inert bits of matter that follow mechanical laws, but that there are no empty spaces between or beyond the atoms—in other words, that there is a plenum and that a vacuum is therefore impossible. Boyle himself entertained the possibility that the world is a plenum of the sort Descartes postulated (i.e., even in the absence of air, space is filled with "subtle matter") and he steadfastly refused to take a position on the question of whether a complete vacuum is possible—that is, whether a space can be empty of all matter whatsoever. But he argued vigorously that Nature should not be personified and that matter is inert, not alive and conscious. He understood his Boylean vacuum to be evidence against the nexus of views that even a partial vacuum is impossible because nature abhors a vacuum and that nature, including matter, is alive and enjoys some sort of consciousness.

To justify the hypothesis that the air has pressure, Boyle used the air pump, and his explanation of the pump's efficacy required that a Boylean vacuum be possible, that air be evacuated from receiver even if some other, "subtle" matter remained in it. Certainly these beliefs cohere well with the principle that matter is inert and with the new model of nature as a machine, but they are logically consistent with and can be made coherent with the principles that matter is alive and nature is a person. Both hypotheses, the inertia of matter and the consciousness of matter, explain the experimental data; so Boyle could have adapted, for example, Campanella's conception of the atoms as alive and loving one another, but whereas Campanella argued that their love for one another prevents a vacuum, Boyle could have argued that atoms, like members of the human community, can occasionally be separated even though they love one another. Or he could have remained neutral on this issue as he did on the issue of the complete vacuum. Instead, he argued that matter is inert. What constrained this choice of metaphysical principle?

Franiscus Linus was a Jesuit whose Aristotelian science was an integral part of a religious and political outlook to which Boyle and his fellow virtuosi in England objected, and in arguing against the science that supported Roman Catholic religion and politics, Boyle helped undercut them. However, we will not examine those politics here. Instead, we will look at the natural philosophy, politics, and religion of another group of people Boyle also worried about, a group whose class and gender politics deeply threatened sound Englishmen. By defeating the natural philosophy supporting them, Boyle helped to make his world a good one for bourgeois gentlemen. To understand the way Boyle negotiated class and gender politics in his work on air pressure, then, we must leave his laboratory and look into the political, social and religious upheavals of mid-seventeenth–century England.

The political struggle of the English Civil War was not a two-way struggle between the king and the people but a three-way struggle involving conflicting interests among classes of the people. Thus, the picture of that struggle as one between the Tories (who supported absolute monarchy) and the Whigs (who wanted a strong parliament) is not completely accurate. In fact, the Whigs represented the interests of middle- and upper middle-class merchants, traders, and investors and fought not only against royalist and Tory attempts to suppress their claims to freedom and representation, but also alongside the Tories against the political aspirations and claims of a large group of poor and lower-class women and men.

The English Civil War is sometimes called the Puritan Revolution since the fight was religious as well as political and economic and because many of the political and economic issues were debated in religious terms. The very name Puritan Revolution tells who won: the Puritans defeated the Royalists, but *they also defeated the radicals*. The radicals were included among several groups of "masterless men" and women comprised first, of rogues, vagabonds, and beggars; second, of casual laborers in London, dock workers, watermen, building laborers, and journeymen as well as fishwomen—all those people who made up "the mob" as it was called in Boyle's time; third, of the rural poor, including cottagers and squatters on commons, wastes and in forests; and finally, the protestant sectarians who included townspeople, often immigrants, who were small craftsmen, as well as apprentices and "serious-minded" laborious men." All rejected the state church. Instead of the hierarchical society logically supported by the doctrines of the Church of England, the sectarians preferred a more democratic society, logically supported by their belief that God is in all His saints; they therefore saw no need for priests of the established church to mediate between them and God. They held that each individual has access to God and that each is responsible to God for his or her own soul.[26]

Sectarian political views were supported by a natural philosophy that grew out of certain theological heresies. These heresies in turn derived from the natural magic tradition whose sources included works attributed to Hermes Trismegistus, believed by Renaissance thinkers to have been an Egyptian priest at the time of Moses. Hylozooism, the principle that all matter is alive, was central to Hermeticism. We find in the *Corpus Hermeticum*, for example, that "all that is in the world, without exception, is in movement, and that which is in movement is also in life. Contemplate then the beautiful arrangement of the world and see that it is alive, and that all matter is full of life.[27]

The association between the natural magic tradition and political rebellion could be seen in the work of Paracelsus, the sixteenth-century physician who championed the poor and oppressed and advocated a reformation of religion and of society, including a redistribution of wealth.[28] And the association appears again in the life and work of Thommaso Campanella. In 1600, Campanella was tortured by the Inquisition for rebelling against Spanish rule in Naples in order to set up a "universal republic." Campanella describes the republic in his *City of the Sun*, published in 1623 while he was imprisoned: it is led by a Hermetic magician and characterized not only by eugenics but also by communal ownership of property. Although women are assigned traditional female tasks, they also receive military training and are taught natural science. There is no traditional family; everyone lives in a dormitory and eats in a commons; and children are weaned at two and given over to others to raise. Campanella imagines an ideal human community living together in love, which mirrors his view of nature: the basic constituents of both are credited with life and consciousness. Bodies "enjoy being together and cherish their reciprocal contact with one another," so much so that they abhor any vacuum that would destroy their "community."[29]

In England, the pre-eminent Digger Gerrard Winstanley offers a clear case of the sectarian debt to the natural magic tradition. He held a kind of materialistic pantheism that identified God with the created world and so placed the spirit of life and cause of motion within terrestrial and celestial bodies themselves:

> To know the secrets of nature is to know the works of God. . . . And indeed if you would know spiritual things, it is to know how the spirit or power of wisdom and life, causing motion or growth, dwells within and governs both the several bodies of the stars and planets in the heavens above; and the several bodies of the earth below, as grass, plants, fishes, beasts, birds and mankind.[30]

And Winstanley's revolutionary political commitment to human equality followed from his beliefs about nature. He argued that men can know God's will for themselves by looking at the world around them and do not need priests and bishops as intermediaries to tell them God's will because *all* of nature is full of God or Reason. Not only tithes but the entire institution of a state church should be abolished, and inasmuch as the monarchy and the state church were interdependent institutions, a threat to the church was a threat to the state.

Sectarian emphasis upon the individual soul and the Spirit within had important implications for sectarian women. The Seventeenth Century saw the development of the ideal woman as a bourgeois who was to marry and to stay at home minding the house; while married, she was to own no property. She had no voice in the church or state. Puritan marriage manuals continually reinforced the view that "the man when he loveth should remember his superiority,"[31] and William Gouge, in his popular manual *Of Domestic Duties* of 1622 and 1634, flatly declared that "the extent of wive's subjection doth stretch itself very far, even to all things."[32]

But the rise of sectarianism, with its view that God is in everything and everyone, threatened the sexual status quo. The Leveller John Lilbourne remarked that "every particular and individual man and woman that ever breathed in the world since [Adam and Eve] are and were by nature all equal and alike in power, dignity, authority and majesty, none of them having (by nature) any authority dominion or magisterial power, one over . . . another."[33] Thus, sharing at least spiritual equality, all members of sectarian congregations, including women, debated, voted, prophesied, and even preached. Also, because the sectarians believed that the regenerate must separate from the ungodly, sectarian women were often allowed or encouraged to divorce or separate from their unregenerate husbands.

At various times during the Civil War and the years before the restoration of monarchy, sectarians, Levellers, and others called for a number of more or less revolutionary reforms. They wanted an end to enclosures, a practice which required that the people living on the land be displaced and rendered homeless. They also objected to rent racking, sharp rises in the rent owed by tenant farmers to landlords. Like enclosures, fen drainage also yielded more land for cultivation and was justified by its forcing squatters "to quit idleness and betake themselves to . . . manufactures. . . ."[34] The people whose homes and livelihoods were lost by fen drainage and enclosures fought back by all available means. As early as 1603, women led a revolt against the drainage of Deeping Fen in Lincolnshire and participated in the destruction of enclosures in Braydon Forest in the 1630s, at Buckden in 1641, at York in 1642, and in other places.

Off and on throughout the 1640s, London women petitioned and demonstrated at Parliament, complaining of the "decay of trade" and the high price of food due to the war. In 1642, about 400 women, having petitioned the day before concerning "their wants and necessities by reason of the great decay of trading," returned for an answer and roughed up the Duke of Lenox when he cried, "Away with these women, we were best to have parliament of Women."[35] And in 1649, about 500 Leveller women brought a petition signed by 10,000 women for the release of Leveller leaders, complaining that "Trading is utterly driven away, all kinds of Provision for Food at a most excessive rate, multitudes ready to starve and perish for want of work, employment, necessaries, and subsistance. . . ."

Boyle, and others who later became mechanists, were in and out of London in the late 1640s and would have read and heard accounts of the outrageous activities of women at Parliament. It was precisely during this period that Boyle wrote what we might call his "essays on women." These include the "Letter to Fidelia," dated London, December 2, 1647; the "Letter to Mrs. Dury," dated Stalbridge, April 15, 1647; "The Duty of a Mother's Being a Nurse"; and "The Martyrdom of Theodora." The Boyle revealed in these seldom-read texts eagerly resisted radical change in the social position of women or in the ideology of woman. The "Letter to Mrs. Dury," for example, inveighs against Corisca's painting because painting "invites loose gallants to tempt them [the women who paint]" and may have been written in support of a bill then before Parliament forbidding women to wear makeup, whereas "The Duty of a Mother's Being a Nurse" argues that mothers should breastfeed their own children instead of hiring wet-nurses for them. In these nonscientific works, most of them intended for a private audience, Boyle saw fit to expose a relentless concern that women occupy the domestic space being created for them by bourgeois liberal ideology.

Early in his life, Robert Boyle himself may also have adopted views derived from the naturalist and hylozooist tradition. Certainly he read the works of Paracelsus, Campanella, Telesio, and other naturalist and hylozooist writers because he gives them partial credit, along with Bacon, Gassendi, and Descartes, for weaning him "away from Aristotelian principles." And he shared with the radicals and others the widely held conviction that the natural order on one hand and the moral and social order on the other are mutually reflective. It follows then that Boyle was well-equipped to negotiate against the radicals' class and gender struggles by defeating the natural philosophy used to support them. I suggest that suppressing these struggles provided *one* of the constraints upon the decision by Boyle and other mechanists to adopt the hypothesis that matter is inert by arguing against the hylozooists that the air has spring and weight and that a (Boylean) vacuum is possible.[37]

The restoration of Charles II to the throne in 1660 saw an end to the greater freedoms of the Interregnum that had allowed radicals to voice their thoughts in print and in their assemblies. Thereafter they were harrassed, hounded, imprisoned, and often tortured for their views. Although Boyle and other members of the Royal Society had further work to do before their understanding of nature and society won out, they successfully negotiated the radical challenge during the Restoration.

## Conclusion

The politics of gender and other axes of oppression enter the production of knowledge at many points. Here we have seen that they can be put into play when decisions are made, even over hypotheses that appear to be far removed from gender issues. The historical case sketched above offers an example of the way in which gender considerations enter the production of knowledge. The macronegotiations that took place among social groups in mid-seventeenth–century England over what was to count as the proper understanding of certain natural phenomena had direct implications for the women of that period.

It has seemed to many philosophers that negotiation over knowledge is only salient on constructivist views and that on one or another version of realism, negotiation is epistemologically irrelevant. If, as it were, God created each thing in the world and commanded it to reproduce itself "after its kind," then the things in the world are independent of our minds and presorted into kinds, and the first epistemological project is to name each thing and its kind. The similarity of one thing to one another is not a matter of choice; therefore, the epistemic agent doesn't *decide* that they are similar in any sense other than that he simply *recognizes* that they are. The only decisions to be made are over what names to apply to each similar kind. But because the realist's model epistemic situation is not the one we live in, because phenomena do not in fact wear their identities on their sleeves, there will be rational desagreement over beliefs. Thus, the only way to identify true beliefs (assuming, for the moment that a realist epistemology is the right one) is to *decide* which ones are rationally acceptable given current standards of evidence and so on. But, if we must in fact decide which beliefs are true, then realist accounts are epistemically indistinguishable—that is, indistinguishable in practice— from contructivist ones, and the points made above about epistemic negotiation are valid in any case.

It is understood in philosophy of science that positivist accounts of science have been left behind; the field can be referred to now as "post-Kuhnian" to indicate that we no longer take up positivist projects such as the search for a logic of scientific rationality. But the dream of an algorithm for rationality lingers on. Under the conviction that only bad science can result from the intersection of politics with technical scientific concerns, many philosophers of science still assume that scientific rationality requires the decisions scientists make to be hedged about sufficiently to preclude the "irrational" influence of political opinions. To show the intersection of politics with the content of scientific theories is, then, ipso facto to reveal irrationality in the procedures that led to those theories. Following this line of argument, the case study presented above will be read as an accusation that Boyle and his fellow virtuosi practiced bad science. I take this conclusion to be absurd and to vitiate the line of argument leading to it. Instead, it seems quite reasonable, when the data do not uniquely select one theory, to select the theory that *coheres* with one's world view. As we saw above, people of the seventeenth century understood the natural and social orders to reflect one another; therefore, one would reasonably choose as an explanation of controversial natural phenomena such as suction that account carrying the most congenial social meaning (assuming that the competing accounts have comparable empirical adequacy).

# Notes

I am grateful to Hamilton College for the Faculty Fellowship supporting work upon which this essay is based. I am also particularly grateful to Helen Longino and Linda Alcoff for their comments as well as for the comments of audiences at the Massachusetts Institution of Technology and the Society for Women in Philosophy meeting at Rider College, Lawrenceville, N.J. in November, 1990. This essay extends the argument begun in my "Modeling the Gender Politics in Science," in *Hypatia: A Journal of Feminist Philosophy* 3,3 (Spring 1988): reprinted in *Feminism and Science*, ed. Nancy Tuana (Bloomington: Indiana University Press, 1989).

My first development, with Kathryn Addelson, of the notion of "epistemological individualism" can be found in "Making Knowledge," in Kathryn Pyne Addelson, *Impure Thoughts: Essays on Philosophy, Feminism and Ethics* (Philadelphia: Temple University Press, 1991) reprinted in *(En)Gendering Knowledge: Feminists in Academe*, ed. Joan E. Hartmann and Ellen Messer-Davidow (Knoxville: University of Tennessee Press, 1991).

1.   W.V. Quine, "Epistemology Naturalized," in *Ontological Relativity and Other Essays.* (New York: Columbia University Press, 1969), 83. I take Quine's work as an example because his is an individualist epistemology grounded in the sensory impressions of the individual; although his work tacitly recognizes the socially negotiated character of knowledge, he does not make that central to his philosophical analysis.

2.   Hilary Putnam, "Why Reason Can't Be Naturalized," in *Realism and Reason* (New York: Cambridge University Press, 1983), 236.

3.   The question of whether any given statement really corresponds to the way things are in themselves and the general question of the nature of truth need not be answered for this version of the argument to go through because ordinary people are not held to such a high standard.

4.   Wittgenstein's argument has the merit that it applies regardless of whether the individual is supposed to be interacting only with private objects (notably his own sensations) or with a world that is in principle public but in fact private because there are no other language speakers in it.

5.   This is as Putnam points out in his discussion of Wittgenstein's attack on methodological solipsism. Cf. Putnam, in *Realism and Reason*, 229–247.

6.   The implications of the demise of epistemological individualism are profound; for example, an epistemology based upon the assumption that a belief is fundamentally a state of an individual puts the epistemological cart before the horse. Indeed, "*S* believes that *p*" is not the fundamental explicandum of epistemology. We need a new, richer analysis of beliefs. Cf. Lorraine Code, this volume.

See also Lynn Nelson, *Who Knows?* (Philadelphia: Temple University Press,

1990); Lynn Nelson, this volume, for a sustained argument that the community is the subject of knowledge; and Helen Longino, *Science as Social Knowledge* (Princeton, N.J.: Princeton University Press, 1990) for an extended discussion of the social nature of scientific knowledge.

7.   Wittgenstein, of course, would have disagreed that politics intersect the production of knowledge.

8.   W.V.O. Quine *The Web of Belief* (New York: Random House, 1978).

9.   Mary Hesse *The Structure of Scientific Inference* (Berkeley and Los Angeles: University of California Press, 1974), 52.

10.   Karen D. Knorr-Cetina, "The Ethnographic Study of Scientific Work: Towards a Constructivist Interpretation of Science," in *Science Observed: Perspectives on the Social Study of Science*, ed. Karen D. Knorr-Cetina and Michael Mulkay (Beverly Hills: Sage Publications, 1983) 127.

11.   Karen D. Knorr-Cetina and Michael Mulkay, "Introduction: Emerging Principles in Social Studies of Science," in *Science Observed*, 11.

12.   Bruno Latour and Steve Woolgar, *Laboratory Life: The Social Construction of Scientific Facts* (Beverly Hills: Sage Publications, 1979), 156.

13.   Quoted in Karen D. Knorr-Cetina, "The Ethnographic Study of Scientific Work," in *Science Observed*, 128. I have set the conversation in standard English to aid those of us who are not familiar with the notation used by observers. Knorr-Cetina quotes the original text as follows:

V: How de yew know they're microglia?
H: Uh:   :h
V: I: *mean*
V: (hh) UH YEH KNOW THE'S A BIG QUESTION OF
H: ( )
V: whut i:s microglia, whut is'n microglia an' where does microglia come from
   en-
H: (ahts's ats *fuckin* doesn' make any difference tme noe)
V: O:h its a big doh- big d(hh)d question an-
( ): hah hah hah hah hah
H: I don't worry bou-
   yeh know *thet* s:s ( )
   ah yeh know yew c'n use whatever *wo:rd* yew wonna use=
V: =uh:h
H: say uh Del Rio Hortega (pos'tve cells) fer all I care, *right?*
H: Y'see these liddle things ( )
H: Del Rio Hortega positive cells

14.   I am grateful to my colleague, Dr. Sue Ann Miller, for help in analyzing this interchange.

15.   W.V. Quine and J.S. Ullian, *The Web of Belief* (New York: Random House, 1970), 66–67.

16.   "Because You Are a Woman," *Philosophy* 48 (1973). For the argument

that Plato did not recognize the equality of all women, cf. Elizabeth V. Spelman, *Inessential Woman* (Boston: Beacon Press, 1988), chapter 1.

17.   Thomas E. Hill, "Servility and Self-Respect," *The Monist* 57 (1973): 12–27.

18.   Portions of this discussion are taken from my analysis of the intersection of seventeenth-century gender politics with the production of the technical principle that matter is inert. Cf. Potter "Modeling the Gender Politics in Science," in *Hypatia* 3,3 (Spring 1988).

19.   The spirit of the new paradigm has been captured by the title of Carolyn Merchant's booklength discussion of it, *The Death of Nature* (New York: Harper and Row, 1980).

20.   The men who studied nature in seventeenth-century England referred to themselves as "virtuosi," not as "scientists"; the latter term did not take on its modern meaning until well into the Eighteenth Century.

21.   *Robert Boyle's Experiments in Pneumatics*, ed. James Bryant Conant (Cambridge, Mass.: Harvard University Press, 1950), 14.

22.   Ibid., 16.

23.   All quotations are from "New Experiments Physico-mechanical, touching the Spring of the Air," in *The Works of the Honourable Robert Boyle* (1772; reprint, Hildesheim: Georg Olms Verlagsbuchhandlung, 1965), 1:33–34.

24.   Boyle, "Of the Usefulness of Natural Philosophy," in *Works* 2:37. Essay IV of "Of the Usefulness of Natural Philosophy," from which this quotation is taken, argues against Aristotelian explanations of suction and women's menstruation in terms of the psychological traits and intentional designs of Nature. It is in this essay that Boyle gives one of the earliest of his statements of the mechanical philosophy, likening the motions of inert matter to the clock of Strasburg.

25.   This taxonomy is set out in Merchant, *The Death of Nature*, chapter 4. I have deviated from her categories only in referring to hylozooists where she refers to vitalists. This is, of course, not the only possible taxonomy; Frances Yates, for example, refers to both Bruno and Campanella as magician-philosophers "in the line of the Renaissance Magi descending from Ficino" in *Giordano Bruno and the Hermatic Tradition* (New York: Vintage Books 1964).

26.   Christopher Hill, *The World Turned Upside Down* (New York: Penguin Books, 1982), 40ff.

27.   Frances A. Yates, *Giordano Bruno and the Hermetic Tradition* (New York: Vintage Books, 1964), 31 and 34.

28.   Brian Easlea, *Witch Hunting, Magic and the New Philosophy: An Introduction to Debates of the Scientific Revolution 1450–1750* (Atlantic Highlands, N.J.: Humanities Press, 1980), 102.

29. Ibid., 105.

30. Quoted by Hill in *The World Turned Upside Down*, 142.

31. J. Dod and R. Cleaver, *A Godly Forme of Household Government* . . . (London, 1614); quoted in Keith Thomas, "Women and the Civil War Sects," in *Past and Present* 13 (1958), 43.

32. William Gouge, *Of Domestical Duties* (London, 1622), p. 268. Facsimile by Walter J. Johnson, Inc. Theatrum Orbis Terrarum, Ltd.; Amsterdam, 1976.

33. Quoted in Thomas, "Women and the Civil War Sects," 44.

34. Quoted in Christopher Hill, *The Century of Revolution 1603–1714* (London and Edinburgh: Thomas Nelson and Sons, Ltd., 1961), 203.

35. Patricia Higgins, "The Reactions of Women," in *Politics, Religion and the English Civil War*, ed. Brian Manning (New York: St. Martin's Press, 1973), 185.

36. Ibid., 201.

37. I am indebted to the work of J.R. Jacob, J.R. Jacob and Margaret Jacob, and Peter Rattansi. In many publications over several years, these historians argued that class politics, in particular those between the sectarians and the virtuosi of Boyle's class, influenced the acceptance of the mechanical philosophy. Most useful for my purposes has been J.R. Jacob and Margaret C. Jacob, "The Anglican Origins of Modern Science: The Metaphysical Foundations of the Whig Constitution," in *Isis* 71 (1980): 251–67, in which they show that in adopting the principle that matter is inert, Boyle and his compatriots "outlawed" the radicals' natural philosophy of hylozooism and the radical class politics based upon it. My essay (and the larger project from which it is taken) intend to show that further analysis allows us to see the intersection of gender as well as class politics with the debate, not only over the nature of matter, but also the related fundamental principles regarding the vacuum, the pressure of the air, and finally over Boyle's Law of Gases.

# 8

# Bodies and Knowledges: Feminism and the Crisis of Reason

*Elizabeth Grosz*

---

*If the skin were parchment and the blows you gave me were ink . . .*
— William Shakespeare, *The Comedy of Errors*[1]

My aim in this article is to exacerbate, rather than dissolve, what is commonly regarded as "the crisis of Reason." This crisis has threatened to infect all knowledges, particularly in the humanities and social sciences, although the natural sciences are not immune to its implications either. This crisis has methodological, epistemological, and political implications for metatheoretical conceptions of knowledge or knowledge production; it entails reconceiving the sources, aims, and goals of the form and functioning of knowledges. I intend to outline one of the lines of attack available to feminist theory in its challenge to many of the founding presumptions and methodological criteria governing knowledges by examining (re-) explorations of the body and drawing out some implications of acknowledging the body in the production and evaluation of knowledge.

This crisis of reason is a consequence of the historical privileging of the purely conceptual or mental over the corporeal; that is, it is a consequence of the inability of Western knowledges to conceive their own processes of (material) production, processes that simultaneously rely on and disavow the role of the body. This claim that the body is disavowed in the production of knowledges has implications not only for epistemologists but also for feminist theorists, especially for those attempting to criticize and transform the traditional patriarchal forms that knowledge has thus far taken. If the body is an unacknowledged or an inadequately acknowledged condition of knowledges and if, as I will argue, the body is always sexually specific, concretely "sexed,"

187

this implies that the hegemony over knowledges that masculinity has thus far accomplished can be subverted, upset, or transformed through women's assertion of "a right to know," independent of and autonomous from the methods and presumptions regulating the prevailing (patriarchal) forms of knowledge. This article is an attempt to address the *explicit sexualization of knowledges*, the relationship that models and goals of knowledges have to sexually specific (male) bodies. My aim is to draw out some of the effects that a concept of *sexed corporeality* may have on relations between knowers and objects known and on the forms, methods, and criteria of assessment governing knowledges today.

The first two parts of this article briefly outline the forms the contemporary "crisis of reason" takes, the ways in which it has manifested itself, and the theoretical sites where it has been located and localized in both traditional conceptions of knowledge and in feminist theory. The third and fourth sections examine two important—and possibly contradictory—conceptions of the body, the body understood as a surface of social inscription and as the locus of lived experience, which may prove useful in this project of resexualizing those discourses (i.e., most of them) that have disavowed the role of the specificities of the male body in their production. The fifth section draws out the effects of acknowledging the sexual specificity of the body in conceptions of knowledge; the final two sections explore in preliminary fashion some of the relations between feminist theory, bodies, and knowledges.

In working though the meaning and many ramifications of this crisis in twentieth-century reason, I am not by any means articulating a new concern but echoing an often-voiced anxiety, one that may have originated with skepticism in ancient Greece but that reemerges in distinctively modern terms in the writings of Descartes, considered by many to be the "father" of modern philosophy. For Descartes, this crisis consisted in the fact that knowledge lacked secure foundations. If its foundations remain insecure, then the intellectual structures built upon it will, at best, be shaky. For Hume, in quite different ways, our (scientific) knowledge is in a state of crisis insofar as universal natural laws—the laws it is the task of science to discern—are unable to be rationally justified. There is, for example, no rational basis in our belief that the sun will rise tomorrow. That we believe it will do so is a function of unjustified habit and expectation rather than rationally or scientifically secure knowledge. Descartes and Hume represent rationalist and empiricist approaches to knowledge; neither they nor the traditions they founded have been able to resolve the insecurities and doubts that both imply. The various projects that have attempted to bridge the methodological gaps between rationalism and empiricism are also incapable of such a resolution.

Husserl, in the *The Crisis of European Sciences and Transcendental Phenomenology*, formulated the crisis as a confrontation between a Galilean mathematization of nature (a tendency to mathesis) and a Cartesian concern for the knowing subject (a phenomenological tendency). Through a reading of the history of modern philosophy *The Crisis* attempts to reinsert the Cartesian emphasis on the subject into the realm of the objectivity sought by Galileo and the empiricist tradition. On Husserl's argument, the clash of "transcendental subjectivism" and "physicalist objectivism" is the principle of the "unity of history." Others, such as Heidegger, Habermas, Lyotard, Rorty, Jameson and, in a quite different form, Foucault, Derrida, and Deleuze, have formulated the crisis in *very broadly* similar terms—the mismatch, conflict, or displacement between "objectivity" and "subjectivity." This crisis has been variously described as a crisis of identity, of modernity, of capitalism, of morality, and even of science. It is a crisis of self-validation and methodological self-justification, formulated in different terms within different disciplines and periods; a crisis of reason's *inability to rationally know itself*; a crisis posed as reason's inability to come outside of itself, to enclose and know itself from the outside: the inadequation of the subject and its other.

## 1. The Crisis

The following are what seem to me the most fundamental assumptions within various systems of contemporary knowledges that have been brought into question by the crisis of reason. I will list them numerically for the sake of brevity and clarity:

1. There is the underlying presumption in the humanities and social sciences that reason and knowledges based upon it are *methodologically appropriate* to their object of investigation, the human subject. Methods, procedures, and techniques of socially legitimated knowledges are assumed to be *transparent* and *neutral* instruments, intellectual tools that contribute to the growth of knowledges but are unproblematically disposable by them. They are tools whose influence or productive contributions can be calculated and distinguished from their objects. This instrumentalization of methods is not restricted to realist approaches to knowledge but characterizes any position that accords a recalcitrance to reality or to the object of knowledges. (It may well be that methodological procedures do have largely instrumental value, but this value resides in their relation to goals, ideals,

or strategies, and not in their representative relation to reality). The question, "How does this knowledge, this method, this technique, constitute its object?" cannot be raised or answered. If methods of knowing are indeed transparent and neutral, being either mere tools which could be replaced by others (and thus not integral to knowledge, but convenient for it) or *a priori* necessities, we are assured that knowledges do not *distort*, manipulate, or constrain their objects. Instead, they are presumed to describe and/or explain them, analyzing and synthesizing them without loss or residue. It is only ignorance, false propositions, and invalid arguments and theories that distort or produce their objects. In other words, what is in question here is the adequacy of methods, axioms, and criteria of evaluation in knowledges relative to their objects of investigation and the presumption of the transparent neutrality of ways of knowing to the objects known.

2. There is a presumption about the scope and limits of knowledges. The boundaries that border knowledges constitute the often zealously guarded divisions between particular *disciplines* that comprise the humanities and social sciences. The disciplines are themselves effects of historically concrete, dynamic relations of power.[2] They divide knowledges according to historically specific categories as well: the inside and the outside of the subject (psychology as analysis of "man's" interior and sociology as an analysis of "his" exterior); self and other (anthropology); the universal and the particular (philosophy and history, respectively); appearance and reality (literature or visual arts and natural sciences); and so on. Although the boundaries are not *immutable*, enabling some cross-fertilization between disciplines, nevertheless each defines and is defined by both a mainstream or core and a periphery or margins. These margins and the *spaces between disciplines* are unable to be theorized in the terms of the core—that is, within the discipline itself. Each is concerned with its autonomy and the integrity of its own procedures or those of others, insofar as they cohere with their own repective commitments. Interdisciplinary as well as disciplinary relations *may* be analyzed from *within* a discipline, but the spaces of exclusion *between* disciplines must remain untheorized by the disciplines themeselves.[3]

3. There are presumptions about the criteria by which such knowledges are judged valid and/or true. Clearly, criteria of truth and validity vary enormously from one discipline to another, but it is not clear that truth is relevant at all for the more "interpretive" disciplines, such as literature, psychoanalysis, or film theory. Lacan, for example, actively affirms the radical cleavage of knowledge from truth.[4] In spite of the diversity of criteria by which, say, behaviorism seems to share little with literature or philosophy, there are still a

number of shared assumptions, including clarity, precision, the capacity to be verified or falsified, parsimony, communicability, translatability, and so on. Underlying these is a belief that the object of investigation, whether a text, human behavior, or social interactions, exists independently of knowledge of it, presuming a "reality" resistant to false or invalid methods, misinterpretation, or misrepresentation. There is, in other words, the presumption of a rift between the object of knowledge and knowing such that the knowledges can be judged in terms of their adequacy to the object, as if this object were somehow independently accessible and outside knowledge, a kind of prediscursive referent of knowledges.

4. There is the presumption of the atemporal and transgeographic value and validity of knowledges. Although knowledges are produced at specific times and places, their genesis is considered largely irrelevant (except perhaps for historical purposes) to the knowledge they produce. These processes of production leave no trace in their product. Theories and knowledges are produced in their transparency as *eternally true* or valid, independent of their origins. Knowledge is outside of history, capable of being assessed and reevaluated independently of the time and space of its production. Knowledges do not carry the index of their origins.

5. There is a presumption that though knowledge is produced by individuals, it is in no way personal or merely idiosyncratic if it is to be considered as genuine knowledge. The knowing subject who produces knowledge is, as it were, bracketed off from the knowledges thus produced. Knowledge is considered *perspectiveless*; if it represents a particular point of view, this point of view is accessible to everybody, insofar as we are suitably trained. (Here, I am not claiming a "subjective bias" in knowledge but rather the fact that all knowledges are produced from and occupy particular positions that are not identical to that of their creator.) This process of "suitable training," rather than the regularity of the objects investigated, helps produce the regularity and repeatability of results that is a necessary criterion for objectivity.

In dealing with "man" as the object and subject of analysis, those knowledges comprising the humanities and social sciences are unable to articulate their basis in masculinity, their investments in power relations, and their apparent displacement of power or desire from the knowledges they produce. Insofar as they rely on specific and problematic conceptions of knowledge, they will remain unable to rationally acknowledge and justify themselves on the more limited and circumspect basis as perspectival or, in Donna Haraway's term, as situated (sexually specific) knowledges.

If the subject of knowledge is a "blind spot" in knowledge production and assessment, then all knowledge is necessarily contaminated by an irreducibly arational component at its core. The knower who utilizes and relies upon the principles of reason is not *himself* capable of being included in terms of the reason *he* utilizes.[5] The epistemic and cultural crisis faced by theory today must be located in a number of tendencies and commitments produced within this intellectual tradition. Even so-called radical theory, which includes many forms of feminist or marxist theory, actively participates in a process of salvaging or resuscitating reason. If I can be permitted to merely indicate these tendencies and commitments in point form, this should suffice to recognizably characterize the tradition.

1. First, there is a notable breakdown of confidence in modes of "objectivist" inquiry even among its proponents. The criteria constituting objectivity are subject to stringent criticisms from within even the most "objective" of knowledges—particularly theoretical physics (since the advent of Heisenberg, Einstein, and the principle of uncertainty or, more recently and in a different way, chaos theory). Kuhn, Lakatos, and Feyerbend, among others, question this apsiration to unmediated objectivity. If objectivity means unprejudiced, observer-independent knowledge, some physicists and epistemologists challenge the belief that observers face "facts" directly, in a manner unmediated by theories, presumptions, and values. They deny the prevailing belief in facts, "raw data," and information as being somehow independent of, and unaffected by, the presence of the observer. Objectivity implies a *single* monolithic world, which is posited as external to and autonomous from subjects.

2. Yet, in spite of an occasionally recognized limit to the value of objectivity within the natural sciences—or at least in their most developed forms—part of the current crisis faced by the humanities and social sciences is dependent on their aspiration towards a natural science model of knowledge, which is impossible for them to achieve and which has dire consequences for the types of knowledge they produce. This produces a positivist version of the "Sciences of Man" that reduces its object—humanity—to the status of physical object; behavioral psychology, statistical sociology, and positivist historiography may provide recognizable examples. The crisis faced by pseudo scientific approaches to the human subject is that, by utilizing objective, verifiable, and formalizable techniques, the specificity of the subject is ignored.[6]

3. The humanities and social sciences have been increasingly confronted by the problem, outlined in logic by Gödel, of the impossibility of reason's self-knowledge. If reason is not self-inclusive, then there must be an irrational or nonrational kernel within rationality that subverts its claims to provide methods and systems of judgment for knowledges. I have already suggested that reason's blind spot can be located in its inability to know the knower. This has had particularly traumatic effects on the social sciences insofar as their object and subject are avowedly similar. Kristeva locates the problematic limits of linguistic and literary theory in their failure to adequately conceptualize *the speaking subject*; Lacan admonishes psychology and psychiatry for effacing the *subject of desire*; and Merleau-Ponty locates philosophy's impasses in its failure to understand the nature of a *subjectivity that perceives, thinks, and acts*. All of these shortcomings highlight a particular dilemma for the humanities. A discipline whose object is *man* is necessarily incomplete unless it can include its own production as a discipline within the knowledges it produces.

4. Knowledges lack the means to understand their own self-development as knowledges. They lack the means by which to understand their own historicity and materiality. Indeed, the history of knowledges is explicitly excluded as irrelevant to the contemporary forms of these knowledges. Even a discipline specifically devoted to such histories—the "history of ideas"—does not solve the problem. At best, a history of ideas may provide information and techniques regarding a discipline's history, but it cannot serve as a substitute for a discipline's *self-knowledge* or self-reflection. Moreover, although it outlines histories of knowledges, it is unable to articulate its own history, its own specific mode of self-knowledge. This absence has major stategic effects. If knowledges are not marked by the various, often widely disparate kinds of events that construct them as disciplinary knowledges, they are unaffected by a *political investment in knowledges*; they remain, in a certain sense, value-free. The political investment of knowledges remains external to knowledge and can be seen to be an effect of *external impingements*, an effect of the *application* of knowledges rather than of its being located within knowledges themselves—the distinction between "pure" and "applied" knowledges or between science and technology. A convenient opposition between "pure" knowledges and political "uses" of this "pure" knowledge enables them to protect themselves from political scrutiny. Foucault convincingly argued that the relations between power and knowledge must be considered *internal* to knowledges, providing their condition of possibility and guiding their material effects.

5. Because of the elision of the presumed subject of knowledge and

of the (historical) processes of production of knowledges, the prevailing intellectual paradigms face a crisis of "perspectivism." They cannot acknowledge their perspectival, partial, and limited access to objects of investigation. To admit that knowledges are but perspectives—points of view of the world—is to acknowledge that other, quite different positions and perspectives are possible. This opens up a multiplicity of vantage points or positions in fields that, up to now, have been governed by a singular, exclusive, and privileged access to true representations and valid methods of knowing reality. To accept these limits and their own partisan nature amounts to relinquishing their claim to objective, true, singular, and transhistorical or transgeographic value. Moreover, it is to accept a heterogeneous series of influences—some rational, some not, some universal, some highly particularized—in the production and nature of knowledge.

6. Finally, the crisis of reason consists in the impossibility of rationally deciding between competing methods and paradigms produced from different positions. One certainly makes decisions within disciplines about which theories to rely upon, which methods to use, and which basic premises to assume; these are not based on reason alone but are the products of a variety of psychological, social, political, *and* epistemological forces. This adherence to positions and values that cannot be rationally justified and compete with each other for supremacy within disciplines is not a function of incommensurable theories—for although it may be true that some discourses and paradigms have no basis of comparison or common grounds, it is also true that most actively compete with each other (at any given time) around a cluster of shared issues. Nor am I here affirming a relativism that asserts the equal value of all theories and all positions or perspectives. Relativism amounts to an abdication of the right to judge or criticize a position—any position—and a disavowal of any politics insofar as all positions are rendered equivalent.

Although I have suggested that this crisis is based on an inability to know the subject of knowledge, this can now be understood as a *crisis of specificity*, a crisis of the limits or the particularity of knowledges—a crisis in status and at the level of self-representations of the (sexual) specificities at play in the production of knowledges.

## 2. Feminism and the Body

Although feminists have frequently struggled around issues involving women's bodies—the right to abortion, contraception, maternity, reproduction, self-defense, body image, sexuality, pornography, and so on—there is still a strong reluctance to conceptualize the female body as playing a major role in women's oppression. Few concepts have been as maligned or condemned within feminist theory, with monotonous charges of biologism, essentialism, ahistoricism, and naturalism continuing to haunt those feminists theorizing the body.[7] However understandable these charges may be (in the context of patriarchal reductions of women to *natural* passivity, maternity, dependence, and so on.), they presume that *only* anatomical, physiological, or biological account of bodies are possible, obscuring the possibility of *sociocultural* conceptions of the body. Nonbiologistic, nonreductive accounts of the body may entail quite different consequences and serve to reposition women's relations to the production of knowledges.

How, then, are bodies relevant to feminism and the structure of prevailing knowledges? The following outline presents some answers:

1. Given the prevailing binarized or dichotomized categories governing Western reason and the privilege accorded to one term over the other in binary pairs (mind over body, culture over nature, self over other, reason over passions, and so on), it is necessary to examine the subordinated, negative, or excluded term, *body* as the *unacknowledged condition* of the dominant term, *reason*.

2. Because these binary pairs function in lateral alignments, that are cross-correlated with other pairs—particularly the distinction between male and female—the body has been and still is closely associated with women and the feminine, whereas the mind remains connected to men and the masculine. Exploring these phallocentric alignments is prerequisite to transforming the presuppositions underlying prevailing knowledges.

3. If adequate concepts of the *variety* of human beings are to be developed, *differences* between subjects must be openly accepted. These differences *must* in some way be inscribed on and experienced by and through the body. Sexual differences, like class and race differences, *are* bodily differences, but these are not immutable or biologically pre-ordained.

4. If we take antihumanist critiques of personal identity seriously, feminists can meaningfully talk about women as an oppressed group or a site of possible resistance only be means of the specificity of the female body and its place in locating women's lived experiences and social positions.[8] That is, if subjects are produced, in analogy with the production of commodities, then the only thing capable of acting as raw materials for the production analogy are human (biological) bod-

ies. As pliable flesh, the body is the unspecified raw matter of social inscription, producing subjects as subjects of a particular kind.

5. Power can thus be seen to operate directly on bodies, behaviors, and pleasures, extracting from them information necessary for the emergence of the knowledges constituting the social sciences and humanities. Knowledges require the interaction of power and bodies; correlatively, power requires knowledges of bodies and behaviors in order to remain effective and "in play." The disciplines (including psychology, criminology, sociology, psychiatry, and so on) are, as Foucault argues, formed through the interaction of disciplinary regimes and institutions—prisons, asylums, clinics, doctor's surgeries, the psychoanalyst's couch—functioning to inscribe bodies in distinctive ways. Bodies are thus essential to accounts of power and critiques of knowledge. Feminist conceptions of the body are unlike those of their male counterparts (Nietzsche, Freud, Lacan, and Foucault, among others) insofar as the bodies and pleasures of individuals and groups are always *sexually specific* and may well entail different regimes of power and their associated knowledges.[9]

### 3. The Body as Surface of Inscription

Two broad kinds of approach to theorizing the body can be discerned in twentieth-century radical thought. One is derived from Nietzsche, Kafka, Foucault, and Deleuze, which I will call "inscriptive"; the other is more influenced by psychology, especially psychoanalysis and phenomenology. I will refer to this second approach as the "lived body." The first conceives the body as a surface on which social law, morality, and values are inscribed; the second refers largely to the lived experience of the body, the body's internal or psychic inscription. Where the first analyzes a *social*, public body, the second takes the body-schema or imaginary anatomy as its object(s). It is not clear to me that these two approaches are compatible or capable of synthesis. Nevertheless they may provide some of the theoretical terms necessary to problematize the major binary categories defining the body—inside/outside, subject/object, active/passive, fantasy/reality, and surface/depth.

The body can be regarded as a kind of *hinge* or threshold: it is placed between a psychic or lived interiority and a more sociopolitical exteriority that produces interiority through the *inscription* of the body's outer surface. Where psychoanalysis and phenomenology focus on the body as it is experienced and rendered meaningful, the inscriptive model is more concerned with the processes by which the body is marked, scarred, transformed, and written upon or contructed by the various regimes of institutional, discursive, and nondiscursive power as a particular kind of body. In this section I will explore the inscriptive model of corporeal subjectivity and in the next, the notion of the lived body, the body as it is experienced.

In *The Genealogy of Morals*, Nietzsche outlines a basic account of corporeal inscription. At the horizon of culture, he argues, social morality and memory are not inscribed by man's unique reason, compassion or morality, but by *mnemotechniques*—methods of branding or permanently etching the body. A genealogy of morals reveals a history of corporeal cruelty.

> The poorer the memory of mankind has been, the more terrible have been its customs. The severity of all primitive penal codes gives us some idea of how difficult it must have been for man to overcome his forgetfulness and to drum it into these slaves of momentary whims and desires a few basic requirements of communal living. . . . (Nietzsche 1969)

For Nietzsche, economic equivalence, the capacity to exchange and to make contracts, does not derive from a sense of social justice, because justice itself derives from a primitive notion of "corporeal compensation," a kind of originary social violence by which damages are retrievable from the body of the guilty party. Debt is ultimately expiated by flesh and blood. Civilization carves meanings onto and out of bodies; it does not, as it professes, "enlighten the masses" by reason and education but instead ensures its cohesion through coercion and cruelty. So-called primitive societies practice a kind of ritualized body-inscription that is no more and no less painful or primitive than our own forms of initiation ceremonies. Scarring, tattooing, circumcizing, excising, and remaking parts of the body by surgical means, processes of stretching, marking, and distorting the lips, teeth, ears, necks, feet acculturate the body and its parts. The body is adorned with color, mud, feathers, or stones and marked by processes securing, at least ideally, its social integration. Inscriptions mark the surface of the body, dividing it into zones of intensified or de-intensified sensation, spreading a libidinal concentration unevenly over the written-and-erotic living surface:

> The body-image . . . may be transformed by clothes, by decoration or by jewelry, but it is also possible . . . to change the body itself as such; holes may be drilled into the body, ears, nose, lips, the genitals may be perforated, parts may be cut away, metal and wood may be inserted into the different parts of the body . . . one may also try to change the body-image in a less violent way by gymnastics of all kinds. (Schilder, 1978)

Ritualistically inscribed scars and incisions become the marks of one's social location and position, creating a (provisional) fixity from the flux of the body's experiential intensities. As a receptive surface, the body's boundaries and zones are constituted in conjunctions and through linkages with other surfaces and planes: the lips connected with the breast in orality, possibly accompanied by the hand in conjunction with an ear, each system in perpetual motion and interrelation with the other; toes in connection with sand in the obsessional's fixation with his shoes and calluses. These linkages are assemblages that harness and produce the body as a surface of interchangeable and substitutable elements. Libidinal intensities do not function through biologically predesignated zones or invest or radiate outward from them to other sites that borrow their force; they extend out from orifices and activate bodily organs to stretch erotogenicity to other sites, surfaces, organs, protusions, and openings, thereby creating by inscription and bordering of these loci. They libidinize the body in its capacity to form linkages with other bodies, animate and inanimate.[10]

Libidinal intensifications of bodily parts are *surface effects*, interactions occuring on the surface of the skin and various organs. These surface effects, however, are not simply superficial, for they generate an interior, an underlying *depth*, individuality, or consciousness much like a möebius strip (a two-dimensional flat plane, which, when rotated in space, creates both—and in a sense, neither—an inside and an outside). Tracing the outside of the möebius strip leads one directly to its inside without at any point leaving its surface. This *depth* is one of the distinguishing features marking out the modern, Western capitalist body from other kinds. Our body forms are considered expressions of an interior, not inscriptions of a flat surface. By constructing a soul or psyche for itself, the "civilized body" forms libidinal flows, sensations, experiences, and intensities into needs, wants, and commodified desires that can gain a calcuable gratification. The body becomes a text, a system of signs to be deciphered, read, and read into. Social law is incarnated, "corporealized", correlatively, bodies are textualized, "read" by others as *expressive* of a subject's psychic interior. A storehouse of inscriptions and messages between its internal and external boundaries, it generates or constructs the body's movements into "behavior," which then have interpersonally and socially identifiable meanings and functions within the social system.

Cuts on the body's surface serve, through pain, to organize the interior or lived body. This, no doubt, is in part the purpose of institutionally sanctioned forms of interrogation through torture: not the extraction of information, nor control over the prisoner's movements, but an *unmaking* of the subject's lived experience and agency.[11]

Foucault outlines various systems for the normalization of bodies within a regime of disciplinary control; as procedures of punishment developed, there was a transition from a macropolitics of spectacular display (a kind of intimidatory and exemplary, or ostentatious, power) to a microphysics of intricate bodily supervision and surveillance. Punishment remains coupled with knowledges—either those produced by legal "proofs," confessions, and expert opinions, or those originating in the minds and behaviors of the spectators of punishment. Disciplinary normalization, a contemporary mode of power, culminates in an increasingly medicalized discourse: health, well-being, clinical supervision, and surgical intervention become ever more crucial to legal, juridical, and political domains. These are agencies for regimenting, observing, and inspecting "delinquent bodies" (those of the sick, insane, or criminal); through them, the normalized body is surveyed as well. Epistemic and coercive relations create what Foucault describes as the "modern soul" (which, for him, imprisons the body), the psychological interior or subjectivity so central to the "Sciences of Man."

The increasing medicalization of the body, based on processes of removal (incision, cutting, removing, and reduction) or addition (inlaying, stitching, and injection), demonstrate a body pliable to power, a *machinic* organism in which "components" can be altered, adjusted, removed, or replaced. The body becomes increasingly regarded as functional, composed of organic parts capable of mechanical/cybernetic duplication.[12] Correlatively, there is an ever more insistent inscription by physico-cultural object-signs on the surface of the body. Clothing, jewelry, makeup, cars, living spaces, and work all function to mark the subject's body as deeply as any physical incision, binding individuals to systems of significance in which they become signs to be read (by others and themselves). Food, dieting, exercise, and movement provide meanings, values, norms, and ideals that the subject actively ingests, incorporating social categories into the physiological interior. Bodies *speak*, without necessarily talking, because they become coded with and as signs. They speak social codes. They become *intextuated*, narrativised; simultaneously, social codes, laws, norms, and ideals become *incarnated*.[13]

If bodies are traversed and infiltrated by knowledges, meanings, and power, they can also, under certain circumstances, become sites of struggle and resistance, actively inscribing themselves on social practices. The activity of *desiring, inscribing bodies* that though marked by law, make their own inscriptions on the bodies of others, themselves, and the law in turn, must be counterposed against the passivity of the inscribed body.[14]

## 4. The Lived Body

Freud describes the process by which the child acquires an image of its own body as "primary narcissism."[15] The subject acquires an underlying sense of unity beneath the disparate, heterogenous sensations it experiences. This sense of a unity or identity is the end result of the processes that construct the ego. For Freud, the ego does not result from a pre-ordained, biological order but from a specific psychical intervention into the child's "natural" development:

> We are bound to suppose that a unity comparable to the ego has to be developed.... There must be something added to auto-eroticism—a new psychical action—in order to bring about narcissism. (Freud 1914, 69)

He claims that the genesis of the ego is dependent on a *psychical map* of the body's libidinal intensities. In *The Ego and the Id* (1923), he argues that the ego is not so much a thing as a bodily tracing, a map of the erotogenicity of the body, an internalized image of the intensity of sensations in the body:

> The ego is first and foremost a bodily ego; it is not merely a surface entity, but is itself the projection of a surface. If we wish to find an anatomical analogy for it we can best identify it with the "cortical homunculus" of the anatomists, which stands on its head in the cortex, sticks up its heels, faces backwards and as we know, has its speech-area on the left hand side. (Freud 1923, 364–365.)[16]

The ego or sense of self derives from a *libidianal, narcissistic* investment in the *specular*, or visually perceived, body outline. Erotogenic orifices and the skin's surface form privileged points of intensity, special zones requiring registration in the psychical cartography that is the subject's interior. The ego is like an internal screen onto which the illuminated images of the body's outer surface are projected. For Freud, the ego is not a *photograph* of the body but a map of its degrees of erotogenicity. The ego is thus an image of the body's *significance* for the subject. Freud asserts that this is as much a function of fantasy and desire as it is of sensation. He illustrates this with the example of hypochondria, in which attitudes about one's body are not congruent with the body's physiological or "real" status. The libidinal energies investing the sexual zones auto-erotically provide the energy for this psychical inscription of the subject's corporeality.

Lacan and Merleau-Ponty, whatever their differences in other respects, take their lead from Freud and the elaborations of his work by a number of psychoanalysts and neurophysiologists who worked on body image in the 1920s and 1930s: Sir Henry Head, Henri Wallon, Paul Guillaume, Charlotte Bühler, and Paul Schilder (who all analyze the first year of psycho-physiological life). The body image or corporeal schema is not gradually acquired by the child piece by piece through an aggregation and location of its experiences or sensations. The direct transposition of sensations into perceptual images, *cenesthesia*, is considered impossible, for there is no ground or spatial field where such sensations can be, as it were, "put together" or located by the child in a continuous, coherent surface or space. There is a discontinuous leap from a body image that is largely fragmentary and dislocated to a unified, total image of the body, positioned in space and in relation to other bodies. The body image is the precondition, not the effect, of the child's acquisition of a notion of space and its bodily location within it. The *body gestalt* is the condition of self-representation and identity; it serves to distinguish the child as a distinct being separate from others, bounded by its skin.

Lacan elaborates Freud's account of primary narcissism with his postulate of *the mirror-stage*. At around its sixth month, the child develops a fascination with mirror-images, especially of itself. Lacan sees this as the "specific psychical action" that Freud left unelaborated in his account of primary narcissism. For Freud, narcissism mediates between auro-erotic sensations and a stable identity; for Lacan, the ego is an effect of the unmediated conflict between kinaesthetic sensations of fragmentation and visually coordinated experiences of unity, based on the child's identification with the image of itself in the mirror. The ego is an effect of the internalized image or *imago*. Lacan calls the body schema thus internalized through mirror representation the "imaginary anatomy," an anatomy derived from the *fantasy* of the body. The imaginary anatomy is revealed most clearly in the *phantom doubles* or doppelgängers that haunt suicidal patients, in the doubling and mirror-inversion of the subject so common in dreams, and in the symptoms of the phantom limb and hysteria. Hysterical symptoms conform to an anatomy that bears only superficial resemblance to organic lesions or neuronal connections that govern organic paralyses.[17]

In the case of the phantom limb, the subject feels a pain in the place where the real limb should have been before its amputation. This illustrates the "laws" of the body gestalt, which are distinct from organic or biological "laws":

> The phantom in the beginning usually takes the shape of the lost extremity but in the course of years, it begins to change its shape and parts of it disappear. When there is a phantom of the arm, the hand comes

nearer to the elbow, or in extreme cases, may be immediately in the place of the amputation. Also the hand may become smaller and be like the hand of the child. . . . The position of the phantom is often a rigid one and . . . it is often in the position in which the patient lost his limb. It is as if the phantom were trying to preserve the last moment in which the limb was present. (Schilder 1978, 63–64.)[18]

## 5. Sexed Bodies

Sexual differences *demand* social representation insofar as social roles and procreative functions are not governed by instincts or "nature" but are socially required, produced, and regulated. Sexually differential biological processes—menstruation, pregnancy, childbirth, lactation, and sexual maturation in women and phallic maturation, paternity, emissions, and so on in men—*must* be signified in all cultures. These differences ensure that even if the text to be written is the "same" one, the body's positive contribution to the "text" produced ensures that the inscribed message will be different. The inscribed surface is not neutral but may require different typographical procedures and result in very different kinds of meanings, depending on the type of (sexed) materiality to be inscribed.

On a psychic level, the pre-oedipal child may not experience its body as *different from the other (sex)*, but whether it exercized this comparative faculty or not, the social and psychical significance of sexual differences are signified to it long before the Oedipus complex. Its body is *always already* sexually coded in terms of the meanings each sex has for the parental generation and within a given cultural position (which includes class, race, and historical factors). The child's body means different things (for the parents and for others) according to its sex. The parental-social meaning of the child's body is not externally imposed but is actively incorporated by means of its narcissistic identifications with others and their formative role in the establishment of the ego. Although both Lacan and Merleau-Ponty suggest that sex makes a difference as to the kind of body image and subjectivity available for the subject, this difference is explained for the former, in terms of a binary structure of active and passive, presence and absence, which grants primacy to male sexuality. For the latter, the body's sex seems more an afterthought, a detail within an otherwise sexually neutral sensory and perceptual body subject. If women are to be granted a position *congruous* with but independent of men, the female body must be capable of autonomous representation. This demands a new use of language and new forms of knowledge capable of articulating femininity and women's specificity in ways quite different from prevailing alternatives. Biological sciences, for example, would have to be drastically modified so that distinctively female processes are no longer considered passive *a priori* or by definition, in opposition to the activity attributed to men's biological processes. Female characteristics are considered aberrations of the male norm. It is significant that in listing some of the defining characteristics of the two sexes earlier, I had to resort to specifying the female sex only; this is not surprising, given the presumption that men provide the ideal by which women are judged.[19] They also require transformations in social practices and exchanged relations—sexual or otherwise—between men and women, so that women's bodies are no longer treated as inert, passive, incapable, and dependent but in terms relevant to women's specificity.

If bodies are objects of power and sites of social inscription that are densely inhabited by psychic and social meaning, what effect is an understanding of the *sexually differential* forms of body going to have on our understanding of power, knowledges, and culture? What is the effect of acknowledging *autonomous differences* between kinds of human bodies on our understanding of subjectivity and the epistemological presumptions governing theory development?

## 6. Knowledge and Sexual Difference

Nietzsche regarded knowledge as an unrecognized product of bodies and as an instrument that bodies can utilize in order to act, to expand one's capacities. Just as all morality, virtue, and justice are for him passions and bodily states miscontrued as divinely ordained or intellectually formulated moral laws, he also believed knowledges, truths, and sciences to be the results of the knower's corporeality an material position.[20]

Knowledges are not purely conceptual or merely intellectual; they are not governed by a love of truth, of absolutes, or of a will to comprehension. The self-images of knowledges have always been, and remain today, bereft of an understanding of their own (textual) corporeality. Knowledge is an activity; it is a *practice* and not a contemplative reflection. It *does things*. As product or thing, it denies its historicity and asserts its indifference to questions of politics in such a way that it functions as a tool directed to any particular purposes its user chooses. Knowledges are effects of a drive for mastery, a visceral force or impulse to appropriate and subdue, a will to power:

(a) sort of malicious destruction of the valuations by which men live, an unsatisfied soul that feels the tamed state as a torture and finds voluptuous pleasure in a morbid unravelling of all bonds that tie it to such a state. (Nietzsche 1968, 461)

Knowledges are the product of a drive to live and conquer, a will to power that is also, and primarily, exhibited corporeally. They misrecognize themselves as cerebral, a product of ideas, thoughts, and concepts, forgetting or repressing their own corporeal genealogies and processes of production. They are products of bodily impulses and forces that have mistaken themselves for products of mind.

Like others I have cited, however, Nietzsche is guilty of abstracting and reducing the body to a singular masculine model. He, along with Foucault, Freud, Lacan, Merleau-Ponty, and others, assumes the corporeality of knowledge production, evaluation, and use; yet the corporeality invoked is itself not concrete or tangible, but ironically, "philosophical." Once the universal is shown to be a guise for the masculine and knowledges are shown to occupy only one pole of a (sexual) spectrum instead of its entirety, the possibility of other ways of knowing and proceeding—the possibility of feminine discourses and knowledges—is revealed. Only through developing alternative modes of representational and inscriptional etching of femal bodies can the singular domination of the universal by the masculine be made explicit. And conversely, it is only through a careful reading of phallocentric texts and paradigms that the rifts, flaws, and cracks within them can be utilized to reveal spaces where these texts exceed themselves, where they say more than they mean, opening themselves up to a feminine (re-)appropriation. Any theoretical evocation of an autonomous, positive femininity involves both an interrogation and supercession of masculinist norms and at the same time, an invention and remaking of signifying, representational, and epistemic norms.

The masculinity or maleness of knowledges remains unrecognized as such because there is no *other knowledge* with which it can be contrasted.[21] Men take on the roles of neutral knowers, thinkers, and producers of thoughts, concepts, or ideas only because they have evacuated their own specific forms of corporeality and repressed all traces of their *sexual* specificity from the knowledges they produce. In appropriating the realm of mind for themselves, men have nonetheless required a support and cover for their now-disavowed physicality. Women thus function as *the* body for men—correlative with the effacement of the sexual concreteness of their (womanly) bodies.[22]

If women are represented as the bodily counterparts to men's conceptual supremacy, women's bodies, pleasures, and desires are reduced to versions or variants of men's bodies and desires. Women are thus conceptualized as castrated, lacking, and incomplete, as if these were inherently qualities (or absences) of their (natural) bodies rather than a function of men's self-representations.

Women's reduction to the status of "neutral" bodies for men is an effect of the male sexualization of knowledges, a point-by-point projection of men's sexualized bodies onto the structures of knowledges and, conversely, of the power of inscription that knowledges, discourses, and representational systems impose on bodies to constitute them as such.

This correspondence between prevailing discursive models and forms of male sexuality and corporeality, described by Irigaray (1985) in terms of isomorphism, is not the result of a male conspiracy to create knowledges in their own image; rather, the hierarchical organization of men's bodies under the dominance of the phallus is the result of marking social meanings, values, and knowledges on the boy's body. This correspondence is a function of the systems of representation that traverse and constitue both men's bodies as such and the criteria for the evaluation of knowledges. It is needless to add here that women's bodies are also represented and inscribed by the same systems that regulate men's bodies. Instead of seeing man as the active creator of discursive and epistemic values, the male body must be seen as an inscribed product of the intervention of meanings into the way men live their bodies. It is not really a question of *blaming men* but of understanding that certain perspectives are particular to their social and corporeal interests. These consequently may not be relevant to women except insofar as they are oppressively imposed on them. Many features of contemporary knowledges—knowledges based on the presumption of a singular reality, pre-existent representational categories, and an unambiguous terminology able to be produced and utilized by a singular, rational, and unified knowing subject who is unhampered by "personal" concerns—can be linked to man's *disembodiment*, his detachment from his manliness in producing knowledge or truth.

The (sexual) position(s) of a text cannot be identified with the position(s) occupied by the author. Nor can it be identified directly with the contents of a text—with what it says.[23] Rather, it is a result of the position(s) a text occupies within a history of other texts and the degrees of adherence it exhibits to that position. It is an effect of the ways in which texts support or challenge prevailing and historically formative paradigms occupied by knowledges. This position is sexually coded insofar as access to positions of enunciation are sexually regulated and theoretical paradigms and values serve sexually specific interests.

## 7. Feminism and the Crisis

Feminism has a complex relation to this crisis in contemporary knowledges. Its unprecedented development over the last twenty years is both a product of and a response to the dilemmas such a crisis poses for current knowledges. Feminist theory is implicated in this crisis in sometimes unrecognized ways. I will attempt to outline some of the major factors involved in this complex interaction.

For the purposes of my argument here, it may be convenient to divide feminist theory into two very broad categories. The first is committed to the introduction, analysis, and affirmation of "women," of "the feminine" as viable objects of knowledge. It aims to include women in those domains where they have been hitherto absent. It aspires to an ideal of a knowledge adequate to the analysis or representation of women and their interests and exhibits varying degrees of critical distance from the male mainstream. What distinguishes this group from the second are its interests in focusing on woman or femininity as *knowable objects*. This must be distinguished from a second type of feminist theory, concerned with articulating knowledges that take woman as the *subject* of knowledges.

The first category of feminism is committed to the basic precepts and indeed implicit values governing mainstream knowledges and disciplines (or interdisciplines). To somewhat crudely characterize their views, their major contention with mainstream knowledges lies in the neglect or active exclusion of issues related to women and the feminine. This means that their works are largely confined to rewriting and supplementing existing knowledges: adding and suitably altering, say, marxism, psychoanalysis, history, or literary theory where these leave out the contributions of women. This, of course, is no easy task, for it soon becomes clear that this does not merely involve adding a neglected "object" to knowledges that are already more or less methodologically complete, merely rectifying an oversight. It involves a more thorough questioning of the theoretical frameworks and intellectual ideals governing knowledges. It is simply not possible to supplement knowledges by adding women to an otherwise neutral or objective knowledge: knowledges have not just "forgotten" women. Their amnesia is strategic and serves to ensure the patriarchal foundations of knowledges. This was an early, memorable lesson in feminist scholarship: the fundamentally patriarchal or phallocentric, rather than neutral, orientation of knowledges. Many recognized that if knowledges were to encompass women and femininity without reduction to male interests, they must be submitted to a thorough and critical overhaul. Their patriarchal investments needed to be understood and challenged if they were to adequately *know woman*.

Feminist attempts to supplement existing knowledges were nevertheless extremely fertile in feminist terms, particularly during the 1970s. Mitchell's work on "reading" psychoanalysis; the project of socialist or marxist feminists to utilize marxist categories of economic production and historical materialist analysis of class relations; and the work of women within academic disciplines such as history, in which both "forgotten women" and women's unrecognized contributions to historical events were being treated serve as some examples of this remarkable productivity.

Yet many such projects are implicated in the challenge posed by the crisis of reason. The degree of commitment of mainstream knowledges to reason is an index of the extent to which feminist contributions to knowledges are themselves put into crisis. Where feminist theory questions mainstream knowledges either to augment them; to replace them with competing, feminist knowledges; or to dispense with them altogether, reverting to an anti-theoretical, anti-intellectual reliance on "experience" or "intuition," it remains in an unresolved relation to this crisis. In other words, where feminism remains committed to the project of *knowing women*, of making women objects of knowledge, *without in turn submitting the position of knower or subject of knowledge to a reorganization*, it remains as problematic as the knowledges it attempts to supplement or replace. A structural reorganization of positions of knowing, their effects on the kinds of object known, *and* our pregiven ways of knowing them is necessary for recognition of the implications and effects of the crisis of reason. If reason is an effect not of reason itself but of something unreasonable (i.e., power), then adhering to even an altered, modified reason is no solution. Nor is the abandonment of knowledges and the reversion to experience or (women's) common sense. These are the two poles around which this questioned reason oscillates—an unbridled "irrationalism" that verges on a celebration of ignorance and entrapment in what is (sociopolitically) *given* and a project of ever-improving progress towards perfection, both of which are equally unacceptable.

A second broad approach within feminist theory grew out of this disillusionment, the recognition that knowledges cannot be neutral or objective. But they can be distinguished from this first category in several ways:

1. They attempt to create new subject positions of knowing as well as the object known.
2. They seem more prepared to reject existing models of knowing without attempting a "correction" or "supplementation".
3. They subject the methodological and criteriological commit-

ments of knowledges to scrutiny and reject their claims to completion, universality, and in some cases, even limited relevance. Yet they do not scorn theory production nor shirk from dealing with patriarchal or phallocentric knowledges.

Instead of taking women and the feminine as the object of their analyses, feminists within this second category take patriarchal knowledges as their objects and starting point. What distinguishes their work from the mire of competing male theories, each of which attempts a critique of the prevailing norm, is that these feminists have had to develop altogether *different* forms and methods of knowing and positions of epistemological enunciation, which are marked as *sexually* different from male paradigms.

Arguably the most developed—and neglected—example of this second category is Luce Irigaray. Although I cannot do justice to the richly complex work she has written regarding questions of epistemology in the space I have left, nonetheless I would like to conclude with a broad outline of those elements of her work that seem to me to accommodate the problems posed by the crisis of reason. She champions one among many possible strategies that feminists may develop and utilize in rethinking knowledges as the products of sexually specific bodies.

1. Irigaray takes as her critical object of investigation neither "Woman" nor women. Instead, she examines key examples of phallocentric knowledges—particularly psychoanalysis and the history of idealist philosophy (from Plato through Descartes, Kant, and Rousseau to Levinas). Yet she does not simply analyze these objects neutrally or indifferently. Her readings of philosophical and psychoanalytic texts are designed to demonstrate not simply male " bias" or "domination" at the level of theory—such terms imply the possibility of a corrected, "purified," unbiased knowledge—but the deeper implications of their *phallocentrism*—their representations of women and femininity in terms that are chosen by and affirm masculinity. Phallocentrism, however, is not limited to men's representations of women but must also include the elision of any *maleness* or masculinity in the perspectives and enunciative positions constitutive of knowledges, an isoporphism of theory with male (sociohistorical) bodies.

2. She spells out how the supposedly neutral, sexually *indifferent* or universal status of knowledges or truths hides the specifically masculine interests that produce them. If men have in part rationalized their domination of the production of knowledges by claiming their interests are universal or sexually neutral, this is only because they

rely upon a culturally inscribed correlation of men with the category of mind and of women with the category of body. Men are able to dominate knowedge paradigms because women take on the function of representing the *body*, the *irrational*, the *natural*, or other episte-mologically devalued binary terms. By positioning women as *the* body, they can project themselves and their products as *disembodied*, pure, and uncontaminated. Irigaray's project consists in part in returning the male body to its products.

3. This implies that knowledges must be seen as *perspectival*, par-tial, limited, and contestable products, as the results of historically specific political, sexual, and epistemological imperatives. Prevailing knowledges, in being recognized as male and as representing men's perspectives, are not thereby rendered redundant or useless (though this may be the effect on some) but are instead limited to a narrower, more constricted position: as partial views, commensurable or in-commensurable with other perspectives and possible perspectives. This challenges the dominant positions accorded to masculine or phal-locentric knowledges and enables women to learn from them and from their various crises in developing different positions.

4. Irigaray's work thus remains indifferent to such traditional val-ues as "truth" and "falsity" where these are conceived as correspon-dence between propositions and reality), Aristotelian logic (the logic of the syllogism), and accounts of reason based upon them. This does not mean her work could be described as "irrational," "illogical," or "false." On the contrary, her work is quite logical, rational, and true in terms of quite *different criteria*, perspectives, and values than those dominant now. She both combats and constructs, strategically ques-tioning phallocentric knowledges without trying to replace them with more inclusive or more neutral truths. Instead, she attempts to reveal a *politics* of truth, logic, and reason.

5. To be more explicit, she does not present a more encompassing knowledge but rather a *less* encompassing knowledge, one committed to the struggles in and around specific texts and debates, not a new eternal truth or answer. In other words, her texts are openly acknowl-edged as historical and contextual, of strategic value in particular times and places, but not necessarily useful or valid in all contexts. Knowledges, however, do not simply *reflect* the social and historical contexts out of which they were developed; rather, they help to actively inscribe or engender the meaning of the social. The challenge to pre-vailing norms of knowledge is not thus simply a narrowly institution-alized, "ivory tower" critique of theories. It is an attempt to stretch, rupture, and proliferate new meanings and modes of representation such that women may adequately represent themselves and the world.

6. She works strategically from a borderline or marginal position that is strategically both within and beyond the bounds of existing theory. Only from such a tenuous and ambiguous marginal position can she both challenge patriarchal texts at their most fundamental levels and, at the same time, prevent any co-option and integration that patriarchal systems use to transform serious threats to their operations. She aims to subvert the ready-made boundaries between knowledges—not by ignoring them or pretending they do not operate but by strategically harnessing precisely the most tension-ridden and contrary disciplines so that the presuppositions of each are challenged. Positions within, say, the philosophy of science and epistemology are dramatically counterpointed by her use of so-called poetic language; high- and low-profile knowledges, serious and pleasurable concerns are all mingled together in an occasionally scandalous drawing out of the conditions of existence of discourses.

Irigaray has demonstrated that there is a plurality of possible techniques, procedures, and methods within knowledges. She shows that there are always *other ways* of proceeding, other perspectives to be occupied and explored, than those contained within our history. The fact that a single contested paradigm (or a limited number thereof) governs current forms of knowledge demonstrates the role that power, rather than reason, has played in developing knowledges. This power, although not as clearly visible as other forms of patriarchal coercion, is nonetheless integral to women's containment within definitions constituted by and for men. Unlike phallocentric and patriarchal models, her work is openly proclaimed as partial, partisan, and motivated. It is a political intervention into a politically unacknowledged field of intellectual warfare. Her tactics are hit-and-run: strategic forays into the "enemies' camp," the camp defined by male theory; skirmishes involving the use of the enemies' own weapons against them seems to be her goal. For her, the crisis of reason does not represent an impasse but rather a path for women to explore and judge for themselves. Her work is a facing up to the implications of this crisis— to know (as woman, as other) the knower (as man has been and woman is now becoming). Her work poses the question of the partiality, that is, the sexualization of all knowledges. It entails an acknowledgment of the sexually particular positions from which knowledges emanate and by which they are interpreted and used.

**Notes**

1. William Shakespeare, *The Comedy of Errors*, ed. Harry Levin (New York: New American Library, 1965), III.1.v. 13–14 (Dromio the slave to Antipholus his master).

2. This is precisely Foucault's claim in "The Discourse on Language": that the division of knowledge into disciplines is one of the internal modes of regulation and supervision that power exerts over discourses.

3. Here I do not want to affirm an interdisciplinary approach, considered in terms of prevailing models of inter- or cross-disciplinary research, which broaden the bases of knowledges without necessarily questioning their founding theoretical commitments. My point is rather that the ways in which disciplines classify propositions either as "their own" or as "outside" their disciplinary boundaries is a *political* and not simply an *intellectual* matter.

4. See Lacan, *The Four Fundamental Concepts of Psychoanalysis* (1977).

5. I use the masculine pronoun here on purpose, for the only socially validated and acknowledged knower has historically been male. This article addresses precisely the question of what role the sex or sexed body of the knower might have on the kinds of knowledge he *or* she produces.

6. This is not to advocate its inverse—a romantic subjectivism or relativism whereby all things are judged according to what individuals think or feel about them. Both objectivism and subjectivism are equally problematic; neither provides a solution to the status of the knower in the production of knowledge.

7. See my paper, "A Note on Essentialiam and Difference" (1990).

8. Among the relatively few feminists to actively rethink the body outside the terms of the mind–body split or beyond the representations of rationalism or empiricism are Luce Irigaray (as I will later discuss), Rosi Braidotti (1991), Iris Marion Young (1990), Judith Butler (1989), Vicki Kirby (1987, 1991), and Moira Gatens (1988, 1991). In refusing to accept the body as simply an object and seeing it as constitutive of subjectivity, these and other feminists seem to have moved beyond the impasse in which feminists themselves denigrated the body.

9. In the second volume of his history of sexuality, *The Uses of Pleasure* (1985), Foucault seems to recognize more sharply than in his earlier works that the regimentation and self-understanding of sexual pleasures is *sexually specific*, such that generalizing from one sex to the other is not clearly possible. Although he acknowledges this sexual specificity, nevertheless he leaves unexplained what women's "use of pleasure" must have been in the classical period. His rationale is rather feeble; it relies on a claim that the regulation of female sexuality was only elaborated at a much later date:

Later, in European culture, girls or married women . . . were to become themes of special concern; a new art of courting them, a literature that was basically romantic in form, an exacting morality that was attentive to the integrity of their bodies and the solidity of their matrimonial commitment—all this would draw curiosity and desire around them. . . . It seems clear, on the other hand, that in classical Greece the problematization was more active in regard to boys. . . . (p. 213)

10. See Alphonso Lingis, "Savages," in *Excesses. Eros and Culture* (1984).

11. It is for this reason that there is a disproportionate use of familiar, domestic objects and even loved ones in the ritualized operations of political torture. In surveying global forms of political interrogation and torture, Elaine Scarry makes this observation:

. . . the contents of the room (in which torture occurs), its furnishings, are converted into weapons: the most common instance is the bathtub that figures so prominently in numerous countries. . . . Made to participate in the annihilation of the prisoners, made to demonstrate that everything is a weapon, the objects themselves, and with them, the facts of civilisation are annihilated: there is no wall, no window, no door, no bathtub, no refrigerator, no chair, no bed. (Scarry 1985, 40–41)

12. There has, of course, been considerable feminist literature on this notion. See, for example, the special issue of *Hypatia* on "Feminism and the Body" (vol. 6, no. 2, 1991); and also Donna Haraway, "Manifesto for Cyborgs" (1985).

13. The inscription of the body's insides and outsides is an effect of historically and politically specific signifying practices and representational systems that penetrate it using a 'social tattooing' system. Codes mark bodies and trace them in particular ways, constituting the body as a living, acting, and producing subject. In turn, bodies leave their trace in laws and codes. A history of bodies is yet to be written, but it would involve looking at the mutual relations between bodily inscription and lived experience.

14. There has of course been considerable feminist literature on the Foucauldian metaphorics of body writing. See, in particular, Probyn and McNay in *Hypatia* (1991); and Diamond and Quinby (1988).

15. See Freud, "On Narcissism: An Introduction" (1914).

16. This confirms a point Freud made earlier, in "On Narcissism":

We can decide to regard erotogenicity as a general characteristic of all organs and may then speak of an increase of decrease of it in a particular part of the body. For every such change in the erotogenicity of libidinal zones there might be a parallel change of libidinal cathexis in the ego. (p. 77)

17. Cf.:

I would emphasize that the imaginary anatomy referred to here varies with the ideas (clear or confused) about bodily functions which are prevalent in a given culture. It all happens as if the body-image had an autonomous existence of its own, and by autonomous, I mean here autonomous from objective structure. (Lacan 1953, 13)

18. In summary, the body image can be seen as an effect of the following:

a. the libidinal cathexes that circulate through the child's body and concentrate particularly in the erotogenic zones (mouth, anus, eyes, ears, and genitals) and at the point of greatest receptivity to external, extroceptive relations—the hands (especially the fingers), the feet, the face, and the surface of the skin

b. the body schema's function with respect to organic changes and processes:

Every change in the organic function is liable to bring forth with it psychic mechanisms which are akin to this organic function. (Schilder 1978, 33)

(The amputation of limbs, lesions, or organic disorders creates a "somatic compliance" with psychic representational functions, enabling infantile afflictions to take on hysterical characteristics or a range of other sorts of meaning by "deferred action" or retrospective.)

c. the corporeal schema as an effect of the interaction with the corporeal schemas of others, particularly the nurturer in the gestural treatment the child receives from the other

d. the body image as a function of the social and idiosyncratic meanings that our bodies and organs have for others and ourselves within a determinate social context

19. Cf. Irigaray, "Is the Subject of Science Sexed?" (1985b).

20. Through the long succession of millenia, man has not known himself physiologically: he does not know himself even today. To know, e.g., that one has a nervous system (—but no "soul"—) is still the privilege of the best informed. But man is not content not to know this is not the case. One must be very humane to say "I don't know that," to afford ignorance. (Nietzsche 1968, 229)

21. "The problem is that of a possible alterity in masculine discourse. . . ." (Irigaray 1985a, 140).

22. In the system of production that we know, including sexual production, men have distanced themselves from their bodies. They have used their sex, their language, their technique, in order to go further and further in the construction of a world which is more and more distant from their relation to the corporeal. But they are corporeal. It is therefore necessary for them to reassure themselves that some woman is indeed the guardian of their body for them. (1981)

23. I have tried to address the relations between textuality and sexed incarnation more directly in a forthcoming paper, "Sexual Signatures: Feminism and the Death of the Author", presented to the conference on "Feminism: An International Debate" held in Glasgow, July 1991, to be published in *Sexual Signatures*, eds. Sandra Kemp and Judith Squires, Routledge.

# References


Braidotti, R. 1991. *Patterns of Dissonance*. Cambridge: Polity Press.

Butler, J. 1990. *Gender Trouble. Feminism and the Subversion of Identity*, New York: Routledge.

Bordo, S. 1989. "The Body and the Reproduction of Femininity: A Feminist Appropriation of Foucault." In *Gender/Body/Knowledge. Feminist Constructions of Being and Knowing*. Edited by A.M. Jagger and S. Bordo. New Brunswick and London: Rutgers University Press.

———. 1988. "Anorexia Nervosa: Psychopathology as the Crystallization of Culture." In *Feminism and Foucault: Reflections on Resistance*. Edited by I. Diamond and L. Quinby. New York: Methuen.

I. Diamond and L. Quinby, eds. 1988. *Feminism and Foucault: Reflections on Resistance*. New York: Methuen.

Foucault, M. 1972. "The Discourse on Language." In *The Archaelogy of Knowledge*. Translated by A.M. Sheridan Smith. New York: Harper Colophon.

———. 1980. *The History of Sexuality, Volume 1: An Introduction*. Translated by R. Hurley. New York: Vintage/Random House.

———. 1985. *The Use of Pleasure, Volume 2 of the History of Sexuality*. Translated by R. Hurley. New York: Pantheon.

———. 1986. *The Care of the Self, Volume 3 of The History of Sexuality*. Translated by R. Hurley. New York: Pantheon.

Freud, S. 1914. "On Narcissism. An Introduction." Translated by J. Strachey. *Penguin Edition of the Complete Psychological Works*, Vol. 11, Harmondsworth: Penguin.

———. 1923. "The Ego and the Id." Translated by J. Strachey. *Penguin Edition of the Complete Psychological Works*, Vol. 11, Harmondsworth: Penguin.

Gatens, M. 1991. "A Critique of the Sex/Gender Distinction." In *A Reader in Feminist Knowledges*. Edited by S. Gunew. New York and London: Routledge.

———. 1988. "Towards a Feminist Philosophy of the Body." In *Crossing Boundaries. Feminism and the Critique of Knowledges*. Edited by B. Caine, E. Grosz, and M. de Lepervanche. Sydney: Allen and Unwin.

Grosz, E. 1989. *Sexual Subversions: Three French Feminists*. Sydney: Allen and Unwin.

———. 1990. "A Note on Essentialism and Difference." In *Feminist Knowledge: Critique and Construct*. Edited by S. Gunew. London and New York: Routledge.

———. 1993. "Sexual Signatures: Feminism and the Death of the Author."

In *Sexual Signatures.* Edited by S. Kemp and J. Squires. London and New York: Routledge.

Haraway, D. 1985. "A Manifesto for Cyborgs." *Socialist Review* 15, 2.

———. 1988. "Situated Knowledges." *Feminist Studies* 3.

Husserl, E. 1970. *The Crisis of European Sciences and Transcendental Phenomenology.* Translated by D. Carr. Evanston: Northwestern University Press.

Irigaray, L. 1981. *Le corps-à-corp avec la mére.* Montréal: Les editions de la Pleine Lune.

———. 1985a. *This Sex Which Is Not One.* Translated by C. Porter. Ithaca: Cornell University Press.

———. 1985b. "Is the Subject of Science Sexed?" *Cultural Critique* 1.

Kirby, V. 1987. "On the Cutting Edge: Feminism and Clitoridectomy." *Australian Feminist Studies* 5.

———. 1991. *"Corpus Delicti*: The Body at the Scene of Writing." In *Cartographies. Postsructuralism and the Mapping of Bodies and Spaces.* Edited by R. Diprose and R. Ferrell. Sydney: Allen & Unwin.

Lacan, J. 1953. "Some Reflections on the Ego." *International Journal of Psychoanalysis* 34.

———. 1977. *The Four Fundamental Concepts of Psychoanalysis.* Translated by A. Sheridan. London: Tavistock.

Lingis, A. 1984. *Excesses: Eros and Culture.* New York: State University of New York Press.

McNay, L. 1991 "The Foucauldian Body and the Exclusion of Experience." *Hypatia* 6, 2 (1991).

Morgan, K. 1991. "Women and the Knife: Cosmetic Surgery and the Colonization of Women's Bodies." *Hypatia,* 6, 2 (1991).

Nietzsche, F. 1969. *On the Genealogy of Morals.* Translated by W. Kaufman and R.J. Hollingdale. New York: Vintage Books.

———. 1968. *The Will to Power.* Translated by W. Kaufman. New York: Vintage Books.

Probyn, E. 1991. "This Body Which Is Not One: Technologizing an Embodied Self." *Hypatia* 6, 2 (1991).

Scarry, E. 1985. *The Body in Pain: The Making and Unmaking of the World.* Oxford: Oxford University Press.

Schilder, P. 1978. *The Image and Appearance of the Human Body: Studies in the Constructive Energies of the Psyche.* New York: International Universities Press.

Whitford, M. 1991. *Luce Irgaray: Philosophy in the Feminine.* London and New York: Routledge.

Young, I.M. 1990. *Throwing Like a Girl and Other Essays in Feminist Philosophy and Social Theory.* Bloomingtom: Indiana University Press.

# 9

# Are "Old Wives' Tales" Justified?

*Vrinda Dalmiya and Linda Alcoff*

## Introduction

Traditional women's beliefs—about childbearing and rearing, herbal medicines, the secrets of good cooking, and such[1]—are generally characterized as "old wives' tales." These "tales" may be interwoven into the very fabric of our daily lives and may even enjoy a certain amount of respect and deference as a useful secret-sharing among women. But nevertheless, it remains the case that they are considered to be *mere tales* or unscientific hearsay and fail to get accorded the honorific status of *knowledge*.

Contemporary epistemological theories have validated this practice of what might be called "epistemic discrimination" by developing definitions of knowledge and stipulating requirements for justification that traditional women's beliefs have generally not met and, in fact, cannot meet. Cognitively successful agents are supposed to have the "right to be sure."[2] But the conditions required for earning this right virtually entail that our "old wives" are banished to the epistemological fringes. In this paper we shall argue that a more egalitarian epistemology is not only possible but also desirable on *purely epistemic grounds*. So, even though the investigation of why more men's voices (rather than women's) have the "right to be sure" seems more appropriate to a sociological study than to a philosophical one, we will show here that the delegitimation of traditional women's knowledge is not only politically disturbing but also epistemologically specious.

Before exploring the roots of this epistemic discrimination, it will be helpful to look at an episode called "The Devoted Wife" from the Indian epic *The Mahābhārata*.[3] Yudhiṣṭhira, one of the principal players in the epic, has a request:

217

Sir, I wish to hear you tell of the greatness of women and the subtleties of the Law. . . . Pray, my lord, tell of the greatness of devoted wives who continuously think of their husbands as gods, while restraining their senses and controlling their minds. This appears to me quite difficult my lord, a woman's (service[4]) to her father, mother and husband. I do not see anything harder than the terrible Law[5] of the woman. . . . What is more marvelous than to be born a woman who is devoted to her husband, speaks the truth, and carries a child for ten months in the womb?[6]

In response, Yudhiṣṭhira is told the following story. The sage Kauśika was once sitting under a tree, deep in the study of the Vedas, when a heron flying above him defecated on his head. Angered by this rude interruption, the brahmin[7] unleashed his supernatural powers and caused the unsuspecting bird to drop dead from the sky. However, realizing the folly of his vengeance almost immediately, Kauśika was overcome with disgust at the fact that all of his scholarship had proved so utterly ineffective in preventing his overreaction, if not outright sinning. Convinced that he had to start all over again in his study of the Laws of Righteousness, the sage set out on a journey of penance. One day, with begging bowl in hand, he found himself at the doorstep of a "devoted wife." This housewife, preoccupied as she was with her domestic chores, kept her honored guest waiting while she tended to the needs of her husband. Once again enraged by such disrespectful behavior, Kauśika stormed:

What is the meaning of this? You told me to wait, fair woman, and delayed me without dismissing me! . . . You make your husband superior! While living by the householder's Law[8] you belittled the Brahmin![9]

The reprimanded woman was contrite but, disagreeing with Kausika, she responded thus:

I do not belittle the brahmins, they are equal to Gods. . . . Surely I have heard of the plentiful powers of the scholars of the Brahman[10]: great is the wrath of those great-spirited beings, and so is their favor, brahmin. Now do excuse me for this transgression, blameless sage. The Law that I must obey one husband is pleasing to me. Among all the deities my husband is my paramount God. I must obey my Law by him without discrimination, best of brahmins. Just look at the result of my [service][11] to him: through it I know that you irately burned a female heron; but ire, good brahmin, is the enemy that lives in a man's body, and the Gods know him for a brahmin who abandons both ire and folly.

She ended her speech with the following:

Many a time the Law has been seen as subtle, great brahmin, and you too are aware of the Law devoted to study, and pious; yet, sir, I do not think you know the Law really. A hunter who lives in Mithila, one obedient to his father and mother, true-spoken, in command of his senses, shall explain the Laws to you. Good luck to thee, go there, if you please, best of brahmins. If I have talked too much, please forgive it all, blameless sir, for women are inviolate to all folk who know of the Law.[12]

The episode concludes with Kauśika acknowledging the truth of the housewife's words. Trusting her, he goes in search of the hunter from whom he ultimately learns the Law in the next episode called "The Colloquy of the Brahmin and the Hunter."

Now, we are not concerned with the moral that *The Mahābhārata* itself draws from this story. Certainly the description given of the woman—"virtuous of conduct, pure, clever, and concerned with the well-being of the family, she always acted in the husband's interest. She was always in command of her senses, and obedient to the Gods, guests, dependents, and parents-in-law"[13]—does not wave any feminist flags! Yet what is evident is that an epistemological hierarchy has been overturned in the story. Yudhiṣṭhira's initial request is interesting in itself. He, a man, is recognizing that the "Law" set down for women seems unnaturally constrictive, and the fact that women can abide by such "terrible" constraints and perform certain duties suggests to him a "greatness" in womankind. The story goes on to explain and account for this superiority in what seem to be clearly *epistemological* terms. Leaving the significance of the hunter aside for the moment (but to which we shall return), it is evident that Kauśika, the master of theoretical knowledge, has *learned the truth* from an ordinary and nameless housewife. His new *guru* is no scholar in any traditional sense but rather spends her time in mundane domestic chores; she is presented in the story as simply a "good wife" performing the duties of her station. Yet she is quite confident in telling the sage, "*I do not think you know the Law really.*" And it also becomes clear during their conversation that the woman has some supernatural powers of her own that give her *access to facts*, for she has knowledge of Kauśika's debacle with the bird: "Just look at the result of my [service] to him: *through it* I know that you irately burned a female heron," (our emphasis), she says. Thus in this episode the housewife, *because and in virtue of her role as housewife*, is both a superior and an extraordinary epistemic agent. The theoretician Kauśika is inferior to her and must ultimately accept her epistemic authority "because of her convincing mention of the heron, and her Law-like and virtuous discourse."[14]

In this tale, then, we discern an alternative to the epistemological paradigm we began with—we see here a model that does not delegitimate the skills required of an ordinary housewife or what we have termed "traditional women's knowledge" but accords the agent of such skills a higher epistemological status. The contrast between these two paradigms causes us to pose the following two questions: (1) What *epistemological* reason (if any) is there for the undermining of women's knowledge in Anglo-American epistemology? (2) What consequences for epistemology would emerge if we were to take seriously the suggestion of the *Mahābhārata* story given above, that a housewife *qua* housewife can be a genuine, if not a superior, epistemic agent? The answer to the first question will result in a philosophical diagnosis of what we will call "epistemic discrimination," which is meant to imply a discriminatory effect rather than an intention. An answer to the second question will require us to sketch the contours of a utopian epistemology in which no such discrimination exists. We turn to these issues in the next section beginning with an analysis of the cause of epistemic discrimination.

**I.**

Discussions of knowledge within professional philosophy have generally focussed on an analysis of the schema "*S* knows that *p*"—where *S* stands for an individual cogniser and *p* stands for a proposition. The favored examples of *p* that we discuss in epistemology seminars include "Jones owns a Ford," "That is my friend David approaching from a distance," "That is a barn in the field," "I am not a brain in a vat," "There exist other minds in the world besides my own," and the like. Now there are many things that might be said about the unexamined assumptions involved in this approach to epistemology that have worked to exclude women and present solitary or sometimes collective male activities as the paradigm of knowing. Lorraine Code, for example, has explored the strategies by which the *S* in "*S* knows that *p*" has been constructed as universal and homogeneous through an undertheorized representation of the epistemic subjective norm.[15]

The point we wish to focus on in our critique, however, is the way in which the schema "*S* knows that *p*" is assumed to be adequate for all possible knowledge and as a consequence of this assumption, all knowing becomes *propositional*. The epistemic invalidation of old wives' tales has been caused, in part, by the fact that modern epistemology has forgotten the lesson from Aristotle that knowledge can come in two forms: propositional and practical. Since Descartes, epistemology has restricted its principal definiendum to propositional knowledge. This nearly exclusive focus on propositional knowledge has had a significant impact on the types of epistemologies developed, the questions taken to be central to the enterprise, and the range of possible answers to such questions that are considered plausible. Our claim here is that this almost exclusive preference for "knowing that" lies at the root of epistemic discrimination, which is informed by something like the following argument:

1. All cases of knowing can be formulated in terms of the schema "*S* knows that *p*".
2. Traditional women's knowledge, however, cannot be so represented.
3 Therefore, traditional women's knowledge is not, in fact, *knowledge*.

It is premise 1 that we shall challenge. Our case rests on claiming that there are *kinds* of genuine knowing that cannot be forced into the schema "*S* knows that *p*." Before we develop this argument, however, we need to look at premise 2 and see how and why it is the case that traditional women's knowledge cannot be adequately represented in the propositional form suggested by the prevalent schema.

Consider Sheba's knowledge of how to bake a successful tortilla or soothe an upset newborn. How many of us have followed a recipe from a cookbook without missing a single instruction, only to have the dish fail anyway? Similarly, reading "how-to" manuals on parenting infants may help in regard to some specific tasks, but there are many sorts of knowledge one learns only through observing another person, participating in an activity with another, or simply trying it out ourselves alone. Some of what we acquire in the process can be expressed in propositional form (e.g., "Newborns often like to be rocked gently to mimic the feeling of the womb"), but the manner in which a newborn needs and prefers to be held can only be learned fully through observation and practice. And the ability to tell from an infant's manner of crying and behavior just what she or he needs is an ability that cannot be taught or expressed in a manual. Here, old wives, like Ryle's wit, "when challenged to cite the maxims, or canons, by which (s)he constructs and appreciates jokes, is unable to answer. (S)he knows how to make good jokes and how to detect bad ones, but (s)he cannot tell us or (her)himself any recipes for them."[16] Sheba knows that *p* is then neither a sufficient nor a necessary condition for her possessing the knowledge that she does.

The history of midwifery in the Western world is particularly instructive here. In Europe and the USA before the nineteenth century, midwives were most often, literally, older wives past their own childbearing years who were widely respected members of the community because of their knowledge and skill in helping women with pregnancy, childbirth, and lactation.[17] The term "old wives' tales" thus began as a reference to the lore of the midwife. Midwives could turn the baby in the womb to avoid a breech presentation, they could perform abortions, and they provided a wealth of practical guidance on everything from inducing conception to curing breast infections. Midwives also had knowledge of herbal remedies that could hasten a protracted labor, reduce the pain of childbirth, and inhibit the chances of miscarriage; many of these herbal concoctions are still used today in modern pharmacology.[18] Up until the nineteenth century and even into the beginning of the twentieth, midwives were recognized by many doctors to be just as successful—or more so—in their occupation as were trained physicians.[19] Certainly among women, midwives had "the right to be sure" in matters concerning childbirth.

Midwives usually had a wealth of experience, including direct personal experience of childbirth. Their training consisted in sharing information and stories of difficult births among themselves and being present at births from an early age. A few midwives in urban areas conducted training classes. Most midwives, like most women, were illiterate.

Although there were many male physicians who were sensitive and conscientious (and certainly there were some poorly skilled and uncaring midwives), a comparison of general methods between the groups reveals some significant differences. Midwives had a different orientation to their work than professionally trained obstetricians, then or now, do. Midwives attended women throughout the entirety of their labor, rather than only for the delivery. They provided psychological as well as physical support, and they were much less prone to invasive and interventionist techniques.[20] Male physicians, by contrast, sometimes practiced such radical techniques as squeezing and trampling on the abdomen to force the baby's descent in a difficult birth or hanging the woman from a tree.[21] It was male physicians who invented caesarean sections, the use of forceps, and the infamous "twilight sleep," which rendered the woman semiconscious, unable to remember the experience afterward, and completely inactive and vulnerable to the doctor's decisions. And it was male physicians who introduced the lithotomy: the manner of giving birth from a supine position. Midwives, by contrast, often carried an obstetrical stool with them so that women could give birth while sitting up, thus making use of women's physiology and increasing the possibility of women's active control over the process.

In Europe, when physicians were finally able to wrest obstetrics from the monopoly of the midwife, the result was an epidemic of death for the mothers. The cause was puerperal, or "childbed," fever, which afflicted women by the thousands across European cities in the nineteenth century. This fever was produced by the unclean hands of the birth attendant, and although midwives at the time were just as ignorant as physicians about the bacterial sources of disease, they had the advantage over physicians in that they saw no other patients and thus were unlikely to carry germs from dying patients to the absorptive tissues of the open womb. But the insistence by physicians at the time that it was the midwife who was "ignorant and dirty" and that women would be safest in their hands at the public hospitals resulted in their unwittingly causing the death of generations of women.

The point of this brief history is to suggest that an advantage in instrumental success cannot account for the rise of the male obstetrician and the demise of the midwife. Many causal elements were at play here, most obviously having to do with the consolidation of a medical institution aligned with the male-dominated endeavors of science and technology. And this was not simply a triumph of men over women; lower-class males who had practical knowledge were also discredited in this process (e.g., apothecaries and barber surgeons). It was a triumph of propositional knowledge over practical knowledge.

One of the common reasons given to justify this turnover to obstetricians was the charge that midwives were *ignorant* and *uneducated* and, having learnt their vocation through "hearsay," were *unreliable*. These charges were self-fulfilling, since women were systematically excluded from entering universities, medical schools, and training clinics as these began to arise. Even today, in a typical contemporary textbook for midwives, the historical transformation of midwives is characterized as a progression "from the unqualified birth attendants of previous centuries to the highly trained professional of the 1980s."[22] And in typical contemporary historical accounts, midwives of the past are said to have been "ignorant and superstitious."[23]

But in what sense could midwives be regarded as ignorant and unqualified and their claimed knowledge labeled "superstition"? Their skill was based on a combination of direct empirical sources, practice, experience, and a reliance on the body of beliefs accumulated by the acknowledged community of experts on childbirth (that is, other midwives)—not unlike the knowledge of modern scientists. Also, as we have seen, their practices enjoyed a high rate of instrumental success and corroboration. So it is not at all obvious why they could be so easily discredited. However, despite the similarities between the way in which midwife knowledge and scientific knowledge was gathered, there remained one striking difference: midwife knowledge was rarely, if ever, codified or written down. Although there were a few manuals for midwives (some of them written by men on the basis of their interviews with midwives), most midwives were illiterate and could not use such manuals even if they were available. Their knowledge remained preliterate: it was *oral, practical,* and *experiential.* Where the "discoveries" of modern science and medicine became recognized as such via their documentation, the developments and successes of midwives were rarely rendered in a written form. Although women in nearly all cultures were the traditional healers, women became automatically disqualified from the profession when medicine was formalized and training institutions were developed, which primarily consisted of reading classical texts.[24] (This process of disqualification is currently underway in much of the "nonindustrialized" world.) The historians and reporters of knowledge were men who were generally either ignorant of the knowledge among women (which was often kept secret from men for reasons of modesty) or were disdainful of it or both.

Thus, the claim that midwives were unqualified resulted from the fact of their *illiteracy.* And male physicians who received medical training with no clinical component were authorized as more expert than the midwives who had abundant lay experience.[25] The "ignorance" of midwives consisted in the fact that they did not receive their knowledge in these sanctioned training centers. Their knowledge was mere "hearsay" because it was not rendered in written linguistic form. It eventually came to be seen as not knowledge at all but merely a set of hunches and tales circulated among gullible and prerational "old wives." The differences in literacy between midwives and physicians, then, resulted in two dissimilarities in their belief systems: (1) Midwife knowledge was generally unrecorded, undocumented, and thus unauthorized according to the terms of authorization increasingly in use in the emerging medical establishment: publication in written form. (2) Midwives gained their knowledge through practice and "hearsay" rather than through "authoritative" books that collected "facts" and stated them in the form of propositions.

For our purposes, the important point here is not so much the contingent one that knowledge of midwives was not recorded in books but that *it could not be.* Midwifery as a skill was not and could not be a matter of following rules codified in conditional propositions. Ryle has persuasively argued that to reduce skills to a two-step process of apprehending rules and criteria and then acting in accordance with them ends in infinite regress or a vicious circle. "Rules of correct reasoning," he explains, "were first extracted by Aristotle, yet men knew how to avoid and detect fallacies before they learned his lessons, just as men since Aristotle, and including Aristotle, ordinarily conduct their arguments without making any internal reference to his for-mulae."[26] Analogically, we can say that the rules and formulae for attending childbirth were first extracted and formulated by modern obstetrics, but such care was prevalent for centuries among women who conducted their practice without any reference to propositions telling them how such care should be given. Obstetrics as a scientific "methodology" *presupposes* the "application of methods" in midwi-fery—that is, practice is prior to the process of codification.

The points just noted indicate what midwives *were not* (institution-ally trained) and what they *did not have* (codified rules) in comparison to medical practitioners. However, there was also a clear difference in the way in which physicians and midwives respectively practiced their profession. The history of midwifery as given above indicates that a crucial aspect of a midwife's skill was her capacity to be em-pathetic and sensitive to the situation of her patients as well as to allay their fears and inspire them to have forbearance and hope. This was possible in part because midwives relied so heavily on their personal experience of childbirth. Thus, we can surmise two further ways in which midwifery can be contrasted with prevalent medical practice: (3) Midwives often gained their knowledge from their own embodied experience of childbirth; they were even proud of this fact. (4) Much of midwife knowledge was empathic, and much of their skill in as-sisting in childbirth was based on this ability to identify with the ex-pectant mother. This empathy was produced partly by a subjective or first-person knowledge of what it is like (for example) to be a woman going through labor, whereas the knowledge of physicians was grounded in a self-conscious quest for "objectivity."

These factors—that midwives *did not* rely on manuals but *did* em-phasize personal experience—explain why the practice of midwifery disregards traditional propositional knowledge. The relatively little importance of or need for manuals and the emphasis on personal experience undermines the importance of information transmitted through impersonal propositions. Therefore, we would suggest that the contrast between beliefs in modern obstetrics and midwifery (taken as an example of "traditional women's knowledge,") which has been typically characterized as a contrast between *knowledge* and *nonknowledge*, is really only a contrast between conformity and non-conformity to the schema "*S* knows that *p*."

In light of this example, we can now offer a simple answer to our first question: What epistemological reason (if any) is there for the undermining of women's knowledge in Anglo-American epistemology? Our answer is that women's knowledge happily ignores the modern epistemic definiendum "*S* knows that *p*." But now we need to show that the fact that midwives do not have ordinary *propositional knowledge* does not, by itself, lead to the conclusion that they do not have *knowledge* at all. This exploration will have important implications for epistemology as a whole, because it will bring to the forefront two different processes of knowing that mainstream epistemology has generally ignored.

## II.

The first set of differences between midwifery and modern obstetrics [(1) and (2) above] hinged on the fact that traditional "old wives" were not institutionally trained and did not follow codified rules—but nevertheless, there is a plausible sense in which they *knew how* to deliver babies in spite of not being able to spell out the steps and rules in propositional form. They were *skilled* in their trade—practicing it even in comparatively complicated situations. Now, this distinction between "knowing how" and "knowing that" is not new to epistemology. We have already made reference to Aristotle and to Ryle, and the latter went so far as to propose a reduction of knowing that to knowing how. But the cognitive importance of knowing how has not been widely accepted. Modern texts on epistemology generally start with a hand-waving gesture towards the different colloquial uses of the word *know* but then go on to the business of identifying the "important" and "epistemically interesting" sense of *know* as the one expressed in the locution "knowing that *p*." Assenting to propositions or attributing epistemic characterizations to propositions remains at the heart of contemporary epistemology.[27]

We have focused on the case of midwives to resurrect the importance of knowing how. But it is likely that much of the knowledge that has been traditionally exclusive (or nearly so) to women can be analyzed similarly. Most women remain illiterate even today, and their knowledge consists in successful practice. And it is not only *women's* knowledge that has been delegitimized in this way. Many men have also had practical knowledge which has been discredited as the "superstitions" or "unscientific beliefs" of peasants.

This brings us back to the *Mahābhārata* and "The Colloquy of the Brahmin and the Hunter." The brahmin, Kauśika, is ultimately sent in his search for truth to a low-caste hunter actively engaged in the (reprehensible) business of selling meat. The sage is taken aback at having been forced into the company of a humble hunter whose only expertise besides his ability to kill, skin, and chop animal carcasses is "living by the Law"—which in his case is the practice of a trade and righteous conduct. On seeing Kauśika, the hunter addresses him respectfully:

> I greet you, reverend sir, be welcome, great brahmin. Hail to thee, I am but a hunter: what can I do? Command me! *A faithful wife has told you to come to Mithila; I know the full reason why you have come here*[28] (our emphasis).

The hunter's greeting indicates that he too had some supernatural access to *facts*, even though he is a symbol of someone who simply *knows how* to practice a trade. The hunter later defends his vocation:

> I know this is *my* Law, and I will not give it up, good brahmin. I know it is due to my old acts, and I live by this job. It is considered lawless here, brahmin, if a man abandons his job.[29]

Kauśika naturally begins by considering this man to be epistemically inferior. But in the course of their conversation, the hunter proves quite adept at discoursing on subtle metaphysical questions such as the nature of the soul and the ultimate constituents of Reality. Kauśika is so impressed by this that he can only exclaim in surprise "Nothing is found in the world that is unknown to you!"[30] Clearly an epistemological paradigm switch has taken place—we find a subject who has mastered *knowing that* (Kauśika) bowing down before a practitioner of *knowing how* (the hunter).

Once again, it is important to note that the hunter's epistemic superiority is acquired *because* of his adeptness in the practice of his Law. He is skilled in the performance of the "duties of his station": "See with your own eyes, best of the twice-born,"[31] the hunter says, "the Law that is mine *by virtue of which* I have attained to success"[32] (our emphasis). It is the hunter's practical activity and his performance of his skill that have enabled him, in the story, to have access to truths, thus conforming to the Rylean notion that propositional knowledge can be traced to practice. Our interest in this episode is its illustration of the fact that skillful practice can produce an epistemic authority, and even superiority, on the part of the agent. Of course, one still has to show if and why a mere *skill* is epistemically important; and in the next section, we will offer support for the claim that knowing how is an alternative cognitive process.

Besides knowing how, the history of midwifery indicates one other kind of knowledge that is embodied in the emphasis midwives placed on personal experience and empathy with the pregnant woman. This difference from the practitioners of modern obstetrics [points (3) and

(4) of the previous section] suggests another nontraditional way of knowing, which might be called "gender-specific experiential knowing" ("G-experiential" for short) as a species of the more general "experiential" knowledge.[33]

Experiential knowledge can be described as knowing "from the inside" or knowing "what it is like to be . . . ," a terminology obviously reminiscent of the work of Thomas Nagel—and we derive the notion of G-experiential knowledge by using and extending Nagelian ideas. According to Nagel, "the fact that an organism has conscious experience *at all* means, basically, that there is something it is like to *be* that organism."[34] These irreducibly "subjective" or "perspectival facts" (of what it is like to be an organism $x$ having an experience $e$) are essentially connected to a specific point of view. To use his example, granting that bats have experience, there is a certain fact of the matter as to what it is like to be a bat experiencing $e$. Trying to grasp this fact through an extrapolation from my own case is bound to be self-defeating, for I remain confined to imaging what it is like *for me* to experience $e$. To grasp the bat's experience, I would have to become a bat myself. Nagel concludes from this that subjective facts like the ones in question embody a specific "point of view" and are accessible only to the subjects who occupy that point of view or perspective.

The notion of a "point of view" is crucial here. Nagel fleshes this out in species-relative terms. To occupy a bat's point of view is to be a member of a type of organism, which means, among other things, having the specific neurophysiological constitution of bats. But Nagel points out that, although bats and humans have markedly different neurophysiological constitutions, "the problem is not confined to exotic cases . . . for it exists between one person and another. The subjective character of the experience of a person deaf and blind from birth is not accessible to me, for example, nor presumably is mine to him."[35] In *What Does It All Mean?* Nagel develops this to formulate a version of the problem of other minds. What it is like to be me eating an ice cream cone is different from what it is like to be Rita eating one. Consequently, I can be skeptical about the content of Rita's experience of ice cream cones even though I know what it feels like for me to eat one.

It is clear then that Nagelian points of view are "sortals" or "types" where the individual-that-I-am is the limiting case of a type with just one member. If this is correct, then it is reasonable to speak of a *gender-specific* point of view in which the subject's being of a particular gender becomes essential or constitutive of the characteristic "inner feel" of a particular gender related experience. The terminology of a "point of view" was introduced primarily as a way to capture the phenomenological features of experience, or how an experience feels to a person from "within." But to talk of "gender-specific points of view" is to imply that "inner" features of an experience are structured not only by neurophysiological but also by social and cultural factors.

Just as there is a fact of the matter as to what it is like to be a bat, a Martian, or Thomas Nagel experiencing *e*, so also there is a fact of the matter as to what it is like to be a *woman* experiencing childbirth, or pregnancy, or patriarchal marriage. Of course, the experience of all women need not be identical—just as the subjective fact of my eating ice cream differs from the corresponding subjective fact involving Rita. All that is necessary to meaningfully speak of a "woman-specific point of view" is that there be a *determinable* quality to the fact of a *woman* having experience *e*, under which we may subsume different *determinate* characteristic feels of varying generality that are dependent, for example, on more specific circumstances like the cultural background of the woman in question down to the unique "subjective fact" associated with a *particular* woman experiencing *e*. Negatively put, the justification for speaking of a "gender-specific point of view" is to say that there are some gender-specific "subjective facts" that are not accessible to subjects who are not of that gender. This is not to deny that a male obstetrician can form *some* conception about experiences like childbirth. By virtue of sharing the determinable "human" point of view with women, he can have some conception of the even more general fact of what it feels like for a *human* to have pain (as opposed to, say, a Martian having pain). But like Nagel trying to empathize with the bat, a man's conception of giving birth will necessarily be drawn from his own gender-specific point of view. Women have a kind of collective privacy in this regard. We will call knowing such gender-specific facts "gender-specific experiential knowing" or simply "G-experiential knowledge."

In light of this, it can now be argued that midwives have G-experiential knowledge in that they have access to the "perspectival fact" of childbirth, which male obstetricians do not and cannot have. And they *use* their knowledge of such facts in their practice in a way that a traditionally trained female obstetrician does not. Not only has it been the case that such experiential knowing has *not* been seen as conferring on women any epistemic advantages, but women who do make use of such knowledge (e.g., some female obstetricians) are discredited as "soft."

It remains an interesting agenda for feminist epistemology to explore the relationship between such G-experiential knowledge and the traditional "knowing that"—the details of which will ultimately depend on a philosophy of language. The crucial question is whether what is acquired from a gender-specific point of view can be expressed as a *proposition* instantiating the schema "S knows that p." The problem here is that propositions are traditionally thought to be intersubjectively available, and G-experiential knowledge is clearly *not* available to all subjects speaking a common language. Reflections on what it is like to be a bat lead Nagel "to the conclusion that there are facts that do not consist in the truth of propositions expressed in a *human* language"[36] (our emphasis). The introduction of a gender-specific point of view and gender-specific facts seems to suggest the conclusion that the truth of some propositions are not expressible in a *gender-neutral language*. Along these lines one could say that G-experiential knowledge is propositional, but these propositions are peculiar in being expressible only in a gender-*specific* idiolect. The details of this, of course, need to be worked out. Whether or not gender-specific facts will be expressible as propositions depends on how we understand propositions. If propositions are conceived as being intersubjectively available to all subjects using a (gender-neutral) language, the answer is no. If however, we are willing to concede the gender-specificity of idiolects, then G-experiential knowledge can become propositional and accessible to (gendered) subjects using a specific idiolect.

In either case, G-experiential knowledge would be different from the usual cases of knowledge found in epistemology. Epistemologists have been sensitive to the fact that the schema "S knows that p" has to be complicated in order to accommodate first-person knowledge of oneself. The logic of knowing the proposition "S is a shabby pedagogue" is very different from that of knowing, "I, myself, am a shabby pedagogue" (even when I happen to be S) because the *latter is an inherently subjective or "perspectival" fact*. What emerges from our discussion is that the logic of the traditional schema "S knows that p" has to be modified not only to deal with propositions involving first-person indexicals but also to accommodate gender-specific facts of experience. Working out these details is beyond the scope of this paper.

What has been established thus far is that stipulating the definiendum of epistemology as propositional knowledge schematized by "S knows that p" has made it possible to discredit certain forms of women's knowing that we have identified as (I) "knowing how" and (II) "G-experiential knowledge." A study of the history of midwifery has helped us to locate these processes. However, what still needs to be established is that these two are genuinely *cognitive* activities, or that the word "know" in "knowing how" and "G-experiential knowing" is to be taken seriously and is not a simple orthographic accident. It is quite possible for critics to agree that the practices of midwives involve these two processes but to deny that (I) and (II) have any significance for epistemology. Succinctly put, our case depends on this argument:

1. Traditional women's knowledge, like knowing what it is like to give birth (G-experiential knowing) and knowing how to soothe a crying baby (knowing how) are not cases of "knowing that" as represented by the traditional schema "*S* knows that *p*".

2. "Experiential knowing" and "knowing how" are epistemic states.

3. Therefore, "knowing that" as represented by "*S* knows that *p*" does not exhaust the sphere of the epistemic.

4. Contemporary epistemology has generally taken "knowing that" as the paradigm of knowledge.

5. Therefore, contemporary epistemology is epistemically discriminatory or inadequate.

What needs to be argued for now is premise (2) above. Why isn't contemporary epistemology *justified* in leaving out knowing how and G-experiential knowing from its domain of discourse? Our claim that epistemology is unjustified in ignoring knowing how and G-experiential knowing assumes that these two processes have a right to be considered epistemically significant. Can this be established?

## III.

In trying to make a case for the cognitive status and epistemic importance of "knowing how" and G-experiential knowledge, we are led straight into the "paradox of definition": instances of knowledge are generally identified as what satisfies the definition of knowledge. But here our argument has been that the very definition of knowledge is restrictive because it unduly limits the scope of the definiendum by excluding some instances of knowing. But because an appeal to the *definition* of knowledge is obviously ruled out, it is unclear on what basis one can *argue* for an expansion of the definiendum. One way out of the problem is to appeal to pretheoretic intuitions about what we count as uncontroversial cases of knowing.

It is interesting to note that this need to expand the traditional scope of epistemology has been felt by other theorists as well, though for different reasons. The traditional narrow conception of knowledge embodies what has been called the "intellectualist legend." According to this picture, the mind has three distinct faculties—thinking, feeling, and willing (which can translate into doing). The "cognitive" or "epistemic" faculties are restricted to the domain of thinking, which is said to be the detached and objective apprehension of propositions. Consequently, knowledge according to this picture becomes an assent to true propositions or a pristine "knowing that." Several philosophers have already begun to break free from the constraints of this model. For example, Alison Jaggar and Martha Nussbaum have suggested kinds of knowledge that originate in emotions.[37] The writings of Nietzsche and Sartre are suggestive as well of the ways in which both feeling and willing contribute to cognition. Thus, the cognitive has begun to seep out of the narrow compartment to which it has usually been confined. The processes of knowing how and G-experiential knowing, as has been argued, do not involve thinking as defined purely in terms of assent to intersubjectively available propositions and, consequently, our concern to establish them as examples of the cognitive is aligned with the general effort to replace the intellectualist model.

It may appear that Ryle has already done the work of showing the cognitive nature of knowing how. It is true that, in arguing that intelligence is not simply "the apprehension of truths," Ryle's main aim was to critique the intellectualist dogma; and in fact he went so far as to demonstrate that *all* knowing is ultimately a kind of knowing how, a capacity or disposition. However, for our purposes the Rylean project needs to be taken farther for a number of reasons. First, Ryle's principal insight is that pure concepts of cognition or forms of "knowing that" do not constitute the core of mental conduct because "the consideration of propositions is itself an operation the execution of which can be more or less intelligent, less or more stupid."[38] Rather, it is mental conduct concepts "ordinarily surnamed 'intelligence' " that signify the basic fact of mentality. But, as the Rylean argument continues, to describe a person by an *intelligence* epithet is not to ascribe to him or her a grasp of propositions but rather the "ability . . . to do certain sorts of things."[39] Consequently, these skills form the essence of mental life. Now *our* question is not simply about the ascription of *intelligence* or whether certain skills embody consciousness or a mind at work, but is rather the subsequent one: whether such conscious acts are *cognitive*. Unlike Ryle, we are not interested in the existence of mentality per se but in whether knowing how exemplifies the *kind of mentality* that is called "knowing" or "cognition." The simple claim that midwives are skilled *conscious* agents (i.e., superior to robots, for example) does not entail that they have the specific mental state called "knowledge." Second, on Ryle's theory the different *kinds* of mental functioning would reduce to a difference in the logic of the underlying abilities or dispositions. But the attempt to identify the uniqueness of knowing (as opposed to merely believing or feeling, for example) along these lines runs into severe problems. Knowledge is conceived as both a "capacity" and an "achievement," and Ryle's positive account of "know" turns out to be inconsistent because of the incompatibility of the logics of these two concepts.[40] Thus, the attempt to construe knowing how along the lines of Ryle's dispositional theory of knowledge would lead to a logical howler. Third, a deference to the Rylean tradition would result in a serious inconsistency in our project. Note that we want to establish the "knowledgehood" of *both* knowing how and G-experiential knowing. The latter is the apprehension of the phenomenological features of a conscious experience that are inherently private to a point of view. Taking G-experiential knowledge seriously thus amounts to taking consciousness seriously and allowing "qualia" and "feels" into one's ontology. But the problem is that the logical behaviorism of Ryle is sharply opposed to any such "privacy." The main purpose of *The Concept of Mind* is to expunge Cartesian ghosts and to make mental life publicly accessible. Consequently, we cannot support a purely dispositional analysis in the case of knowing how while at the same time incorporating G-experiential knowledge into epistemology. Finally, the Ryleans were happy with a *reductionist* account of knowing that in terms of knowing how. But our project is to *expand* the scope of knowledge—we want to *add* to the received list of types of knowing rather than to redefine or substitute it by one single notion.

The cumulative effect of these four observations is to force us to defend the cognitive import of certain skills in a non-Rylean manner and to establish knowing how in nondispositional terms. Why then (because we reject Ryle's analysis) are some skills instances of *knowledge* or *knowing* how? A simple answer would be to insist on the adequacy of common usage. We do *say* such things as "He *knows* how to care for infants," and there seems no reason to doubt the appropriateness of this usage. This move shifts the burden of proof to the skeptic who denies that cases of knowing how can be "knowing." What reasons other than the question-begging adherence to the intellectualist legend could be given for *withholding* cognitive status from knowing how?

Of course, the proponent of knowing how would need to face the charge that "knowledge" here is radically different from "knowing" in the traditional propositional sense—for example, knowing how can be a matter of degree, quite unlike knowing that, which is an all-or-none affair. But because our program here is not reductionistic, this asymmetry in what remain genuine cases of knowing need not be a worry. Moreover, there are interesting parallels between skills and the received paradigms of knowledge that make the according of cognitive status to the former less problematic. After all, it is commonplace to regard "knowledge" as an "achievement word"—and this idea of achievement is taken very seriously (and literally!) in cases of knowing how. A person who *knows how* to do *x*, more often than not, does *succeed* in doing *x*. Moreover, in performing skills we achieve goals *nonaccidentally* just as cases of knowing are distinguished from lucky guesses. But what then of the observation that, although we can be more or less skilled, we either know or simply do not know? To diffuse the force of this, we could note that though grasping the truth is not a matter of degree, *justification* can be so, and a belief that fails to reach truth but which is *justified* has epistemological significance even though it does not amount to knowledge. Similarly, it would be unreasonable to insist that the infant never cry or never get diaper rash before we can say we "know" how to look after babies. There can be an absoluteness to the concept of "succeeding" (once the goal is unambiguously specified), and we expect someone who is skilled to succeed; yet even a skilled agent can, on a particular occasion, be closer or farther away from an actual success. Given that there are degrees of epistemic worth, the fact that the ascription of skills is not necessarily absolute is no argument for denying its *epistemic* significance. But still, one may argue that knowing that entails truth but knowing how does not *entail* success. Even an undeniably skilled person can and does sometimes fail. But once again, all this proves is that the logic of the two kinds of knowing (knowing that and knowing how) are different. It does nothing to detract from the *epistemic* value of a skill, just as "being justified" remains a cognitive and epistemic appraisal even though it does not entail truth.

Of course, in conceiving of knowing how in terms of *probable* rather than actual success, the open-minded epistemologist would not be satisfied with "success" conceived simply in mechanical and statistical terms. This would have to be defined carefully in terms of the actual goal being sought. Thus a midwife is not characterized as knowledgeable only because her rate of mother and infant mortality is low. If we recall the description of midwife practices given earlier, it is clear that the midwife's skill was not simply oriented towards avoiding death but towards ensuring a certain quality of care. Clearly, both failure and success need to be measured by a range of complex criteria.

The above case for knowing how suggests the need for a pragmatic turn in epistemology. We need not look *beyond* skills to some apprehension of truths in order to characterize skills as epistemically significant. We *know* when we nonaccidentally succeed (in the above sense). But does a pragmatic strategy compromise our ability to claim that knowing how is, indeed, a form of *knowing*? After all, replacing "truth" with "success" might appear to play right into the traditional critic's point that the "pragmatic" is not the "epistemic." On the other hand, this is where the strength of the new epistemology might lie. The critic here is clearly not only buying into the myth of the "supremacy of the factual"[41] but is also going on to *identify* the epistemic with fact seeking. On the other hand, this strategy for legitimizing knowing how is informed by the attempt to question and overthrow these assumptions about knowledge and to dislodge truth as the sole epistemological norm. Knowing is not necessarily a matter of saying and representing what is the case but can also be a kind of practical involvement with the world. So the short and direct route of justifying the cognitive import of knowing how is to simply take the bull by the horns and *deny* the watertight distinction between the pragmatic and the epistemic.

Alternatively, it is also interesting to explore whether we can have genuine cases of knowing how while retaining the link between cognition and truth. But you might ask here, "Why bother with such traditionalism at all when we can simply replace it as above?" There are several reasons for pursuing this alternative. First, traditional epistemology not only conceives of knowledge as essentially involving true propositions but it also has a fixed monolithic view of *how* propositions figure in knowing. Trying to establish knowing how while retaining propositions may reveal alternative *ways* in which propositions can become relevant for epistemology. This not only has an intrinsic worth as a reconceptualisation of the role of propositions in cognitive life but it also, as will become evident when we turn to the details, is in conformity with the general line of our criticism of traditional epistemology as underplaying the significance of practice for knowledge. Second, there might still be among us some who would demur at the much more drastic (and admittedly the more interesting and challenging) framework change suggested by the above "pragmatist" strategy. Do we want to lose these opponents in our dialogue at this point, and do we want to give them the escape route of clinging to their exclusionist views by charging *us* with "changing the rules of the game"? It is important to note that in pursuing this line of thought we are not buying into the traditionalist framework. The move is logical—like that in a reductio argument. If we can show that knowing how can be a genuine case of knowing *even when knowledge is conceived as involving propositions*, then the discriminatory exclusionism of traditional epistemology becomes all the more suspect *on its own terms*. Showing the inadequacy of a framework while retaining its defining contours is disrupting it from within.

But can this be done? *If* cognition is linked to propositions, how can we have cases of knowing how without interpreting them as instances of the traditional schema "*S* knows that *p*"?

Manipulation of the environment that leads to a desired goal may or may not be intelligent; but when it is a repeatable intelligent act we have a *skill*. However, according to the presuppositions of our present strategy, all skills do not embody knowledge, and to capture a genuine "*knowing* how" we need to add something to a *mere* skill. This extra element, which is meant to bear the cognitive burden, is (given the constraints of the traditional framework we are working within), some reference to true propositions. Now obviously this cannot consist in (i) the act *being describable* by a set of conditional propositions or rules. Almost all systematic procedures can be codified or described in conditional propositions by a third person without being relevant in any way to the agent (of the act in question); and without access to the propositions—the entities meant to carry epistemic weight—the agent can hardly be said to *know* in any sense even though she can successfully *do*. Neither can it be argued that a cognitively relevant skill (ii) involves the tandem activity of explicitly *apprehending and formulating propositions* or rules while or before performing the act. As Ryle has shown, this condition would rule out most skills and thereby severely restrict the pool from which we can draw on. Ultimately, instances of knowing how are a subset of skills. Moreover, it would not be surprising if this analysis of a skill is interpreted as the innocuous thesis that some cases of "knowing that *p*" *give rise* to actions. But to say that a skill or knowing how is the effect or consequence of a knowing episode is not to say that it is a knowing itself. The answer then seems to lie between (i) and (ii). The agent of the skill must have access to the rules or conditional propositions while performing the action, but *this propositional awareness cannot be a separate act of knowing that*. Such a middle ground can be carved out by the notion of (iii) the agent being able to *recognize* conditional propositions and rules underlying her skill if and when they are formulated for her. The feeling of familiarity when confronted with the propositions in question (implied by recognition) is supposed to explain that the subject did have some access to the propositions even though she did not and could not explicitly formulate or express this in propositional form. Thus a genuine instance of knowing how is a skill in which the subject has such a nascent grasp of the rules and principles underlying her activity that enable her to "recognize" a clear formulation of them, and it is the latter that makes her simple skill *cognitively* relevant.[42] Thus, I may be a skilled (and *merely* so) swimmer if I am completely at a loss when I confront someone's formulation of the "rules" of swimming. But a midwife practices her trade *with knowledge* because, when confronted with a manual that supposedly codifies the rules of midwifery, she can react with agreement or disagreement (unless of course, the idiom in which the rules are coded is designed to exclude her).

The obvious objection to the above strategy is the claim that (iii) is really nothing but an implicit form of (i). Being able to recognize implies an initial apprehension and because we cannot *recognize p* without having first grasped *p*, do we not after all have here a reduction of knowing how to knowing that? An answer to such a criticism would clarify what we have in mind here.

Clearly the above analysis of knowing how tries to cash out the cognitive content of some skills in terms of (possible) recognition of propositions and, given the parameters of a traditional view of the "epistemic," this *reference* to propositions is required. But it is important to note that a mere reference to propositions in this manner need not amount to a *reduction* of knowing how to knowing that, where the latter is schematized as "*S* knows that *p*." An analogy should make this point evident. We may hold that perceptual awareness, for example, involves sensation and memory without maintaining that this *reduces* perception to sensation and memory. Similarly, involving a propositional core does not, by itself, make knowing how a form of knowing that—there is more to knowing how than simply making reference to a proposition.

Let us carefully look at the two formulae "*S* knows that *p*" and "*S* knows how to do *x*." The former embodies the knowing relation as that of *justified assent* between the subject *S* and the (traditional) proposition *p*. "*S* knows how to do *x*," on the other hand, is a relation between *S* and her ability to *do x*. Now according to our strategy, this is conceived as a cognitive relation only if it involves an implicit grasp of the (conditional imperative) propositions or rules of the form "if *q*, then do *r*." Let us call this conditional proposition *p*. It might seem then that "*S* knows how to do *x*'" is simply the *implicit form* of "*S* knows that *p*." However, the difference between the two formulae is much deeper. When *S* knows that *p*, *S* grasps the proposition *p* and goes on to *assent* to it in a "knowing way" (i.e., *S* believes it with justification). When *S* knows how to do *x*, *S* is still required to grasp *p*, but this is not expressed in a consequent *justified belief* that *p* but rather in a *use* of *p* for achieving a desired goal. Thus, the grasp of propositions would lie at the heart of a broadened epistemology that would, however, concede that such a grasp does not necessarily issue in statements of the form "S knows that p." A proposition merely "grasped" can be (a) "assented to" as a full-blooded belief for a case of "knowing that" or can be (b) "put to use" for an instance of "knowing how." And a proposition can be *used* in this way without being *explicitly assented to*. Consequently, what emerges is a distinction between two epistemic attitudes to propositions that have been grasped—(a) believing or assenting to p and (b) using it/being guided by it/acting in accordance with it. "Grasping" the proposition itself is like "sensation" in the perception case—it is mere understanding, which need not be a strict epistemic attitude at all. Knowing that embodies (a), and knowing how is an instance of (b).

The structural difference spelled out above between knowing that and knowing how involves making conceptual distinctions between grasp of a proposition, using it, and believing/assenting to it. This has further consequences for the notion of *truth*. Spelling this out is important in order to counter possible qualms about designating the use of a proposition (along with assent) as an "epistemic" relation. Assent or belief in a proposition is epistemic because such belief is itself true if the proposition assented to is true. How can the *use* of a proposition be "true" in a similar vein? We need to develop a concept that will parallel the traditional notion of truth and yet be applicable to cases of knowing how.

Now "S knows that p" when p is a proposition made true by a state of affairs in the world and where "made true" can be a simple correspondence or a "picturing" of the world. In "S knows how to do x," the propositional core consists of conditional propositions like "If circumstances . . . occur, then you should do———." These cannot be "true" in the straightforward correspondence or "picturing" sense, and our broad-minded epistemologist would consequently have to adopt a more broad-minded notion of truth in any case or give up her project. It is the *normative dimension* of truth that is important for epistemology. Truth is the value or the norm sought by traditional knowers, and as norm it implies a "disvalue"—falsity—which cognisers are constrained to avoid. Epistemological judgments are made to the extent that truth is achieved and error avoided. This normative dimension of the ordinary notion of truth *can* be retained in a modified form in the "how to" schemas. We make judgments that a person does *not* know how to care for infants, for example, implying thereby that there is a "correct" and an "incorrect" way of handling newborns that is not *only* dependent on instrumental success or achieving some goals. So there clearly is some content to the notion of a *correct way of using* propositions or rules to achieve success, which could parallel the idea of a true proposition correctly "picturing" the world. Of course, this need not suggest that there is a culturally invariant, ahistorical, and objectively "right" way—the truth-parallel notion in cases of knowing how need not simulate that admittedly problematic aspect of traditional correspondence. What we want to emphasize is that the fact that we make such judgements underscores the normative or valuative dimensions of our "knowing how to" ascriptions. Consequently, it is not merely the *belief/assent* to propositions that can be evaluated but also the *way these propositions are used*. Because evaluation or normativity is essential for epistemologically relevant processes, "S knows how to do *x*" passes muster.

Summing up the discussion of knowing how, we can say that there are two alternative ways of arguing for the cognitive import of some practices. The first amounts to a paradigm shift in which the fact-stating emphasis of the traditional account of knowledge is rejected; the second works within the traditional framework of the supremacy of the factual and thereby of propositions and truth.

Establishing the cognitive status of G-experiential knowing is easy by comparison. If we take the notion of consciousness seriously, we must accept that there are "subjective facts" in Nagel's sense, and we have argued for the existence of gender-specific facts. Now in its most minimal and uncontroversial sense, knowledge is that which gives us *information* about the world. Even supporters of the first alternative above who object to knowing as exclusively fact-stating would be hard pressed to claim that I do *not* know when I make the statement "The cat is on the mat" as descriptive of the world when the cat *is* on the mat—though, of course, they might broaden the view of "describing" and of what is a fact. Given the ontological admission of gender-specific *facts*, an access to these facts is an increase in information and, consequently, G-experiential knowledge, which consists in such an access to special facts, can be a knowledge claim. If there is a fact of the matter as to what it is like to give birth, then apprehension of this fact in a gender-specific experience could count as knowledge as much as apprehending the objective fact about the cat being on the mat.

The informational value of G-specific knowing can be emphasized in other ways as well. Despite the extreme variability in experience of childbirth, there is usually *some* similarity; those who share the experience can discuss it with each other in a deeper, richer, and more nuanced manner than they can with people who have not had the experience. Even women who have had very different sorts of deliveries might be able to share some of the experiences of fear, surprise, and the ultimate shock at how much their lives are changed as a result of giving birth. The conversation between people who have shared a type of experience has a richer quality to it that may not be observable by a simple recounting of their statements. The quality of such conversation could serve as the basis for saying that there is *content* to an "empathic" conversation, which is what makes it richer (informationally) than a mere objective discourse. The practice of midwifery, as we have seen, found this extra information useful.

A recent article in *Time* magazine, entitled "A Lesson in Compassion," offers support for this conclusion.[43] The article's subtitle is reminiscent of Nagel in asking: "What's it like to be a patient? For more and more aspiring doctors there's only one way to find out." Some medical schools are asking new residents to engage in role-playing programs in which, with the help of cosmetics and crutches, they play the role of patients with differing illnesses and symptoms. These students "spend part of the first day of school as hobbled patients. A few male students are even subjected to an indignity familiar to women: waiting in the stirrups for a doctor to arrive." As this training program suggests, the mastery of objective facts or facts in propositional form is sometimes, or perhaps often, insufficient. Dr. Simon Auster of the Uniformed Services Medical School comments: "By concentrating on symptoms and lab data, we ignore a *wealth of information* that can affect patient's well-being" (our emphasis). The physicians behind these training programs obviously recognize that "knowing what it is like to be a patient" (to the extent that a healthy doctor *can* occupy the point of view of a patient) enhances their care-giving ability but cannot be fully imparted by traditional methods of study, a fact understood long ago by midwives.

Of course, in a realist framework the mere admission of a kind of fact in ontology does not entail a corresponding epistemological process of accessing those facts. But the peculiarity of "subjective facts" is that they are like Lockean secondary qualities: their being is a dimension of the subjects' *experience* of something. Being in part constituted by a subject's experience, such facts are *defined* in terms of their manifestation to a (particular) subjective point of view. Thus, if there are gender-specific facts, then there must be a subjective point of view from which such "qualia" are grasped. A point of view cannot exist in isolation from the viewing done through it. What would such a viewing be but experiential knowing? This way of putting the matter enhances the epistemic import of G-experiential awareness. Knowledge after all, is not any haphazard access to facts but rather is *justified* assent. Since gender-specified facts *consist* in the way a certain experience *feels like* to a subject, the G-experiential awareness from that particular subjective point of view cannot be mistaken and, consequently, is justified. In G-experiential knowing we have a kind of "collective privacy" and another variety of "privileged access."

## Conclusion

If epistemology is concerned with knowing, it needs to incorporate accounts of knowing how and experiential knowledge along with propositional knowledge. For too long cognition has been exclusively pictured as "knowing that." Even if science is taken as the paradigm case of knowledge, some philosophers have begun to argue that it is more accurate to say that science is "a field of practices rather than a network of statements."[44] According to Joseph Rouse, for example, we will understand science better if we conceive of it not as a network of statements or system of theories but as an interrelated configuration of practices and techniques that are guided by the need to generate new research opportunities. Modern epistemology has taken the observatory to be the model site of research; Rouse suggests that an epistemology that more accurately and realistically represents science will be based on the laboratory.[45] If this is right, then the focus of epistemology on propositional over practical forms of knowing has unjustifiably excluded many important sites of knowing: not only the birthing room and the kitchen but the laboratory as well. Moreover, the emphasis on objectivity and intersubjective accessibility has blocked our ability to acknowledge certain inherently "subjective" features of reality. There is nothing embarrassingly limited about the midwife's perspectival (and hence partly exclusionary) knowledge; rather, it ensures a higher level of holistic care by taking into account certain perspectival facts that are necessarily beyond the reach of traditional forms of knowing.

Incorporating these substantively distinct forms of knowing into epistemology increases the complexity of our notion of the epistemic and the cognitive. Uniform criteria of justification and a unitary notion of the epistemic norm of truth, for example, can no longer stand for all cases of knowing. All modes of knowing, according to the traditionalist, can be *said*; we suggest that some knowledge can only be *shown* and other knowledge can only be said in an inherently perspectival language. These differences, however, need not be structured into a hierarchy or used as an excuse for discriminating against certain cognisers. Like the sage Kauśika, contemporary epistemology needs to recognize that knowledge can be found in unexpected places.

# Notes

We would like to thank Elizabeth Potter, Alessandra Tanesini and Arindam Chakrabarti for helpful comments on this paper.

1. It may seem anachronistic to characterize *women's* knowledge in terms of "old wives' tales," premodern midwifery, or practical household knowledge. Many of the examples we will use are historically past rather than contemporary. However, three points can be made in defense of the continued relevance of this analysis: (1) The conceptualization of women's doxastic features in the past continues to affect present conceptualizations. Nowhere yet has the subordination of women been eradicated, and old ideas continue to permeate and influence present thinking. (2) Moreover, there is no justifiable reason for always taking women of the industrialized countries and educated classes as the norm or the center of an account about women's beliefs in general. (3) In most of the world today, women continue to rely on midwives, herbal cures, and the shared "lore" of motherhood passed down through generations. And this knowledge continues to be called in question as concoctions of superstitious and illiterate women. Midwives who still practice in the nonindustrialized countries are under attack, and midwives in industrialized countries are enjoined to become "professionalized" through training programs that sharply subordinate traditional midwifery to Western "medicine." Thus, the traditional women's knowledge we discuss in this paper continues to exist and to be under attack today.

2. A. J. Ayer, *The Problem of Knowledge* (London: Penguin, 1956).

3. J. A. B. van Buitenen, trans. and ed., *The Mahābhārata* (Chicago: University of Chicago Press, 1975). See Book 3, (37.e) and 37.f).

4. Translation altered. "Obedience" is inadequate to capture the original Sanskrit term *susrusa*. The latter conveys the idea of nurturing service or caretaking and connotes *performance* of actions.

5. The "Law" here stands for the almost untranslatable notion of *dharma*. It signifies the "dos and don'ts," or duties associated with one's *station* in life.. A person's station is determined by the position he or she occupies in the *four-fold caste system*—Brahmin, Kṣatriya, Vaiśya and Śūdra—and the location in the fourfold *stages* of life—which are celibate student, householder, retiree, and monk.

6. Ibid; 614.

7. "Brahmin" refers to one of the categories in the four-fold caste system of the Hindus (cf. footnote 5). Etymologically, it means "He who has mastered *Brahman*, or Ultimate Reality."

8. See note 5. One of the duties of a householder is to serve guests and particularly brahmins.

9. *The Mahābhārata*, 616.

10. See note 7.

11. See note 4.

12. Ibid., 617.

13. Ibid., 616.

14. Ibid., 618.

15. See her article in this volume, "Taking Subjectivity Into Account."

16. Gilbert Ryle, *The Concept of Mind* (London: Penguin Books, 1949), 30. The gender of the quotation has been altered.

17. See Jean Towler and Joan Bramall, *Midwives in History and Society* (London: Croon Helm, 1986); Barbara Ehrenreich and Deirdre English, *Witches, Midwives, and Nurses: A History of Women Healers* (Old Westbury, N.Y.: The Feminist Press, 1973); Jane Sharp, *The Midwives' Book* (New York: Garland, 1985); Adrienne Rich, *Of Woman Born* (New York: Bantam Books, 1976); Janet Carlisle Bogdan, "Losing Birth: the Erosion of Women's Control Over and Knowledge About Birth, 1650–1900" in *Changing Education*, ed. Joyce Antler and Sari Knopp Biklen (Albany: SUNY Press, 1990); and Judy Barrett Litoff, *American Midwives 1860 to the Present* (London: Greenwood Press, 1978).

18. Ehrenreich and English, *Witches, Midwives, and Nurses*, 14 See also Billie Potts, *Witches Heal*, 2nd ed. (Ann Arbor: DuReve Publications, 1988).

19. Litoff, *American Midwives*, 76; Bogdan, "Losing Birth," 95.

20. See Ehrenreich and English, *Witches, Midwives, and Nurses*, 34.

21. Rich, *Of Woman Born*, 122–123. See also Suzanne Arms, *Immaculate Deception* (Boston: Houghton Mifflin, 1975), 10.

22. Maureen A. Hickman, *Midwifery*, 2nd ed. (Oxford: Blackwell Scientific Publications, 1985), 487.

23. Thomas Roger Forbes, *The Midwife and the Witch* (New Haven: Yale University Press, 1966), 112.

24. Towler and Bramall, *Midwives*, 29. See also Bogdan, "Losing Birth," 93.

25. Ehrenreich and English, *Witches, Midwives, and Healers*, 23.

26. Ryle, *The Concept of Mind*, 30–31.

27. For example, Keith Lehrer, in *Theory of Knowledge* (Westview, Boulder & San Francisco 1990), begins by distinguishing three senses of *know* but then goes on to say: "In our study we shall be concerned with knowledge in the information sense. It is precisely this sense that is fundamental to human cognition and required both for theoretical speculation and practical sagacity." Posing the problem of an analysis of this sense of knowledge, he adds, "(a) philosopher might be concerned with precisely the question of what conditions are necessary and sufficient for a person to have knowledge, or *more precisely, to know that p*" (our emphasis) (pp. 2–6).

28. *The Mahābhārata*, 619.

29. Ibid., 624.

30. Ibid, 633.

31. Members of the Brahmin, Kshatriya, and Vaishya castes were supposed to have a "second birth" after their natural birth in a ritualistic initiation that gave them the right to study the Vedas.

32. Ibid., 634.

33. Thomas Nagel, "What Is It Like To Be a Bat?" in *Mortal Questions* (Cambridge: Cambridge University Press, 1979), 166.

34. Ibid., 170.

35. Nagel, "What Is It Like To Be A Bat?" 171.

36. See Alison Jaggar, "Love and Knowledge: Emotion in Feminist Epistemology," reprinted in Ann Garry and Marilyn Pearsall, eds., *Women, Knowledge, and Reality* (Boston: Unwin Hyman, 1989); and Martha Nussbaum, "Love's Knowledge," in Amelie Rorty, ed., *Self Deception* (Berkeley: University of California Press, 1986).

37. Ryle, *The Concept of Mind*, 31.

38. Ibid., 28

39. See Isreal Scheffler, "On Ryle's Theory of Propositional Knowledge," in *Journal of Philosophy* 22 (1968); and also Raziel Abelson, "Knowledge and Belief," in the same journal.

40. A phrase used by Alessandra Tanesini.

41. Michael Dummett, in *The Logical Basis of Metaphysics* (Cambridge, Mass.: Harvard University Press, 1991), particularly pp. 93–100, suggests something along these lines in explicating our practical knowledge of language. Thomas Nagel's "Linguistics and Epistemology," in *Language and Philosophy*, ed. Sidney Hook (New York: New York University, 1969) also formulates a similar criterion of knowledge in his discussion of whether or not Chomsky's theory of Transformational Generative Grammar can count as a theory of innate *knowledge*.

42. Anastasia Toufexis, "A Lesson in Compassion" in *Time*, 23 December 1991.

43. Joseph Rouse, *Knowledge and Power: Toward a Political Philosophy of Science* (Ithaca: Cornell University Pres, 1987), 27.

44. Ibid., 22–23.

# 10

# Feminism and Objective Interests: The Role of Transformation Experiences in Rational Deliberation

*Susan E. Babbitt*

---

The importance of the particular and the personal in feminist accounts of ethics and epistemology has suggested to some that feminist epistemologies are irrationalist or at best relativistic. Feminist theorists have emphasized the importance of interpersonal relations and particular connections in making ethical and epistemic judgments. They have thus sometimes been accused of ignoring the importance of general principles.[1] Although it has sometimes been true in feminist debates that emphasizing the particular *is* set in opposition to the development of general theories, it is often the case that such emphases are advanced as part of a broader reconception of personal relations and knowledge. What is especially insightful in some recent feminist treatments of epistemological issues is the recognition that adequate understanding, both personal and political, often depends upon the actual bringing about of alternative social relations and political structures. Although such discussions are not often advanced as theories about knowledge, in some recent feminist discussions of personal and political relations there exist resources for rethinking and answering some general epistemological and metaphysical issues.[2]

In this article I will argue that some feminist treatments of the role of personal experience in political theorizing ought to be understood as part of a reconception of the notion of objective rational interests. In particular, I suggest that some feminist discussions have offered important criticisms of a standard (liberal) notion of what it means for someone to act in her real interests, as opposed to doing what is right for her according to accepted social norms and values. They have done so by advancing implicit reconceptions of self-knowledge and hence of autonomy. I will argue that the emphasis on personal

245

experience in recent feminist theorizing ought to be understood as an emphasis on the occasional role of personal development and experience in the acquiring of nonpropositional understanding, the understanding people possess in the form of intuitions, attitudes, and so on. When feminist insights about personal development are understood in a more straightforwardly epistemological fashion, it will turn out that rather than undermining the possibility of objective knowledge and general rational principles, as feminist theorists have sometimes been accused of doing, the treatment of personal experience found in some feminist accounts in fact advances the possibility of objective justification for claims about social and political realities.

There is a tradition in political philosophy of distinguishing between actions and interests that people engage in and possess, and actions and interests that are rational for them. We may wonder, for instance, whether the decisions a person makes on the basis of her preferences at a particular time really represent her long-term interests. It may be that the individual's decisions rest on very little information or are the result of dubious influences. Or, even when someone's projects and interests are carefully chosen and reflected upon in light of available facts, we may think she is choosing irrationally because she fails to value the right kinds of things for herself. In some cases in which we think someone falls short of choosing rationally, we may want to say not just that she chooses irrationally because she fails to choose correctly given her ends, but also that she is mistaken about her ends.

The most interesting and controversial formulations of issues about rational interests arise in relation to cases of false consciousness. In situations involving ideological oppression, an individual may fail to possess preferences and desires that adequately reflect an interest in her own human flourishing because she has been beaten down by the circumstances of her situation. She may have been deprived of information about her personal prospects and, more importantly, denied the possibility to develop the self-assurance and integrity that would allow her to pursue her options if they were made available to her. Moreover, individuals who are discriminated against in a society are sometimes not aware of that discrimination, and even when people do become aware of discrimination, they may not be aware of the full extent to which discriminatory practices affect them. The effects of oppression may be such that people are psychologically damaged, possessing interests and desires that reflect their subservient social status. They fail to recognize that social and institutional structures discriminate against them in deep ways and that as a result many of their own perceptions and reactions are not fully representative of their own real needs and aspirations. In such cases we may want to say that an individual possesses an objective interest in goods that go beyond what she would desire for herself even if she were not mistaken about her options or the consequences of pursuing them. We may think, for instance, that an individual has an objective interest in full self-respect and integrity even though it may be true that this is for her both inconceivable and unavailable given current structures.

Questions about the relation between rational choice and objective interests have been approached in several ways. The liberal approach to the question has been to define rational choice in terms of what someone would choose under various types of idealized cognitive conditions.[3] The idea is that an act is rational for a person if it is accessible to that person through a process of rational deliberation in which the conditions for rational deliberation are idealized in a suitably specified way. John Rawls argues, for instance, that a person's rational choice is what she would choose if she possessed adequate instrumental reasoning abilities, full and complete information, and the capacity to vividly imagine the consequences of her actions.[4] In his discussion of paternalism, Rawls argues that in any judgment about what is good for someone, we had better be able to argue that the individual herself would have so decided if she had been able to choose under the right conditions.[5] Otherwise, it would be possible to rationalize "totalitarian" actions. Rawls's view permits identifying desires and aims as a person's rational desires and aims even if they are not the person's current desires and aims but precludes the justification of actions aimed at making the person into someone she previously wasn't—that is, conversion experiences. As long as a person would so choose if she *were* fully rational and adequately informed, we can say that the choices in question are in her real interests.

The liberal view has the virtue, first, that it preserves the centrality of the individual perspective. It defines rational choice in terms of what the individual herself would choose under idealized conditions, so that what might be called a person's objective rational choice is determined by the person's idiosyncratic initial perspective. Thus, the liberal can say that the idealization defines an *individual's* good as opposed to what is good for all people (or all relevant sorts of people, according to general social or moral theories). Especially in cases in which paternalism is justified on the liberal view by the individual's incompetence or incapacity, the argument is that the individual herself would have so chosen under the right conditions. For instance, we might feel justified in preventing someone from harming himself even though he has reflected carefully on his decision and strongly desires the result. If intervention were justified in such a case, the argument would be that the person would not have reasoned as he had if he had been able to consider his options in the absence of certain psychological constraints or distorting circumstantial pressures. The concern here is that if individuals' goods were not defined in terms of current interests and desires, it could turn out that detrimental processes of brainwashing and other wrong licensing of intervention could be held to be rational for an individual.

The second virtue of the liberal account is that it avoids saying that something is in someone's interest if, as a result of just any changes that come about, she ends up desiring it; that is, the liberal view acknowledges the centrality of the individual's perspective but does not claim that anything a person comes to desire is rational for her. If a person is adequately indoctrinated, subjected to psychological pressure, she will indeed desire the situation that results from the process, even if it is quite wrong for her. The liberal view suggests that a future desire is rational for a person at a time if it is desirable to her when reflected upon at that time in light of full and complete information and vivid awareness of the consequences of desiring it. That is, it defines a person's good in terms of what the current person, given her basic desires and interests, would choose for her future self if only she could choose under idealized conditions (i.e., conditions of full information and capacity to reason well instrumentally). It does not consider relevant to defining someone's good what that individual would choose for herself if she were to become some other person—if, for instance, she were to undergo a conversion experience and come to assess her options in terms of a fundamentally different personal perspective.

But there are some cases in which this conception of what is in someone's real interests gives the wrong result. The central insight of this standard account is that what makes a choice rational for someone is that she herself would choose such an option if she were able to choose under the right conditions; it precludes consideration of what the person would choose if she were psychologically pressured or were to undergo a conversion experience. Yet there are some cases in which the effects of social conditioning on a person are such that if rationality is defined ultimately in terms of a person's current desires and interests, even under conditions of more adequate beliefs, continued subordination and degradation turn out to be in the person's best interests. In cases in which someone is the victim of ideological oppression, the failure to act in what we would think to be her real interests may not be just a matter of her mistaken beliefs and inadequate reasoning capacities; it may also be a matter of her not possessing a sense of her self—or even a self at all—that would support a full sense of flourishing. Equipped with ideal cognitive capacities and resources, it is not clear that a person who is degraded and di-minished by social conditioning would have reason to choose goods typically thought to represent flourishing.

Consider for instance the case of Thomas Hill's Deferential Wife, the wife who is utterly devoted to and derives happiness from deferring to her husband.[6] The person in the example does not just subordinate herself to her husband as a means of acquiring happiness; for instance, she does not defer to him in some spheres in return for his deference to her in other spheres. The Deferential Wife defines herself in terms of her subordination. She is proud to subordinate herself to her husband and derives much of her happiness from the fact that she serves him well. As Hill describes the temperament and outlook of the Deferential wife, aspiring toward being in control of her life would cause her more suffering than would be balanced out by the resulting benefits. His proposal is that we can account for our intuitions that she is acting irrationally in subordinating herself by suggesting that she would choose to pursue a sense of self-respect if she were fully informed as to her rights as a moral being and were able to accord the right kind of importance to such rights. Hill uses the example to show that although there are some cases in which it is apparently not instrumentally rational for a person to pursue her rational interest, we might still want to say that that person *has* a rational interest in becoming a fully self-respecting and autonomous human being.

Suppose, however, that in fact the Deferential Wife *is* in control of her life and that deferring to her husband *is* the realization of her actual sense of self—not a result of mistaken beliefs about her self. Suppose she controls the life that she has, appreciates her rights, and has full respect for what she is; suppose, in other words, that her problem is that the life she has and the person she really is are diminished and defective due to deep and long-standing forms of social oppression. If this is so, an alternative interpretation of Hill's example is that rather than failing to have the right beliefs about her situation, the Deferential Wife fails to have an appropriate situation—in particular, she fails to possess an adequate self and sense of integrity. She may not be lacking in imagination or self-concern at all; on the contrary, she may have carved out carefully defined limits as regards deference to her husband and be actively engaged in fulfilling herself in accordance with them.

Of course, in some formulations of his view Rawls adds the restriction that under idealized conditions the person whose good is in question should be concerned about autonomy.[7] He does this in order to guarantee that it be in everyone's good to become an autonomous, valuing agent. But if autonomy is defined so as to rule out the kind of servility that characterizes the Deferential Wife's relationship to her husband, it may not in fact turn out that, with full and complete information, she would desire autonomy. For given her actual sense of her self, which is the position from which she approaches idealized information on liberal views, she may have no reason to desire *that* kind of autonomy. If her social and historical situation is such that it is part of her identity to be inferior to men—in particular to her husband—deferring to him in all decisions *is* a valuing of her autonomy. She already is autonomous and self-respecting to the extent available to her.[8]

In other words, one might think that Rawls's view can account for people in situations like that of the Deferential Wife by simply building into the model the notion that under idealized cognitive conditions people would desire the right kind of autonomy. However, it is important to note that to the extent that some people are in fact deprived of dignity and self-respect in their actual lives, desiring the kind of self-determination that we usually think characteristic of a good life would depend upon their undergoing a change to their actual selves. Insofar as the model would turn out to accommodate the situations of people who are actually degraded, it would risk giving up the very feature supposedly making it a model that preserves individuals' autonomy.

Thus, in situations in which a person's self is degraded, the result of the person's choosing under Rawls-type idealized conditions may be a sense of autonomy that is somewhat thin. It is central to the liberal definition of interests that the self that chooses under idealized conditions be untransformed; that is, it is important that the individual's choices be defined in terms of her own perspective. However, in the case of the Deferential Wife, if she is to choose what is best for *her*—even if she has access to full and complete information about what would be good for her under different conditions—she has no reason to choose a full sense of autonomy. She has not the kind of self to which such a sense of autonomy could be applied. And if Rawls were to stipulate that under idealized conditions the Deferential Wife desires a thick sense of autonomy, he would have to include in his idealization transformations to her self. In order for it to be rational for her to desire autonomy in the sense that rules out her habitual servility, her actual sense of self would have to be transformed so that habitual servility is not what defines it. But defining a person's objective interest in terms of a perspective the person might have but in fact does not is just what the liberal view rules out.[9]

The reasons for denying a role for conversion experiences in defining someone's rational interests are clear. For one thing, it would be hard, otherwise, to see how the *individual*'s good is at issue. If, under idealized conditions, a person chooses from among her various options from a perspective that is not that of her actual self, it is hard to see how such a choice should carry any weight for the actual person whose choices are at issue. Second, if potential psychological transformations are relevant to defining rational choice, it may become possible to rationalize dubious life choices. Not all transformation experiences are beneficial for individuals, and some are quite detrimental. For instance, it might turn out to be possible to say that something is in someone's best interests because if she were to spend weeks being indoctrinated by a religious (or other) cult, she would then desire the thing in question. A third consideration is the rationalization of undesirable forms of paternalism. Given that people may in fact come to desire certain choices after having been coerced into them, we might be forced to say that such coercive interventions are for their own good.

But in some cases, like that of the Deferential Wife, a person's rational interests—or at least what we might intuitively think to be in her individual rational interests—depend precisely upon the kinds of personal and political transformation experiences the liberal accounts want to rule out. In fact, it sometimes looks as though the disruption of a person's secure sense of self is just what is required to make a full state of flourishing individually rational for a person. Consider the member of a marginalized group who has the talent to be a medical researcher but who aspires toward a job in the local pharmacy. The liberal view would attempt to account for our intuitions that the person's aspirations are irrational by suggesting that if the person had access to full and complete information, then he would know that his low expectations for himself are socially induced and would desire more for himself than a career in the local drug store. But if the person has access to full and complete information, then he will not only find out that his aspirations are a result of adverse social conditioning but also that if he pursues a career as a medical researcher, he will then suffer harassment, job discrimination, alienation, and so on. Moreover he will find out that although he has the ability to do such a job well, that fact is irrelevant. For he will not be taken seriously in his work and will spend more of his time fighting civil rights cases than doing what he had desired. At least at the drug store he has the possibility of doing reasonably satisfying work and gaining a steady income. If he inserts himself into the medical establishment, he may then achieve other goals and acquire other goods, but he may not be acting rationally given his current desires and interests.

Now, of course it may *not* be in his rational interests to pursue a career in medical research. It is certainly sometimes true of individuals that they could not cope with the consequences of pursuing what we would intuitively think to be in their long-term interests as human beings. But there *are* cases in which a person actually acquires greater self-respect, strength, and a quite different sense of priorities as a result of the effects upon her of undertaking just such an apparently irrational pursuit. As a result of social and political engagement, she does not just acquire different aims and desires; she also becomes personally changed so as to possess a different interpretive background on the basis of which to weight her desires and interests. Hill's Deferential Wife may in fact be right in thinking she is not being personally deprived by acting out her deferential relationship. Given the dependence of her identity on her social situation, she may really have as part of her self-concept the feature of being inferior to her husband. However, it is likely that if the Deferential Wife were to act in certain ways or even were compelled to act in certain ways by circumstances or forceful persuasion, she would *acquire* desires and interests that would change her position and provide her with a different interpretive background. If she were to acquire, say, greater power or self-respect, she would in fact become such that the actual denial of power and control to her *is* a personal deprivation. Now if Rawls were to include under the effects of vivid imagining the insight people acquire as a result of having their condition and situation transformed in this sort of way, he would in fact be including the role of conversion experiences in his account of a person's good. But he would then have to answer the question, which he does not address, of why some conversion experiences and not others can be beneficial for someone.

The second closely related feature of note about the liberal view is that the full and complete information assumed in the idealizations is mostly propositional; that is, the kind of information in light of which an individual considers her choices is of the type that could be expressed in words and concepts. The individual reflects upon her options in light of a full and complete body of truths that could be put into the form of sentences in her idiolect. The idealizations do not include complete access to a different kind of knowledge—knowledge that people possess in the form of intuitions, attitudes, ways of behaving, orientation, and so on. It is true that for Rawls, a kind of nonpropositional understanding is involved in the idealizations insofar as people are able to vividly imagine being in certain circumstances. But his account does not include the kind of understanding that a person acquires in virtue of being transformed—precisely the kind that is often needed for understanding ideological oppression. This is because this sort of transformation constitutes a different interpretive position; the vivid imaginings provided in a Rawlsian idealization are dependent for their interpretation upon the person's *initial* interpretive position.

It seems clear that people usually know things about their situation that cannot be expressed now. There is always something about an experience of a situation that cannot be expressed, even in principle. But in certain cases what a person knows as a result of being in a situation constitutes understanding of a larger situation. That is, being in a particular personal state and relationship to society sometimes constitutes a kind of understanding of that society that could not be obtained through an examination of the expressible truths about that society. Literary critic Barbara Christian describes something like this knowledge in her discussion of Alice Walker's *The Color Purple*.[10] She cites a passage in which Mister taunts Celie: "Look at you. You black, you pore, you ugly, you a woman. Goddam . . . you nothing at all." Celie retorts: "I'm pore, I'm black, I may be ugly and can't cook . . . but I'm here." Celie is nothing according to the categories that Mister possesses for interpreting the world. Her existence as a person is an anomaly in his terms because according to the conceptual framework he applies, the concept "people" does not include black women. Christian writes that "Celie's affirmation of her existence does not deny [Mister's] categories of powerlessness; rather she insists that nonetheless she exists, that she knows something as a result of being at that intersection of categories that attempt to "camouflage her existence."

But we might think that Celie does indeed challenge Mister's categories, and it is in fact *because* she challenges his categories that she knows something that could not otherwise be known. Celie's experience of existing as a person puts her outside of the categories in terms of which Mister, and the rest of society, make sense of their experience. Not only is there something about Celie's experience that cannot be expressed—that is, something that it feels like to be in her situation—but there is also something about her experience that, if it could be expressed, would contradict presuppositions of the dominant conceptual framework. Celie's assertion of her existence challenges Mister's categories, but it is because her knowledge is in fact a way of existing and acting that her assertion constitutes a threat. If her challenge to Mister's categories were merely verbal or intellectual, it could be answered within the terms of the framework that Mister employs, just as anomalies can usually be explained away in terms of a dominant conceptual framework. However, to the extent that Celie's understanding of what it is like to be in her situation consists in her *acting* against the grain of that conceptual framework, her nonpropositional understanding of her position constitutes a critical interpretive position. As Christian writes, "That contrariness [between prevailing traditional and alternative modes of representing reality] is a measure of health, of the insistence that counter to the societal perception of black women as being 'nothing at all,' their existence is knowledge that relates to us all."[12]

Celie's existing in a certain relation to society constitutes a kind of understanding of that society that cannot entirely be expressed in propositions. In one sense the inexpressibility of Celie's experience is explained simply by the difficulty of expressing any experience of what it is like to be somewhere or in some state. But there is more to be said about inexpressibility in this particular case. In Celie's situation, the inexpressibility of her experience is of particular epistemic significance. For it is not just another dimension of her expressible experience. What she understands but is incapable of expressing provides, or potentially provides, the interpretive standards that could make a more adequate *expressed* experience possible. That is, the conceptual framework that she currently operates with is not adequate for Celie's deliberations about her life and actions because according to that conceptual framework, she doesn't exist as a person. A better conceptual framework, however, cannot be got simply by revising language and concepts because the only available theoretical instruments for carrying out such revision disallow the full humanity of people like Celie. Instead, Celie's proper deliberations depend upon the bringing about of a critical perspective as a result of acting on the basis of that part of her experience that is inexpressible—her nonpropositional understanding of her situation. In this kind of case, then, nonpropositional understanding provides not just another level of understanding but perhaps the only possible access to the kinds of epistemic standards that would permit effective radical criticism.

In another Walker story, a young African-American woman's understanding of her personal situation depends importantly upon the bringing about of social relations in terms of which she can properly interpret her personal perceptions. In *Meridian*, the protagonist comes to understand her political goals primarily as a result of her experiencing what it is like to be part of the "togetherness, communal spirit [and] righteous convergence" of the civil rights movement.[13] Perhaps due in part to her youth, Meridian is at first unable to define her own political commitment. When asked whether she would kill for the revolution, she is unable to make a judgment because she lacks a clear understanding of what such a commitment would entail. At the point in the story when Meridian *does* decide that she can kill for the revolution, the difference is not that she has acquired more theoretical understanding; she had quite a bit of that at the point where she had been confused. Instead, what is different is her situation, particularly her emotional situation. Sitting in the church, feeling the political impetus of the music and the tradition, she recognizes that "the years in America had created them One Life."[14] Certainly, this latter is propositional understanding, but the understanding of this proposition depends heavily on Meridian's changed personal state. The intellectual element of her experience in the church is made possible, it seems, by her emotionally experiencing what it is like to be part of a developing set of social and political interrelations. Her actual situatedness within a network of political and emotional relationships itself provides her with epistemic standards making interpretations possible that were not so previously. What Meridian acquires during her experience in the church is not knowledge of when and where she would or could kill for the revolution; rather, what appears to be the case is that she has acquired relations, attitudes, and ways of behaving that constitute a more adequate interpretive framework.

It looks as though one sort of nonpropositional understanding consists largely in a person, or a group of persons, existing or acting in ways that constitute an interpretive framework. A person's existing in a certain state or a group of persons bringing about certain sets of social or political relations can sometimes constitute understanding of a situation that cannot be entirely expressed theoretically. This kind of understanding is different from the experience of vivid imagination that liberals typically include in their idealizations. In the case of someone like the Deferential Wife, it would be the acquiring of new aims and interests altogether—in fact, her becoming a different person—that would explain her possession of an individual rational interest in human flourishing. Vividly imagining oneself in some position does not usually involve transformations. This is why vivid imaginings are usually different from something like a mind-altering drug experience or a hallucination. When we vividly imagine ourselves in some situation, we are usually in control of the interpretation of that event. In a drug experience or a hallucination, the control is not there, so that often a person experiences herself in a state of emotion, desire, commitment, or relationship that she does not choose. Not only does that person experience herself in that situation, but she also acts and engages according to what she is in this other state, experiencing the consequences and so on. The kind of transformation that would make it possible for the Deferential Wife to properly understand her real possibilities as a person would be one that would provide her with different grounds, and such a transformation would most likely have to be one which transformed her*self*.

Now, it is not just in the case of oppressed people that transformation experiences are relevant to the acquisition of a more adequate understanding of one's life and situation. bell hooks has made the point that it is often difficult for white liberals to acknowledge that there are perspectives that they cannot have access to.[15] By this, I take it that she does not mean that whites can have no understanding of racist oppression at all but rather that there are some things that cannot be understood by whites in advance of somewhat radical change to the social structures and power relations that define the way people see themselves. In particular, I suspect that she means that adequate understanding of racism, on the part of white people, requires personal change, a giving up of power, and an actual change of behavior and commitment. There are plenty of examples of people possessing large amounts of theoretical information about sexism and racism and failing to understand what it means; they fail in particular to grasp the implications of such information for their own behavior and relations. hooks' point appears to be that it is not possible for the relatively nonoppressed to acquire adequate understanding of racism simply by reading or listening to what people of color have to say, unless that reading or listening is of an emotionally and politically engaged sort. Instead, understanding often requires undergoing some kind of transformation experience, particularly of the sort that results in the unsettling of the a person's self and position.

The two features of the liberal view noted above are related in a way that helps explain the inadequacy of the liberal idealization. I have suggested that it is a mistake to think that a person acts autonomously when she chooses in light of correct information in a way that preserves her basic sense of self. For it is often a person's *self* that is diminished and deprived by ideological oppression, and correcting a person's *beliefs* is not an adequate response. But there is definitely a strong grain of truth in the intuition reflected in the liberal view that it is wrong to interfere in a person's carefully thought out choices. It is certainly true that we are often rightly reluctant to try to persuade someone that we care about that she is living her life wrongly, that she is mistaken in her view of what is good for her. It is also true, however, that in cases in which we might be reluctant to say such a thing to someone, we would take action to change that person's situation. We might supply her with increased economic resources, introduce her to different sets of relations, and so on. The grain of truth in our intuitions that it is wrong to tell people how to live their lives may not be that people act autonomously when they act on the basis of their own basic preferences and values and that their choices therefore ought to be respected; rather, it may be that it is often painfully futile and startlingly insensitive to try to help someone out of a difficult situation by simply giving her more information. Telling someone that she is living her life wrongly is not usually helpful and often quite damaging However, by changing someone's situation we are sometimes in fact supplying that person with relevant information. The notion that we ought not interfere with someone's choices does not correctly reflect a concern for autonomy if that person is deprived of the resources to act autonomously. It may, however, correctly reflect the insight that in many cases supplying people with information that would be useful to them in individual deliberations is not a matter of providing increased access to propositional truths; instead, it is a matter of the bringing about of different, more appropriate, social and political situations. The idea that a person acts or chooses in her interests when she proceeds as she would under liberal idealized conditions is mistaken both epistemologically and metaphysically; it mistakenly excludes the role of important kinds of nonpropositional understanding in rational deliberation, and it ignores the occasional importance to proper individual development of the bringing about of conditions that transform a person's aims and values.

Gayatri Spivak is one feminist theorist who sometimes appears to be talking about the role of nonpropositional understanding. Many feminists have talked about the importance of bodily understanding, but such discussions do not often hook up discussions about the body to questions about the development of radical critique. In her intriguing discussion of "The Breastgiver," Spivak suggests that the body is the *place* of knowledge and not merely the instrument.[16] This claim by itself is not striking, but Spivak goes on to suggest that bodily experience can often be the bringing about of different sets of relations, relations that can make things understandable that could not have been understandable previously. Women's full sexual identity, for instance, cannot be properly understood within a conceptual framework that denies women any identity at all. But the *experience* of orgasmic pleasure—*joissance*—is "the place where an unexchangeable excess can be imagined and figured forth."[17] The bodily experience, the bringing about of relations, is necessary in order that experiences that would have no meaning within a dominant conceptual framework are able to be understood. Spivak appears, at least here, to be suggesting that in order for some situations to be understood, it is not just new concepts that need to be introduced but new relations, and new relations sometimes constitute epistemic standards according to which concepts can be more properly evaluated and applied.

Sometimes an alternative conceptual background can be acquired imaginatively through fiction. Spivak points out that emotional involvement in fiction can sometimes "perform the ideological mobilization" that an adequate propositional understanding of the situation cannot.[18] People always understand information from a particular (biased) perspective. If what needs to be understood is the nature and wrongness of the structures and assumptions in terms of which people are interpreting information and themselves, "scholarly demonstrations" are not going to do the job. What is needed is a different perspective, one which can often only be acquired through transformative emotional involvement. Certainly, not just any reading of fiction can help to bring about the "counter-hegemonic ideological production" that Spivak has in mind, for one can read fiction without being unsettled and transformed. The point is that one often *has* to become unsettled in order to understand properly, and fiction is sometimes a vehicle for this.

Audre Lorde is another theorist who sometimes treats personal involvement and commitment epistemically and who also appears to have in mind the important political role of understanding acquired through personal engagement and activity.[19] In her "Uses of the Erotic," she appears to be attributing to experiences of passionate involvement the kind of epistemic significance that can explain radical understanding. The passionate involvement she appears to have in mind is sometimes sexual but also includes activities such as building a bookcase; specifically, she seems to have in mind the occasional spiritual experiences people undergo when they become intensely, creatively involved—with people, art, things, nature, or whatever. In suggesting that the erotic is a source of power and information in our lives, Lorde does not appear to be suggesting that there is propositional information that can be gained through passionate involvement in activities and relationships; she speaks of the erotic as a "lens through which we scrutinize ... [and] evaluate" aspects of our existence.[20] She speaks of the capacity to experience and to engage as a "measure" of the possibilities for a more full human experience, suggesting that the entering into and the bringing about of states, not primarily a theoretical body of truths, provides a more adequate basis for individual deliberation.

There is an important scientific source for this notion of nonpropositional knowledge. In Kuhn's discussion of scientific paradigms, he treats the acquiring of scientific skills as an acquiring of knowledge.[21] He insists that scientific practices and procedures amount to more than the explicit theories that they depend upon and inform, and that precisely for this reason part of the training of professional scientists must be experimental. Whether or not they accept Kuhn's constructivist conclusions about the status of scientific knowledge, philosophers of science are generally agreed that good scientific practice depends upon the acquiring of experimental know-how, including good scientific"hunches" and intuitions. Moreover, one explanation for this is that the practices and procedures of science often constitute a kind of nonpropositional, or tacit, knowledge.[22] One reason the role of nonpropositional understanding of this type would be important in explaining scientific progress is that what needs to be explained in regard to the possibility of objective scientific knowledge is how it is that scientists acquire rational standards that guide them to knowledge of an independent world.[23] To the extent that it is uncontroversial that all aspects of scientific practice are deeply theory-dependent, the possibility that scientists develop practices and skills as a result of interaction with the physical world would help explain how it is that scientific standards are appropriate for the investigation of an independent world and not simply the consequence of the development of a particular tradition. The role of nonpropositional knowledge in explaining reliable scientific practice is thus not *just* the acquisition of skills necessary for carrying out previously defined projects. Rather, it appears importantly to involve the development of standards for defining and evaluating new directions in theory development.

Knowledge people acquire of oppression appears to be of this sort. If it is true, as it seems to be, that all thinking is dependent upon a person's social and historical situation, there is a question about how people can ever know that their current situation is in fact wrong for them. To the extent that people interpret their lives in terms of a conceptual background that represents the status quo, how do they come to learn that that background is in fact mistaken? One answer to this is that in order to continue to act and to make sense of his situation, a person who is a member of an oppressed group will learn certain behaviors and attitudes. For instance, he learns to become aware of racist biases and to make allowance for them. Now it could be that someone learns how to behave appropriately for a situation and continues to understand things in the same way. But often an individual's learning of coping skills in such a situation constitutes a way of interpreting things differently. As a result of learning certain procedures, he comes to see his situation differently and to apply different considerations in deliberating about it.

It seems reasonable that some feminist discussions of personal development could plausibly be understood as a working out of the political implications of the importance of acquiring nonpropositional understanding in choosing and acting rationally. Sarah Hoagland, for instance, makes the important point that engaging in projects and commitments is necessary for discovering one's proper sense of self and that such "self-interest" in fact provides the ground for effective moral action.[24] She emphasizes that her point is *not* that people sometimes need to engage with others to discover the submerged self but rather that engaging with others in personally and politically appropriate ways is necessary to bring about the conditions that make being an integrated self possible in the first place. Her point appears to be that *self*-interest ought not always to be considered egotistical, because serving one's real self-interest often depends upon engaging oneself socially and politically in appropriate ways. The development of the right kinds of community relations provides the social network—especially the transformed power relations—that makes options conceivable that otherwise would not be for a given individual. This makes it look as though the role of community building in Hoagland's account is partly epistemic; it consists, at least in part, in providing a more appropriate background for individual rational deliberation. The striking consequence of the potential epistemic role of personal engagement and community building is that it looks as though rather than requiring information in order to make the right choices, individuals sometimes have to make certain choices and take actions *first* in order to bring about the conditions under which information, if it is available, can be properly approached.

The importance of Hoagland's treatment of rational interests, I suggest, is her emphasis on the ontological significance of social and political engagement. While philosophers commonly note that it is old hat to recognize the social dimensions of personal identity,[25] there are important questions to be raised about the implications of recognizing the fully social nature of identity that are not often addressed. Hoagland's account contributes to this development in demonstrating a more thoroughgoing denial of the centrality of a person's given psychological state in defining an individual's individuality or proper sense of integrity. In particular, her account is important in pointing out the political aspects of defining and acquiring an adequate sense of personal integrity. The suggestion is not that a person's self has to be *discovered* through interaction and engagements—as if it were *always* there to begin with—but rather that in some cases a person's self has to be brought about and discovered through her experience of the effects of actual social and political change and moreover by changes to the external circumstances.

But Hoagland does not herself emphasize the epistemic dimensions of her account. In fact, one finds no answer to the question of why not just any way we choose to create ourselves is rational as long as it emerges from the right kind of community. It is clear that she does not intend that just any kind of interrelational patterns emerging from lesbian community provide conditions for more adequate personal development, for she criticizes the racism and violence of some lesbian communities. She even suggests that people (within lesbian communities) sometimes need to be jolted out of their stupidity and bigotry.[26] Insofar as her emphasis is strictly on community and interaction and not on the occasional epistemological role of transformative personal and political experiences, it is not at all clear how she explains the possibility of justifiably criticizing some community practices and promoting others.

The epistemic component of personal development provides part of an answer to the question of how some transformations can be considered beneficial for someone and others not. The capacity of personal transformations to sometimes provide the insight and capacity to act in ways that promote self-respect, dignity, greater liberation, and so on provides part of a basis for measuring the rational adequacy of such experiences. Now one might think that the appeal to general human goods such as self-respect, dignity, and liberation or even to a notion of adequacy amounts to the importation of abstract, removed ideals, of the sort that the liberal accounts of an individual's good are rightly concerned to avoid. But the constraints on individual development provided by a concern to achieve greater human flourishing, both for individuals and for society, need not be abstract and removed anymore than the principles that guide the acquiring of objective scientific knowledge are of this sort.

It is especially significant here that if knowledge is acquired through processes of action and engagement and if in fact some such knowledge is tacit, it is a mistake to think that a theory of knowledge must provide criteria, justifiable a priori, for distinguishing knowledge from nonknowledge.[27] The worry expressed by some feminists about developing theories of knowledge is sometimes that the development of such theories imposes, a priori, legislative conditions for knowledge. But, in fact, it is one of the virtues of developing an alternative general account of the nature of knowledge and objectivity that it becomes possible to see why such epistemological demands are misguided. If political knowledge depends upon the acquisition of nonpropositional understanding as a result of engagement, then the status of epistemic principles raises a contingent question about the role of such principles in a general process of social, political, and moral development; it is not a question that can be answered, or should be answered, in advance of engagement in and application to that process.

Feminist accounts of the role of personal relations and commitments in self- and social understanding provide reasons for thinking that the standard (liberal) formulations of the issue of an individual's rational interests gets the question backwards. If it is true that the acquiring of adequate personal integrity often depends upon the bringing about of more appropriate personal and political conditions the question of what is good for someone cannot be a question about what an initial individual does *with* information; instead, to the extent that the acquiring of information *is* the bringing about of a more adequate personal situation, the proper formulation of the issue is as a question about what the right kind of information does *to* the individual. The deep problem with liberal views—and with any view that identifies what is good for someone with what the person would herself choose if only she possessed the right amount of propositional information—is that such a model for rational choices misconstrues the metaphysics of individuality. In particular it misconstrues how the acquiring of adequate personal integrity depends upon actual changes to a person's self and situation. Not only do some feminist accounts contribute to our understanding of how we can really know about our social and political situations; in doing so they also indicate the mistake in thinking that issues about genuinely autonomous action are fundamentally issues about an individual's psychological state.

## Notes

I am greatly indebted to Richard Boyd for frequent and fruitful discussions on the issues of this paper. I am also grateful to him for extensive and insightful written comments on countless drafts of the dissertation from which this paper emerges. Others who have offered helpful discussion and comments are Linda Alcoff, Richmond Campbell, Jackie Davies, Libby Potter, Phyllis Rooney, Nicholas Sturgeon, and an audience at the Canadian Philosophical Association Meetings in Kingston, Ontario, May 1991.

1. See, for example, Kai Nielsen, Afterword in Kai Nielsen and Marsha Hanen, eds., *Science, Morality and Feminist Theory* (Calgary, Alta.: University of Calgary Press, 1987).

2. I should say here that I do not agree with characterizations of feminist work according to which feminist epistemology is opposed to the development of theories of knowledge, or even, as is often said, to "mainstream" episte-

mology. Feminists, it seems to me, are clearly developing general theories of knowledge, and in many ways feminist work is continuous with some strains of postpositivist, naturalistic epistemology. While I cannot here make the arguments for this, I suggest that the radical, subversive potential of feminist work is undermined when it is thought of as being somehow *opposed* to the development of general epistemology and metaphysics.

3. I have called this a "liberal" view, not just because it is advanced by liberals but also because it is characterized primarily by its ultimate preservation of the initial individual's perspective and a certain conception of knowledge. I have argued elsewhere ("Rationality and Integrity: The Role of Transformation Experiences in Defining Individual Rational Standards", chapter 2, Dissertation, Cornell, 1991) that Peter Railton, a Marxist, offers an account that shares the same liberal features. While Railton does indeed introduce nonliberal insights that could provide the resources for accommodating the kinds of case I discuss below, I argue that he fails to properly exploit them.

4. John Rawls, *A Theory of Justice* (Cambridge: Harvard University Press, 1971), 417 ff. Similar views have been advanced by Henry Sidgwick, *The Methods of Ethics* (London: Macmillan & Co., Ltd., 1907); Richard Brandt, *A Theory of the Right and the Good* (Oxford: Clarendon Press, 1979); and R. M. Hare, *Moral Thinking* (Oxford: Clarendon Press, 1981).

5. Rawls, *A Theory of Justice*, 248ff.

6. Thomas Hill, "Servility and Self Respect," in *The Monist* 57 (1973): 87.

7. John Rawls, *A Theory of Justice*: 417, "Kantian Constructivism in Moral Theory," in *Journal of Philosophy* 87 (1980): 525–26.

8. There are plenty of examples available to show that people can fail to understand or be motivated by information that they posses and believe and in which the failure can be attributed to the possession of a particular self-concept. When I lived for years in Italy, I failed to learn to make fresh pasta even though I was shown in detail many times and possessed a great desire to learn. I knew all the steps but did not understand the procedure. One main reason for this, I presume, is that I possessed a concept of people who make pasta from scratch as being unusually competent in culinary affairs and of myself as not being such a person. Had I become integrated enough to be able to see making pasta as part of what one does to get along, I would have understood better. A self-concept, including understanding of social positioning, is not something that people are often fully aware of but which is assumed in the interpretation and application of much information. That the possession of a certain self-concept prevents or makes possible understanding of one's situation is indicated by the fact that people often acquire an understanding of their actual situations when they discover the ways in which their self-concepts, unbeknownst to them, are racist, sexist, or whatever.

9. See especially Rawls, *A Theory of Justice*: 248. In fact, liberal accounts allow significant criticism of a person's particular desires—even strongly held

ones—but they stop at criticism of the standards and perspective according to which the current person assesses her desires and options.

10. Barbara Christian, "What Celie Knows That You Should Know," in David T. Goldberg, ed. *The Anatomy of Racism* (Minneapolis: University of Minnesota Press, 1990), 135.

11. Ibid., 135.

12. Ibid., 141–42.

13. Alice Walker, *Meridian* (New York: Pocket Books, 1976),199–200.

14. Ibid.

15. bell hooks, "Talking Race, Resisting Racism," presented at "Feminism and Cultural Imperialism" conference, Cornell University, April 23, 1989.

16. Gayatri Spivak,"A Literary Representation of the Subaltern," in *In Other Worlds* (New York: Methuen Press, 1987), 241–268, esp.258–261.

17. Ibid., 259.

18. Ibid., 256.

19. Audre Lorde, "Uses of the Erotic: The Erotic as Power," in *Sister Outsider* (Freedom, CA: The Crossing Press, 1984), 53–59.

20. Ibid., 53,57.

21. See Thomas Kuhn, *The Structure of Scientific Revolutions* (Chicago, University of Chicago Press, 1970).

22. For discussion of scientific intuitions and their explanation, see Richard Boyd,"Naturalistic Epistemology and Scientific Realism," *Philosophy of Science Association*, 2 (1980); and "How to be a Moral Realist," in G. Sayre-MacCord, ed. *Essays on Moral Realism* (Ithaca: Cornell University Press, 1989).

23. In particular, Boyd op. cit.; and "On the Current Status of Scientific Realism," *Erkenntnis* 19 (1983): 45–90.

24. Sarah Hoagland, *Lesbian Ethics* (Palo Alto, CA: Institute for Lesbian Studies, 1988), esp. chapter 2.

25. Peter Railton, for instance, in "Alienation, Consequentialism and the Demands of Morality," in *Philosophy and Public Affairs* 13 (1984): 167.

26. This point was made in a presentation, "Lesbian Ethics," at Cornell University, March 9, 1990.

27. This point has been made by naturalistic epistemologists. For an overview see Philip Kitcher "The Naturalist's Return" in *The Philosophical Review* 101: January (1992) 33–114.

# 11

# Knower/Doers and Their Moral Problems

*Kathryn Pyne Addelson*

The traditional epistemology of the Anglo-American canon was a theory for *knowledge makers*. It was a normative theory that told how knowledge makers ought to reason to reach knowledge of the true or the good or the right. The fact that it was a theory for knowledge makers was covered up by using several clever strategies—including the democratic claim that anyone might have knowledge if only they used the certified method. So far as knowledge went, we were all interchangeable individuals. The epistemology seemed not to be a theory of knowers or a theory of knowledge makers, even though the abstract individuals were acknowledged as among its basic units. It seemed to be a theory about knowledge itself.

As a matter of fact, the traditional epistemology was a theory for knowledge makers in a straightforwardly political sense; it supported the elites who in fact exercised cognitive authority through knowledge-making institutions. Feminist scholars pointed this out by saying that traditional epistemology supported male dominance and patriarchy. The aim of a feminist epistemology was to criticize the patriarchal epistemology in ways that subverted it and led to the overthrow of male dominance.

How might a feminist epistemology do such a thing?

In this article, I will give some reasons that a feminist epistemology is (and should be) an epistemology for knowledge makers. I don't mean by this that "all women" are included as knowledge makers in the epistemology I sketch here—although I believe that all women are knowledge makers and should be respected as such. Who makes knowledge varies systematically with the politics of a situation. In this academic anthology, it makes sense to speak of (and to) academic knowledge makers. And so I will offer suggestions on a feminist epistemology that shows how elite feminist knowledge makers in the academy and elsewhere make knowledge and how we might do so responsibly.

The epistemology I sketch is descriptive, not normative. It serves as a way of testing, in practice, the usefulness and adequacy of whatever normative epistemologies feminist philosophers cook up. It should help us knowledge makers know ourselves.

## The Knower and the Known

Dominant Anglo-American philosophers approached epistemology as a normative enterprise. Their job in building epistemologies was to evaluate methods of inquiry or strategies of reasoning; analyze what knowledge is and how it differs from mere opinion or false belief; and refute skeptical arguments that no knowledge of reality is possible (Stich, 1990).[1] The goal of the epistemologies was to plot the path to the one truth, the genuine morality, or the one rationality that ought to be used by all (or as the more cautious say, by all of "us").

Like any epistemologies, these carried with them an ontology and a methodology, both of which were based on a set of presuppositions about the nature of knowledge, of knowing beings, and of known objects. One of the deepest assumptions of the Anglo-American epistemology has been that knowing primarily concerns the beliefs of individuals (beliefs being propositions an individual accepts as true); concepts, languages, or conceptual systems; and, in ethics, moral language, or codes and principles. These were the units of the epistemology. With such units, epistemology had its focus on thinking rather than doing. "Conceptual analysis" and providing hypothetical examples seemed to be adequate methods. The strategies of reasoning were designed for all knowers, and so social and cultural differences were declared irrelevant. *Qua* knowledge, individuals were indistinguishable and their social positions irrelevant. And yet the collective life in which knowledge is made and used includes the social arrangements through which cognitive authority is exercised.

Over the past century in the United States, these social arrangements changed as professions developed in the sciences and humanities and as universities, research institutes, and bureaucracies carved out their territories of expertise. There were drastic changes in *who* made the public knowledge. Philosophers of the traditional epistemologies of science ignored these changes, claiming that they had to do not with genuine issues of knowledge (as they construed it) but only with external questions that might be interesting to historians, sociologists, and psychologists. In moral epistemology, the social organization of moral knowledge was brushed aside from the outset—at most it concerned heteronomous morality or mores, never the autonomous morality of genuine moral knowledge. Moral reasoning, not moral doing, was the subject matter of moral epistemology.

This story of the traditional Anglo-American epistemologies is an old story, and the philosophies have been criticized for over 100 years. Here in this anthology on feminist epistemologies, I recollect the old stories because there is still something to be learned from them—some clues and some warnings.

One characteristic claim among feminist philosophers is that traditional epistemology has a concealed political purpose: to support a dominant elite (all men, or higher-class white men of developed nations). Under the guise of an epistemology that plots the one rational route to truth and morality, the traditional philosophers were defining human nature and experience in terms of an ideology that higher-class men of developed nations used to dominate others. As a tool in the domination, those men made knowledge.

Feminist epistemology is often taken to have an opposing political purpose: to overcome male dominance and to do so by taking women's experience seriously.[2] Fulfilling this purpose requires radical changes in the disciplines of philosophy—including feminist philosophy. Fundamentally, it requires dissolving the old distinction between the internal, philosophical matters of epistemology proper and the external, historical, psychological, and sociological issues of social arrangements. For any adequate epistemology, social organization must be shown to be crucial to knowledge. The simple reason is that dominance is exercised through particular social and political organizations, however ideology may rationalize it. Despite the old ideology, *who* makes knowledge makes a difference. Making knowledge is a political act.

To dissolve the separation between knowledge and the social organization of cognitive authority requires that feminists jettison the old assumption that knowing is a matter of the beliefs or conceptual schemes of individuals. Many feminist philosophers (and even some revisionist traditional philosophers) heartily agree with this. However, to reunite knowledge with the social arrangements of cognitive authority requires making epistemology at least in part a descriptive enterprise, with appropriate empirical methods and concepts. It also requires forging appropriate epistemological units—who knows, what they know, and how they know it.

In this paper, I will offer some suggestions or a feminist epistemology. I was asked by the editors of this volume to treat moral epistemology, and that is a fine area in which to argue for radical philosophical change because it is obvious that the knowers of moral epistemology also have to be doers—something that seems easier to forget in epistemology proper, suffused as it has been with myths about scientific knowledge. But moral epistemology has its own myths, and they are particularly difficult to dislodge when they concern the basic units—myths that individuals or persons are the only appropriate knower/doers and that moral schemes (or principles, narratives, or lists of character types and virtues) are the appropriate units for expressing what is known.

There is, however, a very tricky issue that complicates my proposal for such a new epistemology. It reveals another, more intimate side to the need for feminist philosophers to base their work in both a descriptive epistemology and the activities of the real world.

We feminist philosophers who work within the academy are ourselves part of an elite. We are makers of knowledge; we exercise cognitive authority. In the United States, the academic elite has many times operated to support the very dominance structures that the women's movement has worked to overcome. This, of course, is the reason feminists try to change philosophy, using the strategy of undermining from within. However, feminists in the academy in the United States also form an elite among women, an elite in terms of our professional class position; in terms of our race (for the most part); and internationally, as members of an elite institution in a dominant nation.

The social position of feminist philosophers is a dominant one, not only over the positions of most other women but also over the positions of men of other classes, races, ages (both young and very old), and even nations.[3] In such a dangerous position, it is essential to do responsible work—and to be accountable for our work. We need to be accountable in general to all women, children, and men and responsible in particular to our sisters doing activist work outside the academy as well as our sisters in other disciplines within it (here granting the honorific name "sisters" to some men for their feminist work). It is for this positive reason of commitment, responsibility, and accountability that feminist epistemology must have a central descriptive component, grounded in an appropriate empirical science. For reasons of criticizing the old epistemology, we must know how the social organization of knowledge has supported male dominance. For reasons of making the new epistemology, we must know precisely and practically how our work operates to undermine dominant elites—or, alas, how it operates to support them. This means taking knowledge as a dynamic social process, not as a product to be justified, as traditional epistemologies have done.

I offer this descriptive epistemology for feminist knowledge makers, particularly in the academy. I believe, for some purposes, it is appropriate for knowledge makers in general—not only for those in the academy, not only for feminists. But I won't argue that here.

My main effort will be to set out appropriate units for such an epistemology. I'll review some widely known criticisms of traditional epistemology by revisionist philosophers W.V. Quine and Richard Rorty as a way of showing the importance of the units we use to analyze knowledge—a question of what is known, how it is known, and as Lynn Nelson says, of "who knows" (Nelson, 1990). I'll then offer my own proposals for units for a descriptive moral epistemology. As a working start, I will focus on what mainstream ethics classifies as questions of public policy rather than those of personal conscience (or personal decision or choice, or questions of the self). I am making a beginning, not an ending, because questions of the self and the personal are crucial to moral epistemology.[4] My proposed units are based in the idea that moral problems are known by social worlds through a process of making moral problems public in arenas of conflict. The science I work with in describing these things is symbolic interactionism—the line in American sociology that goes back to Jane Addams, John Dewey, and G.H. Mead.[5]

Many feminist philosophers present us with normative epistemologies that are useful for various purposes. The descriptive epistemology that I offer allows us to place the normative epistemologies within the social organization of cognitive authority by asking questions about who these feminists serve and how. To illustrate the procedure, I'll briefly evaluate several feminist normative theories using the abortion controversy as an illustration.

Finally, I'll look briefly at my own efforts as a knowledge maker. After all, I too exercise cognitive authority in our social organization of knowledge. I too am a certified member of an elite profession. I too formulate my questions and solutions out of a discipline of philosophy. Am I claiming to give an epistemology that really captures the truth and provides a method that legitimates the knowledge makers? No. The point is to give an epistemology, rooted in the social organization of knowledge, that may allow knowledge makers to do their work responsibly. The consequence of accepting the epistemology, for feminist knowledge makers in the academy, is a commitment to change the existing social organization of knowledge by changing our own practice—something that hasn't been widely attempted by academic feminists since the mid-1970s.

## Philosophical Work and the Units of Epistemology

In *Philosophy and the Mirror of Nature*, Richard Rorty told a story about Anglo-American epistemology. It originated, he said, in the setting of a problematic: the relation between universals and particulars—or in twentieth-century terms, between meanings and their references (Rorty 1979). The units here are particular things in the world and the abstract entities by virtue of which the particulars are "the same." The epistemological angle enters when we ask the self-interested and practically important questions of how we human beings know what exists and how we ought to find out the truth (often construed as issues in the foundations of knowledge). These questions bring in a third and crucial unit: individuals or persons who know. With the third unit comes a new set of questions concerning the relations of persons with the abstract commonalities and the individual particulars.

The invention of the problematic that Rorty describes was a way of legitimating certain kinds of philosophical work. Philosophers constructed the problematic by creating and interpreting a canon that includes the greats of the academic courses in ancient and modern philosophy, from Plato to Kant. In contemporary philosophy, it includes Quine and, by now, Rorty himself—for his work was in constructing a revisionist canon. The original effort elevated the work of some philosophical disciplines over others, and it gave grounds for determining who was doing philosophy and who was doing something extraneous to philosophy. Most of all, it legitimated philosophy as an intellectual profession—for according to the dominant ideology, a profession must have a monopoly on a difficult and important body of knowledge that requires lengthy training to master and certification to practice.[6] It carved out an area in the division of academic labor as a philosophical bailiwick.

By the mid-twentieth century, philosophy was securely ensconced as a profession in the United States. Epistemology per se had been translated to epistemology of science, and the units of interest were theories and their observation sentences. Persons had dropped into the deep background as objects of analysis, because it was self-evident to the reigning materialist/reductionists that it is individual persons who exist and know. The "norm of universalism" in science also rationalized forgetting about persons; it makes no difference who discovers or states the truth, because scientific knowledge is not relative to personal idiosyncrasy or political or cultural context (Merton 1949). This thesis, of course, helped rule out criticizing gender dominance in science, for the claim was that it was not the scientific knowledge itself that was biased; bias was the result of faulty research by prejudiced practitioners. In fact, knowledgeable, scholarly books were written to prove that science was "fair." The more radical feminist claim was, of course, that science upheld not simply gender bias but also massive support of male dominance, and not through the beliefs or actions of a bigoted few but systematically, as embedded in its deepest premises.

Science was a prestigious institution during most of the twentieth century. But within the traditional epistemology, science was defined as *the knowledge* made in science; more precisely, it was reduced to an idealized product: reconstructed theories and their observation sentences. Science as a dynamic social process of making knowledge dropped out of account in philosophy and was relegated to fields of study considered unimportant to epistemology—to sociology and history of science.[7] In fact, *philosophy* as a social process dropped out of account. The spotlight was on the product, and the professional and institutional processes by which the product was defined and constructed were hidden. The way knowledge was made and implemented was rendered irrelevant and, within the discipline of philosophy, it was invisible. Yet a main result of this epistemology was the production of propaganda veiled as rationality and correct reasoning.

The authors of "logical empiricism" took to themselves the task of legitimating the cognitive authority of science. They talked of the logic of science and the canonical form of theories, and they drew a line between genuine science and pseudoscience. They promoted science and secular humanism and debunked religion and folk practices and beliefs. They hid the fact that they were legitimating the authority of living human beings and institutions by separating scientific knowledge in its "reconstructed" idealized form from the work that flesh-and-blood scientists did in the academy and the research institutes.

Within philosophy, there was eventually an avalanche of mainstream criticism—spearheaded by Quine and Davidson and, much later, Rorty—against this older approach to epistemology of science. Though they did not raise issues of implementation and the social organization of cognitive authority, the criticisms took two directions of interest to me in this article. One, taken particularly by Quine and Davidson, was basically a criticism of the some of the units of epistemology. The other, insisted upon by all three, was a criticism of the task the earlier epistemology had taken to itself: the provision of some sort of foundation for knowledge. The second criticism led Rorty and

Quine to the conclusion that the new epistemology should be moved out of philosophy into some field of science—though they did not agree on which one.

These philosophers of the contemporary mainstream canon roundly criticized meanings, propositions, theories, conceptual schemes, and the like—the abstract units that were used to represent what is common among the particulars. Their conclusions were that epistemology was no longer to be concerned with justification of theories or laws in terms of evidence or with the relation of observation sentences to theories or hypotheses. Rather, according to Rorty at least, justification takes place in an activity of arguing out disputes in conversations. Who has these conversations? Cognitive authorities like Rorty himself, operating out of ethnocentric (and we might suppose androcentric) presuppositions about knowledge, politics, and rationality (Davenport, 1987). I'll return to this below when I discuss the notion of arenas in which social worlds carry out their arguments.

The other unit, the one so deeply presupposed in epistemology of science that it was submerged, is that of a person or individual. It seems equally submerged in the work of these canonical critics. In contrast some feminist philosophers have argued strenuously against taking individual persons as the knowing units. Lynn Nelson raises one of these questions dramatically in the title of her recent book, *Who Knows* (1990). She argues against epistemological individualism, the assumption that individuals are among the basic units (or are the basic units) of epistemology. This assumption has been widely criticized by feminists.[8] The difficulty is how to find an alternative to individuals without making individuals disappear entirely.

One of Thomas Kuhn's great contributions in his work, *The Structure of Scientific Revolutions*, was implicitly to take scientific communities as knowers. Kuhn's work took some account of politics within the scientific disciplines, and recent work in sociology of science and sociology of knowledge scrutinizes the ways that scientific knowledge is constructed in labs, in the field, and in the hallways of the workplace. Lynn Nelson has argued explicitly that communities are knowers in the basic sense and that individuals qualify as such only derivatively (Nelson 1990). In moral epistemology, communities are plausible candidates, but we need a way of understanding communities that allows us to see how they operate as knower/doers in the dynamic processes of making knowledge and upholding or undermining a dominance order. I'll pursue this suggestion below.[9]

By taking communities as knowers, we take a step toward understanding the process of making knowledge rather than being mesmerized by the product. However, this step alone is not sufficient to show how traditional epistemology has supported male dominance and how a feminist epistemology might be liberatory. To do those things requires showing how the knowledge that is made in the professional communities comes to be *implemented* in the larger society. It requires taking account of the social organization of cognitive authority. It requires continued self-consciousness about the fact that we operate as elite professionals. It requires a method by which we can make knowledge responsibly.

The magnitude of this task cannot be underestimated. The academic disciplines are constructed to preserve themselves, their bailiwicks, and the careers and authority of their members. In producing knowledge, they face, as it were, inward contemplation of their own navels. This is as true of feminist philosophy as it is of traditional disciplines. The dangers Daniel Callahan lists in his complaint about the practice of philosophical ethics are dangers for feminist philosophers as well:

> ... The culture of professional philosophy ... is a relatively closed world. The debates in the field usually circle about a small number of dominant figures, analyze a relatively narrow range of theoretical topics ... proceed by what appear to be set procedural rules, and are written for the private language of professional moral theory. As a rule, the references and sources used are those of the writings of other theorists, rarely the external world of human events, actions, and motives (Callahan 1989,22).

Taking communities—or as I'll say, social worlds—as one of the units of epistemology allows us to see Callahan's criticism as one that is central to issues of knowledge. With an appropriate description of social worlds as knower/doers, we will be able to find out, on a case-by-case basis, whom we serve and how well we serve them. Feminist philosophers will be able to test how well our knowledge work subverts male dominance and serves women.

Finally, after this lengthy discussion of the much-criticized epistemology of science, we may enter the fresher air of moral epistemology.

## Moral Epistemology and Philosophical work

Writers of ethics texts make a three-fold distinction that separates meta-ethics (or ethics proper), morality (or moral theory) and practical (or applied) ethics. Moral epistemology falls within ethics proper. In doing work in ethics proper, philosophers analyze the form and nature of the moral theories they produce. "Practical ethics" is a discipline that developed over the past generation, when Anglo-American philosophers found employment by taking the theoretical products out to the world. Feminist work in ethics covers all three of the canonical divisions, but it is rooted in practical ethics.

Philosophers doing practical ethics are said to be concerned with problems in the world—chronic problems like gender dominance or more immediate ones like abortion policy. In the academy, the work of practical ethics includes writing philosophy books and teaching courses but focuses on the public problems of the moment rather than conceptual problems generated entirely within the discipline. For example, multitudes of books and articles have been published on abortion, animal rights, the environment, race- and gender-based discrimination, and equal opportunity. These are generally classed as moral problems of public policy, and feminist philosophers have not only contributed to their clarification but have also changed moral theory on their basis.

Practical ethics includes other work: for example, work in situ by ethicists attached to ethics committees in hospitals. These ethicists are said to offer expert advice in helping personnel come to decisions on particular cases or on general issues of ethics for particular professions or businesses.[10] That work is important to analyze, but in this paper I will stay with moral problems that are made public—which I will sometimes call "public problems" for short.

Philosophers nearly always decide the units of their moral epistemologies on the basis of some normative moral theory that they favor.[11] The knowers of these epistemologies are individuals (either human beings or rational beings). What the individuals know varies with the given normative moral theory—they may know moral principles; or the good, or the right thing to decide in a given circumstance; or their own interests and desires. Usually they know explanations and justifications of what they and others do—they know the rules of the moral language games. This theoretical pattern holds true even for some of the new feminist (or feminine) ethics. For example, in Carol Gilligan's ethics, the units are individuals and their moral reasons and explanations (stated in terms of care and relationship). Gilligan's is an ethics of moral reasoning that takes concepts and principles of care as units. Only in this very derivative sense is it a morality of care and relationship, for it lacks any means of representing social relationships as they exist, to say nothing of showing how the explanations are constructed [see Addelson (1991)].

There is another unit important in practical ethics. In writing or teaching on public policy issues, philosophers often frame their discussions in terms of "positions" (e.g., the pro-life or pro-choice position in abortion; the liberal, conservative, or feminist positions on various issues; and so on).[12] "Position" is one of the explicit units in the dominant moral epistemology dealing with public problems. A position is something that can be reconstructed into a set of principles and "claims" in the form of a logical argument. These abstract, conceptual products substitute for the processes of conflict among groups.

A second unit—the omnipresent individual—is often implicit. Books and articles and classroom lectures in practical ethics are formatted "as if" they were addressed to rational individuals to help them make up their minds about which "position" to take. This, of course, is a liberal approach—philosophically and politically—but it is an approach often taken even by philosophers who argue bitterly against liberalism. Public action is reduced to "policy issues," which are then reduced to verbal controversies over positions about which an individual rationally makes up his or her mind. This is the format for teaching and writing philosophy.

The focus in this philosophical format is on deciding which policy is a good one, as if after the vote the moral issue was settled. But, of course, whatever policy is decided upon has to be implemented. For example, liberalized abortion policy had to be implemented nationally (in 1973) by removing, in practice, obstacles to legal abortion and providing real options for choosing abortion. For the most part, the options were supplied in a laissez-faire manner—clinics sprang up according to market demand, and those who could pay could choose. Initially, funding for those who couldn't pay was implemented through the Medicaid bureaucracies.[13] That implementation was cause of bitter conflict among contestants in the abortion policy arena.

Feminist philosophers have taken implementation of policy very seriously, and in doing so they have altered liberal ethics and political theory to include real options and not simply abstract rights and equalities.[14]

There is a second question of implementation that concerns not policy but philosophical work in ethics: What does moral theorizing have to do with "morality itself" or "the moral institution of life"? How is the theory we make in our offices and seminar rooms implemented out in the world? This is a question about the social arrangements of cognitive authority. It is essential to answer this question properly not only if moral theories are to be tested for adequacy but also if we are to understand and take account of our elite social positions as knowledge makers. Answering the question properly requires finding appropriate units for moral epistemology and an appropriate social science to use as a basis. As I said earlier, my candidate is a modified interactionist sociology, and I offer that candidate for test here.

I spoke earlier not of positions but of "contestents in a policy arena." Contestants in a policy arena are "knower/doers," and they are not reducible to "positions." Their contest is a process, and it cannot be reduced to a reified product. I will interpret these contestants, these "knower/doers," as *social worlds,* and I'll discuss that notion and the notion of an *arena* later.

The crucial activity of these knower/doers is not a conflict over which position is the morally right and justifiable one—though arguments about moral rightness and justifiability are part of their arsenals and, with few exceptions, they believe what they way. I will take these knower/doers to be concerned with moral problems (not positions) and with the process of making moral problems public. For short, I'll speak of *public problems.* The process of making moral problems public is one of the central processes through which dominance is maintained—and changed. It is therefore an important unit for a feminist epistemology.

I have, then, three units for my moral epistemology: social worlds, arenas, and public problems (understood as a process of making moral problems public). To deal with these units more carefully, I will set out a set of working notions, or "sensitizing concepts" as they are called.

Sensitizing concepts are rather different from the usual definitory concepts that philosophers demand. They are not defined by giving necessary or sufficient conditions, and they cannot be articulated by conceptual analysis. They are designed for making sense of data from field studies, which are the basic empirical data in participant-observation studies and in everyday life as well. Sensitizing concepts organize field data in a way that simplifies them and shows important patterns and relationships. A good concept will help make coherent the data from many studies so that, in a sense, the investigator (or the audience) reaches what is common across the studies by using what is distinctive to the empirical instance.[15] I will use several sensitizing concepts in this paper, among them public problems, social worlds, and arenas, and my readers may judge their usefulness.

Our first need is to have a more precise understanding of the process of making moral problems public, one which can lead us to uncover the social worlds that are to be our knower/doers and the arenas in which they act.

## Making Moral Problems Public

In very rough terms, making a moral problem public is a process in which groups of activists work to gain the attention of public officials in order to make them do something about it. The media are usually heavily involved in the process. Examples of recent public problems are abortion, euthanasia, pornography, poverty, racism, homelessness, drugs, teen pregnancy, AIDS, homosexuality, homicide, gangs, unemployment, childcare, working mothers, abuse, incest, child pornography, woman pornography, health care, pregnancy care, child mortality, global warming, toxic waste, banking abuses, and war.

Philosophers pick up these problems as they emerge as public issues and then analyze and reconstruct the moral rhetoric in terms of their moral theories. As they are framed, the public problems involve a variety of moral problems concerning rights, goodness, virtue, obligation, life plans, responsibilities, sanctities, and so on that enter somehow into discussions over their resolution. For example, abortion is said to involve a conflict of rights or (alternatively) the sanctity of life; AIDS and teen pregnancy are said to involve responsible sex or the virtue of chastity; and most of the problems are understood, implicitly or explicitly, in terms of consequences for the good life for human beings and (often) in terms of rational life plans.

Before presenting my own understanding of public problems, it is necessary to disqualify for my purposes here a common-sense or folk understanding that I believe is shared by many traditional philosophers doing practical ethics and even by many feminist philosophers. It is the operative understanding in the political resolution of the problems, and it usually supports dominance orders that feminists claim to find objectionable. And so it is important to make the folk understanding explicit. It has something like the following format: A social condition objectively exists (scientists confirm it) that is problematic because it has morally relevant consequences. The problematic situation comes about through people doing various things for various reasons or causes. The solution lies in understanding and changing the conditions (either the people's behavior or the environment) so that the future will be different (i.e., the social problem will be solved or resolved). Social worlds in the public problems arena seem to accept the folk explanation, at least in their public actions and arguments. Let me illustrate this by presenting the problem of teen pregnancy, which contestants on all sides seem to agree is a problem, though they disagree on cause and solution.

Many teens are getting pregnant (objective condition), and it ruins their lives and costs society a lot of money in welfare payments (morally relevant consequences). As we might expect, the explanation of the causes differs according to the solution one side or another is promoting. For liberal secular humanists and family planners, the cause is that teenagers are ignorant about sex and so act irresponsibly, and the solution is sex education in the schools—the goal being rational behavior. For some Christian groups, the cause is a lack of moral fiber in the teens, and the solution is to instill chastity in our youth—the goal being virtuous behavior. Both sides embrace the "mom and apple pie solution" that parents should overcome their inhibitions and talk to their kids about sex. One side claims its solution leads to rational behavior and a lean social services budget; the other side claims its solution leads to good character, happy family life, and the health of the nation.

It's worth noting that all contestants rely on scientific and other professional authorities, and that the secular humanist analysis relies on some analogue of the traditional epistemology and ontology.

In setting the problem of teen pregnancy, I have already slipped into a different perspective, that of describing the process of making the teen pregnancy problem public. Let me be explicit about it.[16]

In 1976 the Alan Guttmacher Institute discovered an epidemic of teen pregnancy (the emergence of the problem). They placed the cause in ignorance that led to irrational and irresponsible sexual behavior by teens.[17] The Guttmacher institute published a report that included demographic and other data establishing the existence of the problem (legitimating the problem by citing cognitive authorities). Legitimation usually involves data gathered by research institutes to show the problem really exists. It also usually includes cost-benefit data, data from psychologists, and even arguments from philosophers (implementation in the second sense).[18]

In the next stage—the mobilization of action—Planned Parenthood circulated pamphlets; the newspapers and television ran stories giving the statistics and showing sad cases; lobbyists went to work in Washington; and social service professionals became involved. On the other side, conservative groups did their own mobilizing, accepting the problem but differing about cause and solution. [See Petchesky (1983) for an account.]

With all this brouhaha, the Carter administration formulated an official policy and said, "Let there be an office for teens!" Congress voted funding and set policy guidelines. The policy was implemented, and the office was set up. On the national level, the implementation of teen pregnancy policy changed radically from the Carter administration to the Reagan administration. On the local level, there are still struggles in schools, clinics, and so on.

In this description of making moral problems public, knower/doers emerge from several directions. There are the groups of activists (for example family planning groups and Christian groups) who head up the legitimation and mobilization processes. There are the officials.

There are the bureaucrats, social service officials, and so on who implement the official plan. There are also various experts—demographers, biologists, sexologists, educators, and even philosophers—who work with the activists, officials, and bureaucrats. Lest we forget, there are also the individuals who are the source of the social problem—those people who are labeled as doing something that causes the social problem. In this example, they include the teenagers—particularly teenaged young women—and their parents.

What I like about taking public problems as a unit in my epistemology is that in describing the process, I can show precisely how knowledge is made public and how particular people, social worlds, and institutions use and act on that knowledge so as to reinforce or subvert dominance orders. We can find out who knows, what they know, and how. I do not need to talk in some vague way about ideology influencing hearts and minds so that somehow (unexplainedly) dominance and subordination results. Having made that promissory note, I'll now make some vague remarks on how the problem of teen pregnancy, as it was defined, contributed to supporting dominance orders (or hiding their subversion).

First of all, teen pregnancy was isolated from procreative issues in general. This fragmentation of women's issues has been a common feminist complaint, and it is quite clearly a political move. In addition, the sexual and reproductive problems of teens were defined and officially dealt with by mechanisms distinct from those used for adult women—reinforcing, even manufacturing, age dominance. This restriction also led to solutions in terms of educating teens (for safe sex or chastity) rather than of change in male-female relationships or the economic system.

The ahistorical presentation of the problem is also important. From an historical point of view, teens have been getting pregnant ever since public high school was invented (and before, of course). However, there were institutionalized ways to deal with pregnancy. One of the most important was marriage—one authority reports that from 1960 to 1965, 65% of births conceived out of wedlock were legitimated by marriage. (Vinovskis, 1981) Adoption was an important alternative in some circles; even before Roe v. Wade, abortion was an alternative—sometimes very risky, sometimes safe. After Roe, of course, abortion became publicly visible; reliable statistics became available on who was getting abortions. More unmarried white women began keeping their babies—young African-American women had always done so.

These were changes that were made, in part, through the "sexual revolution" and the women's movement. The changes have generally been interpreted as undermining male dominance an the subordination of women. There is clearly a change in the moral selves of young women in this process—from being shamed into hiding the illicit sex and pregnancy to being able to deal with it—even to going public by keeping the child. The process of making teen pregnancy a public problem does not set the changes in this liberatory light. Rather, authorities in the process make knowledge of the problem in a way that upholds the subordination. Feminists often argue this about the Christian recommendation for chastity. It is equally true for the secular humanist recommendation for safe sex, which is played as rational decision in the service of an individual life plan—hiding the dominance structures of the world in which that life will be made.

For both the Christians and the secular humanists, the definition of the problem posits something wrong, something different, about the young women who get pregnant, and the solution is to normalize them. Normalize them to what? A proper answer would require a fuller investigation of how we all make our lives today, but it would certainly include the fact that the young women are to be normalized to a social order marked by dominance and subordination.

I've said these things to indicate why the process of making moral problems public is a useful unit for a descriptive epistemology. It allows us to find out how knowledge is made in circumstances that relate directly to maintenance or subversion of dominance orders.

This gives a rough sense of the epistemological unit of making moral problems public, enough to move on to the sensitizing concepts of a social world and a social arena.

## Social Worlds and Arenas

In my discussion above, I mentioned various categories of people— family planners, demographers, philosophers, bureaucrats, and presidents. People in these categories take part in the interacting social worlds—the communities of knowers/doers. In rough terms, a social world consists of people who, over a period of time, perform some sort of collective action together.[19] Social worlds may be enormous and complex, with many subworlds: for example, a large corporation or the philosophy profession. Or they may be small, with a relatively simple goal: for example, an ad hoc effort to stage a benefit for a family burned out of its home or the world of pick-up basketball at a local park.

Unlike a nation or a community, a social world need not have geographical boundaries or formal membership. The relations among members of a social world are founded in communication, whether it be face-to-face activity with little talk (pick-up basketball, manual work), regular meetings, electronic mail, telephone calls, or form letters. For example, "the philosophy profession" and "feminist philosophy" name social worlds of related, quite complex sorts, held together by a multitude of communicative modes that includes department meetings, conferences, journals, and electronic media.

What is important in this notion of a social world is that we can ask detailed, empirical questions to specify what is done and who does it rather than talk abstractly about "positions" or "the patriarchy" or "the ruling class." In the example I gave above of the public problem of teen pregnancy, I named organizations and dates; I did not talk about "liberal secular humanist" or "family planner" or "fundamentalist" positions. Of course, any adequate discussion of the public problem of teen pregnancy would have to be much more empirically detailed than the one I gave.

The social worlds relevant to public problems consist of group knower/doers whose collective action involves creating and struggling over public problems. They are doers because they (the social worlds) take part in the process of making moral problems public, and they are knowers not only because they know facts (moral or otherwise) about a given problem but also because they organize knowledge and in fact create definitions of the social problem under which to organize and interpret the scientific, philosophical, religious, and other knowledge. They make knowledge and construct morality as they act and know.

In cases of disagreement, either within a social world or among social worlds, an "arena" is created. In arenas, the social worlds involved in a given public problem come together to struggle things out (Strauss et al. 1964, 377). Like social worlds, arenas vary in size from national to very local and "domestic." In my example, I discussed (obliquely) the national arena in which teen pregnancy became a public problem. That arena is part of the larger arena in which reproductive policy is made. Adele Clarke lists the some of the social worlds involved in the reproductive policy arena.

> ... In the broad arena focused on human reproduction, participants include knowledge producers (several kinds of reproductive scientists, geneticists, social scientists), practicing medical personnel (physicians, nurses, other health care providers, public health personnel), their various professional medical organizations, sponsors (public and private funding agencies), consumers (both as organized collective actors and as individuals), the pharmaceutical and medical industries, policy makers, governmental regulatory bodies, organized religious and political groups, and others. (Clarke 1990)

The social worlds of philosophy, including the subworld of feminist philosophy, participate in the reproduction arena as knowledge producers. This is one way in which moral theories are implemented.

At this point, I need to relate these theoretical notions more clearly to feminist work in philosophy. To do so, I'll specify one common sense of "the women's movement" in terms of social worlds. I'll then be able to raise some questions about how some of the feminist moral theories and moral epistemologies serve this social world.

## The Women's Movement: An Illustration

The women's movement in the United States is a very large social world in the sense of a group of people working together toward certain ends, even though the subworlds might not all share all of the ends and even though they might disagree on the means. Although we can discuss the social world of the women's movement in terms of its historical changes, I'll discuss it as it was in the 1980s, trying to avoid the historical gaffe of including what was appropriate twenty years ago but is not appropriate now. To begin, I'll use *Women and Public Policies* by Joyce Gelb and Marian Lief Palley. Gelb and Palley specify the women's movement in terms of women's organizations that move nationally on women's issues. They divide the women's movement into feminist groups and traditional groups. Recently, the feminist groups they mention have been called "the women's community," a social world that refers to groups whose staff meet more or less regularly in Washington, D.C., to trade information and plot strategy or who maintain close communication.

Gelb and Palley include among the feminist groups those that are mass-based, like NOW; specialized groups like The Women's Rights Project and The Reproductive Freedom Project of the ACLU; and single-issue groups like NARAL, The Association for Intercollegiate Athletics for Women, and PEER, which monitors Title IX in educational settings.

These feminists groups claim to represent the social world in many external arenas. It is a standard feature that organizations claim to represent a social world, and these claims often give rise to conflict within a social world (i.e., to internal arenas).

The social world that is the women's movement also includes organizations classed as traditional women's groups but who maintain close communication with the above groups and have a large membership (roughly 2.5 million gross) that is crucial for support. They include the AAUW, B'nai Brith Women, The League of Women Voters, The General Federation of Women's clubs, The National Federation of Business and Professional Women's Clubs, The National Council of Jewish Women, and The United Methodist Women.

There are also millions of people not affiliated with any of these groups who also support them and are part of the large, complex social world of the women's movement but in a weaker sense, in which communication consists of reading about the public problems, receiving mailings, sending in contributions, and being mobilized for marches and other actions.

This is "the women's movement" in one effective sense. The women's movement in this sense has been most successful in arenas in which equity issues are raised to public problems requiring official action on policy. They include, for example, credit discrimination, issues of economic equity, pregnancy discrimination, and all the various Title IX issues of sex discrimination.

There has been widespread support on these issues among women of all classes and races in the United States and widespread support among men as well. These issues unite women.[20]

The case is different in arenas involved in public problems of reproduction, particularly abortion. It is a problem that divides, rather than unites, women even in the social world of the women's movement. Both anti-abortion and pro-choice women agree that the women's movement has broken barriers that keep women from being full partners in society, and both reject the idea that the male should be primary breadwinner: they are more or less in harmony with feminists who focus on issues of equal opportunity, equal pay for equal work, and so on (Fried 1988; Gelb and Palley 1987).

Abortion "pits women against one another" (Gelb and Palley 1987, 133). This makes it a prime problem that calls out for the aid of feminist ethics aimed at the social worlds and arenas of the women's movement. It is taken as a moral problem in the arena, and it divides people within the arena. It is also marks major divisions among feminist philosophers, and unless the philosopher relates herself to a specific social world, it results in a massive, snarling confusion. This makes it a good test area for feminist theory.

## A Test for Normative Moral Theories

I've now sketched some of the basic units for the descriptive core of a moral epistemology. To show some of the uses, I might show how traditional practical (or applied) ethics supports patriarchy by taking part in making moral problems public in ways that support male dominance. I would then demonstrate some of the practices that feminists need to overcome and that would be useful. Instead, I will take up the "more intimate" problem I mentioned in the introduction—the problem that we feminist academics are members of an elite that exercises cognitive authority. The hope is that we exercise it in a way that subverts dominance structures. But that is a hope that needs testing. Once again, I'll use abortion as a sample problem.

Most of the hundreds of philosophical articles written on the topic of abortion use a liberal, secular humanist moral theory as their basis, as do the canonical papers enshrined in ethics texts for the classroom. For the most part, the moral problem is defined in terms of a conflict of rights between the fetus and the pregnant woman. This, I suppose, began as an effort to capture the moral problem in the rhetoric of the political arena where some prominent slogans had to do with a woman's choice—making a focus on individual liberty—or with the right to life—making a focus on fetal viability or fetal personhood. These sorts of philosophical papers tend to feed on each other, as Callahan said. A few have been reprinted in multitudes of copycat anthologies for classroom use, where there is a canonical statement of the moral problem of abortion. In mainstream ethics, the problem has to a good degree become self-contained within the discipline.

Feminists have offered very significant challenges to the usual "conflict of rights" approaches, and some have devised perspicuous alternatives (Hursthouse 1987; Harrison 1983; Whitbeck, 1983). I'll first consider "conflict of rights" approaches, and then look briefly at some alternative feminist proposals.

As I discussed the implementation of moral theory above, the philosophical theorists are members of social worlds. The theorists need not have personal contact with other members of the world. In fact, our academic jobs encourage us to communicate by writing books and articles that others "freely chose" to read—quite a distant mode of participation. Theorists using a "conflict of rights" approach take part in particular social worlds by virtue of the very theories they propose. In the abortion controversy, these may include worlds on both the pro-choice side and, interestingly enough, the anti-abortion side. This is particularly true when, in an effort at detachment, philosophers construct theories that are supposed to accommodate "both sides in the debate" through examining arguments and clarifying concepts. [see Sumner (1981) and Thomson (1971)]. In its implementation, the "conflict of rights" approach shows a class and race bias, as well as a bias toward supporting an elite and arguing against an elite. We can see how if we take social worlds seriously.

According to Mary Jo Nietz's research with anti-abortion Catholic groups, there were two different moral stands against abortion (Nietz 1981). Among educated, higher-class Catholics who are anti-abortion (and this includes members of the Church hierarchy), the arguments primarily concerned the personhood of the fetus. Among the lower- and middle-class Catholics, the arguments concerned the integrity of the family and the care and love that we are bound to show each other. The usual philosophical arguments deal with the first, not the second. The upshot is that developing abortion arguments within one of the liberal moral theories leaves philosophers talking to the elite on both sides and ignoring moral issues the nonelite find crucial. I am saying that philosophers, including feminist philosophers, make public the moral problem of abortion in ways that support the authority and the action methods of elites.

The problem is very serious, because there is some reason to believe that there is a class issue in abortion politics itself—Anne O'Donnell, director of the National Right to Life Committee, once went so far as to say that abortion politics involves a "class struggle" because of the predominantly lower- and middle-class character of grassroots right-to-life activists. On the other hand, a survey of NARAL members showed a membership that was white, female, urban, and relatively young. Many were professionally educated and employed. NARAL membership, of course, has a large overlap with other groups like NOW (Gelb and Palley 1987; 25–44, 149, 151).

One root of the classism is that, in the conflict-of-rights analysis, abortion is removed from the life context in which it has its moral meaning. Feminist philosophers (and other feminists) have insisted that it is a patriarchal bias as well, removing abortion from other problems to which it is connected in many feminist social worlds— problems of healthy childbirth, women's health care in general, healthy families, teen pregnancy, childrearing and education, and even poverty (Addelson, 1991; Harrison, 1983; Whitbeck, 1983). The classism has not gone unnoticed, of course, and these differences in the abortion controversy constitute one of the reasons "the women's movement" has been called white and middle class. Gerrymandering abortion out of the context of women's lives also accounts for the fact that until 1989 African-American and Hispanic groups were very little involved in abortion politics. The conclusion is that, in its implementation in the abortion arenas, the liberal moral theory has racist, ageist, ethnic, and religious consequences, as well as classist ones.

Does this mean that feminists must stop philosophical work on the abortion problem? My own view is that we should change the way we do the work. The descriptive epistemology I have suggested shows how philosophers operate as knowledge makers—and so it shows not only the unfortunate effects of unreflective theoretical work but also a way to deal with them so that we can do responsible knowledge work.

How might we remedy the problem? I believe we can begin to find remedies only by being more fully engaged with the social worlds we serve so that we can find out what they need by way of a moral theory. This means becoming more full-blooded members of the social worlds for which we do our practical ethics. We need to be members involved in face-to-face interchange, putting the full range of our abilities at their service. Then our work will be not only politically useful but also tested in the heat of conflict within important arenas. Let me give an example.

In 1989, Frances Kissling of Catholics for a Free Choice declared to political leaders in the women's movement that the abortion movement was dead in the water unless they broadened their approach. They did so by doing serious networking and holding meetings with groups like the Children's Defense League, the National Black Women's Health Network, the National Hispanic Women's Health Network, and the usual women's movement organizations. But they also required a moral analysis that was different from the conflict-of-rights analysis. They require this for political reasons of unity and effectiveness on the national, and particularly the state, fronts. The analysis had to do what many feminist philosophers have been saying it must do—link abortion with the broad spectrum of reproductive, family, and life issues that women face. Beverly Harrison, a feminist theologian, is one theoretician who has offered a beginning idea for an appropriate moral theory—to speak of procreative choice *in general* (Harrison 1983). Applied in the abortion arena, this might yield media rhetoric that moves the emphasis off abortion and onto women making many kinds of responsible choices.[21]

There are some recent original offerings in feminist ethics that seem to avoid the problems of liberal moral theory but also require testing in the social arenas in which moral problems are made public. For example, Carol Gilligan gave us a moral theory of preserving relationship; Nel Noddings, one of care; Annette Baier, one of trust; and Sara Ruddick, one of mothering. Do these moral theories acknowledge a wider range of procreative experience? Are they useful to pro-choice arenas and the social world of the women's movement? Celia Wolf-Devine (1989) has argued quite convincingly that these ethics essentially support an anti-abortion stance or, if they acknowledge choice (as most explicitly do), the weight of the moral theories is heavily against having an abortion. The authors of these feminist ethics are fairly uniformly pro-choice, and some try to argue that way. But Wolf-Devine claims, with some reason, that they do not succeed.

Might these feminist theorists of care and mothering have something to give to the grassroots, anti-abortion social worlds? Perhaps they might, but they would have to become part of those worlds, in however limited a way, to find out. And if they are proposing their ethics for the social worlds of the women's movement, then they have a lot of work to do to make their theories serviceable. It is work that cannot be done without direct collaboration with the activists of the women's movement. We cannot suppose that moral theorists know, from the vantage point of our ivory tower, the needs of social worlds engaged in battles of public policy arenas. That was the mistake of the old epistemology, and it was a philosophical and a moral error.

### Remarks on My Own Knowledge Making

So what do I think about making normative moral epistemologies, feminist or otherwise? I feel there is an internal, theoretical, and methodological side to the issue. The normative epistemologies have to be taken as rhetoric or as ideologies that are embedded in our folk understandings and our present ways of making moral problems public. This is perfectly compatible with the feminist criticisms that these epistemologies (in their traditional forms at least) support male dominance or patriarchy. However, we must understand even the feminist, normative epistemologies as rhetoric—proposals for new ideologies to be embedded in new institutional ways of making moral problems public. Such a feminist epistemology requires a new social organization of knowledge. That is, it requires that feminists within the academy institute new and responsible practices of making knowledge. In the women's movement of the 1970s, many feminist academics did just that. Today, the trick is to invent ways to subvert the usual practices of the academy and to overcome our own professionalized training. It requires dissolving the walls of the academy to learn how to make knowledge with the women we serve. To do this is to develop an *effective* class consciousness of how the elite academic classes recreate dominance, and to become aware of how we ourselves are complicit in that process.

I must stress that I do not mean that all is relativism and incommensurability, a whir of rhetoric signifying nothing. That is the nihilism embraced by mainstream critics of traditional epistemology. To do normative ethics or feminist theory under such a flag is to succumb to a poisonous and cynical self-interest. I am saying that making knowledge is a political act, and making normative moral epistemology is an act of political rhetoric. To give a theory of moral reasoning—or of women's moral reasoning—is to give a rhetoric, one that may even be used by the people in question and (we hope) be useful to them. It is not to describe "the moral institution of life" or "the patriarchy" or even "the liberal/capitalist/democratic system." It does not capture "our" morality—though it may present moral rhetoric people use in certain situations for certain purposes.

The moral institution of life is a dynamic, creative process of knowing and doing. Normative moral epistemologies play a part in it. But understanding the process of knowing and doing requires a descriptive epistemology, not a normative one. That is what I am suggesting.

And what about myself as a knowledge maker proposing this descriptive epistemology? Am I pretending to offer up the truth while others supply mere rhetoric? Am I giving the hard facts while others muddle along with soft values? These questions come out of the old ways of traditional epistemology—that epistemology created by and for knowledge makers who supported certain dominance orders. That old epistemology defined what it was to be responsible in making knowledge and did so in terms of justification and correct reasoning. In doing so, it supported the cognitive authority of knowledge makers in a liberal, capitalist democracy marked by dominance orders. My descriptive epistemology is designed for different knowledge makers in the hope of a different social order. I suggest a few routes to responsible knowledge making—only a few, for much more is needed. *The measure of any epistemology lies in how well it allows knowledge makers to be responsible.* It does not lie in how well it gives us certified knowledge or the route to the truth of the one reality.

In this article, I gave suggestions on a descriptive epistemology for knowledge makers in the academy. But the world is made up of multitudes of knowledge makers in social worlds large and small. A fuller measure of my descriptive epistemology requires seeing how useful it is for these other knower/doers in the arenas in which they live. If it were useful in this larger scope, then the rhetoric of normative epistemology might come to be known as a metaphor that is useful in some situations for conducting the business of life. Then the normative epistemologies would no longer function as veils to hide dominance orders.

## Notes

Some of the ideas in this paper were worked out in the process of writing "Making Knowledge" (Addelson and Potter 1991). I particularly want to thank

Ellen Davidow, one of the editors of the anthology for which that paper was written, for her detailed and perspicuous criticisms and comments. I also thank Lynn Nelson and the editors of this volume for their helpful comments on this paper.

1.  Stich himself opts for normative epistemology, though he claims to be pluralist in the sense that there are a number of such epistemologies.

2.  Jaggar (1989) gives a brief review of themes in feminist ethics and social philosophy. Criticisms of the traditions of the West abound. See, for example, Elshtain (1981), Harding (1986), Jaggar (1983), and Spelman (1989) as well as anthologies of earlier feminist work, like Osborne (1979).

3.  My peculiar phrasing here in terms of dominance of *positions* is meant to stress the systemic nature of dominance as a relation among groups. The reductionist approach that has each man dominating every woman in some personal, economic, and status mode is not only false but also leads us to ignore issues of class, race, age, and imperialist dominance in which feminist academics, by virtue of our class position, are implicated. The point, of course, is that we try to act from a dominant position to overcome dominance. See Addelson and Potter (1991) for further discussion.

4.  I used interactionist sociology to look at questions of personal morality—choice, explanation, character, and the self—in Addelson (1987).

5.  See my essays in Addelson (1991). Though I find much that is useful in the interactionist tradition, I also have serious criticisms; for example they ignore *systemic* relations of dominance, as well as the class position of the professional researcher.

6.  See discussions in Addelson and Potter (1991). Professions, and their legitimizations, have been exhaustively studied in sociology. See Hughes (1984) for a classic source on theory. Freidson (1982, 1986) does interesting work on professions in medicine. Clarke (1990) contains important work on the development of professions in reproductive science. The necessity of legitimating the philosophy profession is least of all a matter of mere self-importance. It has been necessary if philosophy was to be worthy of departmental status and control of job slots within the universities and colleges and to have funding and access to the means of publication. See the discussion on the development of modern and ancient philosophy in Kucklick (1984). See Oleson and Voss (1979) on the social organization of knowledge in the United States.

7.  Critics like C. Wright Mills were ignored; see Mills (1963). Marxists were, of course, also ignored.

8.  See Scheman (1983) and Jaggar (1983). The term "epistemological individualism" is taken from Addelson and Potter (1991). These criticisms are widespread in feminist philosophy and in feminist studies and are generally presented as criticisms against liberal individualism. They are also widespread among social constructionists, Marxists, and others.

9.   Communities are acknowledged in moral epistemology, of course, but on the side of the "common" (cultures, moral schemes, sets of "our" moral concepts, practices, moral language, and narratives), which sets them as what is known rather than as knowers.

10.   Patricia Flynn (1991) has done a study of ethics committees with interesting results.

11.   Descriptive moral epistemology may sound to many of them like something best left to anthropologists. Some, like Stanley Hauerwas, seem to be doing a priori descriptive epistemology, for example when Stanley Hauerwas analyzes Christian ethics in terms of narratives based on the Bible. Some, like Gilligan or Bellah, use interviews to get individuals' verbal explanations of their normative folk moralities.

12.   Some feminist and other radical philosophers have managed to escape this method by transforming the medium; see, for example, Griffin (1978). For a blatant example of this method in the abortion "controversy," see Sumner (1981).

13.   The Medicaid bureaucracies are themselves results of previous efforts to implement health policy.

14.   See, for example, Meyers (1989), and the discussions of socialist feminism in Jaggar (1983) and many other feminist works.

15.   The term "sensitizing concept" is from Blumer (1969, 148). See also my discussions in Addelson (1991, 91-92). The discussion in Addelson (1991, 126ff) connects Blumer's sensitizing concepts with Strauss's notion of grounded theory, which must be done to see the validity of the notion. [See Strauss (1987)]. In some ways, the notion of sensitizing concepts suits Wittgenstein's understanding of language—but it is crucial to realize that Wittgenstein was talking primarily about folk language; sensitizing concepts are developed within a science for the purposes of the science, not for folk purposes.

16.   See Blumer, (1971); see also Spector and Kitsuse (1977). Both Blumer and Spector and Kitsuse use the term "social problem" rather than "public problem" for the phenomena captured by their format. I am using Joseph Gusfield's (1981) term, "public problems," because it includes only those social problems whose definitions and solutions involve official action (usually by elected or bureaucratic officials), leaving the term "social problems" for a larger and more varied field—to include for example, feminist rape-crisis lines and battered women's shelters, which were solutions to social problems long before those became public problems. ALanon and the Salvation Army (as well as multitudes of other groups) also work in solving social problems.

17.   A 1990 article by Faye Wattleton of Planned Parenthood gives this same analysis.

18.   In this and other problems, philosophers have given testimony about various moral issues like personhood, abortion, the neutrality of evolutionary

theory, whether secular humanism is a religion, and the moral status of animals.

19. For the classic discussion of arenas and social worlds, see Strauss (1964, 1978).

20. So a feminist who did her work on some of the moral problems that this social world found important might work within that traditional ethics to show how traditional interpretations have supported male bias and how they ought to be changed.

21. Some of my information in this paragraph comes from an August 1989 meeting on the abortion problem with social worlds of the women's movement. Kissling has written at very interesting length about these issues for *Conscience*, the publication of Catholics for a Free Choice. Hursthouse (1990) offers an analysis of abortion based in part on an Aristotelian ethics that is complex and interesting, though I won't discuss it here.

# References

Addelson, K., and E. Potter. 1991. "Making Knowledge." In *Engendering Knowledge: Feminists in Academe*. J. Hartman and E.M. Davidow. Knoxville: University of Tennessee Press.

Addelson, K. 1991. *Impure Thoughts: Essays in Philosophy, Feminism, and Ethics*. Philadelphia: Temple University Press.

———. 1987. "Moral Passages." In Women and Moral Theory. E. Feder Kittay and D.T. Meyers. Totowa, N.J.: Rowman and Littlefield.

———. 1983. "The Man of Professional Wisdom." In Discovering Reality. S. Harding and M. Hintikka. Dordrecht: D. Reidel.

Baier, A. 1986. "Trust and Anti-Trust." *Ethics* 96 (January).

———. 1985. "What do Women Want in a Moral Theory?" *Nous* 19 (March).

Bellah, R. 1985. *Habits of the Heart*. Berkeley: University of California Press.

Blumer, H. 1971. "Social Problems as Collective Behavior." *Social Problems* 18 (Winter): 298–306.

———. 1969. *Symbolic Interactionism: Perspective and Method*. Englewood Cliffs, N.J.: Prentice Hall.

Callahan, D. 1989. "Moral Theory: Thinking, Doing, and Living" *J. Social Phil.* xx, 1 and 2 (Spring/Fall).

Clarke, A.E. 1991. "Social Worlds/Arenas Theory as Organizational Theory." In *Social Organization and Social Process: Essays in Honor of Anselm L. Strauss.* Edited by D. Maines. Hawthorne, NY: Aldine de Gruyter.

Clarke, A. 1990. "Controversy and the Development of Reproductive Sciences." *Social Problems.* 37, 1 (February): 18–37.

Davenport, E. 1987. "The New Politics of Knowledge: Rorty's Pragmatism and the Rhetoric of the Human Sciences." *Philosophy of Social Science* 17:377–94.

Elshtain, J. 1981. *Public Man, Private Woman.* Princeton, N.J: Princeton University Press.

Freidson, E. 1986. *Professional Powers: A Study of the Institutionalization of Formal Knowledge.* Chicago: University of Chicago Press.

―――. 1982. "Occupational Autonomy and Labor Market Shelters." In *Varieties of Work.* Edited by P. L. Stewart and M. G. Cantor. Beverly Hills: Sage Publications.

Fried, A. 1988. "Abortion Politics as Symbolic Politics: An Investigation into Belief Systems." *Social Science Quarterly* 69 (March):137–154.

Flynn, P. 1991a. *Just Decisions: Moral Ordering and the Social Construction of Bioethics.* Unpublished PhD. dissertation, University of California at San Francisco, School of Nursing.

―――. 1991b. "Moral Ordering: The Work of Bioethics Committees." Paper presented at Stone Symposium, Society for the Study of Symbolic Interactionism, San Francisco, CA.

Gelb, J., and M.L. Palley. 1987. *Women and Public Policies.* Princeton, N.J.: Princeton University Press (revised edition)

Gerson, E.M. 1983. "Scientific Work and Social Worlds." *Knowledge: Creation, Diffusion, Utilization* 4, 3 (March).

Gilligan, C. 1982. *In a Different Voice.* Cambridge, Mass.: Harvard University Press.

Griffin, S. 1978. *Woman and Nature: The Roaring Inside Her.* New York: Harper and Row.

Gusfield, J. 1981. *The Culture of Public Problems: Drinking, Driving, and the Symbolic Order.* Chicago: University of Chicago Press.

Harrison, B. 1983. *Our Right to Choose: Toward a New Ethic of Abortion.* Boston: Beacon Press.

Harding, S., and M. Hintikka. 1983. *Discovering Reality* Dordrecht: D. Reidel.

Harding, S. 1986. *The Science Question in Feminism.* Ithaca, N.Y.: Cornell University Press.

Hartman, J., and E.M. Davidow. 1991. *Engendering Knowledge: Feminists in Academe.* Knoxville: University of Tennessee Press.

Hauerwas, S. 1981. *A Community of Character: Toward a Constructive Christian Social Ethic*. Notre Dame: University of Notre Dame Press.

Hughes, E.C. 1984. *The Sociological Eye*. New Brunswick, N.J.: Transaction Books.

Hursthouse, Rosalind. 1987. *Beginning Lives*. New York: Basil Blackwell Inc.

Jaggar, A. 1989. "Feminist Ethics: Some Issues for the Nineties." *J. Social Phil.* xx, 1 and 2 (Spring/Fall).

———. 1983. *Feminist Politics and Human Nature*. Totowa, N.J.: Rowman and Allanheld.

Kittay, E.F., and D.T. Meyers. 1987. *Women and Moral Theory*. Totowa, N.J.: Rowman and Allenheld.

Kucklick, B. 1984. "Seven Thinkers and How They Grew: Descartes, Spinoza, Leibniz, Locke, Berkeley, Hume, Kant." *Philosophy in History*. Edited by R. Rorty, J. Schneewind, and Q. Skinner. Cambridge: Cambridge University Press.

Kuhn, T. 1979. *The Structure of Scientific Revolutions*. Chicago: University of Chicago Press.

Merchant, C. 1980. *The Death of Nature: Women, Ecology, and the Scientific Revolution*. San Francisco: Harper and Row.

Merton, R.K. 1949. *Social Theory and Social Structure*. Glencoe, Ill.: The Free Press.

Meyers, D. 1989. *Self, Society, and Personal Choice*. New York: Columbia University Press.

Mills, C.W. 1963. *Power Politics and People*. Edited by I.L. Horowitz. New York: Ballantine Books.

Nelson, L. 1990. *Who Knows: From Quine to a Feminist Empiricism*. Philadelphia: Temple University Press.

Nietz, M.J. 1981. "Family, State, and God: Ideologies of the Right-to-Life Movement." *Sociological Analysis* 42, 3: 265–276.

Noddings, N. 1984. *Caring*. Berkeley: University of California Press.

Oleson, A., and J. Voss. 1979. *The Organization of Knowledge in Modern America*. Baltimore: Johns Hopkins University Press.

Osborne, M. 1979. *Woman in Western Thought*. New York: Random House.

Petchesky, R. 1983. *Abortion and Woman's Choice: The State. Sexuality, and Reproductive Freedom*. New York: Longman.

Quine, W.V. 1963. *From a Logical Point of View*. New York: Harper and Row.

———. 1969. *Ontological Relativity and Other Essays*. New York: Columbia University Press.

Rorty, R. 1979. *Philosophy and the Mirror of Nature*. Princeton, N.J.: Princeton University Press.

Ruddick, S. 1983. "Maternal Thinking." In *Mothering: Essays in Feminist Theory*. Edited by J. Treblicat. Totowa, N.J.: Roman & Allenheld.

Scheman, N. 1983. "Individualism and the Objects of Psychology." In *Discovering Reality*.

Spector, M., and J. Kitsuse. 1977. *Constructing Social Problems* Menlo Park, Calif.: Cummings.

Spelman, E.V. 1989. *Inessential Woman*. Boston: Beacon Press.

Stich, S. 1990. *The Fragmentation of Reason: Preface to a Pragmatic Theory of Cognitive Evaluation*. Cambridge, Mass.: MIT Press.

Strauss, A. 1987. *Qualitative Analysis for Social Scientists*. Cambridge, England: Cambridge University Press.

———. 1973. "A Social Worlds Perspective." Vol. 1 of *Studies in Symbolic Interaction*. Edited by N.K. Denzin. Greenwich, Conn: JAI Press.

Strauss, A., et al. 1964. *Psychiatric Ideologies and Institutions*. Glencoe, Ill.: Free Press.

Sumner, L.W. 1981. *Abortion and Moral Theory*. Princeton, N.J.: Princeton University Press.

Vinouskis, M.A. 1981. "An Epidemic of Adolescent Pregnancy? Some Historical Questions." *J. Family History* 6, 2 (Summer).

Wattleton, F. 1990. "Teenage Pregnancy: A Case for National Action." In *The Black Women's Health Book*. Edited by E.C. White. Seattle, Wash.: Seal Press.

Whitbeck, C. 1983. "'The Moral Implications of Regarding Women as People." *In Abortion and the Status of The Fetus*, edited by W. Bondeson et al. Boston: D. Reidel.

Wolfe-Devine, C. 1989. "Abortion and the Feminine Voice." *Public Affairs Quarterly* 3, 3 (July): 81–97.

# Bibliography of Feminist Epistemologies

N.B.: We have attempted in this bibliography to include only work which fits narrowly into epistemology. Thus, work in the philosophy of science has been excluded unless there is significant epistemological content.

Addelson, Kathryn Pyne. "The Man of Professional Wisdom." In *Discovering Reality: Feminist Perspectives on Epistemology, Metaphysics, Methodology, and the Philosophy of Science*. Edited by Sandra Harding and Merrill Hintikka. Dordrecht, Netherlands: Reidel, 1983.

Addelson, Kathryn Pyne and Elizabeth Potter. "Making Knowledge." In *Engendering Knowledge: Feminists in Academe*. Edited by Ellen Messer-Davidow and Joan E. Hartman. Knoxville, Tennessee: University of Tennessee Press, 1991.

Alcoff, Linda. "Justifying Feminist Social Science." *Hypatia* 2 (Fall 1987): 107–127.

Alcoff, Linda. "How is Epistemology Political?" In *Theory, Power, and Human Emancipation: Dimensions of Radical Philosophy*. Edited by Roger Gottlieb. Philadelphia: Temple University Press, forthcoming.

Arnault, Lynne. "Talking 'Bout a Revolution: Feminism, Historicism, and Liberal Moral Theory." *Logos: Philosophical Issues in Christian Perspective*. 10 (1989): 39–55.

Arnault, Lynne. "The Radical Future of a Classic Moral Theory." In *Gender/Body/Knowledge*. Edited by Susan Bordo and Alison Jaggar. New Brunswick: Rutgers University Press, 1989.

Barrett, Michele. *The Politics of Truth: From Marx to Foucault* (London: Polity Press, 1992).

Belenky, Mary G., B. M. Clinchy, N. R. Goldberger, and J. M. Tarule.

*Women's Ways of Knowing: The Development of Self, Voice and Mind*. New York: Basic Books, 1986.

Bergmann, Sheryle. "Feminist Epistemologies." *Eidos* 6 (Dec. 87): 201–214.

Bordo, Susan. "The Cartesian Masculinization of Thought." *SIGNS* 11 (1988): 619–629.

Bordo, Susan. *The Flight to Objectivity: Essays on Cartesianism and Culture*. Albany: SUNY Press, 1987.

Braaten, Jane. "Towards a Feminist Reassessment of Intellectual Virtue." *Hypatia* 5 (Fall 1990): 1–14.

Code, Lorraine. "Credibility: A Double Standard." In *Feminist Perspectives: Philosophical Essays on Method and Morals*. Edited by Lorraine Code, Sheila Mullett, and Christine Overall. Toronto: University of Toronto Press, 1988.

Code, Lorraine. "Experience, Knowledge, and Responsibility." In *Feminist Perspectives in Philosophy*. Edited by Morwenna Griffiths and Margaret Whitford. Bloomington, Indiana: Indiana University Press, 1988.

Code, Lorraine. "Is the Sex of the Knower Epistemologically Significant?" *Metaphilosophy* 12 (July/October 1981): 267–276.

Cook, Judith A. and Mary Margaret Fonow. "Knowledge and Women's Interests: Issues of Epistemology and Methodology in Feminist Research." *Sociological Inquiry* 56 (1986): 2–29.

Duran, Jane. *Toward a Feminist Epistemology*. Savage, Maryland: Rowman and Littlefield Publishers, 1991.

Fee, Elizabeth. "Women's Nature and Scientific Objectivity." In *Woman's Nature: Rationalizations of Inequality*. Edited by Marian Lowe and Ruth Hubbard. New York: Pergamon Press, 1983.

Fee, Elizabeth. "Critiques of Modern Science: The Relationship of Feminism to Other Radical Epistemologies." In *Feminist Approaches to Science*. Edited by Ruth Bleier. New York: Pergamon Press, 1984.

Flax, Jane. *Thinking Fragments: Psychoanalysis, Feminism and Postmodernism in the Contemporary West*. Berkeley: University of California Press, 1990.

Gergen, Kenneth J. "Feminist Critiques of Science and the Challenge of Social Epistemology." In *Feminist Thought and the Structure of Knowledge*. Edited by Mary McCanney Gergen. New York: NYU Press, 1988.

Gorniak, Krystyna. "Some Remarks on the Need for Communication Between Men's and Women's Ways of Cognition." *Communication and Cognition* 21 (1988): 139–140.

Grant, Judith. "I Feel, Therefore I Am: A Critique of Female Experience as the Basis for a Feminist Epistemology." *Women and Politics* 7:3 (1987).

Grimshaw, Jean. *Philosophy and Feminist Thinking*. Minneapolis: University of Minnesota Press, 1986.

Grosz, E. A. "The in(ter)vention of feminist knowledges." In *Crossing Boundaries: Feminisms and the Critique of Knowledge*. Edited by Barbara Caine, E. A Grosz, and Marie de Lepervanche. Boston: Allen and Unwin, 1988.

Hallberg, Margareta. "Feminist Epistemology—An Impossible Project?" *Radical Philosophy* 53 (Autumn 1989): 3–7.

Hanen, Marsha P. "Feminism, Objectivity, and Legal Truth." In *Feminist Perspectives: Philosophical Essays on Method and Morals*. Edited by Lorraine Code, Sheila Mullett, and Christine Overall. Toronto: University of Toronto Press, 1988.

Hanen, Marsha. "Justification, Coherence, and Feminism." In *Ethics and Justification*. Edited by Douglas Odegard. Edmonton: Academic, 1988.

Haraway, Donna. "Situated Knowledges: The Science Question in Feminism and the Privilege of Partial Perspective." *Feminist Studies* 14 (Fall 1988): 575–599.

Harding, Sandra. "Epistemological Questions." Editor's Conclusion to *Feminism and Methodology: Social Science Issues*. Edited by Sandra Harding. Bloomington: Indiana University Press, 1987.

Harding, Sandra. "Feminist Justificatory Strategies." In *Women, Knowledge and Reality*. Edited by Ann Garry and Marilyn Pearsall. Boston: Unwin Hyman, 1989.

Harding, Sandra. "Is Gender a Variable in Conceptions of Rationality? A Survey of Issues" In *Beyond Domination: New Perspectives on Women and Philosophy*. Edited by Carol Gould. Totowa, New Jersey: Rowman and Allanheld, 1984.

Harding, Sandra. "The Norms of Inquiry and Masculine Experience." In *PSA 1980*. Edited by Peter Asquith and Ronald Giere, 305–324. East Lansing, Michigan: Philosophy of Science Association.

Harding, Sandra. *The Science Question in Feminism*. Ithaca, New York: Cornell University Press, 1986.

Harding, Sandra. *Whose Science? Whose Knowledge?* Ithaca, New York: Cornell University Press, 1991.

Harding, Sandra. "Why Has the Sex/Gender System Become Visible Only Now?" In *Discovering Reality*. Edited by Sandra Harding and Merrill Hintikka. Dordrecht: Reidel, 1983.

Hartsock, Nancy. "Epistemology and Politics: Minority vs. Majority Theories." *Cultural Critique* 7 (1987): 187–206.

Hartsock, Nancy. "The Feminist Standpoint: Developing the Ground for a Specifically Feminist Historical Materialism." In *Discovering Reality*. Edited Sandra Harding and Merrill Hintikka. Dordrecht: Reidel, 1983.

Hawkesworth, Mary E. "Knowers, Knowing, Known: Feminist Theory and Claims to Truth." *SIGNS* 14 (Spring 1989): 533–557.

Hekman, Susan. "The Feminization of Epistemology: Gender and the Social Sciences." *Women and Politics* 7:3 (1987).

Hekman, Susan. *Gender and Knowledge*. Boston: Northeastern University Press, 1990.

Held, Virginia. "Feminism and Epistemology: Recent Work on the Connection Between Gender and Knowledge." *Philosophy and Public Affairs*. 14 (Summer 1985).

Heldke, Lisa. "Recipes for Theory-Making." *Hypatia* 3 (Summer 1988): 15–30.

Heldke, Lisa. "John Dewey and Evelyn Fox Keller: A Shared Epistemological Tradition." *Hypatia* 2 (Fall 1987): 129–140.

Hill Collins, Patricia. *Black Feminist Thought: Knowledge, Consciousness and the Politics of Empowerment*. Boston: Unwin Hyman, 1990.

Holler, Linda. "Thinking with the Weight of the Earth: Feminist Contributions to an Epistemology of Concreteness." *Hypatia* 5 (Spring 1990): 1–23.

Hubbard, Ruth. "Science, Facts, and Feminism." *Hypatia* 3 (1988): 114–144.

Irigaray, Luce. "Le Sujet de la Science: Est-il Sexue?" "Is the Subject of Science Sexed?" Translated by Carol Mastrangelo Bové. *Hypatia* 2 (1987): 65–87.

Jaggar, Alison. *Feminist Politics and Human Nature*. Totowa, New Jersey: Rowman and Allanheld, 1983.

Jaggar, Alison. "Love and Knowledge: Emotion in Feminist Epistemology." In *Gender/Body/Knowledge*. Edited by Susan Bordo and Alison Jaggar. New Brunswick: Rutgers University Press, 1989.

Jarratt, Susan C. "The First Sophists and Feminism: Discourses of the 'Other'." *Hypatia* 5 (Spring 1990): 27–41.

Keller, Evelyn Fox and Christine R. Grontkowski, "The Mind's Eye." In *Discovering Reality*. Edited by Sandra Harding and Merrill Hintikka. Dordrecht: Reidel, 1983.

Keller, Evelyn Fox. *Reflections on Gender and Science*. New Haven: Yale University Press, 1984.

Lazreg, Marnia. "Feminism and Difference: The Perils of Writing as a Woman on Women in Algeria," in *Conflicts in Feminism*, edited Marianne Hirsch and Evelyn Fox Keller (New York: Routledge, 1990), 326–348.

Lloyd, Genevieve. *The Man of Reason: "Male" and "Female" In Western Philosophy*. Minneapolis: University of Minnesota Press, 1984.

Longino, Helen. "Can There Be a Feminist Science?" In *Feminism and Science*. Edited by Nancy Tuana. Bloomington: Indiana University Press, 1989.

Longino, Helen. "Science, Objectivity, and Feminist Values." *Feminist Studies* 14, 31: 561–574.

Longino, Helen. *Science as Social Knowledge*. Princeton: Princeton University Press, 1990.

Longino, Helen. "Scientific Objectivity and Feminist Theorizing." *Liberal Education*. 67: 1981.

Longino, Helen and Ruth Doell. "Body, Bias and Behavior: A Comparative Analysis of Reasoning in Two Areas of Biological Science." *SIGNS* 9 (Winter 1983): 206–227.

Lugones, Maria. "Playfulness, 'World' Traveling, and Loving Perception." *Hypatia* 2 (Summer 1987): 3–19.

Lugones, Maria, and Elizabeth Spelman. "Have We Got a Theory for You! Feminist Theory, Cultural Imperialism, and the Demand for the Woman's Voice." *Hypatia, Women's Studies International Forum* 6 (1983): 578–581.

Messer-Davidow, Ellen. "Knowers, Knowing, Knowledge: Feminist Theory and Education." *Journal of Thought*. 20 (Fall 1985): 8–24.

Mills, Charles. "Alternative Epistemologies." *Social Theory and Practice*. 14 (Fall 1988): 237–263.

Minnich, Elizabeth Kamarck. *Transforming Knowledge*. Philadelphia: Temple University Press, 1990.

Narayan, Uma. "The Project of Feminist Epistemology: Perspectives From a Nonwestern Feminist." In *Gender/Body/Knowledge*. Edited by Susan Bordo and Alison Jaggar. New Brunswick: Rutgers University Press, 1989.

Narayan, Uma. "Working Together Across Differences: Some Considerations on Emotions and Political Practice." *Hypatia* 3 (Summer 1988): 31–48.

Nelson, Lynn Hankinson. *Who Knows: From Quine to a Feminist Empiricism*. Philadelphia: Temple University Press, 1990.

Nye, Andrea. *Words of Power: A Feminist Reading of the History of Logic*. New York: Routledge: 1990.

Pakszys, Elzbieta. "Feminism, Sciences, and Epistemology: Three Issues." *Communication and Cognition* 21 (1988): 141–143.

Potter, Elizabeth. "Locke's Epistemology and Women's Struggles." In *Critical Feminist Essays in the History of Western Philosophy*. Edited by Bat-Ami Bar On. Albany: SUNY Press, forthcoming.

Rooney, Phyllis. "Gendered Reason: Sex Metaphor and Conceptions of Reason." *Hypatia* 6 (Summer 1991): 77–103.

Rose, Hilary. "Beyond Masculinist Realities: A Feminist Epistemology for the Sciences." In *Feminist Approaches to Science*. Edited by Ruth Bleier. New York: Pergamon Press, 1988.

Rose, Hilary. "Hand, Brain and Heart: A Feminist Epistemology for the Natural Sciences." *SIGNS* 9:1 (1983).

Rose, Hilary. "Reflections on the Debate Within Feminist Epistemology." *Communication and Cognition*. 21 (1988): 133–138.

Ruddick, Sara. "Maternal Thinking." *Feminist Studies* 6 (Summer 1980): 342–367.

Ruddick, Sara. *Maternal Thinking: Toward a Politics of Peace*. Boston: Beacon Press, 1989.

Ruddick, Sara. "Remarks on the Sexual Politics of Reason." In *Women and Moral Theory*. Edited by Eva Feder Kittay and Diana T. Meyers. Savage, Maryland: Rowman and Littlefield, 1987.

Russell, Denise. "Feminist Critiques of Epistemology." *Methodology and Science* 22 (1989): 87–103.

Scheman, Naomi. "Othello's Doubt/Desdemona's Death: The Engendering of Skepticism." In *Power, Gender, Values*. Edited by Judith Genova. Edmonton, Alberta, Canada: Academic Printing and Publishing, 1987.

Seller, Anne. "Realism versus Relativism: Towards a Politically Adequate Epistemology." In *Feminist Perspectives in Philosophy*. Edited by Morwenna Griffiths and Margaret Whitford. Bloomington, Indiana: Indiana University Press, 1988.

Soble, Alan. "Feminist Epistemology and Women Scientists." *Metaphilosophy* 14 (J1-O 83): 291–307.

Stenstad, Gail. "Anarchic Thinking." *Hypatia* 3 (Summer 1988): 87–100.

Trebilcot, Joyce. "Dyke Methods, or Principles for the Discovery/Creation of the Withstanding." *Hypatia* 3 (Summer 1988): 1–14.

Tuana, Nancy, ed. *Feminism and Science*. Bloomington: Indiana University Press, 1989.

Turkle, Sherry and Seymour Papert. "Epistemological Pluralism: Styles and Voices Within the Computer Culture." *SIGNS* 16 (Autumn 1990): 128–157.

Vintges, Karen. "Do We Need Feminist Epistemologies?" *Communication and Cognition* 21 (1988): 157–162.

Von Morstein, Petra. "A Message from Cassandra—Experience and Knowledge: Dichotomy and Unity." In *Feminist Perspectives: Philosophical Essays on Method and Morals*. Edited by Lorraine Code,

Sheila Mullett, and Christine Overall. Toronto: University of Toronto Press, 1988.

Walker, Margaret Urban. "Moral Understandings: Alternative 'Epistemology' for a Feminist Ethics." *Hypatia* 4 (Summer 1989): 15–28.

Whitbeck, Caroline. "Love, Knowledge, and Transformation." *Hypatia Women's Studies International Forum* 2 (1984): 393–405.

Whitford, Margaret. "Luce Irigaray's Critique of Rationality." In *Feminist Perspectives in Philosophy*. Edited by Morwenna Griffiths and Margaret Whitford. Bloomington, Indiana: Indiana University Press, 1988.

Winant, Terry. "The Feminist Standpoint: A Matter of Language" *Hypatia* 2 (Winter 1987): 123–148.

Wylie, Alison, Kathleen Okruhlik, Sandra Morton, and Leslie Thielen-Wilson. "Feminist Critiques of Science: The Epistemological and Methodological Literature." *Women's Studies International Forum.* 12:3 (1989).

# Index

# Notes on Contributors

Kathryn Pyne Addelson is a professor in the Department of Philosophy and the Program in the History of the Sciences at Smith College. She is on the board of a conservation land trust and does volunteer work at a shelter for homeless families. She is the author of *Impure Thoughts* (Philadelphia: Temple University Press, 1991).

Linda Alcoff teaches philosophy and women's studies at Syracuse University. Her papers have appeared in *SIGNS, Hypatia, Cultural Critique* and numerous anthologies. She is currently writing a book exploring new coherence epistemologies.

Bat-Ami Bar On is Associate Professor of Philosophy and Director of Women's Studies at SUNY-Binghamton. Her detour into epistemology is motivated by her interests in socio-political and ethical issues and theory, especially those arising in relation to everyday kinds of violence and abuses. She is working on a book about these issues.

Susan E. Babbitt teaches philosophy at Queen's University in Kingston, Ontario, Canada. Originally from Ottawa, she received her PhD from Cornell University in 1991 with a dissertation on rationality and integrity. She currently teaches courses in the philosophy of science, contemporary moral theory, and a graduate seminar on rationality and cultural difference.

Lorraine Code is Professor of Philosophy at York University and a member of the Graduate Programme in Social and Political Thought. In addition to numerous articles on epistemology and feminist philosophy, she is the author of *Epistemic Responsibility*

(1987) and *What Can She Know? Feminist Theory and the Construction of Knowledge* (1991); and co-editor of *Changing Patterns: Women in Canada* (1988) and *Feminist Perspectives: Philosophical Essays on Method and Morals* (1988).

Vrinda Dalmiya is Assistant Professor of Philosophy at Montana State University. She has also taught at the University of Washington. She is the author of "Coherence, Truth, and the Omniscient Interpreter" which appeared in *The Philosophical Quarterly*, January, 1990.

Elizabeth Grosz teaches feminist theory, philosophy and critical theory at Monash University, Australia. She is the author of *Sexual Subversions: Three French Feminists* (Allen and Unwin, 1989) and *Jacques Lacan: A Feminist Introduction* (Routledge, 1990).

Sandra Harding is Professor of Philosophy at the University of Delaware. She is the author of *Whose Science? Whose Knowledge?: Thinking from Women's Lives, The Science Question in Feminism*, and the editor of five books on related issues including *Feminism and Methodology* and *The Racial Economy of Science*, forthcoming from Indiana University press in 1993.

Helen E. Longino teaches philosophy and women's studies at Rice University. She is the author of *Science as Social Knowledge: Values and Objectivity in Scientific Inquiry* (Princeton University Press, 1990) and co-editor with Valerie Miner of *Competition: A Feminist Taboo?* (The Feminist Press at the City College of New York, 1987).

Lynn Hankinson Nelson is Associate Professor of Philosophy at Glassboro State College. She is the author of *Who Knows: From Quine to a Feminist Empiricism* (Philadelphia: Temple University Press, 1990). She is currently working on an exploration of the implications of feminist theory for the notion of experience; she is particularly interested in the understandings of experience and its relationship to knowledge at work and emerging in feminist epistemologies.

Elizabeth Potter is the Alice Andrews Quigley Professor of Women's Studies at Mills College. Her recent work includes "Making Genders/Making Science: Gender Ideology and Robert Boyle's Experimental Philosophy," in *Making a Difference: Feminist Critiques in the Natural Sciences*, edited by Bonnie Spanier, forthcoming from Indiana University Press. She is completing *Gender Politics in Seventeenth-Century Science*, a book exploring the intersections of gender and the production of early modern atomic theory, especially Boyle's Law of Gases.